June 20–22, 2018
Innsbruck, Austria

**Association for
Computing Machinery**

Advancing Computing as a Science & Profession

IH&MMSec'18

Proceedings of the 6th ACM Workshop on

Information Hiding and Multimedia Security

Sponsored by:

ACM SIGMM

Supported by:

Universität Innsbruck

Association for
Computing Machinery

Advancing Computing as a Science & Profession

The Association for Computing Machinery
2 Penn Plaza, Suite 701
New York, New York 10121-0701

ISBN: 978-1-4503-5625-1 (Digital)

ISBN: 978-1-4503-6108-8 (Print)

Additional copies may be ordered prepaid from:

ACM Order Department
PO Box 30777
New York, NY 10087-0777, USA

Phone: 1-800-342-6626 (USA and Canada)
+1-212-626-0500 (Global)
Fax: +1-212-944-1318
E-mail: acmhelp@acm.org
Hours of Operation: 8:30 am – 4:30 pm ET

Printed in the USA.

Preface

We cordially welcome you to the 6th ACM Information Hiding and Multimedia Security Workshop – IH&MMSec'18 – in Innsbruck, Austria. For more than 20 years, the workshop (and its predecessors) has attracted researchers from all over the world, whose efforts brought tremendous advances to the fields of Information Hiding and Multimedia Security.

This year, our call for papers has attracted a total of 40 submissions, both short and full papers, contributed by authors from North America, Europe, Asia, and Africa. Each paper has received at least three independent and double-blind reviews from members of the Technical Program Committee. On this basis, and incorporating the outcome of a paper discussion phase, the Program Chairs have selected the 18 most promising submissions for presentation and publication. The acceptance rate for full papers was 37.5%.

We use this opportunity to thank all the submitting authors and all reviewers for their high quality contributions and help, which has resulted in a strong technical program. The accepted papers cover the fields of steganography and steganalysis, forensics, biometrics, anonymity, and cryptography. We expect them to be of wide interest to researchers working both in academia and industry.

The technical program also features two invited keynote speakers. It is an honour to have as first keynote speaker professor Ross Anderson from Cambridge University, England. Ross is an influential thought leader who hosted the first Information Hiding workshop in 1996, and co-authored one of the most cited surveys on the area. In his keynote, he will present examples and concepts of covert and deniable communications. The second keynote is given by professor Luisa Verdoliva from the University Federico II of Naples, Italy, undoubtedly a "rising star" in our community. She will talk about the exciting discussion and share new insights on the role of deep learning in multimedia forensics.

As for the previous editions, the workshop is structured in three days. The afternoon of the second day is devoted to a social event, designed to foster discussions and help establishing new collaborative research relationships among participants, while enjoying the breathtaking views from the Nordkette mountain range. Moreover, at the end of the first day we have reserved time for a rump session: all participants are invited to discuss their ongoing work, unpublished results, new product demos in five-minute presentations.

We thank the University of Innsbruck, specifically its Department of Computer Science, for hosting and supporting the event. Great thanks belong to Manuela Resch, Birgit Juen and all student volunteers for their invaluable help with the local organization of the event. Further thanks are due to professor Jana Dittmann for the liaison with the ACM and her team at the University of Magdeburg for hosting the conference website. Lastly, we gratefully thank the Steering Committee for entrusting us with this edition of the workshop.

Finally, we really hope that this program will be of great interest to you, and you will have an enjoyable stay in the heart of the Alps.

IH&MMSec'18 General Chairs	*IH&MMSec'18 Program Chairs*
Rainer Böhme	**Giulia Boato**
University of Innsbruck, Austria	*University of Trento, Italy*
Cecilia Pasquini	**Pascal Schöttle**
University of Innsbruck, Austria	*University of Innsbruck, Austria*

Table of Contents

Session: Embedding Impact in Steganography

Session: Encryption, Authentication, Anonymization

IH&MMSec 2018 Workshop Organization

General Chairs: Rainer Böhme *(University of Innsbruck, Austria)*
Cecilia Pasquini *(University of Innsbruck, Austria)*

Program Chairs: Giulia Boato *(University of Trento, Italy)*
Pascal Schöttle *(University of Innsbruck, Austria)*

Local Arrangements Chairs: Manuela Resch *(University of Innsbruck, Austria)*
Birgit Juen *(University of Innsbruck, Austria)*

ACM Liaison: Jana Dittmann *(Otto-von-Guericke University of Magdeburg, Germany)*

Steering Committee: Patrizio Campisi *(University of Roma TRE, Italy)*
George Danezis *(University College London, UK)*
Jana Dittman *(Otto-von-Guericke University of Magdeburg, Germany)*
Jessica Fridrich *(SUNY Binghamton, USA)*
Stefan Katzenbeisser *(TU Darmstadt, Germany)*
Balakrishnan Prabhakaran *(University of Dallas, USA)*

Program Committee: Mauro Barni *(University of Siena, Italy)*
Patrick Bas *(CNRS, University of Lille, France)*
François Cayre *(Grenoble-INP, University of Grenoble Alpes, France)*
Marc Chaumont *(LIRMM Montpellier, Université de Nîmes, France)*
Remi Cogranne *(Université de Technologie de Troyes, France)*
Pedro Comesaña-Alfaro *(University of Vigo, Spain)*
Jana Dittmann *(Otto-von-Guericke University of Magdeburg, Germany)*
Wei Fan *(Dartmouth College, USA)*
Caroline Fontaine *(CNRS & IMT Atlantique, France)*
Jessica Fridrich *(SUNY Binghamton, USA)*
Neil Johnson *(Booz Allen Hamilton, USA)*
Stefan Katzenbeisser *(TU Darmstadt, Germany)*
Andrew D. Ker *(Oxford University, UK)*
Matthias Kirchner *(SUNY Binghamton, USA)*
Christian Kraetzer *(Otto-von-Guericke University of Magdeburg, Germany)*
Qingzhong Liu *(Sam Houston State Universtiy, USA)*
Wojciech Mazurczyk *(Warsaw University of Technology, Poland)*
Fernando Pèrez-Gonzàlez *(University of Vigo, Spain)*
Tomáš Pevný *(Czech Technical University in Prague, Czech Republic)*
Alessandro Piva *(Università degli Studi di Firenze, Italy)*
William Puech *(Université de Montpellier, France)*
Thomas Schneider *(TU Darmstadt, Germany)*
Matthew Stamm *(Drexel University, USA)*

Covert and Deniable Communications

Keynote Abstract

Ross Anderson
Cambridge University
JJ Thomson Avenue, Cambridge CB3 0FD
Ross.Anderson@cl.cam.ac.uk

ABSTRACT

At the first Information Hiding Workshop in 1996 we tried to clarify the models and assumptions behind information hiding. We agreed the terminology of cover text and stego text against a background of the game proposed by our keynote speaker Gus Simmons: that Alice and Bob are in jail and wish to hatch an escape plan without the fact of their communication coming to the attention of the warden, Willie. Since then there have been significant strides in developing technical mechanisms for steganography and steganalysis, with new techniques from machine learning providing ever more powerful tools for the analyst, such as the ensemble classifier. There have also been a number of conceptual advances, such as the square root law and effective key length. But there always remains the question whether we are using the right security metrics for the application. In this talk I plan to take a step backwards and look at the systems context. When can stegosystems actually be used? The deployment history is patchy, with one being Trucrypt's hidden volumes, inspired by the steganographic file system. Image forensics also find some use, and may be helpful against some adversarial machine learning attacks (or at least help us understand them). But there are other contexts in which patterns of activity have to be hidden for that activity to be effective. I will discuss a number of examples starting with deception mechanisms such as honeypots, Tor bridges and pluggable transports, which merely have to evade detection for a while; then moving on to the more challenging task of designing deniability mechanisms, from leaking secrets to a newspaper through bitcoin mixes, which have to withstand forensic examination once the participants come under suspicion.

We already know that, at the system level, anonymity is hard. However the increasing quantity and richness of the data available to opponents may move a number of applications from the deception category to that of deniability.

To pick up on our model of 20 years ago, Willie might not just put Alice and Bob in solitary confinement if he finds them communicating, but torture them or even execute them. Changing threat models are historically one of the great disruptive forces in security engineering.

This leads me to suspect that a useful research area may be the intersection of deception and forensics, and how information hiding systems can be designed in anticipation of richer and more complex threat models. The ever-more-aggressive censorship systems deployed in some parts of the world also raise the possibility of using information hiding techniques in censorship circumvention. As an example of recent practical work, I will discuss Covertmark, a toolkit for testing pluggable transports that was partly inspired by Stirmark, a tool we presented at the second Information Hiding Workshop twenty years ago.

KEYWORDS

Deception, forensics, mixes, steganography, privacy enhancing technology, censorship resistance

ACM Reference Format:
Ross Anderson. 2018. Covert and Deniable Communications: Keynote Abstract. In *IH&MMSec '18: 6th ACM Workshop on Information Hiding and Multimedia Security, June 20–22, 2018, Innsbruck, Austria*. ACM, New York, NY, USA, 1 page. https://doi.org/10.1145/3206004.3206023

1 BIOGRAPHY

Ross Anderson organised the first Information Hiding Workshop in 1996. He is Professor of Security Engineering at Cambridge University and a Fellow of both the Royal Society and the Royal Academy of Engineering.

Deep Learning in Multimedia Forensics

Luisa Verdoliva
University Federico Ii of Naples
Naples, Italy
verdoliv@unina.it

ABSTRACT

With the widespread diffusion of powerful media editing tools, falsifying images and videos has become easier and easier in the last few years. Fake multimedia, often used to support fake news, represents a growing menace in many fields of life, notably in politics, journalism, and the judiciary. In response to this threat, the signal processing community has produced a major research effort. A large number of methods have been proposed for source identification, forgery detection and localization, relying on the typical signal processing tools.

The advent of deep learning, however, is changing the rules of the game. On one hand, new sophisticated methods based on deep learning have been proposed to accomplish manipulations that were previously unthinkable. On the other hand, deep learning provides also the analyst with new powerful forensic tools. Given a suitably large training set, deep learning architectures ensure usually a significant performance gain with respect to conventional methods, and a much higher robustness to post-processing and evasions.

In this talk after reviewing the main approaches proposed in the literature to ensure media authenticity, the most promising solutions relying on Convolutional Neural Networks will be explored with special attention to realistic scenarios, such as when manipulated images and videos are spread out over social networks. In addition, an analysis of the efficacy of adversarial attacks on such methods will be presented.

CCS Concepts/ACM Classifiers

• Surveys and overviews ~ Security and Privacy

Author Keywords

Multimedia forensics; forgery detection and localization; deep learning; convolutional neural networks.

BIOGRAPHY

Dr. Luisa Verdoliva is Assistant Professor in the Department of Electrical Engineering and Information Technology at University Federico II of Naples and holder of the National Habilitation for Associate Professor in Telecommunications. Her research activity focuses on deep learning for multimedia forensics, in particular on source identification, image and video forgery detection and localization. She is member of the IEEE Information Forensics and Security Technical Committee and Associate Editor for IEEE Transactions on Information Forensics and Security. She has been serving on the technical program committees of numerous image processing and digital forensics conferences. She is the Principal Investigator for the Research Unit of University Federico II of Naples in the DISPARITY (Digital, Semantic and Physical Analysis of Media Integrity) project funded by DARPA (Defense Advanced Research Projects Agency) under the MEDIFOR program. She led her research group in several international contests, including the recent 2018 IEEE Signal Processing Cup on camera model identification (first prize) and the 2013 IEEE Image Forensics Challenge (first prize both in the detection and localization task).

IH&MMSec '18, June 20-22, 2018, Innsbruck, Austria.
© 2018 Copyright is held by the owner/author(s).
ACM ISBN 978-1-4503-5625-1/18/06.
DOI: https://doi.org/10.1145/3206004.3206024

Defining Joint Distortion for JPEG Steganography

Weixiang Li
CAS Key Laboratory of
Electromagnetic Space Information
University of Science and
Technology of China
Hefei, Anhui, China
wxli6049@mail.ustc.edu.cn

Weiming Zhang*
CAS Key Laboratory of
Electromagnetic Space Information
University of Science and
Technology of China
Hefei, Anhui, China
zhangwm@ustc.edu.cn

Kejiang Chen
CAS Key Laboratory of
Electromagnetic Space Information
University of Science and
Technology of China
Hefei, Anhui, China
chenkj@mail.ustc.edu.cn

Wenbo Zhou
CAS Key Laboratory of
Electromagnetic Space Information
University of Science and
Technology of China
Hefei, Anhui, China
welbeckz@mail.ustc.edu.cn

Nenghai Yu
CAS Key Laboratory of
Electromagnetic Space Information
University of Science and
Technology of China
Hefei, Anhui, China
ynh@ustc.edu.cn

ABSTRACT

Recent studies have shown that the non-additive distortion model of Decomposing Joint Distortion (*DeJoin*) can work well for spatial image steganography by defining joint distortion with the principle of Synchronizing Modification Directions (SMD). However, no principles have yet produced to instruct the definition of joint distortion for JPEG steganography. Experimental results indicate that SMD can not be directly used for JPEG images, which means that simply pursuing modification directions clustered does not help improve the steganographic security. In this paper, we inspect the embedding change from the spatial domain and propose a principle of Block Boundary Continuity (BBC) for defining JPEG joint distortion, which aims to restrain blocking artifacts caused by inter-block adjacent modifications and thus effectively preserve the spatial continuity at block boundaries. According to BBC, whether inter-block adjacent modifications should be synchronized or desynchronized is related to the DCT mode and the adjacent direction of inter-block coefficients (horizontal or vertical). When built into *DeJoin*, experiments demonstrate that BBC does help improve state-of-the-art additive distortion schemes in terms of relatively large embedding payloads against modern JPEG steganalyzers.

*Corresponding author

IH&MMSec'18, June 20–22, 2018, Innsbruck, Austria
© 2018 Association for Computing Machinery.
ACM ISBN 978-1-4503-5625-1/18/06...$15.00
https://doi.org/10.1145/3206004.3206008

KEYWORDS

Steganography; JPEG image; non-additive model; joint distortion; block boundary continuity

ACM Reference Format:
Weixiang Li, Weiming Zhang, Kejiang Chen, Wenbo Zhou, and Nenghai Yu. 2018. Defining Joint Distortion for JPEG Steganography. In *Proceedings of 6th ACM Information Hiding and Multimedia Security Workshop (IH&MMSec'18)*. ACM, New York, NY, USA, 12 pages. https://doi.org/10.1145/3206004.3206008

1 INTRODUCTION

Modern steganography is a science and art of covert communication that changes the original digital media slightly in order to hide secret messages without drawing suspicions from steganalysis [5, 13]. Currently, the most effective steganographic schemes are based on the framework of minimizing distortion, which defines the distortion as the sum of embedding cost at each individual cover element. And Syndrome-Trellis Codes (STCs) [4] provide a general and efficient coding method that can asymptotically approach the theoretical bound of average embedding distortion for arbitrary additive distortion function.

As a widely adopted format for image storage and transmission, JPEG steganography has become a research hotspot over the past few years. To date, there exist many content-adaptive algorithms designed for JPEG steganography, such as J-UNIWARD [10], UED [7], UERD [8], IUERD [15], HDS [18], RBV [19]. The embedding distortion of J-UNIWARD (UNIversal WAvelet Relative Distortion) [10] is computed as a sum of relative changes of coefficients in a directional filter bank decomposition of the decompressed cover image. Followed by the concept in spirit of "spread spectrum communication", UED (Uniform Embedding Distortion) [7] and UERD (Uniform Embedding Revisited Distortion) [8] with low complexity uniformly spread the embedding modifications to DCT coefficients of all possible magnitudes. IUERD (Improved UERD) [15] works quite well in the intersections between smooth and texture regions by exploring the correlation among neighboring DCT blocks more efficiently. After decompressing the image, HDS (Hybrid DiStortion) [18] exploits block fluctuation via the prediction error of pixel and combines quantization step to form a hybrid distortion function, while RBV (Residual Block Value) [19] uses a wavelet filter bank to filter the decompressed image and obtains residual block values to measure block fluctuation, which can effectively identify complex discernible objects and their orientation from the spatial domain.

Above adaptive steganographic methods are based on additive distortion model, in which the modifications on cover elements are assumed to be independent and thus minimizing the overall distortions is equivalent to minimizing the sum of costs of all individual modified elements. Intuitively, non-additive distortion model is more suitable for natural images because the embedding changes on adjacent cover elements will interact mutually and the interplay among them would sometimes disturb the spatial continuity and correlation in natural images. Recent studies on spatial image steganography show that non-additive distortion models work best in resisting modern steganalysis equipped with high-dimensional features. Li et al. [14] and Denemark et al. [2] independently introduced a similar and effective strategy for exploiting the mutual impact of adjacent modifications. In [14], the cover image is decomposed into several sub-images, and additive distortion is individually minimized in each of the sub-images while the costs of cover elements within each sub-image are dynamically updated according to the modification directions of the embedded sub-images. The strategy used in [14] and [2] is generalized as "updating distortion" (abbreviated to $UpDist$) in this paper. Since that how to design efficient coding schemes for non-additive distortion function is commonly recognized as an important open problem for steganography by the academia [11], Zhang et al. [20] proposed a general framework called $DeJoin$ attempting to solve this problem, in which the joint distortion of cover element block is firstly defined and then decomposed into additive distortion on individual elements. It has been proved that $DeJoin$ can approach the lower bound of average joint distortion for a given payload. We mainly use $DeJoin$ for JPEG non-additive distortion steganography, and also combine it with $UpDist$ to enhance the steganographic security in this paper.

With the aforementioned non-additive models, finding some rules or principles for defining reasonable joint distortion or updating distortion availably in various kinds of covers has become a critical issue for non-additive distortion steganography. Regrettably, there emerges only one practical principle for defining non-additive distortion that works well for spatial images. The principle of Synchronizing Modification Directions (SMD) used in [2, 14, 20] aims to cluster modification directions of adjacent pixels by decreasing the costs on changes in the same direction and increasing that in the opposite direction. However, experimental results show that SMD could not be directly applied to JPEG images, meaning that simply pursuing the synchronization of modification

directions among adjacent DCT coefficients (intra-block or inter-block) does not improve the security of steganography. Intuitively, the interplay among adjacent modifications is more complicated since changing one DCT coefficient will make diverse impacts on the whole 8×8 block. As for the most popular image format, it is still unclear how to define non-additive distortion for JPEG steganography.

In this paper, we present a principle called Block Boundary Continuity (BBC) for exploiting the interactive impact of changes between adjacent inter-block coefficients. Inspecting the embedding change from the spatial domain, the goal of the principle is to preserve spatial continuity at block boundaries via restraining blocking artifacts caused by adjacent modifications on inter-block coefficients, and thus effectively maintain the spatial continuity and neighboring relativity in natural images. According to BBC, the encouraged modification direction is not only related to the mode of DCT coefficient but also the adjacent direction of inter-block coefficients (horizontal or vertical), so the changed directions of some adjacent inter-block coefficients may be the same whereas others should be the opposite. When built into $DeJoin$, experimental results show that BBC can help improve the performances of recent additive distortion schemes in resisting the state-of-the-art JPEG steganalyzers.

The rest of this paper is organized as follows. In Section 2, the model of $DeJoin$ for non-additive distortion steganography are briefly reviewed. We elaborate the principle of BBC and show its effectiveness in resisting steganalysis via a simulation experiment in Section 3. The definition of JPEG joint distortion with BBC is provided in Section 4. Experimental results and comparisons are presented in Section 5. The paper is concluded in Section 6.

2 MODEL OF DECOMPOSING JOINT DISTORTION

In this paper, sets and matrices are written in boldface, and k-ary entropy function is denoted by $H_k(\pi_1, \cdots, \pi_k)$ for $\sum_{i=1}^{k} \pi_i = 1$. The embedding operation on cover element is ternary embedding with $\mathbf{I} = \{+1, -1, 0\}$, where 0 denotes no modification.

Previous adaptive steganography usually defines additive cost c_i on single cover element e_i for $i = 1, \cdots, n$. In the model of $DeJoin$ established in [20], joint distortion on element block need to be defined firstly according to the additive distortion and a specific principle. The joint distortion of each block is still additive, but it is unpractical to directly apply STCs because the number of modification patterns within a block is large that causes a high computational complexity. Therefore, $DeJoin$ carries out a two-round embedding strategy by decomposing the joint distortion into distortions on individual elements, and thus STCs can be used to embed message efficiently. Without loss of generality, Figure 1 illustrates the example of the decomposition coding process on the 1×2 block.

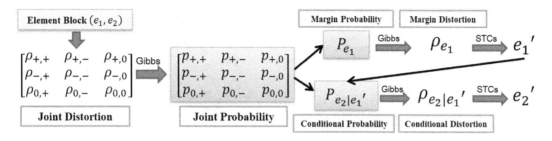

Figure 1: Illustration of *DeJoin* on 1×2 element block.

Assume that the joint distortion of the block $(e_{i,1}, e_{i,2})$ is $\rho^{(i)}(l, r)$, which denotes the distortion introduced by modifying $(e_{i,1}, e_{i,2})$ to $(e_{i,1} + l, e_{i,2} + r)$ for $(l, r) \in \mathbf{I}^2$. For a given message length L, following the maximum entropy principle, the optimal joint modification probability $\pi^{(i)}$ has a Gibbs distribution [3], and is given by

$$\pi^{(i)}(l, r) = \frac{\exp\left(-\lambda \rho^{(i)}(l, r)\right)}{\sum_{(p,q) \in \mathbf{I}^2} \exp\left(-\lambda \rho^{(i)}(p, q)\right)}, (l, r) \in \mathbf{I}^2, \quad (1)$$

which satisfies $L = \sum_{i=1}^{N} H_9(\pi^{(i)})$, where N is the number of element blocks.

In the first round, the margin probability $\pi_1^{(i)}$ on $e_{i,1}$ is calculated by

$$\pi_1^{(i)}(l) = \sum_{r \in \mathbf{I}} \pi^{(i)}(l, r), l \in \mathbf{I}. \quad (2)$$

As proved in [3], $\pi_1^{(i)}(l)$ can be transformed to the corresponding distortion $\rho_1^{(i)}(l)$ by

$$\rho_1^{(i)}(l) = \ln \frac{\pi_1^{(i)}(0)}{\pi_1^{(i)}(l)}, l \in \mathbf{I}, \quad (3)$$

and after that, ± 1 STCs can be applied to embed message into $e_{1,1}, \cdots, e_{i,1}, \cdots, e_{N,1}$ efficiently.

In the second round, the conditional probability $\pi_{2|l}^{(i)}(r)$ on $e_{i,2}$ is calculated by

$$\pi_{2|l}^{(i)} = \frac{\pi^{(i)}(l, r)}{\pi_1^{(i)}(l)}, r \in \mathbf{I}, l \in \mathbf{I}, \quad (4)$$

which denotes the probability such that $e_{i,2}$ is changed to $e_{i,2} + r$ under the condition of $e_{i,1}$ having been changed to $e_{i,1} + l$ in the first round. After transforming the conditional probability to the corresponding distortion as done in the first round, message is embedded into $e_{1,2}, \cdots, e_{i,2}, \cdots, e_{N,2}$ with ± 1 STCs.

Demonstrably, we will embed $L_1 = \sum_{i=1}^{N} H_3(\pi_1^{(i)})$ bits of message in the first round and $L_2 = \sum_{i=1}^{N} \sum_{l \in I} \pi_1^{(i)}(l) H_3(\pi_{2|l}^{(i)})$ in the second round. By chain rule, totally $L_1 + L_2 = \sum_{i=1}^{N} H_9(\pi^{(i)}) = L$ bits of message are embedded into the cover image. It has been proved in [20] that *DeJoin* can minimize the joint distortion defined on element blocks of any size, such as *DeJoin* on 2-element blocks (abbreviated to *DeJoin*$_2$) and 4-element blocks (abbreviated to *DeJoin*$_4$).

Obviously, *DeJoin* implicitly introduces non-additivity by distinguishing the joint distortions of different joint modification patterns in element block and executing a decomposition coding algorithm for embedding. Note that the definition of joint distortion is guided by some specific and instructive principles for various kinds of covers. We will discuss an effective principle for defining JPEG joint distortion in the next section.

3 THE PRINCIPLE OF BLOCK BOUNDARY CONTINUITY

Currently, there is no effective principle proposed to instruct the definition of joint distortion for JPEG steganography. In this section, we elaborate a principle called Block Boundary Continuity (BBC), which considers the spatial interactions of modifications on coefficients at the same DCT mode in adjacent blocks. The pair of coefficients at the same DCT mode in adjacent blocks is called the inter-block neighbors for short.

3.1 Embedding Change in Spatial Domain

In JPEG standard, the image is split into blocks of 8×8 pixels, and each block is converted to a frequency-domain representation by 2-D DCT transform

$$F(u, v) = \frac{1}{4} \xi(u)\xi(v) \left[\sum_{x=0}^{7} \sum_{y=0}^{7} f(x, y) \cdot \cos \frac{(2x+1)u\pi}{16} \cdot \cos \frac{(2y+1)v\pi}{16} \right], \quad (5)$$

where $f(\cdot)$ and $F(\cdot)$ are respectively the pixel value and the DCT coefficient. (x, y) represents the location of pixel in the spatial block where $x, y \in \{0, 1, \cdots, 7\}$ are respectively the row and column coordinate, and (u, v) is the DCT mode where $u, v \in \{0, 1, \cdots, 7\}$ are the horizontal and vertical spatial frequency respectively.

$$\xi(u), \xi(v) = \begin{cases} 1/\sqrt{2} & \text{if } u, v = 0 \\ 1 & \text{otherwise} \end{cases} \quad (6)$$

are the normalizing scale factors to make the transformation orthonormal. Then the quantized DCT coefficient $F_q(u, v)$ is computed with a selected quality factor and rounded to the nearest integer by

$$F_q(u, v) = round\left(\frac{F(u, v)}{Q(u, v)}\right), \quad (7)$$

where $Q(u, v)$ is the quantization step of the DCT mode(u,v), and JPEG steganography embeds message by modifying these quantized DCT coefficients. In view of the neighboring relativity in natural images, we attempt to inspect the embedding change from the spatial domain according to 2-D IDCT transform

$$f(x, y) = \frac{1}{4}\left[\sum_{u=0}^{7}\sum_{v=0}^{7}\xi(u)\xi(v)R(u,v)\cdot\cos\frac{(2x+1)u\pi}{16}\cdot\cos\frac{(2y+1)v\pi}{16}\right],$$
(8)

where $R(u, v) = F_q(u, v) \times Q(u, v)$ is the reconstructed approximate coefficient after inverse quantization. Suppose that a single quantized coefficient $F_q(u, v)$ is modified to $F_q'(u, v) = F_q(u, v) + \Delta F$, and equivalently $R'(u, v) = R(u, v) + \Delta R(u, v) = R(u, v) + Q(u, v) \times \Delta F$, the change on the spatial block can be computed by

$$\Delta f_{u,v}(x, y, \Delta F)$$
$$= f'(x, y) - f(x, y)$$
$$= \frac{1}{4}\xi(u)\xi(v)\cdot\Delta R(u,v)\cdot\cos\frac{(2x+1)u\pi}{16}\cdot\cos\frac{(2y+1)v\pi}{16}$$
$$= \frac{1}{4}\xi(u)\xi(v)\cdot[Q(u,v)\times\Delta F]\cdot\cos\frac{(2x+1)u\pi}{16}\cdot\cos\frac{(2y+1)v\pi}{16}.$$
(9)

For a given mode(u,v), we can draw the spatial change image $\Delta\mathbf{I_{u,v}}$, which consists of 64 gray values $\Delta f_{u,v}(x, y, \Delta F)$ representing positive or negative increment of the original pixel at position (x,y). We call $\Delta\mathbf{I_{u,v}}$ the DCT base image at mode(u,v). Without loss of generality, we select the quantization matrix $\mathbf{Q}$ of quality factor 75, and take $\Delta F = +1$ for illustration since $\Delta F = +1$ and $\Delta F = -1$ result in equal and merely opposite spatial change. Obviously, for quality factor 75 and $\Delta F = +1$, there are 64 DCT base images in total for all modes, and we draw them together in Figure 2(a). To clarify, the increments within each base image are normalized respectively, and like $\Delta\mathbf{I_{7,7}}$ in Figure 2(a), whiter means larger increment and darker means larger decrement within a base image.

In this paper, we just concentrate on the directions of changes on original pixel values, i.e. increase or decrease. When the magnitude is being neglected, the spatial change can be binarized to $\Delta f_{u,v}^B(x, y, \Delta F) = sgn\big(\Delta f_{u,v}(x, y, \Delta F)\big)$ by the sign function

$$sgn(\phi) = \begin{cases} 1 & \text{if } \phi > 0 \\ 0 & \text{if } \phi = 0 \\ -1 & \text{if } \phi < 0 \end{cases}.$$
(10)

Since $sgn(\phi_1\phi_2) = sgn(\phi_1) \times sgn(\phi_2)$, the binarized spatial change

$$\Delta f_{u,v}^B(x, y, \Delta F) = sgn\big(\Delta f_{u,v}(x, y, \Delta F)\big)$$
$$= sgn\big(\Delta F\cdot\cos\frac{(2x+1)u\pi}{16}\cdot\cos\frac{(2y+1)v\pi}{16}\big)$$
$$= \begin{cases} 1 & \Longrightarrow increase \\ -1 & \Longrightarrow decrease \end{cases}.$$
(11)

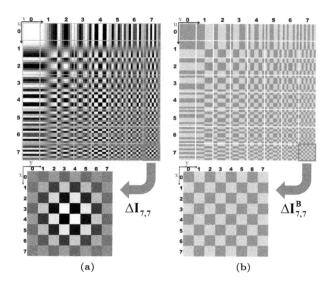

Figure 2: Two kinds of DCT base images associated with quality factor 75 and $\Delta F = +1$, and the corresponding examples of mode(7,7). (u, v) represents the DCT mode where $u, v \in \{0, 1, \cdots, 7\}$ are respectively the horizontal and vertical spatial frequency, and (x,y) represents the location of pixel in the spatial block where $x, y \in \{0, 1, \cdots, 7\}$ are respectively the row and column coordinate. (a) 64 base images $\Delta\mathbf{I_{u,v}}$, and a close-up of $\Delta\mathbf{I_{7,7}}$. (b) 64 binarized base images $\Delta\mathbf{I_{u,v}^B}$ with blue representing increase and red representing decrease, and a close-up of $\Delta\mathbf{I_{7,7}^B}$.

We also make $\Delta F = +1$ and plot 64 binarized base images $\Delta\mathbf{I_{u,v}^B}$ in Figure 2(b) with blue representing increase and red representing decrease. From $\Delta\mathbf{I_{u,v}^B}$, it is easy to make out the positive or negative change patterns on the spatial block when the single DCT coefficient $F_q(u, v)$ is modified by $\Delta F = +1$. For instance, modifying the DC coefficient $F_q(0, 0)$ by $+1$ generates increases on all the 8×8 pixels; modifying $F_q(0, 1)$ causes increases on the left half and decreases on the right half of the spatial block, while modifying $F_q(1, 0)$ causes increases on the upper half and decreases on the lower half of the spatial block. Obviously, with the mode being higher, $\Delta\mathbf{I_{u,v}^B}$ becomes more complicated in horizontal and vertical direction.

3.2 Impact of Simultaneous Modifications on Inter-block Neighbors

In the process of steganography, the cases of simultaneously modifying inter-block neighbors are possible and common, especially among coefficients of low frequency in textured regions, for that we need to observe the combined influence on adjacent spatial blocks. Denote the inter-block neighbors at mode(u,v) by $\big(F_q^1(u, v), F_q^2(u, v)\big)$ and the simultaneous modifications on them by $(\Delta F_1, \Delta F_2)$. The simultaneous modifications contain four pairs of nonzero joint modification patterns, i.e., $(\Delta F_1, \Delta F_2) \in \big\{(+1, +1), (+1, -1), (-1, +1), (-1, -1)\big\}$,

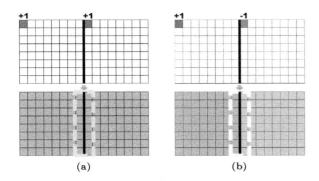

Figure 3: Combined impact on adjacent spatial blocks when modifying horizontal inter-block neighbors at mode DC with two kinds of joint modification patterns. (a) Pattern (+1,+1). (b) Pattern (+1,-1).

where $(+1,+1), (-1,-1)$ correspond to synchronizing modification directions and $(+1,-1), (-1,+1)$ denote desynchronizing modification directions. Without loss of generality, we take $(+1,+1)$ and $(+1,-1)$ as examples of synchronization and desynchronization, respectively.

As illustrated in Figure 3, when modifying the horizontal $\left(F_q^1(0,0), F_q^2(0,0)\right)$, the joint modification pattern of $(+1,+1)$ simultaneously increases pixel values of both adjacent blocks and thus preserves the consistency of boundary between the adjacent blocks, whereas $(+1,-1)$ causes increases on the left block but decreases on the right block, which leads to a discontinuity at block boundary, i.e. blocking artifact. In view of the neighboring relativity in natural images, $(+1,-1)$ is notably unreasonable because it breaks the local continuity on adjacent blocks and brings about blocking artifact, which would be captured and utilized by steganalysis as well. Hence for a higher steganographic security, $(+1,+1)$ is encouraged and $(+1,-1)$ should be avoided for DC inter-block neighbors.

Similarly, we need to maintain spatial continuity at block boundaries if simultaneously modifying horizontal or vertical inter-block neighbors at other modes. To clarify, the block boundary consists of two columns or rows bordering two adjacent spatial blocks, i.e., the union of the 7th column in the left block and the 0th column in the right for the horizontal, or the union of the 7th row in the upper block and the 0th row in the lower for the vertical.

As illustrated in Figure 2(b), since $\Delta\mathbf{I}_{u,v}^{B}$ are distinct with different DCT modes, $(+1,+1)$ may be not invariably suitable for each mode (differs from SMD in spatial images). Figure 4 displays the combined impacts on adjacent blocks when modifying horizontal or vertical $\left(F_q^1(0,1), F_q^2(0,1)\right)$ and $\left(F_q^1(1,0), F_q^2(1,0)\right)$, where $(+1,-1)$ seems to be more preferable for some modes. In Figure 4(a)-(b) of horizontal inter-block neighbors, $(+1,-1)$ preserves the spatial continuity at block boundary for mode(0,1) but breaks that for mode(1,0), so it should be encouraged for mode(0,1) but discouraged for mode(1,0). The results about the vertical can be observed from Figure 4(c)-(d), and Table 1 reports the

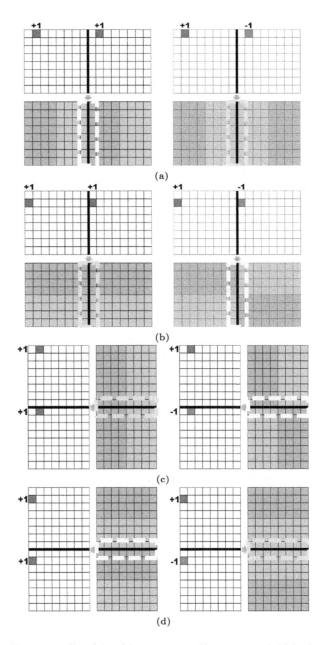

Figure 4: Combined impact on adjacent spatial blocks when modifying horizontal or vertical inter-block neighbors at mode(0,1) or mode(1,0) with (+1,+1) and (+1,-1). (a) Horizontal inter-block neighbors at mode(0,1). (b) Horizontal inter-block neighbors at mode(1,0). (c) Vertical inter-block neighbors at mode(0,1). (d) Vertical inter-block neighbors at mode(1,0).

corresponding encouraged joint modification patterns, which indicates that encouraged joint modification patterns are related to the mode of coefficient and the adjacent direction of inter-block neighbors.

Table 1: The encouraged joint modification pattern on horizontal or vertical inter-block neighbors at mode(0,1) or mode(1,0).

Mode	Horizontal	Vertical
(0,1)	(+1, −1)	(+1, +1)
(1,0)	(+1, +1)	(+1, −1)

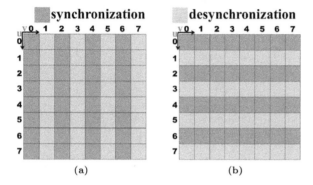

(a)   (b)

Figure 5: Encouraged joint modification patterns of 64 DCT modes with two types of adjacent direction, where green represents synchronization and orange represents desynchronization. (a) Horizontal inter-block neighbors. (b) Vertical inter-block neighbors.

3.3 Principle of BBC

Through observation from $\Delta \mathbf{I}_{u,v}^{B}$, we summarize the strategy associated with encouraged joint modification patterns of all the 64 DCT modes and two adjacent directions of inter-block neighbors, as shown in Figure 5. The strategy is named the principle of Block Boundary Continuity (BBC) as follows.

Principle of BBC.

(i) *For horizontal* $\left(F_q^1(u,v), F_q^2(u,v)\right)$ *at mode(u,v), the encouraged joint modification pattern*

$$(\Delta F_1, \Delta F_2) = \begin{cases} (+1,+1) \text{ and } (-1,-1) & \text{for } v = 0,2,4,6 \\ (+1,-1) \text{ and } (-1,+1) & \text{for } v = 1,3,5,7 \end{cases}.$$

(ii) *For vertical* $\left(F_q^1(u,v), F_q^2(u,v)\right)$ *at mode(u,v), the encouraged joint modification pattern*

$$(\Delta F_1, \Delta F_2) = \begin{cases} (+1,+1) \text{ and } (-1,-1) & \text{for } u = 0,2,4,6 \\ (+1,-1) \text{ and } (-1,+1) & \text{for } u = 1,3,5,7 \end{cases}.$$

According to the principle of BBC, it is encouraged to synchronize modification directions at modes of $v = 0,2,4,6$ and desynchronize that at modes of $v = 1,3,5,7$ for horizontal inter-block neighbors, and meanwhile for vertical inter-block neighbors, synchronization should be encouraged at modes of $u = 0,2,4,6$ and desynchronization at modes of $u = 1,3,5,7$. With BBC, the neighboring relativity in natural images is maintained, thus the modifications in DCT domain would be more secure.

Here we take modifications on horizontal inter-block neighbors as an example to prove the correctness of the BBC principle. We further derive the formulas for judging whether the joint modification pattern should be encouraged or not, which are needful for the definition of joint distortion.

PROOF. The block boundary of horizontally adjacent blocks is the union of the $7th$ column in the left block and the $0th$ column in the right block. Let $\Phi_{u,v}(x, \Delta F_1, \Delta F_2) = \Delta f_{u,v}^{B}(x, 7, \Delta F_1) \cdot \Delta f_{u,v}^{B}(x, 0, \Delta F_2)$ determine the consistency of the binarized spatial changes at two columns, and $\Phi_{u,v}(x, \Delta F_1, \Delta F_2) = 1$ means continuity while conversely $\Phi_{u,v}(x, \Delta F_1, \Delta F_2) = -1$ means discontinuity. From (11),

$$\Phi_{u,v}(x, \Delta F_1, \Delta F_2)$$
$$= sgn\left(\Delta F_1 \cdot \Delta F_2 \cdot \cos^2 \frac{(2x+1)u\pi}{16} \cdot \cos \frac{15v\pi}{16} \cdot \cos \frac{v\pi}{16}\right)$$
$$= sgn\left(\Delta F_1 \cdot \Delta F_2 \cdot \cos \frac{15v\pi}{16} \cdot \cos \frac{v\pi}{16}\right)$$
$$= sgn\left(\Delta F_1 \cdot \Delta F_2 \cdot \cos(v\pi - \frac{v\pi}{16}) \cdot \cos \frac{v\pi}{16}\right)$$
$$= sgn\left(\Delta F_1 \cdot \Delta F_2 \cdot [\cos v\pi \cdot \cos \frac{v\pi}{16} + \sin v\pi \cdot \sin \frac{v\pi}{16}] \cdot \cos \frac{v\pi}{16}\right)$$
$$= sgn\left(\Delta F_1 \cdot \Delta F_2 \cdot \cos v\pi \cdot \cos^2 \frac{v\pi}{16}\right)$$
$$= sgn\left(\Delta F_1 \cdot \Delta F_2 \cdot \cos v\pi\right)$$
$$= \Delta F_1 \cdot \Delta F_2 \cdot \cos v\pi$$
$$= \begin{cases} \Delta F_1 \cdot \Delta F_2 & \text{if } v = 0,2,4,6 \\ -\Delta F_1 \cdot \Delta F_2 & \text{if } v = 1,3,5,7 \end{cases}.$$

So, taking $\Delta F_1 \cdot \Delta F_2 = 1$ (synchronization) for $v = 0,2,4,6$ and $\Delta F_1 \cdot \Delta F_2 = -1$ (desynchronization) for $v = 1,3,5,7$, can maintain the continuity $\left(\Phi_{u,v}(x, \Delta F_1, \Delta F_2) = 1\right)$, which derives the principle about horizontal inter-block neighbors. □

Since $\Phi_{u,v}(x, \Delta F_1, \Delta F_2)$ is independent of x, we denote it by

$$\Phi_{u,v}^{hor}(\Delta F_1, \Delta F_2) = \Delta F_1 \cdot \Delta F_2 \cdot \cos v\pi. \quad (12)$$

Similarly, for vertical inter-block neighbors, $\Phi_{u,v}(y, \Delta F_1, \Delta F_2) = \Delta f_{u,v}^{B}(7, y, \Delta F_1) \cdot \Delta f_{u,v}^{B}(0, y, \Delta F_2)$ is denoted by

$$\Phi_{u,v}^{ver}(\Delta F_1, \Delta F_2) = \Delta F_1 \cdot \Delta F_2 \cdot \cos u\pi. \quad (13)$$

Obviously, $\Phi_{u,v}^{hor}(\Delta F_1, \Delta F_2), \Phi_{u,v}^{ver}(\Delta F_1, \Delta F_2) = 1$ correspond to encouraged joint modification patterns, and conversely $\Phi_{u,v}^{hor}(\Delta F_1, \Delta F_2), \Phi_{u,v}^{ver}(\Delta F_1, \Delta F_2) = -1$ correspond to discouraged joint modification patterns, which will be used in the definition of joint distortion.

3.4 Verifying the Practicability of BBC

To verify whether the BBC principle is reasonable for JPEG steganography, we perform a simulation as follows. Firstly, 10,000 gray-scale images of size 512×512 pixels from BOSS-Base1.01 [1] are JPEG compressed with quality factor 75, and coefficients at mode(u,v) are extracted from DCT blocks to form a sub-image of size 64×64, which is then divided into non-overlapping blocks of size 8×16. Secondly, a noise pattern is added to each image block to simulate the effect of data embedding. Two kinds of noise patterns in Figure 6 are

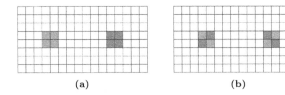

Figure 6: Two kinds of noise patterns where blue means +1 and red means -1. (a) Noise pattern A. (b) Noise pattern B.

Table 2: The MMD and the steganalytic performance of individually adding noise pattern A or B on coefficients at mode DC or mode(1,1).

Mode	Pattern	MMD	Testing Error
DC	A	2.494×10^{-3}	0.2540
	B	5.716×10^{-3}	0.0777
(1,1)	A	7.446×10^{-3}	0.0478
	B	5.443×10^{-3}	0.0879

used, where modification directions are the same in Pattern A but the opposite in Pattern B both in horizontal and vertical directions. Thirdly, the DCTR-8,000D [9] features of the first 1,000 images are obtained and the MMD (maximum mean discrepancy) [16], which quantifies the distance between the feature set of cover images and that of stego images, is computed for each noise pattern. Finally, we employ modern steganalyzer with DCTR-8,000D to evaluate the performance of each noise pattern on resisting steganalysis. Generally, a lower MMD or a higher classification error corresponds to a higher level of security.

Without loss of generality, we only demonstrate the example of noise addition on coefficients at mode DC or mode(1,1) individually. The results in Table 2 show that noise addition of Pattern A is more secure for mode DC while Pattern B is less harmful for mode(1,1), which ideally conforms to the strategy in Figure 5. We also perform simulations with BBC on coefficients at other modes and come to the same conclusion. Consequently, it is reasonable to employ the BBC principle on directing the definition of joint distortion for JPEG steganography.

4 DEFINING JPEG JOINT DISTORTION WITH BBC

Under the guidance of the BBC principle, we define joint distortion for DCT coefficients at the same mode. Firstly, the initial distortion on single coefficient is defined by state-of-the-art additive methods. Secondly, coefficients at each mode are extracted from DCT blocks to form a sub-image $\mathbf{D}_{u,v}$ of size $\frac{m}{8} \times \frac{n}{8}$ (assume the size of the image is $m \times n$), which is then divided into non-overlapping joint blocks of the needed size. The joint distortion on joint block in each sub-image

$\mathbf{D}_{u,v}$ is computed on the basis of the initial distortion and the BBC principle. Finally, joint distortions from all $\mathbf{D}_{u,v}$s are composed into a sequence of joint distortion that can be sent into *DeJoin*.

The division of a JPEG image into 1×2 joint blocks (abbreviated to 2-Coeffs) and 2×2 joint blocks (abbreviated to 4-Coeffs) is depicted in Figure 7. For 2-Coeffs, $\mathbf{D}_{u,v}$ is divided into the joint block sequence $B_{u,v}^{(i)} = (d_{u,v}^{i,1}, d_{u,v}^{i,2})$ for $i = 1, \cdots, N$ where $N = (\frac{m}{8} \times \frac{n}{8})/2$. For 4-Coeffs, $\mathbf{D}_{u,v}$ is divided into the joint block sequence $B_{u,v}^{(i)} = \begin{pmatrix} d_{u,v}^{i,1}, d_{u,v}^{i,2} \\ d_{u,v}^{i,3}, d_{u,v}^{i,4} \end{pmatrix}$ for $i = 1, \cdots, N$ where $N = (\frac{m}{8} \times \frac{n}{8})/4$.

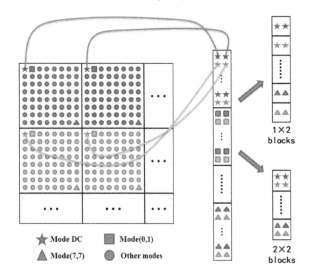

Figure 7: The division of a JPEG image into 1×2 joint blocks and 2×2 joint blocks.

4.1 Defining Horizontal 2-Coeffs Joint Distortion

For the joint block $B_{u,v}^{(i)} = (d_{u,v}^{i,1}, d_{u,v}^{i,2})$ in $\mathbf{D}_{u,v}$, denote the initial cost on $d_{u,v}^{i,1}$ by $c_{u,v}^{i,1}(\Delta F_1)$ for $\Delta F_1 \in \mathbf{I}$ and the initial cost on $d_{u,v}^{i,2}$ by $c_{u,v}^{i,2}(\Delta F_2)$ for $\Delta F_2 \in \mathbf{I}$. The joint distortion on $B_{u,v}^{(i)}$ is defined by

$$\rho_{u,v}^{(i)}(\Delta F_1, \Delta F_2) = \omega_{u,v}(\Delta F_1, \Delta F_2) \times \left(c_{u,v}^{i,1}(\Delta F_1) + c_{u,v}^{i,2}(\Delta F_2) \right), \quad (14)$$

and the scaling function $\omega_{u,v}(\Delta F_1, \Delta F_2)$ is computed by

$$\omega_{u,v}(\Delta F_1, \Delta F_2) = \begin{cases} 1/\alpha & \text{if } \Phi_{u,v}^{hor}(\Delta F_1, \Delta F_2) = 1 \\ \alpha & \text{if } \Phi_{u,v}^{hor}(\Delta F_1, \Delta F_2) = -1 \\ 1 & \text{otherwise} \end{cases}, \quad (15)$$

where $\alpha > 1$ is to differentiate the costs of encouraged and discouraged joint modification patterns. According to (12), $\Phi_{u,v}^{hor}(\Delta F_1, \Delta F_2) = 1$ corresponds to the encouraged joint modification patterns, of which the costs will be reduced by dividing α, and $\Phi_{u,v}^{hor}(\Delta F_1, \Delta F_2) = -1$ corresponds to the discouraged joint modification patterns, of which the costs will be enlarged by multiplying α. A larger α means a better differentiation but inevitably causes more modifications. Since too many modifications would make a greatly bad influence on steganographic security, α could not be too large. We set $\alpha = 1.5$ experimentally, and embed message by using $DeJoin_2$ on 2-Coeffs from all $\mathbf{D_{u,v}}$s to minimize the joint distortion defined in (14).

4.2 Combining $DeJoin_2$ with $UpDist$

Since the joint distortion on horizontal 2-Coeffs only reflects the mutual impact of modifications in horizontal direction, we can incorporate the mutual impact in vertical direction by applying $UpDist$ upon 2-Coeffs if taking 2-Coeffs as a super-coefficient. To do that, we firstly embed half of payload into the 2-Coeffs in *odd* rows by using $DeJoin_2$. As illustrated in Figure 8, the joint distortion on the 2-Coeffs in *even* rows will be updated according to the changed results of the *odd* 2-Coeffs (in the same $\mathbf{D_{u,v}}$) above and under it. We finally embed the rest payload into the *even* 2-Coeffs by using $DeJoin_2$ on the updated joint distortion that considers the impact of modifications both in horizontal and vertical directions. The combination of $UpDist$ and $DeJoin_2$ is abbreviated to $UpDist\text{-}DeJoin_2$.

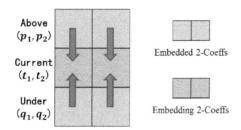

Figure 8: Illustration of $UpDist$ upon 2-Coeffs.

Assume that in the first round, the above *odd* block (p_1, p_2) has been changed to $(p_1 + \Delta F_1', p_2 + \Delta F_2')$ and the under *odd* block (q_1, q_2) has been changed to $(q_1 + \Delta F_1'', q_2 + \Delta F_2'')$, and then the joint distortion $\rho_{u,v}(\Delta F_1, \Delta F_2)$ on the current *even* block (t_1, t_2) will be updated to $\rho_{u,v}^{update}(\Delta F_1, \Delta F_2)$ by

$$\rho_{u,v}^{update}(\Delta F_1, \Delta F_2) = \prod_{(\Delta_1, \Delta_2)} \varepsilon_{u,v}(\Delta_1, \Delta_2) \times \rho_{u,v}(\Delta F_1, \Delta F_2),$$

(16)

where

$$\varepsilon_{u,v}(\Delta_1, \Delta_2) = \begin{cases} \beta & \text{if } \Phi_{u,v}^{ver}(\Delta_1, \Delta_2) = 1 \\ 1 & \text{otherwise} \end{cases},$$ (17)

and

$$(\Delta_1, \Delta_2) \in \left\{ (\Delta F_1, \Delta F_1'), (\Delta F_1, \Delta F_1''), (\Delta F_2, \Delta F_2'), (\Delta F_2, \Delta F_2'') \right\}$$

corresponds to four pairs of vertically adjacent modifications. With (13), $\beta < 1$ has the same effect as α in (15), and we set $\beta = 0.6$ experimentally in this paper.

4.3 Defining 4-Coeffs Joint Distortion

For the joint block $B_{u,v}^{(i)} = \begin{pmatrix} d_{u,v}^{i,1}, d_{u,v}^{i,2} \\ d_{u,v}^{i,3}, d_{u,v}^{i,4} \end{pmatrix}$ in $\mathbf{D_{u,v}}$, denote the initial cost on $d_{u,v}^{i,j}$ by $c_{u,v}^{i,j}(\Delta_j)$ for $j \in \{1, 2, 3, 4\}$. The joint distortion on $B_{u,v}^{(i)}$ is defined by

$$\rho_{u,v}^{(i)}(\Delta_1, \Delta_2, \Delta_3, \Delta_4) = \omega_{u,v}(\Delta_1, \Delta_2, \Delta_3, \Delta_4) \times \sum_{j=1}^{4} c_{u,v}^{i,j}(\Delta_j).$$

(18)

The scaling function $\omega_{u,v}(\Delta_1, \Delta_2, \Delta_3, \Delta_4)$ is a ratio between the number of discouraged modification pairs (determined by $o_{u,v}(\Delta_p, \Delta_q)$) and the number of encouraged modification pairs (determined by $s_{u,v}(\Delta_p, \Delta_q)$), which is computed by

$$\omega_{u,v}(\Delta_1, \Delta_2, \Delta_3, \Delta_4) = \frac{\theta + \sum_{(p,q)} o_{u,v}(\Delta_p, \Delta_q)}{\theta + \sum_{(p,q)} s_{u,v}(\Delta_p, \Delta_q)},$$ (19)

where

$$s_{u,v}(\Delta_p, \Delta_q) = \begin{cases} 1 & \text{if } \left(mod(p+q, 2) = 1 \ \&\& \ \Phi_{u,v}^{hor}(\Delta_p, \Delta_q) = 1 \right) \\ 1 & \text{if } \left(mod(p+q, 2) = 0 \ \&\& \ \Phi_{u,v}^{ver}(\Delta_p, \Delta_q) = 1 \right) \\ 0 & \text{otherwise} \end{cases},$$

(20)

$$o_{u,v}(\Delta_p, \Delta_q) = \begin{cases} 1 & \text{if } \left(mod(p+q, 2) = 1 \ \&\& \ \Phi_{u,v}^{hor}(\Delta_p, \Delta_q) = -1 \right) \\ 1 & \text{if } \left(mod(p+q, 2) = 0 \ \&\& \ \Phi_{u,v}^{ver}(\Delta_p, \Delta_q) = -1 \right) \\ 0 & \text{otherwise} \end{cases},$$

(21)

and $(p, q) \in \left\{ (1, 2), (1, 3), (2, 4), (3, 4) \right\}$ corresponds to four pairs of horizontally $\left(mod(p + q, 2) = 1 \right)$ or vertically $\left(mod (p + q, 2) = 0 \right)$ adjacent modifications within $B_{u,v}^{(i)}$. With (12) and (13), $\theta > 1$ has the same effect as α and β. We set $\theta = 3$ experimentally and embed message by using $DeJoin_4$ on 4-Coeffs from all $\mathbf{D_{u,v}}$s to minimize the joint distortion defined in (18).

5 EXPERIMENTAL RESULTS AND ANALYSIS

In this section, experimental results are presented to demonstrate the feasibility and effectiveness of the BBC principle. We compare the performances of BBC-based schemes with several state-of-the-art additive schemes, including UERD [8], J-UNIWARD [10], IUERD [15], HDS [18] and RBV [19], on resisting the detection of DCTR-8,000D [9] and GFR-17,000D [17] under several quality factors.

5.1 Experiment Setup

All experiments are conducted on BOSSBase 1.01 [1], which contains 10,000 gray-scale images of size 512×512 pixels. All of the images are compressed into JPEG domain with quality factor $QF = 50, 75, 90$ respectively, which are then adopted as datasets for experimental comparisons. We replace STCs with an optimal embedding simulator [6] to reduce experimental complexity. The payloads range from 0.1 to 0.5 bpnzac (bit per nonzero AC coefficient) with a step of 0.1 bpnzac. The detector is trained by using state-of-the-art DCTR-8,000D [9] and GFR-17,000D [17] with the FLD ensemble [12] by default, which minimizes the total classification error probability

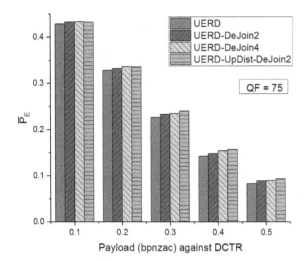

Figure 9: Detection errors for UERD and the corresponding BBC-based schemes against DCTR under QF=75.

under equal priors $P_E = \min_{P_{FA}} \frac{1}{2}(P_{FA} + P_{MD})$ where P_{FA} and P_{MD} are the false-alarm probability and the missed-detection probability respectively. The ultimate security is qualified by average error rate $\overline{P_E}$ averaged over 10 random 5000/5000 splits of the dataset, and larger $\overline{P_E}$ means stronger security.

5.2 Comparison and Visualization of $DeJoin_2$, $DeJoin_4$ and $UpDist$-$DeJoin_2$

Taking UERD as the initial distortion, we compare the steganographic securities of $DeJoin_2$, $DeJoin_4$ and $UpDist$-$DeJoin_2$ on resisting DCTR-8,000D with payloads of 0.1-0.5 bpnzac under $QF = 75$. As reported in Figure 9, three BBC-based schemes can outperform UERD, and because of incorporating the mutual impact of modifications in vertical direction, $DeJoin_4$ and $UpDist$-$DeJoin_2$ are more secure than $DeJoin_2$. For intuitively understanding the effect of BBC in JPEG steganography, an example is provided in Figure 10 to visualize the embedding changes in spatial domain. The sample cover image of size 128×128 pixels, containing smooth, edges and textured regions, is cropped from the full-size image "1013.jpg". It is clear that BBC-based schemes do maintain spatial continuity at block boundaries, and $UpDist$-$DeJoin_2$ preserves a wider range of continuity so that it can slightly outperform $DeJoin_4$. Hence, we select $UpDist$-$DeJoin_2$ for the following experiments.

5.3 Comparison with State-of-the-art Additive Distortion Functions

Since UERD and J-UNIWARD have become the mainstream methods in JPEG steganography, we compare the steganographic securities of UERD-$UpDist$-$DeJoin_2$ and J-UNI-$UpDist$-$DeJoin_2$ with that of the initial distortion UERD and J-UNIWARD against DCTR-8,000D and GFR-17,000D

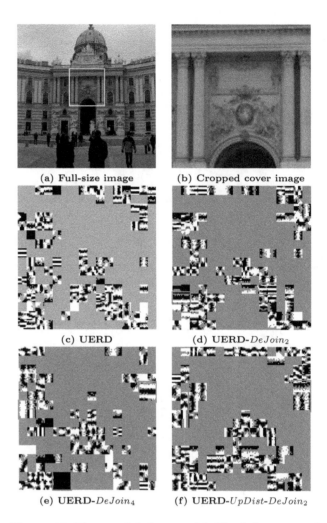

(a) Full-size image   (b) Cropped cover image

(c) UERD   (d) UERD-$DeJoin_2$

(e) UERD-$DeJoin_4$ (f) UERD-$UpDist$-$DeJoin_2$

Figure 10: The spatial changes (c)-(f) of the cropped cover image (b) with payload 0.5 bpnzac, QF=75, using UERD and the corresponding BBC-based schemes respectively, where white represents increase (≥ 1) and dark represents decrease (≤ -1).

under $QF = 50, 75, 90$. For $QF = 75$ in Figure 12, the BBC-based schemes perform better than the initial distortions in all cases, and improvements are larger than 1% at high payloads (≥ 0.3bpnzac) both for UERD and J-UNIWARD. As shown in Figure 11, improvements are more outstanding for $QF = 50$, even with small payloads. However for $QF = 90$ in Figure 13, promotions from BBC are relatively mild. We attribute this phenomenon to the degree of blocking artifact caused by modifications on inter-block neighbors with different QFs. It is clear in (9) that with the QF becoming smaller and equivalently the quantization matrix $\mathbf{Q}$ becoming larger, modifying a DCT coefficient is creating a larger impact on spatial block, so unreasonable joint modifications would inevitably lead to more severe blocking artifacts. Although the magnitudes of spatial changes are neglected in this paper,

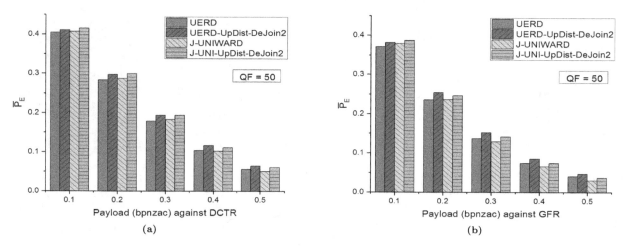

Figure 11: Detection errors for UERD, J-UNIWARD and their corresponding BBC-based $UpDist\text{-}DeJoin_2$ **against two steganalysis features under QF=50. (a) DCTR. (b) GFR.**

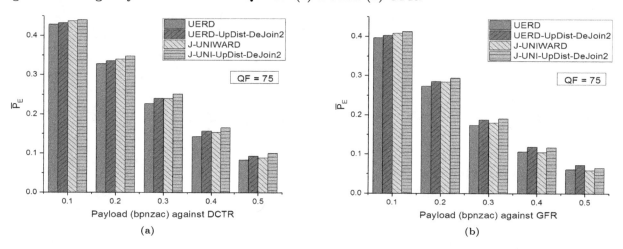

Figure 12: Detection errors for UERD, J-UNIWARD and their corresponding BBC-based $UpDist\text{-}DeJoin_2$ **against two steganalysis features under QF=75. (a) DCTR. (b) GFR.**

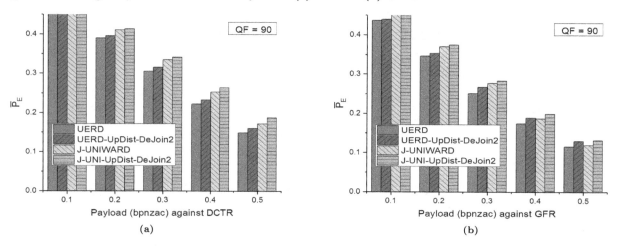

Figure 13: Detection errors for UERD, J-UNIWARD and their corresponding BBC-based $UpDist\text{-}DeJoin_2$ **against two steganalysis features under QF=90. (a) DCTR. (b) GFR.**

Table 3: Detection errors at 0.3 bpnzac for three novel additive schemes (IUERD, HDS and RBV) and their corresponding BBC-based schemes on BOSS-base1.01 using the FLD ensemble classifier with two feature sets under quality factor 75.

Embedding Method	DCTR	GFR
IUERD	$.2287 \pm .0019$	$.2011 \pm .0020$
IUERD-$UpDist$-$DeJoin_2$	$.2447 \pm .0017$	$.2198 \pm .0025$
HDS	$.2292 \pm .0022$	$.1841 \pm .0024$
HDS-$UpDist$-$DeJoin_2$	$.2420 \pm .0018$	$.1993 \pm .0023$
RBV	$.2420 \pm .0019$	$.1996 \pm .0027$
RBV-$UpDist$-$DeJoin_2$	$.2541 \pm .0014$	$.2171 \pm .0021$

the principle of BBC is in reality designed to utilize blocking artifacts, so the BBC-based schemes can work better with small QFs and correspondingly the highly compressed JPEG images. Table 4 reports the security performances of the involved schemes against two steganalysis features under quality factor 50, 75 and 90.

We also test three novel additive distortions IUERD, HDS, RBV and their corresponding BBC-based $UpDist$-$DeJoin_2$ at 0.3bpnzac under $QF = 75$, to verify whether the BBC principle can be generalizable to other additive schemes. It confirms in Table 3 that deploying BBC into non-additive scheme is beneficial to steganographic security. To date, RBV-$UpDist$-$DeJoin_2$ achieves the state-of-the-art security performance for JPEG steganography when resisting DCTR-8,000D, while IUERD-$UpDist$-$DeJoin_2$ and RBV-$UpDist$-$DeJoin_2$ receive the same best security against GFR-17,000D, of which the improvements to the initial distortions are apparent by about 1.8%.

6 CONCLUSION

Nowadays, non-additive distortion schemes with the principle of SMD have been proved to be tremendously beneficial for spatial image steganography. However, experimental results show that SMD could not be directly applied to JPEG steganography, and thus finding some principles appropriate for JPEG steganography has become an essential and interesting research problem.

In this paper, we introduce a principle of Block Boundary Continuity (BBC) for defining JPEG joint distortion, which tactfully and initiatively inspects the combined embedding changes on adjacent blocks from the spatial domain. According to BBC, the changed directions of some inter-block neighbors may be the same while others should be the opposite, which is related to the DCT mode and the adjacent direction of inter-block neighbors (horizontal or vertical). The principle aims at preserving spatial continuity at block boundaries through restraining blocking artifacts caused by joint modifications, so the neighboring relativity in natural images is maintained and thus modifications in DCT domain would be more secure. Experiments demonstrate that when

configured into the model of *DeJoin*, BBC does help improve state-of-the-art JPEG additive schemes in terms of relatively large embedding payloads against modern JPEG steganalyzers.

Since the magnitude of spatial change is neglected in this paper, we only exploit the spatial continuity at block boundaries in a simplified and rough way. How to precisely measure the degree of continuity or blocking artifact to enhance the security of JPEG steganography will be further explored in the future.

ACKNOWLEDGMENTS

This work was supported in part by the Natural Science Foundation of China under Grant U1636201 and 61572452. The authors would like to thank DDE Laboratory of SUN-Y Binghamton for sharing the source code of steganography, steganalysis and ensemble classifier on the webpage (http://dde.binghamton.edu/download/).

REFERENCES

[1] Patrick Bas, Tomáš Filler, and Tomáš Pevný. 2011. Break Our Steganographic System: The Ins and Outs of Organizing BOSS. In *Information Hiding*. Springer, 59–70.
[2] Tomáš Denemark and Jessica Fridrich. 2015. Improving steganographic security by synchronizing the selection channel. In *Proceedings of the 3rd ACM Workshop on Information Hiding and Multimedia Security*. ACM, 5–14.
[3] Tomáš Filler and Jessica Fridrich. 2010. Gibbs construction in steganography. *IEEE Transactions on Information Forensics and Security* 5, 4 (2010), 705–720.
[4] Tomáš Filler, Jan Judas, and Jessica Fridrich. 2011. Minimizing additive distortion in steganography using syndrome-trellis codes. *IEEE Transactions on Information Forensics and Security* 6, 3 (2011), 920–935.
[5] Jessica Fridrich. 2009. *Steganography in digital media: principles, algorithms, and applications*. Cambridge University Press.
[6] Jessica Fridrich and Tomas Filler. 2007. Practical methods for minimizing embedding impact in steganography. In *Electronic Imaging 2007*. International Society for Optics and Photonics, 650502–650502.
[7] Linjie Guo, Jiangqun Ni, and Yun Qing Shi. 2014. Uniform embedding for efficient JPEG steganography. *IEEE transactions on Information Forensics and Security* 9, 5 (2014), 814–825.
[8] Linjie Guo, Jiangqun Ni, Wenkang Su, Chengpei Tang, and Yun-Qing Shi. 2015. Using statistical image model for JPEG steganography: uniform embedding revisited. *IEEE Transactions on Information Forensics and Security* 10, 12 (2015), 2669–2680.
[9] Vojtěch Holub and Jessica Fridrich. 2015. Low-complexity features for JPEG steganalysis using undecimated DCT. *IEEE Transactions on Information Forensics and Security* 10, 2 (2015), 219–228.
[10] Vojtěch Holub, Jessica Fridrich, and Tomáš Denemark. 2014. Universal distortion function for steganography in an arbitrary domain. *EURASIP Journal on Information Security* 2014, 1 (2014), 1.
[11] Andrew D Ker, Patrick Bas, Rainer Böhme, Rémi Cogranne, Scott Craver, Tomáš Filler, Jessica Fridrich, and Tomáš Pevný. 2013. Moving steganography and steganalysis from the laboratory into the real world. In *Proceedings of the first ACM workshop on Information hiding and multimedia security*. ACM, 45–58.
[12] Jan Kodovsky, Jessica Fridrich, and Vojtěch Holub. 2012. Ensemble classifiers for steganalysis of digital media. *IEEE Transactions on Information Forensics and Security* 7, 2 (2012), 432–444.
[13] Bin Li, Junhui He, Jiwu Huang, and Yun Qing Shi. 2011. A survey on image steganography and steganalysis. *Journal of Information Hiding and Multimedia Signal Processing* 2, 2 (2011), 142–172.
[14] Bin Li, Ming Wang, Xiaolong Li, Shunquan Tan, and Jiwu Huang. 2015. A strategy of clustering modification directions in spatial image steganography. *IEEE Transactions on Information Forensics and Security* 10, 9 (2015), 1905–1917.

Table 4: Detection errors for UERD, J-UNIWARD and their corresponding BBC-based schemes on BOSS-base1.01 using the FLD ensemble classifier with two feature sets under quality factor 50, 75, 90.

QF	Feature	Embedding Method	0.1 bpnzac	0.2 bpnzac	0.3 bpnzac	0.4 bpnzac	0.5 bpnzac
50	DCTR	UERD	.4048 ± .0026	.2830 ± .0013	.1782 ± .0017	.1036 ± .0010	.0559 ± .0010
		UERD-$UpDist$-$DeJoin_2$	.4104 ± .0024	.2972 ± .0016	.1932 ± .0017	.1162 ± .0011	.0639 ± .0010
		J-UNIWARD	.4069 ± .0019	.2869 ± .0015	.1825 ± .0015	.1019 ± .0014	.0500 ± .0005
		J-UNI-$UpDist$-$DeJoin_2$	.4153 ± .0025	.2992 ± .0025	.1934 ± .0024	.1105 ± .0017	.0607 ± .0011
	GFR	UERD	.3705 ± .0038	.2353 ± .0028	.1369 ± .0015	.0739 ± .0009	.0408 ± .0009
		UERD-$UpDist$-$DeJoin_2$	.3813 ± .0032	.2534 ± .0035	.1524 ± .0018	.0849 ± .0010	.0468 ± .0011
		J-UNIWARD	.3793 ± .0026	.2360 ± .0034	.1287 ± .0014	.0654 ± .0011	.0302 ± .0008
		J-UNI-$UpDist$-$DeJoin_2$	.3868 ± .0026	.2462 ± .0028	.1413 ± .0012	.0739 ± .0007	.0370 ± .0009
75	DCTR	UERD	.4284 ± .0029	.3280 ± .0024	.2263 ± .0021	.1424 ± .0010	.0829 ± .0012
		UERD-$DeJoin_2$	.4327 ± .0017	.3316 ± .0021	.2315 ± .0026	.1476 ± .0015	.0888 ± .0009
		UERD-$DeJoin_4$	.4333 ± .0029	.3359 ± .0015	.2352 ± .0024	.1536 ± .0020	.0897 ± .0016
		UERD-$UpDist$-$DeJoin_2$	.4326 ± .0028	.3351 ± .0038	.2401 ± .0015	.1566 ± .0020	.0927 ± .0016
		J-UNIWARD	.4375 ± .0011	.3399 ± .0023	.2392 ± .0017	.1535 ± .0027	.0883 ± .0014
		J-UNI-$UpDist$-$DeJoin_2$	.4402 ± .0021	.3476 ± .0021	.2511 ± .0016	.1651 ± .0020	.0998 ± .0022
	GFR	UERD	.3962 ± .0031	.2729 ± .0023	.1739 ± .0012	.1059 ± .0011	.0611 ± .0008
		UERD-$UpDist$-$DeJoin_2$	.4024 ± .0027	.2856 ± .0021	.1877 ± .0019	.1183 ± .0016	.0721 ± .0011
		J-UNIWARD	.4081 ± .0024	.2836 ± .0014	.1797 ± .0013	.1043 ± .0015	.0587 ± .0008
		J-UNI-$UpDist$-$DeJoin_2$	.4121 ± .0027	.2935 ± .0024	.1906 ± .0020	.1168 ± .0012	.0651 ± .0009
90	DCTR	UERD	.4611 ± .0025	.3902 ± .0031	.3054 ± .0022	.2219 ± .0022	.1484 ± .0010
		UERD-$UpDist$-$DeJoin_2$	.4634 ± .0022	.3955 ± .0019	.3154 ± .0033	.2327 ± .0028	.1600 ± .0020
		J-UNIWARD	.4728 ± .0024	.4106 ± .0033	.3348 ± .0022	.2524 ± .0021	.1715 ± .0014
		J-UNI-$UpDist$-$DeJoin_2$	.4737 ± .0014	.4135 ± .0016	.3412 ± .0030	.2638 ± .0025	.1869 ± .0015
	GFR	UERD	.4366 ± .0028	.3464 ± .0042	.2507 ± .0015	.1742 ± .0013	.1154 ± .0014
		UERD-$UpDist$-$DeJoin_2$	.4396 ± .0015	.3533 ± .0046	.2668 ± .0031	.1891 ± .0008	.1297 ± .0024
		J-UNIWARD	.4523 ± .0025	.3703 ± .0020	.2770 ± .0031	.1868 ± .0021	.1196 ± .0020
		J-UNI-$UpDist$-$DeJoin_2$	.4536 ± .0023	.3748 ± .0025	.2830 ± .0027	.1990 ± .0017	.1315 ± .0018

[15] Yuanfeng Pan, Jiangqun Ni, and Wenkang Su. 2016. Improved Uniform Embedding for Efficient JPEG Steganography. In *International Conference on Cloud Computing and Security*. Springer, 125–133.

[16] Tomás Pevný and Jessica J Fridrich. 2008. Benchmarking for Steganography.. In *Information Hiding*, Vol. 5284. Springer, 251–267.

[17] Xiaofeng Song, Fenlin Liu, Chunfang Yang, Xiangyang Luo, and Yi Zhang. 2015. Steganalysis of adaptive JPEG steganography using 2D Gabor filters. In *Proceedings of the 3rd ACM Workshop on Information Hiding and Multimedia Security*. ACM, 15–23.

[18] Zichi Wang, Xinpeng Zhang, and Zhaoxia Yin. 2016. Hybrid distortion function for JPEG steganography. *Journal of Electronic Imaging* 25, 5 (2016), 050501–050501.

[19] Qingde Wei, Zhaoxia Yin, Zichi Wang, and Xinpeng Zhang. 2017. Distortion function based on residual blocks for JPEG steganography. *Multimedia Tools and Applications* (2017), 1–14.

[20] Weiming Zhang, Zhuo Zhang, Lili Zhang, Hanyi Li, and Nenghai Yu. 2017. Decomposing joint distortion for adaptive steganography. *IEEE Transactions on Circuits and Systems for Video Technology* 27, 10 (2017), 2274–2280.

Facing the Cover-Source Mismatch on JPHide using Training-Set Design

Dirk Borghys
Royal Military Academy, Dept. of
Mathematics
Brussels
Dirk.Borghys@rma.ac.be

Patrick Bas
CNRS, École Centralle de Lille, Univ.
of Lille, CRIStAL Lab
Lille
Patrick.Bas@centralelille.fr

Helena Bruyninckx
Royal Military Academy, Dept. of
Mathematics
Brussels
Helena.Bruyninckx@rma.ac.be

ABSTRACT

This short paper investigates the influence of the image processing pipeline (IPP) on the cover-source mismatch (CSM) for the popular JPHide steganographic scheme. We propose to deal with CSM by combining a forensics and a steganalysis approach. A multi-classifier is first trained to identify the IPP, and secondly a specific training set is designed to train a targeted classifier for steganalysis purposes. We show that the forensic step is immune to the steganographic embedding. The proposed IPP-informed steganalysis outperforms classical strategies based on training on a mixture of sources and we show that it can provide results close to a detector specifically trained on the appropriate source.

KEYWORDS

Digital image steganalysis, JPEG domain, cover-source mismatch, image processing pipeline, forensics-aware steganalysis

ACM Reference Format:
Dirk Borghys, Patrick Bas, and Helena Bruyninckx. 2018. Facing the Cover-Source Mismatch on JPHide using Training-Set Design. In *IH&MMSec '18: 6th ACM Workshop on Information Hiding and Multimedia Security, June 20–22, 2018, Innsbruck, Austria.* ACM, New York, NY, USA, 6 pages. https://doi.org/10.1145/3206004.3206021

1 INTRODUCTION

For digital images, machine learning based steganalysis is currently the methodology that achieves the best performances in a controlled environment, i.e. whenever the steganographic scheme, the payload size and the image source are known. However if one of these three parameters remains unknown, the performance of the steganalysis scheme can be jeopardized. The problem of Cover-Source Mismatch (CSM) occurs when the analyzed image sources are unknown. To the best of our knowledge, it has been identified in 2008 by the pioneering works of Cancelli *et al.* [5] and confirmed during the BOSS contest [2]. It states that a mismatch can occur and consequently degrades the classification performances if the source of the testing set is different from the source of the training set. As

an example, during the BOSS contest and when applying the detectors optimized on BossBase (processed in a specific manner), to "real-world" images, it was noted that the performance dramatically drops.

Note that the CSM effect may be particularly observable when the training set comes from BossBase images. Indeed, if this database enables to compare steganographic and steganalysis results, its development pipeline is however extremely formatted: RAW images are first transformed into spatial (ppm) images using the free software DCraw with specific parameters. The images are then rescaled such that the largest dimension was 512 pixels and converted to greyscale, and for JPEG steganalysis the ppm images are compressed using standard quantization tables. All operations are performed using the 'convert' Unix command, which is very restrictive.

If the CSM can easily be observed, accurate characterization of the source in the literature is not straightforward. The term 'source' has been coined in 2011 [2, 6] and became an important topic in steganalysis research from 2012 onwards (e.g. [7–9, 11, 13, 14, 16]), definitions of a source are diverse and stay informal.

Ker and Pevny characterize a source as an actor [9], i.e. one user uploading a set of images on his social network account. The authors provide options to mitigate the CSM by normalizing independently the features of each user. Pasquet [16] *et al.* consider a source as a cluster of features, and they combine unsupervised and supervised training to conduct steganalysis. Finally, Kodovsky *et al.* [13] proposed to deal with different sources (here cameras) by training on a mixture of images coming from different sources and Lubenko and Ker [14] proposed to adopt a similar strategy on millions of images using a simple on-line classifier.

Recently Giboulot *et al.* [7] conducted an investigation to characterize the set of parameters that specify a 'source'. This paper considered the case were RAW images were acquired using various cameras and developed to JPEG images using photographic development softwares. The impact of the choice of camera, the acquisition parameters and the image processing pipeline (IPP) were considered. The paper showed that the acquisition parameters (including the camera type) have only a minor impact, but that the image processing parameters as well as the quantization table have the largest impact. The investigated processing parameters were sharpening, denoising, color adjustments and the choice of the development software.

The current paper follows the same methodology as [7] while investigating some complementary development pipelines such as white-balancing and demosaicing. It focuses on the popular JPHide embedding scheme. This scheme has been selected because the

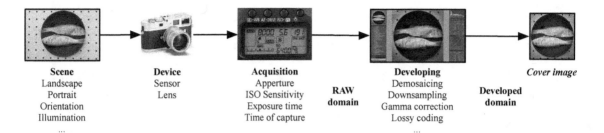

Figure 1: Pipeline of the cover image generation process which can be decomposed into four main steps (scene, device, acquisition, developing) representing parameters of the whole process.

embedding is fast, and its detectability has already been analyzed within the CSM paradigm by Ker and Pevny [9]. Moreover, this work enables to highlight complementary conclusions with respect to [7].

A strategy to mitigate the impact of the CSM due to the image processing pipeline is also proposed. This strategy consists first of a forensics analysis by using steganalysis features to identify a processing pipeline similar to the one applied on the test image. Similarly to [7, 15], we show that the best detection results are obtained when the training is performed on an image database coming from a source similar to the one generating the test images.

1.1 The Image Processing Pipeline

A source can be defined w.r.t. the image generation process depicted in Figure 1 which shows that the creation of a cover image is linked to the succession of different parameters represented by (1) the scene that is captured, (2) the device which is used, (3) the acquisition settings used during the capture and (4) the developing step.

Each parameter is linked with a set of sub-parameters. The scene fluctuates according to the subject, but also according to the illumination or the orientation of the camera. The device is composed mainly of two elements: the sensor (which can be CMOS, CCD; color or monochrome) and the lens.

The acquisition phase relies on three parameters originating from the device: the lens aperture, the ISO sensitivity and the exposure time and one parameter which is the time of capture.

Finally, the developing step which is studied in this paper, contains a lot of processing steps and we list here the most important ones:

- the white-balance is a color transform needed to adjust to human perception of color under different illuminations,

- Gamma correction is a sample-wise transform which maps to a different tone,

- the demosaicing or Color Filter Array (CFA) interpolation step predicts two missing color components for each pixel from neighboring photo-site values,

- and the user can also apply other image processing operations such as denoising or sharpening.

2 METHODOLOGY

The methodology explored in this paper for reducing the CSM (cf. Figure 2) consists in first determining the image processing pipeline

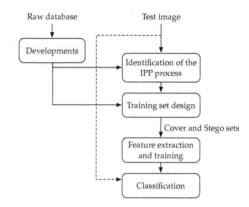

Figure 2: Schematic overview of the examined methodology.

(IPP) that was applied to an image, and then exploiting that information for building an adequate training set that is used to train the steganalysis detectors. First, a multi-classifier is trained to identify the closest development process among a set of predefined ones. This operation is possible by extracting features from databases specifically developed from a database of RAW images. Secondly, the closest database of cover images is used as a training database for steganalysis by generating a corresponding set of stego images. Finally, a classical steganalysis methodology is applied by extracting features and training a classifier which is afterward used on the test image. Note that such a methodology is an example of forensics-aided steganalysis which was already briefly explored by Barni *et al.* [1] for distinguishing camera images from computer generated images before performing steganalysis.

3 EXPERIMENTAL SETUP

We chose to study a specific camera (the Leica M9) and in order to have a complete control of the image processing pipeline, the RAW images available in the BossBase are used in our experiments. In the original BossBase 2758 RAW images of the Leica M9 are available. These are used for creating test images corresponding to different choices of the processing parameters. After processing, the 2758 images are cropped into non-overlapping 512x512 images, resulting in a total of over 160000 images. This procedure thus allows an artificial increase of the image database. The selected cropping method results in a very high variation in scene content between different sub-images but the local statistics caused by the processing pipeline are the same as for the full-sized images.

Three photographic development tools were used in the experiment: the open-source software DCraw v9.25 (denoted "DC" in this paper) and RawTherapee v4.1.0 (http://rawtherapee.com/) ("RT") and the commercial software Adobe Lightroom© v6.0 ("LR6").

The three softwares were used for converting the RAW images into color JPEG images with a standard quantization table with quality factor 100 (STD100) for DCraw and RawTherapee and the Adobe Level 12 quantization table (Adobe12) for Lightroom. A 4:2:2 color sub-sampling was used in the JPEG conversion.

The steganographic method used in the current investigation is JPHide.

As mentioned in Giboulot et al.[7] the IPP in general modifies the content details of a picture and, hence, the resulting number of non-zero AC coefficients (nzac). In order to perform a fair comparison between the photographic developments performed by different IPPs, the payload size should remain constant over the different developments. Contrary to [7], note that we did not use the same message length for all images. The image contents of the different crops is so diverse that we decided to fix the message length for each of the crops but to keep it constant over the different developments applied to each cropped image. The message length is set to 10% of the nzac in the images developed by a specific processing chain (i.e. DCraw using a bilinear CFA interpolation). However, we believe that using a constant payload through all images and developments or using a constant payload only through developments should lead to similar conclusions.

For each of the investigated processing parameters, stego/cover pairs were created for the 160000 cropped images.

The used steganalytic detector is the Ensemble Classifier (EC) [12] based on the CC-JRM feature set [10] and used in a clairvoyant scenario, i.e. both the steganographic method and the embedding rate are known to the steganalyst. The false alarm, missed-detection and total error probabilities, (P_{fa}, P_{md} and $P_E = (P_{fa} + P_{md})/2$) were considered as performance metrics. In order to estimate these performance metrics, 10000 cover/stego image pairs were randomly selected from the set of 160000 images for training the detector. Another (disjoint) set of 10000 image pairs was used for validation. This was repeated five times in order to obtain an average value and a standard deviation for the performance metrics. For compactness, the paper reports only the average values for P_E.

4 IMPACT OF IMAGE PROCESSING PARAMETERS

Because Giboulot et al. [7] already investigated many image processing parameters, the current paper focuses on parameters not yet examined in that paper. These include white balancing, gamma correction, CFA demosaicing and the choice of the development software. For investigating the impact of white balancing and gamma correction, DCraw was used.

4.1 Impact of white balancing

The choice of the white balancing method influences the color appearance of an image. By default, DCraw uses a fixed white balance based on a color chart illuminated with a standard D65

lamp (cf. user manual of DCraw), which roughly corresponds to the average midday light in Northern/Western Europe.

Besides this default white balancing (WBdef) method, DCraw also allows to select two other types of white balance: camera (WBcam) and average (WBave). In WBcam the white balance is defined by the camera. In practice the photographer can choose between automatic white balancing (AWB) or a number of preset values depending on the lighting conditions (e.g. sunset, clear sky, clouded sky, ...). Each choice determines a color temperature applied in the white balancing [4].

In WBave the white balance is calculated by averaging over the complete image.

The white balance is thus partly defined by the camera during image acquisition, but can be overridden by the development software.

In the current experiment DCraw is used with all of its parameters set to their default value. Only the white balancing method is varied. The three available white balancing methods are applied and compared.

Figure 3 shows the results obtained for P_E for a steganalysis detector trained on images created by one of the three white balancing modes of DCraw (shown on the left of the table) and applied to images created by each of the three methods (top of the table). A colormap is assigned to the values for an easier visualization of the mismatch. The values on the diagonal correspond to the matched case and represent the "intrinsic difficulty" of the considered source [7].

The figure shows that the largest mismatch if found when training on WBdef and applying the trained detector to any of the two other methods. Training on WBdef and applying to the two other modes results in a more than tenfold increase of P_E. The mismatch between the two other modes is much milder.

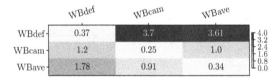

Figure 3: Influence of white balancing (P_E in %).

4.2 Impact of gamma correction

While [7] examines a range of manual tone adjustments in their investigation of the dependence on color adjustment, the current paper focuses on the more automatic process of gamma correction (GC).

In DCraw four gamma correction methods are available: BT-709, Adobe, ProPhoto and sRGB. BT709 is the default GC method in both DCraw and RawTherapee. Details on the various gamma correction methods and their parameters can be found in [18, 19]. The impact of gamma correction on the CSM is illustrated in figure 4. The largest mismatch is found between the default GC (GCdef) and the three other methods. Training on GCdef and applying the trained detector to the images created using the other three GC methods leads again to a more than tenfold increase of P_E w.r.t. the respective

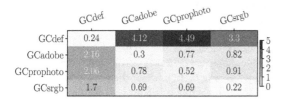

Figure 4: Influence of gamma correction (P_E in %).

fully-matched cases. Between the three other methods the relative increase in P_E is between 1.3 (for training on GCsrgb images and testing on GCprophoto) and 4.1 (for training on GCprophoto and testing on GCsrgb). GCprophoto exhibits a higher intrinsic difficulty (i.e. the value on the diagonal corresponding to the fully-matched case) than the three other methods.

4.3 Impact of CFA interpolation and development software

For the conversion from RAW image to JPEG in this paper three development softwares are used: DCraw (DC), RawTherapee (RT) and Adobe Lightroom 6.0 (LR6). The first step in the conversion from RAW is the CFA interpolation (demosaicing). In this section the combined effect of the CFA interpolation and the choice of development software is investigated. Eleven IPPs were defined and examined. The results of the mismatch between them is presented in figure 5. Details about the eleven IPPs are given below. DCraw and RawTherapee were used with all parameters set to their default values. Only the demosaicing method was varied. For DCraw the (bi)linear, AHD, VNG and PPG interpolations were used (resp. denoted DClin, DCahd, DCvng, DCppg on the figure's axes). For RawTherapee AHD, Amaze and IGV were applied (RTahd, RTamaze and RTigv).

LR6 uses a proprietary demosaicing method for which no detailed documentation is available. For LR6 we considered four processing pipelines. In LR6Def all parameters were left to their default value. LR6 uses its own quantization tables (QTs) and in particular the QT at highest quality (level 12) differs from the standard table at quality factor QF=100. Therefore we also created LR6 images with the standard QT at QF=100 (LR6Std), consistent with the one used in the two other softwares. The LR6Std images were created using LR6 with all parameters set to their default value, but by exporting TIFF images instead of JPEG. The TIFF images are then converted to JPEG using the Python PIL library. The only difference between LR6Def en LR6Std is thus the QT.

LR6 performs several operations by default (denoising, sharpening, etc.). The default sharpening in LR6 is set to "level 25". For LR6 we also applied two other sharpening methods: a rather extreme sharpening in the development module at "level 125" (LR6DS125) and the "standard screen" (LR6SScr) method in the export module.

Figure 5 shows the results of the study of the mismatch between the various demosaicing methods and choice of the development softwares.

The figure clearly exhibits a block structure corresponding to the three softwares. The largest mismatch is thus obtained between different development softwares. Note that in [7] the development

software was found to have only moderate impact. The different result we observe here is probably due to the different choice of the feature set; DCTR in [7] versus CC-JRM in the current paper. We intend to examine this further.

The difference in QT seems to be an important factor in the mismatch found between LR6 and DCraw. LR6Std shows indeed a much smaller mismatch w.r.t. DCraw than LR6Def.

The intrinsic difficulty of a source is lowest for images processed by DCraw and much higher for images processed by RT and LR6. The LR6DS125 images have the highest intrinsic difficulty. The authors think this is caused by the highly non-linear character of the sharpening applied in LR6 which leads to a high variability within the corresponding training set.

The largest relative increase of P_E due to a mismatch in demosaicing method (within the same development software) is between 2.2 (for training on RTigv and testing on RTamaze) and 4.8 (for training on DCvng and testing on DClin).

5 IMAGE PROCESSING PIPELINE (IPP) CLASSIFIER

The fact that steganalysis results depend on the IPP suggests that the used steganalysis feature set is sensitive to this IPP. We have therefore investigated whether it is possible to use the same feature set for detecting the IPP. Several papers have been published showing the usefulness of steganalysis features for digital image forensics and in particular for detecting image manipulations [3, 17].

The ensemble classifier (EC) yielding excellent results for steganalysis using large feature sets, in the current paper the EC is also used for constructing a supervised classifier of the IPP.

For assigning one of the N examined IPPs to a given test image an N-class classifier is needed. For constructing this classifier from the binary ECs, an aggregation of one-to-one EC classifiers is applied: each EC is trained to distinguish between two IPPs. This is done for all pairs of IPPs, leading to $N(N-1)/2$ binary classifiers each voting for one of the IPPs in its pair. For assigning an IPP to an image under test, these $N(N-1)/2$ classifiers are applied and the final decision is the IPP that receives the majority of the votes.

For training the IPP-classifier we considered only the 11 IPPs discussed in section 4.3.

Figure 6 shows the results of the classification obtained after training and validation on 10000 cover images of each processing pipeline. The figure shows the confusion matrix of the classification. The value in row i, column j is the probability that an image created by the IPP noted on row i is classified as being created by the IPP in column j. For the sake of clarity, zero values are omitted.

The results show that the classifier is capable to identify the different IPPs with a very high accuracy. In particular, it is possible to distinguish between the different types of CFA interpolation. Note also that, except for the LR6Std there is no confusion between the LR6 generated images and those from DC or RT.

Interestingly, when applying the IPP-classifier trained on the cover images for classifying the IPP of the stego images, a very similar classification accuracy Acc [1] is obtained. The obtained Acc is 96.1% and 95.9% for resp. the cover and stego images. This means

---

[1] Acc=ratio of correctly classified items to the total number of classified items; expressed as a percentage

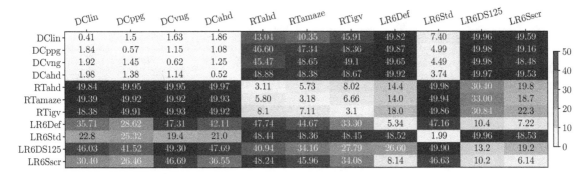

	DClin	DCppg	DCvng	DCahd	RTahd	RTamaze	RTigv	LR6Def	LR6Std	LR6DS125	LR6Sscr
DClin	0.41	1.5	1.63	1.86	43.04	40.35	45.91	49.82	7.40	49.96	49.59
DCppg	1.84	0.57	1.15	1.08	46.60	47.34	48.36	49.87	4.99	49.98	49.16
DCvng	1.92	1.45	0.62	1.25	45.47	48.65	49.1	49.65	4.49	49.98	48.48
DCahd	1.98	1.38	1.14	0.52	48.88	48.38	48.67	49.92	3.74	49.97	49.53
RTahd	49.84	49.95	49.95	49.97	3.11	5.73	8.02	14.4	49.98	30.40	19.8
RTamaze	49.39	49.92	49.92	49.93	5.80	3.18	6.66	14.0	49.94	33.00	18.7
RTigv	48.38	49.91	49.93	49.92	8.1	7.11	3.1	18.0	49.86	30.84	22.3
LR6Def	35.71	28.62	47.31	42.11	47.74	44.67	33.30	5.34	47.16	10.4	7.22
LR6Std	22.8	25.32	19.4	21.0	48.44	48.36	48.45	48.52	1.99	49.96	48.53
LR6DS125	46.03	41.52	49.30	47.69	40.94	34.16	27.79	26.60	49.90	13.2	19.2
LR6Sscr	30.40	26.46	46.69	36.55	48.21	45.96	34.08	8.14	46.63	10.2	6.14

Figure 5: Influence of demosaicing and development software (P_E in %).

that, while steganalysis performance is highly dependent on the processing chain, the detection of the processing chain suffers only a minor influence of the presence of steganography (for the experiments conducted in this paper).

6 MITIGATION OF THE CSM - THE IPP-INFORMED DETECTOR

The results of the IPP-classifier can be used for selecting the detector that was trained on the closest (and possibly same) source, i.e. an IPP-informed detector. For each tested image, the IPP-classifier discussed in section 5 is applied. In the second step the steganalysis detector that was trained on the detected IPP is applied for deciding whether the test image is cover or stego. This is done for 10000 randomly picked images for each of the considered IPPs.

In this test we also include images developed with DCraw/ AHD/ GC=Prophoto (DCCGPP) and DCraw /AHD/ WB= Camera (DCWBcam). Note that neither of these two processing pipelines were used for training the IPP-classifier or for training the steganalysis detectors.

In the test we also included 10000 JPEG images collected from Flickr. The selected images correspond to images acquired with the Leica M9 camera and with quantization table corresponding to Adobe level 12. The images were center-cropped to a size of 512×512 in a way that preserves the DCT structure. The corresponding stego-images were created with an embedding rate of 0.1 bpnac.

Figure 7 compares steganalysis results obtained by four different detection strategies:

- 'Fully matched' case: training and test images come from the same source. This is the baseline for the comparison. It represents the best results that can be obtained using the chosen feature set and the EC classifier.
- 'Class Boss': training on the classical BossBase, i.e. resized (spatially interpolated) images developed with DCraw using PPG demosaicing as explained in the introduction of the paper,
- 'Mixed training': the results of training the EC on a mix of the 11 sources (consisting of 1000 images from each source) as proposed in [13],
- 'IPP informed': the results of the proposed IPP-informed steganalyzer.

For DCGCPP and DCWBcam the values of the 'Fully matched' case in figure 7 are extracted from figures 3 and 4. For the images downloaded from Flickr the presented values for the 'Fully matched' case are the average results over five 5000/5000 random splits of the available images. For the 'Mixed training' of the Flickr images, we decided to use only images from LR6Def, LR6DS125 and LR6SScr for training (3400 of each IPP).

Figure 7 shows that the 'Class Boss' method clearly suffers the most of the CSM. The 'Mixed training' considerably reduces the impact of the CSM compared to the 'Class Boss' approach, except for the case where the latter is almost fully-matched (DCppg and DCahd). The 'IPP informed' method proposed in the current paper results in the smallest increase of P_E with respect to the fully-matched detector.

The proposed method also behaves better than 'Mixed training' for the two processing pipelines that were not used for training the IPP-classifier or the steganalysis detectors. Note that the increase of P_E w.r.t. the fully matched case is the highest for DCWBcam. However, the increase for both DCWBcam and DCGCPP is much smaller than the mismatch found in respectively figure 3 and 4 between WBdef/WBcam and GCdef/GCprophoto. The type of approach as presented in this paper thus also provides some robustness with respect to unknown IPPs. For the Flickr images the IPP-informed and the mixed training detectors obtain similar results. The large difference w.r.t. the 'Fully matched' case suggests that the LR6 developments used for training our models should be expanded, particularly w.r.t. the down-sampling operations that are present in the Flickr database. We also noted that the IPP-classifier classes 99.7% of the Flickr images as one of the three LR6 developments. The remainder is classified as RT developments.

7 CONCLUSIONS AND FURTHER WORKS

The paper investigates the influence of the image processing pipeline on the cover-source mismatch for JPHide. It also proposes a simple classifier of the IPP and shows how it can be exploited for reducing the CSM due to the IPP. We show that within this setup, the proposed IPP-informed steganalysis outperforms approaches based on mixed training over the examined sources. Partitioning the image data prior to steganalysis thus seems a promising approach for mitigating the CSM (see also [16]).

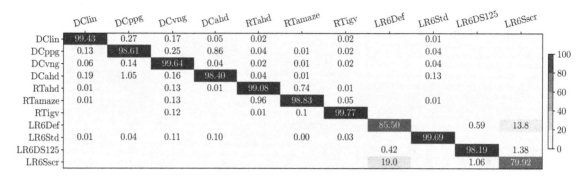

Figure 6: Confusion matrix for the supervised classification of the image processing pipeline (IPP).

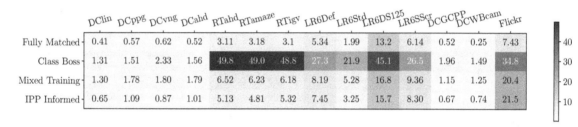

Figure 7: Comparison of P_E (in %) for the four detection strategies.

According to [7], the impact of the image processing pipeline on the CSM is more important than the choice of camera or the image acquisition parameters. The current paper additionally shows that the CSM can be significantly reduced by combining IPP classification with training set design. For the latter the RAW images of BossBase can be used for generating training databases that match or are close to the IPP of the images under investigation. The authors expect that for mitigating the impact of image acquisition a similar approach could be followed, based on a carefully designed expansion of the BossBase, i.e. spanning a larger variation of acquisition parameter settings.

Future work will assess the current methodology on other steganographic schemes in the pixel or JPEG domain.

ACKNOWLEDGMENTS

The authors would like to thank Samuel Tap who, in the frame of an internship at the Royal Military Academy, coded most of the Python™ scripts used for generating the results presented in this paper. This work was partially supported by the French ANR DEFALS program (ANR-16-DEFA-0003) and by the Belgian Royal Higher Institute for Defence (projects DAP16-01 and DAP18-01).

REFERENCES

[1] M. Barni, G. Cancelli, and A. Esposito. 2010. Forensics aided steganalysis of heterogeneous images. In *Int. Conf. on Acoustics Speech and Signal Processing (ICASSP)*. IEEE, 1690–1693.

[2] P. Bas, T. Filler, and T. Pevny. 2011. Break our Steganographic System - the ins and outs of organizing BOSS. In *13th workshop on Information Hiding*. Springer, Prague, Czech Republic, 59–70.

[3] M. Boroumand and J. Fridrich. 2017. Scalable Processing History Detector for JPEG Images. In *Media Watermarking, Security, and Forensics*. IS&T.

[4] Cambridge in Colours 2017. Photography tutorials: White balance. (2017). Retrieved Jan 24, 2018 from http://www.cambridgeincolour.com/tutorials/white-balance.htm

[5] G. Cancelli, G. Doerr, M. Barni, and I. J. Cox. 2008. A comparative study of ±1 steganalyzers. In *IEEE 10th Workshop on Multimedia Signal Processing*. 791–796.

[6] J. Fridrich, J. Kodovský, V. Holub, and M. Goljan. 2011. Breaking HUGO - The Process Discovery. In *13th Int. Conf. on Information Hiding*. 85–101.

[7] Q. Giboulot, R. Cogranne, and P. Bas. 2018. Steganalysis into the Wild: How to Define a Source?. In *Media Watermarking, Security, and Forensics*. IS&T.

[8] A.D. Ker, P. Bas, R. Böhme, R. Cogranne, S. Craver, T. Filler, J. Fridrich, and T. Pevný. 2013. Moving steganography and steganalysis from the laboratory into the real world. In *Workshop on Information Hiding and Multi-media Security (IH&MMSEC)*. ACM, 45–58. http://doi.acm.org/10.1145/2482513.2482965

[9] A. Ker and T. Pevny. 2014. A Mishmash of Methods for Mitigating the Model Mismatch Mess. In *Electronic Imaging, Media Watermarking, Security and Forensics*, Vol. SPIE Vol. 9028. SPIE, San Francisco, 90280I.

[10] J. Kodovsky and J. Fridrich. 2012. Steganalysis of JPEG Images Using Rich Models. In *Electronic Imaging, Media Watermarking, Security and Forensics*. SPIE, San Francisco.

[11] J. Kodovsky and J. Fridrich. 2013. Steganalysis in Resized Images. In *Proc. ICASSP*.

[12] J. Kodovsky, J. Fridrich, and V. Holub. 2012. Ensemble classifiers for steganalysis of digital media. *IEEE TIFS* 7, 2 (2012), 432 – 444.

[13] J. Kodovsky, V. Sedighi, and J. Fridrich. 2014. Study of Cover Source Mismatch in Steganalysis and Ways to Mitigate its Impact. In *Electronic Imaging, Media Watermarking, Security and Forensics*. SPIE, SPIE, San Francisco, California, 90280J.

[14] I. Lubenko and A. Ker. 2012. Going from small to large data in steganalysis. In *Media Watermarking, Security, and Forensics*, Vol. 8303. SPIE, 83030M–83030M–10. https://doi.org/10.1117/12.910214

[15] F. Comby M. Yedroudj, M. Chaumont. 2018. How to augment a small learning set for improving the performances of a CNN-based steganalyzer?. In *Media Watermarking, Security, and Forensics*. IS&T.

[16] J. Pasquet, S. Bringay, and M. Chaumont. 2014. Steganalysis with Cover-Source Mismatch and a small learning database. In *Proc. EUSPICO*.

[17] X. Qiu, H. Li, W. Luo, and J. Huang. 2014. A universal Image Forensic Strategy based on Steganalytic Model. In *Workshop on Information Hiding and Multi-media Security (IH&MMSEC)*. Salzburg.

[18] Rawpedia 2015. Gamma differential. (2015). Retrieved Jan 29, 2018 from https://rawpedia.rawtherapee.com/Gamma_-_Differential

[19] M.S. Tooms. 2016. *Colour Reproduction in Electronic Imaging Systems: Photography, Television, Cinematography*. John Wiley & Sons, Chapter Appendix H: Deriving the Standard Formula for Gamma Correction, 667–672.

Cover Block Decoupling for Content-Adaptive H.264 Steganography

Yun Cao
State Key Laboratory of Information Security, Institute of Information Engineering, Chinese Academy of Sciences, Beijing, China
School of Cyber Security, University of Chinese Academy of Sciences, Beijing, China
caoyun@iie.ac.cn

Yu Wang
State Key Laboratory of Information Security, Institute of Information Engineering, Chinese Academy of Sciences, Beijing, China
School of Cyber Security, University of Chinese Academy of Sciences, Beijing, China
wangyu9078@iie.ac.cn

Xianfeng Zhao[*]
State Key Laboratory of Information Security, Institute of Information Engineering, Chinese Academy of Sciences, Beijing, China
School of Cyber Security, University of Chinese Academy of Sciences, Beijing, China
zhaoxianfeng@iie.ac.cn

Meineng Zhu
Beijing Institute of Electronics Technology and Application, Beijing, China 100091
zmneng@163.com

Zhoujun Xu
Beijing Information Technology Institute, Beijing, China 100094
pl_xzj@uestc.edu.cn

ABSTRACT

This paper makes the first attempt to achieve content-adaptive H.264 steganography with the quantised discrete cosine transform (QDCT) coefficients in intra-frames. Currently, state-of-the-art JPEG steganographic schemes embed their payload while minimizing a heuristically defined distortion. However, porting this concept to schemes of compressed videos remains an unsolved challenge. Because of H.264 intra prediction, the QDCT coefficient blocks are highly depended on their adjacent encoded blocks, and modifying one coefficient block will set off a chain reaction in the following cover blocks. Based on a thorough investigation into this problem, we propose two embedding strategies for cover block decoupling to inhibit the embedding interactions. With this methodology, the latest achievements in the JPEG domain are expected to be incorporated to construct H.264 steganographic schemes for better performances.

ACM Reference Format:
Yun Cao, Yu Wang, Xianfeng Zhao, Meineng Zhu, and Zhoujun Xu. 2018. Cover Block Decoupling for Content-Adaptive H.264 Steganography. In *IH&MMSec '18: 6th ACM Workshop on Information Hiding and Multimedia Security, June 20–22, 2018, Innsbruck, Austria.* ACM, New York, NY, USA, Article 4, 8 pages. https://doi.org/10.1145/3206004.3206014

---

[*]The corresponding author.

---

1 INTRODUCTION

Steganography is the art and science of hiding communication, a steganographic system thus embeds hidden content in unremarkable cover media so as not to arouse an eavesdropper's suspicion [15]. And video steganography, as the name implies, uses digital video, which is almost the most influential media in the entertainment industry, as the cover media.

In literature, so far most achievements are made for the still image steganography. Compared to JPEG, the most common image format in use today, H.264 receives much less attention from the stego community, and there are large gaps between the two technologies. It is important to note that, unlike JPEG compression, H.264 implements data compression mainly based on the block-based prediction technologies. During the encoding process, one pixel block has to be predicted using previously encoded blocks in either the same frame (intra prediction) or the other frame(s) (inter prediction), and only the residual block with some supplementary information are further coded and transmitted. This means for compressed videos, there exist high correlations among QDCT coefficient blocks, which raises new challenges to the H.264 steganographic designing.

This paper focuses on the issues of steganographic designing using the QDCT coefficients of the 4×4 luminance blocks in intra-frame (I-frame). The current relational works can be classified into two types: compressed domain embedding and joint compression embedding [12]. In the first category, the compressed I-frames are partially decompressed to get the QDCT coefficients which are then modified and instantly re-compressed again into video streams. Approaches of this type are usually computational efficient, but suffer from a serious problem of I-frame distortion drift. Because the embedding error propagates, preserving quality is the main issue for such methods. In the literature, there are generally two methodologies for distortion drift prevention, i.e., to restrict modifications to coefficients that are not used in future encodings (e.g. [13, 14]) and to generate compensation signals to be added to the corrupted

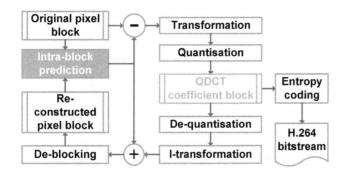

Figure 1: The reconstruction loop of H.264 intra-block coding.

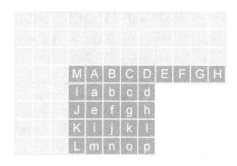

Figure 2: Predicted and reference pixels in a 4×4 luminance block.

signals (e.g. [9]). However, both methodologies are compromises which sacrifice the capacity and security a lot. In the second category, just as suggested by Z. Shahid *et.al.*, the secret message bits should be embedded during the encoding process by taking into account the reconstruction loop [17]. In H.264 intra-block coding, each 4×4 pixel block is subjected to the prediction process, and the associated encoding procedure can be modeled as a reconstruction loop depicted in Figure 1. In this way, since the modified block is reconstructed and used as reference for the following coded blocks, the distortion drift can be avoided. As the cost paid for the capacity gain, the in-loop embedding fashion is computationally expensive since full decompressing and recompressing the video stream are required. However, we believe that it is worthwhile to make the deal. In terms of steganography, the computational cost constrain is not a significant issue since few applications necessitate real-time response, not to mention the considerable strides in technologies for video processing acceleration these years.

Most current steganographic schemes embed the secret payload by minimizing a heuristically defined distortion [16]. Practically, content-adaptive embedding is realized by first defining the cost of changing each element, and then using the efficient coding method, syndrome-trellis codes (STCs) [6], to embed the secret message while minimizing the sum of costs of all changed elements. Unfortunately, this design methodology cannot be directly applied to the H.264 steganography, neither for compressed domain nor joint compression embedding. The intrinsic reasons are specified in Section 3.

The main contribution of this paper is a practical solution to achieve content-adaptive H.264 steganography which serves as a bridge between JPEG and H.264 steganographic designs. Based on a thorough investigation into the mechanism of I-frame coding, we perceive the interactive impact of modifications among adjacent cover blocks and propose two decoupling strategies to prevent the embedding impact from propagation. With this methodology, content-adaptive embedding can be carried out with STCs and any properly designed distortion function.

The rest of the paper is structured as follows. In Section 2, the basic concepts of H.264 intra-block coding and the model of minimal distortion steganography are introduced. In Section 3, the reasons why the distortion minimization framework cannot be applied to H.264 steganography is discussed in details. In Section 4, we

study the embedding interactions among adjacent cover blocks, and put forward two cover block decoupling strategies for inhibition. Section 5 describes comparative experiments which are conducted to prove the reasonability and feasibility of our design methodology. Finally, Section 6 draws conclusions and addresses possible future works.

2 PRELIMINARIES

2.1 H.264 Intra-Block Coding

As a major departure from the previous coding standards, H.264 introduces intra prediction to remove the spatial redundancies, and Figure 1 demonstrate the general flowchart of the intra-block coding. In H.264, two block sizes, i.e., 4×4 and 16×16, are supported. For concreteness, and without loss of generality, only the 4×4 luminance blocks are considered for data hiding in this paper.

Specifically, to encode one 4×4 luminance block $\mathbf{B} = \{b_{i,j}\}(0 \leq i,j \leq 3)$, first its prediction block $\mathbf{P}$ is predicted based on the previously encoded adjacent blocks. As illustrated in Figure 2, the samples in $\mathbf{P}$, i.e., a...p, are predicted based on the reconstructed samples, i.e., A...M, according to the prediction formula corresponding to its intra prediction mode (IPM) $M_\mathbf{B}$. H.264 provides nine optional IPMs for each 4×4 luminance block and four for each 16×16 luminance block [19], and the encoder makes sure that the one with the minimum prediction cost is assigned.

After intra prediction, $\mathbf{P}$ is subtracted from $\mathbf{B}$ to get the residual block $\mathbf{R} = \{r_{i,j}\}(0 \leq i,j \leq 3)$, and $\mathbf{R}$ is subjected to DCT transformation and quantisation to get the DCT coefficient block $\mathbf{Q}$ and the QDCT coefficient block $\tilde{\mathbf{Q}} = \{\tilde{q}_{i,j}\}(0 \leq i,j \leq 3)$ respectively. Then on the one hand $\tilde{\mathbf{Q}}$ is further entropy coded into H.264 video streams and on the other hand, $\tilde{\mathbf{Q}}$ is de-quantised and inverse transformed to $\tilde{\mathbf{R}}$ which is added to $\mathbf{P}$ to get the reconstructed pixel block $\tilde{\mathbf{B}} = \{\tilde{b}_{i,j}\}(0 \leq i,j \leq 3)$. Note that, it is $\tilde{\mathbf{B}}$, but $\mathbf{B}$ that serves as a reference in subsequential block codings.

2.2 Content-Adaptive Steganography by Distortion Minimization

Today, the most secure approach to steganography in digital images represented either in the spatial or JPEG domain is to embed the payload while minimizing a suitably defined distortion function. And the design of the distortion is essentially the only task left to the steganographer since efficient practical codes exist that embed near the payload-distortion bound [8].

For steganographic methods using QDCT coefficients, we denote the cover sequence as $\mathbf{x} = (x_1, x_2, \ldots, x_n)$, where x_i is an integer representing the QDCT coefficient value and n is the cover length. Given a relative payload α, an αn-bit message $\mathbf{m}$ is expected to be embedded by modifying $\mathbf{x}$ into $\mathbf{y}$. If any modification applied on x_i is mutually independent, the distortion introduced by changing single element can be thought to be additive. In this additive distortion model, each x_i is assigned a scalar γ_i to express the changing cost correlated with statistical detectability, and the overall embedding impact $D(\mathbf{x}, \mathbf{y}) = \sum_{i=1}^{n} \gamma_i [x_i \neq y_i]^1$ can be minimized using a flexible coding method known as STCs [6], which can approach the lower bound of average distortion. In syndrome coding, the embedding and extraction mappings can be formulated as

$$\text{Emb}_{\text{STC}}(\mathbf{x}, \Gamma, \mathbf{m}) = \arg \min_{\mathcal{P}(\mathbf{y}') \in C(\mathbf{m})} D(\mathbf{x}, \mathbf{y}') = \mathbf{y}, \qquad (1)$$

$$\text{Ext}_{\text{STC}}(\mathbf{y}) = \mathcal{P}(\mathbf{y})\mathbf{H}^T = \mathbf{m}. \qquad (2)$$

Here, Γ is the distortion scalar vector, $\mathcal{P} : \mathcal{J} \to \{0, 1\}$ can be any parity check function, $C(\mathbf{m})$ is the coset corresponding to syndrome $\mathbf{m}$, and $\mathbf{H} \in \{0, 1\}^{\alpha n \times n}$ is the parity-check matrix of the code C, which has to be shared between the sender and the receiver. For more details of the STCs, please refer to [6].

Actually, the changes on adjacent cover elements will interact and thus a nonadditive distortion model will be more suitable for adaptive steganography. Fortunately, for image steganography, approximating the non-additive distortion function in an additive form is a good solution to balance the simplicity and effectiveness [4]. The mutual impact of adjacent modifications can be exploited by synchronizing modification directions [3, 10].

3 APPLICATION PROBLEMS OF THE DISTORTION MINIMIZATION FRAMEWORK

As mentioned in Section 1, for QDCT-based H.264 steganography, there are generally two approaches: compressed domain embedding and joint compression embedding [12]. Next, in each case, the feasibility of applying the distortion minimization framework to H.264 steganography is discussed.

3.1 Distortion Minimization in the Compressed Domain Embedding

For the compressed domain embedding, if feasible, the STC-based embedding is supposed to be carried out by executing the following steps.

- **Step 1**: Partially decompressed the compressed cover video to get the cover vector $\mathbf{x}$, meanwhile calculate the distortion scalar vector Γ.
- **Step 2**: Obtain the stego vector $\mathbf{y}$ by solving equation (1).
- **Step 3**: Replace each $x_i \in \mathbf{x}$ with $y_i \in \mathbf{y}$.
- **Step 4**: Re-compressed the modified coefficients into H.264 bit streams to get the stego video.

---

[1]The Iverson bracket $[I]$ is defined to be 1 if the logical expression I is true and 0 otherwise.

Note that, the basic feasibility precondition here is the steganographer having the full freedom to manipulate the cover vector $\mathbf{x}$, because the syndrome coding result is not controllable or predictable. However, this requirement cannot be fulfilled due to a serious problem known as distortion drift [14], and the cause of this problem is explained as follows.

Suppose for data embedding, a QDCT coefficient block $\tilde{\mathbf{Q}}$ is arbitrarily modified to $\tilde{\mathbf{Q}}'$. Then at the decoder, the corresponding pixel block is decoded as $\tilde{\mathbf{B}}' = \mathbf{P} + \tilde{\mathbf{R}}'$. Consequently, its subsequent block, e.g., the right block, will be decoded as $\tilde{\mathbf{B}}'_{\rightarrow} = \mathbf{P}'_{\rightarrow} + \tilde{\mathbf{R}}_{\rightarrow}$ instead of $\tilde{\mathbf{B}}_{\rightarrow} = \mathbf{P}_{\rightarrow} + \tilde{\mathbf{R}}_{\rightarrow}$. In this way, the embedding induces deviation in the decoded block, and the deviation will propagate and accumulate very quickly as the decoding process continues [14]. To avoid the distortion drift, both the embedding positions and the embedding fashions are severely restricted. This implies that in the context of compressed domain embedding, the STC-based distortion minimization framework cannot be applied.

3.2 Distortion Minimization in the Joint Compression Embedding

For the joint compression embedding, if feasible, the STC-based embedding is supposed to be carried out by executing the following steps.

- **Step 1**: If the cover video is already compressed, decode it to the raw format, otherwise compress it. During this process, record all qualified coefficients to form the cover vector $\mathbf{x}$, meanwhile calculate the associated distortion scalar vector Γ.
- **Step 2**: Obtain the stego vector $\mathbf{y}$ by solving equation (1).
- **Step 3**: Subject the raw format video to H.264 compression, and sequentially replace each output coefficient $x_i \in \mathbf{x}$ with $y_i \in \mathbf{y}$ as the encoding process continues.

In this context, the steganographer has the full freedom to control the encoding process, and is able to modify the cover coefficients arbitrarily. Nevertheless, it is still not enough to ensure distortion minimization. This is mainly due to the fact called "cover block coupling" which is explained as follows.

For the joint compression embedding, the embedding process is combined with the intra-block coding without changing the encoding order. For instance, once $\tilde{\mathbf{Q}}$ is modified to $\tilde{\mathbf{Q}}'$, its reconstructed block would be $\tilde{\mathbf{B}}'$. Next, the right block $\mathbf{B}_{\rightarrow}$ will be predicted using $\tilde{\mathbf{B}}'$ instead of $\tilde{\mathbf{B}}$. Consequently $\mathbf{B}_{\rightarrow}$'s QDCT block would be updated from $\tilde{\mathbf{Q}}_{\rightarrow}$ to $\tilde{\mathbf{Q}}'_{\rightarrow}$. In this way, modification made to one cover block may change the coefficient values of the following cover blocks even before they are used. In this paper, this interaction among adjacent cover blocks is called "cover block coupling". As a result, the cover $\mathbf{x}$ keeps updating with the embedding continues. This makes the distortion scalar vector Γ meaningless, hence makes the efforts to minimize distortion end in failure.

However, not like performing compressed domain embedding, there are still chances to apply the distortion minimization framework to joint compression embedding as long as coupled cover blocks could be properly decoupled.

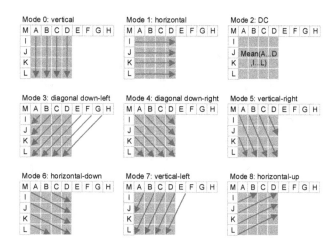

Figure 3: Intra prediction modes for 4×4 blocks.

Table 1: Block's IPM and the associated reference block(s)

$M_\mathbf{B}$	B's reference block(s)
Mode 0: vertical	$\tilde{\mathbf{B}}_\uparrow$
Mode 1: horizontal	$\tilde{\mathbf{B}}_\leftarrow$
Mode 2: DC	$\tilde{\mathbf{B}}_\uparrow, \tilde{\mathbf{B}}_\leftarrow$
Mode 3: diagonal down-left	$\tilde{\mathbf{B}}_\uparrow, \tilde{\mathbf{B}}_\nearrow$
Mode 4: diagonal down-right	$\tilde{\mathbf{B}}_\nwarrow, \tilde{\mathbf{B}}_\uparrow, \tilde{\mathbf{B}}_\leftarrow$
Mode 5: vertical-right	$\tilde{\mathbf{B}}_\nwarrow, \tilde{\mathbf{B}}_\uparrow, \tilde{\mathbf{B}}_\leftarrow$
Mode 6: horizontal-down	$\tilde{\mathbf{B}}_\nwarrow, \tilde{\mathbf{B}}_\uparrow, \tilde{\mathbf{B}}_\leftarrow$
Mode 7: vertical-left	$\tilde{\mathbf{B}}_\uparrow, \tilde{\mathbf{B}}_\nearrow$
Mode 8: horizontal-up	$\tilde{\mathbf{B}}_\leftarrow$

4 COVER BLOCK DECOUPLING FOR CONTENT-ADAPTIVE EMBEDDING

According to Section 3.2, to achieve content-adaptive H.264 steganography, the most intractable issue emerged is to eliminate, or if not possible, to attenuate the embedding interactions among cover blocks to an acceptable level, which is called "cover block decoupling", and CBD for short. In essence, successively coded blocks are coupled, only because the encoded blocks still serve as prediction references of the following blocks. In this section, the dependance of adjacent blocks is carefully studied, based on which we suggest two embedding strategies for impact separation.

4.1 Intra-Block Dependance

Referring to Figure 2, one luminance block **B** is predicted using samples of four encoded and reconstructed blocks, i.e., its upper-left block $\tilde{\mathbf{B}}_\nwarrow$, its upper block $\tilde{\mathbf{B}}_\uparrow$, its upper-right block $\tilde{\mathbf{B}}_\nearrow$ and its left block $\tilde{\mathbf{B}}_\leftarrow$. As illustrated in Figure 3, H.264 provides nine optional IPMs for each 4×4 luminance blocks. The block dependance varies according to the assigned IPM, which is summarized in Table 1.

On the other hand, after **B** is encoded, the reconstructed block $\tilde{\mathbf{B}}$ might be used as a reference to predict its right block $\mathbf{B}_\rightarrow$, its lower-left block $\mathbf{B}_\swarrow$, its lower block $\mathbf{B}_\downarrow$ and its lower-right block

Table 2: IPMs Indicating Referencing.

$\mathbf{B}_{(\cdot)}$	$\mathcal{M}^r_{(\cdot)}$
$\mathbf{B}_\rightarrow$	1, 2, 4, 5, 6, 8
$\mathbf{B}_\swarrow$	3, 7
$\mathbf{B}_\downarrow$	0, 2, 3, 4, 5, 6, 7
$\mathbf{B}_\searrow$	4, 5, 6

$\mathbf{B}_\searrow$. These four adjacent blocks are denoted as the set $\mathcal{A}_\mathbf{B} = \{\mathbf{B}_\rightarrow, \mathbf{B}_\swarrow, \mathbf{B}_\downarrow, \mathbf{B}_\searrow\}$. For any block $\mathbf{B}_{(\cdot)} \in \mathcal{A}_\mathbf{B}$, the set of IPM(s) indicating $\tilde{\mathbf{B}}$ is used for prediction is denoted as $\mathcal{M}^r_{(\cdot)}$, and the relationships are summarized in Table 2. For example, $\mathbf{B}_\rightarrow$'s IPM $M_{\mathbf{B}_\rightarrow} \in \mathcal{M}^r_\rightarrow$ indicates $\tilde{\mathbf{B}}$ is used for prediction when encoding $\mathbf{B}_\rightarrow$.

4.2 Strategies for CBD

Considering the intra-block dependence, once B's QDCT coefficient block $\tilde{Q}$ is arbitrarily modified to $\tilde{Q}'$, each block in the set $\mathcal{A}_{\tilde{Q}} = \{\tilde{Q}_\rightarrow, \tilde{Q}_\swarrow, \tilde{Q}_\downarrow, \tilde{Q}_\searrow\}$ is supposed to be accordingly updated. This does not comply with the basic requirement of distortion minimization framework that the rest of the cover elements remain unchanged after changing the current one. Given this, two CBD strategies are proposed.

4.2.1 Passive Decoupling Strategy. Intuitively, if $\tilde{\mathbf{B}}$ is not referenced for prediction, the modification applied to $\tilde{Q}$ would not affect the rest cover blocks. Referring to Table 2, such blocks are called no-referenced blocks (NRBs) defined by Definition 4.1.

Definition 4.1. **No-Referenced Block.** Let B be a 4×4 intra-block and $M_{\mathbf{B}_{(\cdot)}}$ be the IPM of block $\mathbf{B}_{(\cdot)}$, **B** is called a no-referenced block, if for any adjacent block $\mathbf{B}_{(\cdot)} \in \mathcal{A}_\mathbf{B}$, $M_{\mathbf{B}_{(\cdot)}} \notin \mathcal{M}^r_{(\cdot)}$.

Hence the passive decoupling strategy suggests the NRBs's QDCT coefficient blocks be used as the cover blocks with priorities.

4.2.2 Active Decoupling Strategy. Unfortunately, in H.264 intra-block coding, only a small proportion of the 4×4 blocks are NRBs. Referring to Table 3, the ratio varies from 5% to 10%. To ensure adequate capacity, a more active decoupling strategy is needed. In the joint compression embedding, once $\tilde{Q}$ is chosen as one of the cover blocks, all the blocks in $\mathcal{A}_{\tilde{Q}}$ would be inevitably updated. So as the active decoupling strategy, we suggest to distribute embedding changes to nonadjacent blocks. For example, as illustrated in Figure 4, only the darkest 4×4 block of each macroblock (MB) is allowed to be modified during intra-block coding, while the others are normally encoded.

In this distributed embedding system, lighter blocks serve as the buffering zone used to suppress the embedding interactions. Here, it is essential to realize that the main characteristic of the prediction based intra-block coding is self-correction. To be more specific, as described in Section 2.1, the original pixel block $\mathbf{B} = \mathbf{P} + \mathbf{R}$ is coded and reconstructed as $\tilde{\mathbf{B}} = \mathbf{P} + \tilde{\mathbf{R}}$, hence the coding loss mainly comes from $\Delta \mathbf{R} \triangleq \tilde{\mathbf{R}} - \mathbf{R}$. According to Lemma 4.2 below, the elements in $\Delta \mathbf{R}$ have a zero mean, so each element in the block $\Delta \mathbf{B} \triangleq \tilde{\mathbf{B}} - \mathbf{B}$ is also expected to have a zero mean. This ensures that the buffering

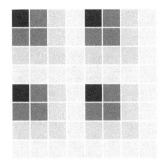

Figure 4: Distributed Embedding.

zone be well maintained after regular intra-block coding, and the lighter the block is, the less it is affected by data embedding.

LEMMA 4.2. *As to an element in a residual pixel block, the difference between its original value and its reconstructed value has a zero mean, i.e.,* $E[\Delta r] = E[\tilde{r} - r] = 0, \tilde{r} \in \tilde{\mathbf{R}}, r \in \mathbf{R}$.

PROOF. In intra-block coding, a 4×4 residual block $\mathbf{R}$ is DCT transformed to $\mathbf{Q}$. As pointed out by F. Bellifemine *et al.*, the 2D-DCT coefficients of the differential signal tend to be less correlated [1]. Thus the distribution of any $q \in \mathbf{Q}$ can be well modeled with the Laplacian probability density function [11] as

$$f_q(q) = \frac{\alpha}{2} \exp^{-\alpha |q|}. \tag{3}$$

Since the H.264 quantiser divides the sample by integer Q_{step} and rounds to the nearest integer, the probability that q will be quantised to $\tilde{q} = iQ_{step}$ is simply the probability that the sample is between $(i - 1/2)Q_{step}$ and $(i + 1/2)Q_{step}$ calculated as

$$p_i = \int_{(i-1/2)Q_{step}}^{(i+1/2)Q_{step}} f_q(q)dq. \tag{4}$$

Then the expectation of the difference introduced by quantisation is

$$\begin{aligned} E[\tilde{q} - q] &= \sum_{i=-\infty}^{+\infty} \int_{(i-1/2)Q_{step}}^{(i+1/2)Q_{step}} (iQ_{step} - q)f_q(q)dq \\ &= 0, \end{aligned} \tag{5}$$

i.e., $E[\tilde{q}] = E[q]$. Because $\tilde{r}$ and r are linear combinations of the samples in $\tilde{\mathbf{Q}}$ and $\mathbf{Q}$ respectively, there is $E[\tilde{r}] = E[r]$, i.e., $E[\Delta r] = E[\tilde{r} - r] = 0$. □

4.3 Distortion Definition

In the distortion minimization framework described in Section 2.2, the STC is leveraged to minimize the overall embedding impact under a given payload. And the key element of this framework is the distortion, which needs to be carefully designed to indicate the applicability of each cover elements. In this paper, the distortion scale of each QDCT coefficient $\tilde{q} \in \tilde{\mathbf{Q}}$ depends on two factors, i.e., its block dependence and its modification impacts on the reconstructed MB, and is defined as

$$\gamma(\tilde{q}) = \frac{1}{K}D(\tilde{q}). \tag{6}$$

Here, K is the number of blocks in $\mathcal{A}_{\tilde{\mathbf{Q}}}$ that do not use $\tilde{\mathbf{B}}$ for prediction and $D(\tilde{q})$ represents the embedding impact on the reconstructed MB.

To acquire $D(\tilde{q})$, we allow $\tilde{q}$ be modified either to $\tilde{q} - 1$ or $\tilde{q} + 1$, and the associated distortions are respectively calculated as

$$D^-(\tilde{q}) = \sum_{i=0}^{15} \sum_{j=0}^{15} |\frac{\tilde{b}_{i,j}^{-1} - \tilde{b}_{i,j}}{\tilde{b}_{i,j}}| \text{and} \tag{7}$$

$$D^+(\tilde{q}) = \sum_{i=0}^{15} \sum_{j=0}^{15} |\frac{\tilde{b}_{i,j}^{+1} - \tilde{b}_{i,j}}{\tilde{b}_{i,j}}|, \tag{8}$$

where $\tilde{b}_{i,j}^{-1}$, $\tilde{b}_{i,j}^{+1}$ and $\tilde{b}_{i,j}$ are pixel values of the reconstructed MBs corresponding to different embedding fashions, i.e., $\tilde{q} - 1$, $\tilde{q} + 1$ and unchanged. Therefore $D(\tilde{q})$ is determined as

$$D(\tilde{q}) = \min\{D^-(\tilde{q}), D^+(\tilde{q})\}. \tag{9}$$

4.4 Practical CBD Embedding with Single I-Frame

This paper deals with the issues of H.264 steganography with I-frames, and for concreteness and without loss of generality, the proposed CBD embedding scheme is described in a practical way using one I-frame as the cover object.

- **Step 1**: If the cover frame is already compressed, decode it to the spatial domain, otherwise compress it. During this process, mark all the 1st 4×4 blocks of each MB and all the NRBs as the cover blocks, and record their QDCT coefficients to form the cover vector $\mathbf{x}$, meanwhile calculate the associated distortion scalar vector Γ by function (6).
- **Step 2**: Obtain the stego vector $\mathbf{y}$ by solving equation (1).
- **Step 3**: Subject the raw format frame to I-frame coding, and sequentially change each output coefficient $x_i \in \mathbf{x}$ according to $y_i \in \mathbf{y}$ as the encoding process continues.

Compared to the embedding process, the message extraction is much easier. With the received compressed frame, the recipient can use any standard H.264 decoder to read the QDCT coefficients of all cover blocks, rebuild the binary channel, and extract the secret message by solving equation (2).

5 EVALUATION

5.1 Experiment Setup

Our experiment is conducted based on the H.264 reference encoder software JM 19.0, created by the joint video team (JVT). The baseline profile is used which supports only I and P frames. The encoder used a fixed quantisation step parameter of 20 for I-frames and an intra-period of 3 (group of picture IPP). To implement our proposed CBD embedding scheme, a good STCs listed in [5] is used, with the relative payload α set to 1/5 and constraint height h set to 7. For comparison, X. Ma *et al.*'s method, referred to as CDE (compression domain embedding), is also implemented. The test set comprises of 20 standard CIF sequences in the 4:2:0 YUV format, part of which is shown in Figure 5. The frame size varies from 90 to 376 at the frame rate of 30 frames per second, and the number of I-frames varies from 30 to 125. All sequences are compressed by the standard encoder, referred to as STD, to produce the class of clean videos. On

Table 3: Test results of some used sequences. (SN (Sequence Name), FN (Frame Number), NR(NRB Ratio (%)), EM (Embedding Method), AC (Average Capacity (bit/I-frame)), PSNR (dB), FS (File Size (KB)))

SN	FN	NR	EM	AC	PSNR	FS
bus	150	8.37	STD	N/A	40.29	2076
			CDE	967	39.31	2135
			CBD	1040	40.16	2087
city	300	7.62	STD	N/A	41.49	2948
			CDE	893	40.18	3092
			CBD	997	41.34	2963
coastguard	300	6.65	STD	N/A	40.41	3733
			CDE	1019	39.33	3833
			CBD	1050	40.26	3768
flower	250	5.62	STD	N/A	40.07	4491
			CDE	915	38.87	4603
			CBD	950	39.94	4501
harbour	300	7.64	STD	N/A	39.78	4476
			CDE	1017	38.63	4552
			CBD	1124	39.67	4491
mobile	300	5.56	STD	N/A	39.21	6133
			CDE	908	38.59	6259
			CBD	1186	39.06	6150
stefan	90	7.69	STD	N/A	39.97	1267
			CDE	791	38.92	1332
			CBD	856	39.84	1273
tempete	260	5.52	STD	N/A	39.78	3898
			CDE	905	38.89	4003
			CBD	975	39.64	3913

Table 4: Average Steganalysis Results (%).

	Intra			All		
	TN	TP	AR	TN	TP	AR
CBD	62.79	55.36	59.07	49.62	53.09	51.36
CDE	73.75	86.01	79.88	59.39	70.88	65.13

to the DCTR (Discrete Cosine Transform Residual) feature [7] used for JPEG steganalysis, it is engineered as the histograms of noise residuals from the decompressed frames using 16 DCT kernels. The second sub-set is designed as the residual histograms from the similar blocks linked by motion vectors between inter-frames.

In our experiments, since embedding is carried out in I-frames, the first sub-set is intentionally used to test the detectability of I-frame. Besides, the whole feature set is used to test all the sequence frames.

5.3.2 Training and Classification. To measure steganographic security levels of the CDE and the proposed CBD scheme, in each run, 12 pairs of compressed sequences (clean and stego) are randomly picked for the training purposes, and the remaining 8 are left for testing. The steganalytic features are extracted from each frames or just I-frames. The classifier is implemented using Chang's support vector machine (SVM) [2] with the Gaussian kernel.

5.3.3 Steganalytic Results. After each run, the true negative (TN) rates, true positive (TP) rates are computed by counting the numbers of detections in the test sets. The performances of the steganalyzers with two feature sets are tested, and the average results of 10 runs are recorded in Table 4. Besides, the detector receiver operating characteristic (ROC) curves of the two steganalyzers are plotted in Figure 8.

It is observed that with the considered embedding strength, the used steganalytic features cannot reliably detect the proposed scheme, and CBD outperforms its competitor, which indicates the advantage of the distortion minimization framework.

the other hand, for CBD and CDE, all sequences are subjected to compression with random messages embedded to create the class of stego videos with comparable embedding capacities (average bits per I-frame).

5.2 Impacts on Coding Performance

The embedding impacts on video coding performance is evaluated from two aspects, i.e., the achieved visual quality and compression efficiency, which are measured by the peak signal-to-noise ratio (PSNR) and the compressed file size (KB) respectively. Corresponding results of several used sequences are recorded in Table 3. What's more, we take a closer look at one specific sequence "stefan.yuv" and plot the dynamic changes in PSNR and the compressed size compared to the STD along I-frames in Figure 6 and Figure 7. It is observed that, with the embedding capacities around 1000 bits per I-frame, both the CBD and CDE scheme have limited impacts on video coding performance, and CBD holds a lead.

5.3 Steganalysis

5.3.1 Steganalytic Features. In order to test the achieved steganographic security, we chose state-of-the-art steganalytic method against the QDCT-based schemes [18] for benchmarking. The used feature set comprises of two sub-sets. The first sub-set is designed to capture the embedding disturbance in the spatial domain. Similar

6 CONCLUSION AND FUTURE WORK

In this paper, we make the first attempt to achieve content-adaptive embedding for H.264 steganography. We analyze the inherent causes why the distortion minimization framework cannot be applied, and point out that the cover blocks must be decoupled during I-frame coding. Based on this, two CBD strategies, i.e., the passive one and the active one, are proposed to inhibit the embedding interactions among cover blocks. In addition, we design a distortion function for QDCT coefficients considering both the modification impacts on the coding performance and the degree of block coupling. Experimental results show that, satisfactory levels of coding performance and security are achieved, which fully embodies the advantage of the distortion minimization framework.

In the near future, the proposed CBD embedding scheme would be further optimized by testing on different distortion functions and embedding structures. Meanwhile, attempts of further steganalysis are to be carried out under more complicated steganalytic models to ensure security. What's more, the application scope is to be extended to inter-frames.

Figure 5: Part of the used sequences.

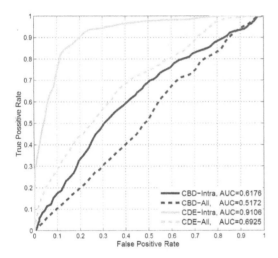

Figure 8: ROC curves of the used steganalyzers.

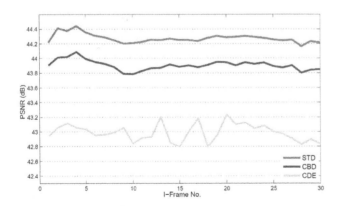

Figure 6: Dynamic changes of I-frame PSNRs.

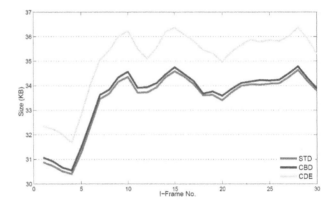

Figure 7: Dynamic changes of I-frame sizes.

ACKNOWLEDGMENTS

This work is supported by NSFC under Grant No.: U1636102 and U1736214, Fundamental Theory and Cutting Edge Technology Research Program of IIE, CAS, under Grant No.: Y7Z0371102iijŇand National Key Technology R&D Program under Grant No.: 2016YFB0801003 and 2016QY15Z2500.

REFERENCES

[1] Fabio Bellifemine, A Capellino, Antonio Chimienti, Romualdo Picco, and R Ponti. 1992. Statistical analysis of the 2D-DCT coefficients of the differential signal for images. *Signal Processing: Image Communication* 4, 6 (1992), 477–488.
[2] Chih-Chung Chang and Chih-Jen Lin. 2011. LIBSVM: a library for support vector machines. *ACM transactions on intelligent systems and technology (TIST)* 2, 3 (2011), 27.
[3] Tomáš Denemark and Jessica Fridrich. 2015. Improving steganographic security by synchronizing the selection channel. In *Proceedings of the 3rd ACM Workshop on Information Hiding and Multimedia Security*. ACM, 5–14.
[4] Tomáš Filler and Jessica Fridrich. 2010. Gibbs construction in steganography. *IEEE Transactions on Information Forensics and Security* 5, 4 (2010), 705–720.
[5] Tomáš Filler, Jan Judas, and Jessica Fridrich. 2010. Minimizing embedding impact in steganography using trellis-coded quantization. In *Media Forensics and Security II*, Vol. 7541. International Society for Optics and Photonics, 754105.
[6] Tomáš Filler, Jan Judas, and Jessica Fridrich. 2011. Minimizing additive distortion in steganography using syndrome-trellis codes. *IEEE Transactions on Information Forensics and Security* 6, 3 (2011), 920–935.
[7] Vojtěch Holub and Jessica Fridrich. 2015. Low-complexity features for JPEG steganalysis using undecimated DCT. *IEEE Transactions on Information Forensics and Security* 10, 2 (2015), 219–228.
[8] Vojtěch Holub, Jessica Fridrich, and Tomáš Denemark. 2014. Universal distortion function for steganography in an arbitrary domain. *EURASIP Journal on Information Security* 2014, 1 (2014), 1.

[9] Weijing Huo, Yuesheng Zhu, and Hongyuan Chen. 2011. A controllable error-drift elimination scheme for watermarking algorithm in H. 264/AVC stream. *IEEE Signal Processing Letters* 18, 9 (2011), 535–538.

[10] Bin Li, Ming Wang, Xiaolong Li, Shunquan Tan, and Jiwu Huang. 2015. A strategy of clustering modification directions in spatial image steganography. *IEEE Transactions on Information Forensics and Security* 10, 9 (2015), 1905–1917.

[11] Xiang Li, Norbert Oertel, Andreas Hutter, and André Kaup. 2009. Laplace distribution based Lagrangian rate distortion optimization for hybrid video coding. *IEEE Transactions on Circuits and Systems for Video Technology* 19, 2 (2009), 193–205.

[12] Eugene Ted Lin and Edward J Delp. 2005. Video and image watermark synchronization. *Center for Education and Research in Information Assurance and Security* (2005).

[13] Tseng-Jung Lin, Kuo-Liang Chung, Po-Chun Chang, Yong-Huai Huang, Hong-Yuan Mark Liao, and Chiung-Yao Fang. 2013. An improved DCT-based perturbation scheme for high capacity data hiding in H.264/AVC intra frames. *Journal of Systems and Software* 86, 3 (2013), 604–614.

[14] Xiaojing Ma, Zhitang Li, Hao Tu, and Bochao Zhang. 2010. A data hiding algorithm for H. 264/AVC video streams without intra-frame distortion drift.

IEEE transactions on circuits and systems for video technology 20, 10 (2010), 1320–1330.

[15] Niels Provos and Peter Honeyman. 2003. Hide and seek: An introduction to steganography. *IEEE security & privacy* 99, 3 (2003), 32–44.

[16] Vahid Sedighi, Rémi Cogranne, and Jessica Fridrich. 2016. Content-adaptive steganography by minimizing statistical detectability. *IEEE Transactions on Information Forensics and Security* 11, 2 (2016), 221–234.

[17] Zafar Shahid, Marc Chaumont, and William Puech. 2013. Considering the reconstruction loop for data hiding of intra-and inter-frames of H. 264/AVC. *Signal, Image and Video Processing* (2013), 1–19.

[18] Peipei Wang, Yun Cao, Xianfeng Zhao, and Meineng Zhu. 2017. A Steganalytic Algorithm to Detect DCT-based Data Hiding Methods for H. 264/AVC Videos. In *Proceedings of the 5th ACM Workshop on Information Hiding and Multimedia Security*. ACM, 123–133.

[19] T. Wiegand, G. J. Sullivan, G. Bjøntegaard, and A. Luthra. 2003. Overview of the H.264/AVC video coding standard. *IEEE Trans. Circuits Syst. Video Technol.* 13, 7 (2003), 560–576.

Do EEG-Biometric Templates Threaten User Privacy?

Full Paper

Yvonne Höller
Department of Neurology, Paracelsus Medical University Salzburg
Salzburg, Austria
yvonne.hoeller@sbg.ac.at

Andreas Uhl
Department of Computer Sciences, University of Salzburg
Salzburg, Austria
uhl@cosy.sbg.ac.at

ABSTRACT

The electroencephalogram (EEG) was introduced as a method for the generation of biometric templates. So far, most research focused on the optimisation of the enrolment and authentication, and it was claimed that the EEG has many advantages. However, it was never assessed whether the biometric templates obtained from the EEG contain sensitive information about the enrolled users. In this work we ask whether we can infer personal characteristics such as age, sex, or informations about neurological disorders from these templates.

To this end, we extracted a set of 16 feature vectors from EEG epochs from a sample of 60 healthy subjects and neurological patients. One of these features was the classical power spectrum, while the other 15 features were derived from a multivariate autoregressive model, considering also interdependencies of EEG channels. We classified the sample by sex, neurological diagnoses, age, atrophy of the brain, and intake of neurological drugs.

We obtained classification accuracies of up to .70 for sex, .86 for the classification of epilepsy vs. other populations, .81 for the differentiation of young vs. old people's templates, and .82 for the intake of medication targeted to the central nervous system. These informations represent privacy sensitive information about the users, so that our results emphasise the need to apply protective safeguards in the deployment of EEG biometric systems.

CCS CONCEPTS

• **Security and privacy → Privacy protections**;

KEYWORDS

EEG-Biometrics; user privacy; multivariate autoregressive model

ACM Reference Format:
Yvonne Höller and Andreas Uhl. 2018. Do EEG-Biometric Templates Threaten User Privacy?: Full Paper. In *IH&MMSec '18: 6th ACM Workshop on Information Hiding and Multimedia Security, June 20–22, 2018, Innsbruck, Austria.* ACM, New York, NY, USA, 10 pages. https://doi.org/10.1145/3206004.3206006

1 INTRODUCTION

The electroencephalogram (EEG) is a neurological examination method used for clinical purposes, such as the diagnosis of epilepsy [45], the monitoring of anaesthesia [31], or the diagnosis of brain death [55], among others. Clinical evaluation of the EEG exists since Hans Berger has established the EEG as an assessment tool of brain activity in humans the 1930ies. This approach is based on qualitative assessment of the raw signal, that allows to examine the presence of natural rhythms such as the alpha rhythm at 8-12 Hz (Figure 1, left), and the detection of epileptiform phenomena such as polyspikes (Figure 1, middle). Qualitative EEG can be used in order to detect diffuse or focal pathological changes, by means of slowing of the background rhythm from the α (8-12 Hz) to $\delta - \theta$ range (0-7 Hz) [8, 24]. This slowing is regionally limited for focal pathologies such as brain tumors [22], transient or permanent ischemia [59], e.g. resulting from stroke, brain hemorrhage, traumatic injury, malformations of cortical development, focal epileptic spikes, neurodegeneration, arteriovenous malformations, and infections such as bacterial cerebritis or viral encephalitis [8, 24]. Generalized slowing can be found under medication with certain drugs [48], neurogenerative disorders, neurodevelopmental pathologies, hydrocephalus, metabolic or toxic encephalopathy, CNS infection disorders, and certain brain lesions [8, 24]. However, the EEG cannot be used in order to determine individual aspects such as sex, age, or in order to differentially classify pathological aspects, such as dementia.

In contrast, quantitative analysis of the EEG has emerged alongside with digital signal processing [37], where the raw signal is processed to form feature vectors such as spectral frequency decomposition or multivariate autoregressive modelling. In this field, the EEG has been shown to yield significant information for the early differential diagnosis of dementia [32].

Today, the EEG is being perceived as a promising technique to generate biometric templates, because the measured activity of the brain is universal, can not easily be circumvent, and there are also studies that evidenciate uniqueness and permanence of specific features extracted from the EEG [1, 4, 7, 11–14, 35, 43, 53, 63]. Moreover, modern mobile systems are small and cheap, so that the biometric characteristic can be captured quickly and easily [23, 33]. EEG biometric features can be captured during rest, or during stimulation or cognitive effort [5, 38, 39, 41, 52, 54, 64, 65].

Qualitative review of the generated templates might not allow to draw any conclusions about characteristics of the investigated individual, since EEG experts are not trained to read such a representation of the information contained in the EEG, in contrast

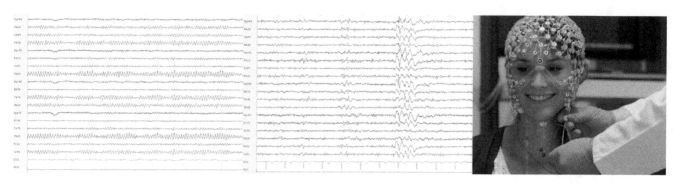

Figure 1: Can we extract informations about sex, age, and health from electroencephalographic biometric templates?

to their well-trained eye for raw EEG signals. Nevertheless, quantitative analysis of the templates is likely to reveal information about factors pertinent to the individuals, such as age, sex, and pathology. The EEG is highly indicative for epilepsy [42], and as for many other biometric characteristics, the EEG is heavily affected by healthy and pathological ageing [46]. For example, there are specific expectations of changes for sub-bands of EEG coherence [60]. In addition, sex affects the EEG [61, 62], and also the menstrual cycle in women [9].

In this work, we aim to demonstrate that it is technically possible to extract privacy sensitive information form EEG biometric templates. To this end, we classified EEG biometric templates by sex, age, diagnosis of neurological diseases, the intake of medication that affects the central nervous system, and neuroradiological pathological findings in the memory region hippocampus of the brain. The neurological diseases included in the analyses were patients with subjective cognitive complaints (SCC) or with mild cognitive impairment (MCI), and temporal lobe epilepsy (TLE). We included also healthy controls (HC), in order to compare them to the neurological populations. Both, SCI and MCI are claimed to be a prodromal phase of Alzheimer's disease, with conversion rates from MCI to Alzheimer's disease of up to 70% [46]. TLE is a disease with medically uncontrollable and unpredictable seizures, therefore affecting all aspects of life. Nevertheless, the disease cannot be recognized unless one witnesses a seizure or performs qualitative analysis of an EEG with epileptiform activity. The burden and stigma of TLE is significant, so that patients try to keep the diagnosis confidential.

The paper is structured as follows: In Section 2 we describe which features we extracted from the EEG, what scenarios of templates and EEG data we examined, how we performed feature subset selection and classification, which informations we tried to extract, and finally, which sample data set we used. In Section 3 we present the results and Section 4 concludes the work.

2 METHODS

2.1 Feature extraction

We used a data sample as described in Section 2.7 with resting EEG recordings and 27 sensors.

We estimated **power spectral density (PSD)** as the single-sided amplitude spectrum from the Fast Fourier Transform of the signal.

Furthermore, we estimated autoregressive coefficients, from which we extracted a set of 14 measures of interaction between

all of the 27 selected sensors. The estimation was based on the multivariate autoregressive model (MVAR) [19, 29]:

$$Y(t) = \sum_{k=1}^{P} A(k)Y(t-k) + U(t) \qquad (1)$$

where $Y(t) = [y_1(t), ..., y_M(t)]^T$ is a vector holding the values of the M channels at time t, P is the model order, $A(k)$ are $M \times M$ coefficient matrices in which the element $a_{ij}(k)$ describes the dependence of $y_i(t)$ on $y_j(t-k)$ and $U(n)$ is the innovation process, which is assumed to be composed of white and uncorrelated noise. We used the functions mvfreqz.m and mvar.m from the BioSig toolbox [50] with model order $P = 41$. The model order was chosen in order to obtain a large ratio $N/(M \cdot P)$ which is needed to get an accurate model estimation [49]. In this study, this resulted in a ratio of $20.5 \cdot 500/(27 \cdot 41) = 9.26$, which is well above an acceptable threshold. In order to estimate the multivariate autoregressive model we used partial correlation estimation with unbiased covariance estimates [29], which was found to be the most accurate estimation method according to [49].

Thus, the matrices $A(k)$ of size $M \times M$ formed the second feature, representing the **multivariate autoregressive coefficients (AR)**.

The other 14 features were obtained as follows. The estimated MVAR model was transformed from the time-domain into the z-domain and the f-domain, which yields accordingly two transfer functions. The multivariate parameters in the frequency domain that can be derived from these transfer functions were computed for 1 Hz frequency steps between 1 and 125 Hz.

- **Direct causality (DC):** Direct causality was developed by [21] to overcome the problem that the directed transfer function does not distinguish between direct and indirect information flows. Direct causality is the only measure that is not computed for each frequency.

- **Spectrum (S):** This contains the auto- and the cross-spectrum, which is the Fourier transform of the cross-covariance function [34]

- **Transfer function (hh):** This transfer function is related to the non-normalized directed transfer function [15].

- **Transfer function polynomial (AF):** This is the frequency transform of a polynomial describing the transfer function. The absolute of the squared transfer function polynomial is the non-normalized partial directed coherence [15].

- **Real valued coherence (COH):** By considering the real part of the complex-valued coherence [36], the result is an ordinary coherence [50]. We will refer to it as coherence.
- **Complex coherence (iCOH):** By considering the imaginary part of the complex-valued coherence [36], we get complex coherence.
- **Partial coherence (pCOH):** This is the partial coherence, calculated with an alternative method as provided in the biosig-toolbox. Partial coherence, also known as Gersch causality, was first designed to identify epileptic foci by [17]. The authors proposed that one channel is said to drive the other channels if the first channel explains or accounts for the linear relation between the other two. The real part of the partial coherence was used.
- **Partial directed coherence (PDC):** Partial directed coherence as an extended concept of partialized coherence, is a measure of the relative strength of the direct interaction between pairs of regions [2].
- **Partial directed coherence factor (PDCF):** The partial directed coherence factor [2] is an intermediate step between partial coherence and partial directed coherence. It adds directionality to partial coherence, but includes instantaneous causality, which is undesirable when examining processes that evolve over time like an epileptic seizure [51].
- **Generalized partial directed coherence (GPDC):** The major advantage of generalized partial directed coherence [3] over partial directed coherence is its robustness against scaling differences between the signals [57].
- **Directed transfer function (DTF):** Like directed coherence, directed transfer function represents information that flows from one region to another over many possible alternative pathways [20].
- **Direct directed transfer function (dDTF):** The direct directed transfer function extends the concept of directed transfer function by distinguishing between direct and indirect causal relations of signals [25]. As such, the concepts of partial coherence and directed transfer function are combined.
- **full frequency directed transfer function (ffDTF):** The difference between the directed transfer function and the full frequency directed transfer function [25] is that the directed transfer function is normalized by the total frequency content of the considered frequency band, while the full frequency directed transfer function is normalized with respect to all the frequencies in the predefined frequency interval. As such, the full frequency directed transfer function priorizes those frequencies which contribute the most to the power of the signal [58].
- **Geweke's Granger Causality (GGC):** This is a modified version of Geweke's Granger Causality [18], concretely the bivariate version as in [6].

Next, all frequency-dependent measures of interaction, that is, all but DC, and the PSD were averaged in classical frequency ranges delta (δ, 2-4 Hz), theta (θ, 5-7 Hz), alpha (α, 8-13 Hz), beta (β, 14-30 Hz), and gamma (γ, 31-80 Hz).

All frequency dependent measures were analyzed once with this 5-band frequency configuration, and once when including only the 3 frequency ranges θ, α, and β, since this range has been shown to be more informative by Maiorana et al. [27]. The non-frequency dependent measures DC and AR were calculated on the band-pass filtered data (5-30 Hz) for this purpose.

2.2 Feature fusion

The autoregressive coefficients were obtained as 27×27 matrices for each $k = 1...P$ where P is the model order, in our case $P = 41$. We concatenated these values as one long feature vector, i.e. all $27 \times 27 \times 41$ coefficients. For PSD, we concatenated the values from all 27 electrodes from all 5 frequency bands, thus resulting in 27×5 values in the feature vector. For each of the 14 measures derived from the autoregressive model, we obtained interaction matrices of size 27×27, thus, one value for each electrode combination. Depending on whether the value was frequency specific (all measures but DC) or not (DC), these interaction matrices were available separately for each of the 5 frequency ranges. Depending on whether the measure was directed or not, this matrix was symmetric (not-directed measures, e.g. coherence) and thus redundant or not symmetric (directed measures, e.g. directed transfer function). We concatenated all of the non-redundant values from these interaction matrices for all frequencies of interest. For non-directed measures we took the upper triangular of the interaction matrix and concatenated these values for each frequency range. For measures without time-lagged auto-correlation, the diagonal of the interaction matrix was excluded because it contained no information. This resulted in high-dimensional feature vectors of lengths ranging from $27 \times 27 = 729$ (DC as the only measure without frequency dimension) to $27 \times 27 \times 5 = 3645$ (all directed measures with autocorrelation).

2.3 Single epochs and templates

We tested the information content in the feature vectors from the single epochs and templates. A single epoch is a segment of the signal, in our experimental data of 20.5 seconds length. A template consists of the average feature vector calculated for several equal sized epochs $e_1...e_k$ that belong to one subject p. Thus, one element i in the template feature vector of subject p was obtained as

$$template_{p,i} = 1/k \sum_{l=1}^{k} z(feat_{p,e_l,i}) \qquad (2)$$

We obtained templates as the average of 3 epochs.

We performed the experiment with the following configurations:

(1) single epochs
   (a) single epochs EEG session 1
   (b) single epochs EEG session 2
   (c) single epochs from both EEG sessions
(2) templates
   (a) templates from EEG session 1
   (b) templates from EEG session 2
   (c) templates from both EEG sessions

We computed receiver operating characteristic (ROC) curve, the area under the curve (AUC) alongside with 95% confidence intervals on the true positive rate by threshold averaging and sampling using bootstrap and 1000 replicas.

2.4 Classification

We used support vector machines for classification, because they deal with non-linear properties of the data even when a linear kernel is used. When data are only non-linearly separable, the data is mapped into a feature space in which the linear separating hyperplane can be used. We performed a classification in the sense of supervised learning with a linear kernel function (dot product) and quadratic programming in order to find the separating hyperplane, resulting in a 2-norm soft-margin support vector machine, by using the matlab functions `svmtrain` and `svmclassify` from the statistics and machine learning toolbox.

2.5 Feature selection algorithm

The high-dimensional vectors are likely to contain redundant information, since neighbouring frequencies and neighbouring electrodes are likely to share information. We implemented a feature subset selection algorithm in a three-layered cross-validation procedure. With three layers the optimization is not done towards the test data population and thus, increases the generalizability of the result. The procedure, illustrated in Figure 2, was as follows:

(1) In the outer layer, we randomly partitioned the set of epochs or templates from 60 subjects into 5 sets for a 5-fold cross-validation. Thus, in 5 iterations, each time the epochs/templates of 20% of the subjects were left out as the *test set*, the other 80% are submitted to the middle layer as the *training set*.

(2) In the middle layer, the included subjects were again divided into 5 subsets, for a 5-fold cross-validation. Thus, in 5 iterations, each time 20% of the subjects were left out as the *left-out set*, the other 80% were submitted to the inner layer as the *optimization set*.

(3) In the inner layer, the subjects that formed the *optimization set* were used in order to optimize the feature vector as follows:

    (a) A *t*-test was calculated between the two groups.

    (b) The resulting *p*-values were sorted in ascending order.

    (c) The feature vector was initiated by taking the feature with the smallest *p*-value, thus, the initial length of the feature vector was one.

    (d) For this feature vector, the classification accuracy was calculated with 5-fold cross-validation, i.e. a model was trained 5 times with a *model-generating set*, and the accuracy was determined in each iteration by the respective *validation set*.

    (e) Then, the next feature from the sorted list was added. For this feature vector, the classification with 5-fold cross-validation was repeated.

    (f) The resulting accuracy for the feature vector with two entries was compared to the previous result of a feature vector with the first entry. The added entry to the feature vector was included only if the condition constraints were met as follows:

      • the resulting classification accuracy was at least as high as the maximum of the previously obtained classification accuracies; that is, the second accuracy had to be larger than the first entry, or the 6th accuracy had to

be larger than each of the five previous classification accuracies.

      • If the so far best sensitivity/specificity, or in other words, accuracy for members of the first/second group, respectively, was lower than 0.75, then the obtained sensitivity had to be at least as large as this maximum.

      • If the so far best specificity/sensitivity, was lower than 0.5, then the obtained specificity had to be larger than this maximum.

    (g) This way, features were added and tested for their contribution to the classification accuracy until all available features were used, or until the feature vector reached a maximum of 30 entries, or if more than a consecutive number of 200 features was not added to the feature vector. We limited the maximally acceptable length of the feature vector to 30 entries in the inner loop of the feature vector optimization process, and 31 entries as a final selection.

(4) The average length N of the resulting 5 optimised feature sets was calculated. The occurrences of the features across the 5 sets was counted. A final feature vector was formed by including only those features which were selected at least in 2 of the 5 iterations. If this resulted in no features, all features were included that were selected at least in 1 out of 5 iterations. If the resulting feature vector included more than N features, only the top-most N selected features were included.

(5) The resulting feature vector was used in order to train a support vector machine on the outer-layer training set, and the resulting model was used to classify the outer-layer test set. From the 5 classifications, the general classification accuracy and the within-group accuracy for the two groups (i.e. sensitivity/specificity) were determined.

The threshold of 0.75 was selected as rough estimator for above-chance classification; a value of 0.75 can be considered to be clearly above chance, since the expected chance level would be around 0.5.

Please note again that the separation into training, evaluation and test set was done subject wise, so that the multiple epochs or templates from one subject were always all included into one of these three sets. That is, we had 6 or 12 epochs per subject when single epochs were classified, and 2 or 4 templates when the templates were classified. Moreover, all subsets were drawn in order to maintain the original proportion of the two groups, but the composition of the 5 subsets for the 5-fold cross validation was obtained by randomized assignment of the subjects to the 5 subsets.

Sorting the features initially by the *p*-values is a trivial but nevertheless efficient way to shorten the time-consuming step of a wrapper-style feature subset selection procedure. Please note that similar approaches implemented principal component analysis [40, 44], independent component analysis [56], or benchmarked the feature selection according to principal component analysis by the ratio of within-subject to between-subject variability [28].

2.6 Classifications

We examined the following pairwise classification scenarios:

sex female vs. male subjects

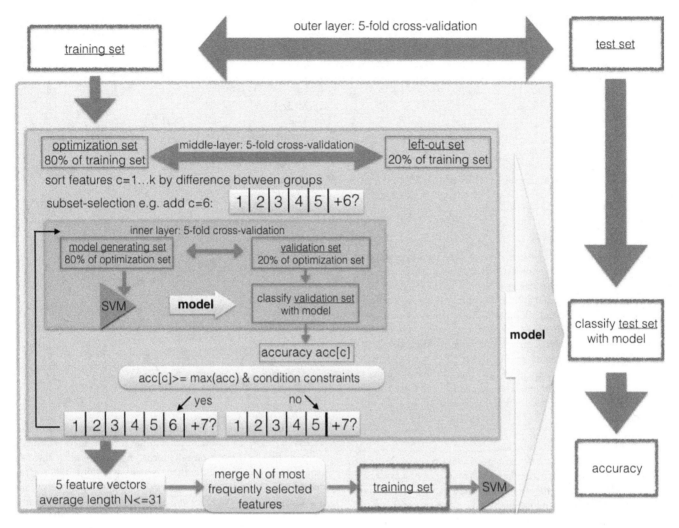

Figure 2: Feature subset selection algorithm in a three-layered cross-validation procedure, in order to shorten and optimize the feature vectors.

age *age* < 36 vs. 35 < *age* < 63, *age* < 36 vs. 62 < *age*, and 35 < *age* < 63 vs. 62 < *age*

clinical diagnosis MCI/SCC vs. TLE, MCI/SCC vs. HC, and TLE vs. HC

medication patients with vs. without medication that affects the central nervous system, that is, anti-epileptic or psychiatric drugs

hippocampal pathology patients with vs. without neuroradiological findings on a structural magnetic resonance imaging examination in the memory-region hippocampus, because anomaly in this region is a correlate of TLE and a precursor of dementia

2.7 Experimental data

2.7.1 Sample. We examined a total sample of 60 participants, with two EEG recordings from each participant obtained during two sessions, separated by two weeks. Participants with EEG that was of poor quality were excluded beforehand (N=3). Poor quality of the EEG was defined as less than 4 sec in at least one of the two recordings after excluding segments of 500 ms according to the automatic data inspection (see Section 2.7.3). Table 1 gives an overview of the demographic characteristics of patients included in the subgroups.

We obtained 8 participants that were younger than 36 years, 27 participants that were up to 62 years old, and 27 participants that were aged 63 years or older.

In order to provide the same amount of data for each participant, data was shortened to the shortest available length across participants, which was 123 seconds. This signal was divided into 6 equal-sized epochs of size 20.5 seconds, which are considered as the input samples to the system. Thus, with two recording sessions, we obtained 12 epochs for each participant.

2.7.2 Data registration. EEG was recorded in two sessions separated by two weeks and took place in the same setting, that is, in a

Table 1: Sample Overview

	MCI/SCC	TLE	HC
N	27	13	20
median age	64	48	61.5
age range	48-76	21-66	23-74
N women	13	9	14
N right-handed	26	12	18
N CNS medication	3	13	0
N hippocampal pathology	13	10	9

N= number; MCI= mild cognitive impairment; SCC= subjective cognitive complaints; TLE= temporal lobe epilepsy; l= left; r= right; HC= controls; age= median age; CNS: central nervous system

Table 2: Best classification accuracies

	single δ-γ	single α-β	template δ-γ	template α-β
sex	.68	.65	.70	.70
MCI/SCC-TLE	.76	.77	.86	.82
MCI/SCC-HC	.64	.60	.66	.66
TLE-HC	.78	.75	.85	.77
young-middle	.74	.75	.74	.78
young-old	.77	.79	.81	.84
middle-old	.61	.67	.61	.63
hippocampus	.63	.63	.63	.67
CNS drugs	.76	.75	.82	.75

MCI=mild cognitive impairment; SCC=subjective cognitive complaints; TLE=temporal lobe epilepsy; HC=controls; young=$age < 36$; middle=$35 < age < 63$; old=$62 < age$; CNS drugs: intake of drugs affecting the central nervous system; hippocampus=hippocampal pathology

quiet room. Participants were instructed to close their eyes and stay awake. Eyes closed is a condition that allows to reduce artefacts from blinking, and thus variability of the recorded EEG. Recordings lasted for 2-3 min. We used a BrainCap with a 10-20 system and a BrainAmp 16-bit ADC amplifier (Brain Products GmbH, Germany). The sampling rate was 500 Hz. Of the 32 recorded channels, one was used to monitor the lower vertical electrooculogram and one was used to measure electrocardiographic activity. Two were positioned at the earlobes for re-referencing, which was conducted in order to remove the bias of the original reference, which was placed at FCz. Data analysis was conducted for data collected from the remaining 27 electrodes F3, F4, C3, C4, P3, P4, O1, O2, F7, F8, T7, T8, P7, P8, Fz, Cz, Pz, FC1, FC2, CP1, CP2, FC5, FC6, CP5, CP6, TP9, and TP10. Impedances were kept below 10 kΩ.

The two EEG sessions were arranged to take place at the same time of the day. For most participants, this requirement was met by performing EEG within the same time-range around noon (1 pm). This means that we aimed to keep the time difference between the two recordings below three hours. For three participants (HC, SCC, TLEl) the time difference was approximately four hours, for two patients (MCI, TLEr) the time difference was six hours, and for one HC the time difference was 11 hours.

2.7.3 Data preparation. Data was pre-processed with Brain Vision Analyzer (Version 1.05.0005, Brain Products GmbH). In order to re-reference all channels, a new reference was built by averaging the signal of earlobe electrodes. Butterworth Zero Phase Filters were used for a high-pass filter from 1 Hz (time constant 0.1592 s, 48 dB/oct) and an additional notch filter (50 Hz) was applied.

An automatic artefact detection was carried out in order to exclude highly contaminated datasets. Please note that the automation of this procedure ensures objectivity, which means at the same time that it is reproducible. Nevertheless, the nature and number of artefacts surely depends on the specific recording and participant. Maximal allowed voltage step per sampling point was 50 μV (values which exceeded this threshold were marked within a range of ±100 ms); maximal allowed absolute difference on an interval of 200 ms was 200 μV and lowest allowed absolute difference during an interval of 100 ms was 0.5 μV (values which exceeded this were marked with a surrounding of ±500 ms). The result of this artefact detection was reviewed visually in order to determine whether the

automated detection yielded reasonable results and whether poor data quality was due to noise on the reference electrodes, which led to exclusion of the dataset.

The preprocessed data was exported into a generic data format and imported to Matlab® (release R2016b, The Mathworks, Massachusetts, USA).

3   RESULTS

Table 2 indicates the best classification results that were obtained across the 16 examined features and the three scenarios of using only the first or the second EEG recording or of pooling the data from both recordings. Interesting results were obtained for the classification of patients with epilepsy vs. other pathological groups, and for the classification of young participants vs. old participants, and the intake of CNS active drugs. Figures 3-6 show the details for the four configurations of using the single epochs with the whole bandwidth (Figure 3) or restricting the bandwidth to θ-β (Figure 4), as well as the use of templates obtained as averages from each 3 single epochs, again with the whole bandwidth (Figure 5) or restricting the bandwidth to θ-β (Figure 6).

According to Table 2 the whole-bandwith analysis of templates yields highest classification accuracies. From Figure 5 we can infer that the most informative features are h, AF, and AR for the identification of patients with TLE and the intake of drugs, while the classification of young vs. old participants was more accurate when based on features such as pCOH, DTF, and ffDTF.

For most features and classifications, the results when using only the first or second EEG or when pooling both sessions are quite comparable. The differentiation between these three scenarios is important, because the EEG varies considerably from day to day, so that the results of single vs. multisession studies on EEG biometrics may lead to different conclusions [27]. However, the two scenarios of using single epochs vs. templates do not only differ with respect to the way the templates were obtained, but also with respect to the sample size that can be used for classification. It seems that the larger sample size in the single-epoch scenarios does not beneficially contribute to the accuracy to an extent that

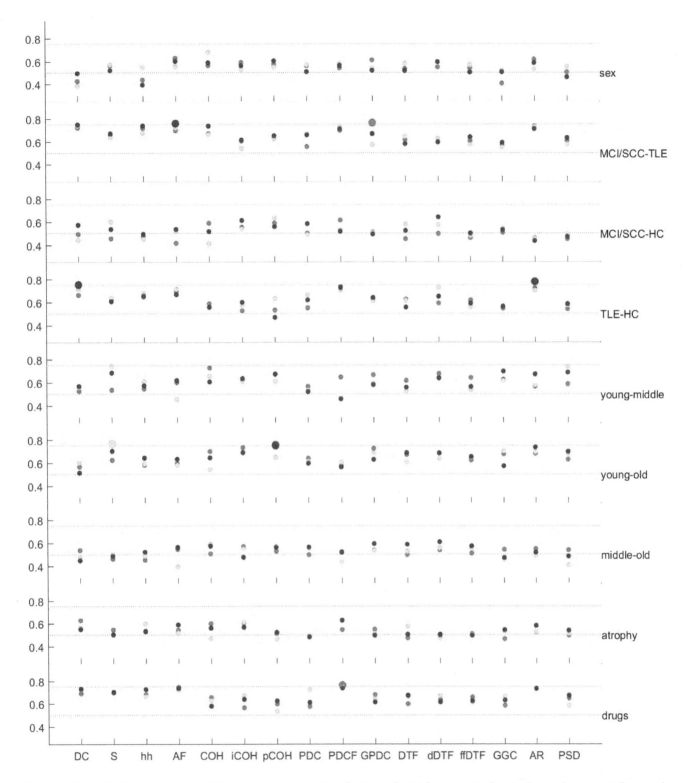

Figure 3: Classification accuracies of the pairwise group classifications for 16 features, in the single epoch scenario for epochs from first EEG only (red), second EEG only (green), both EEGs pooled (blue). Horizontal lines indicate the range between 0.5 and 0.75. Larger markers indicate values ≥ 0.75.

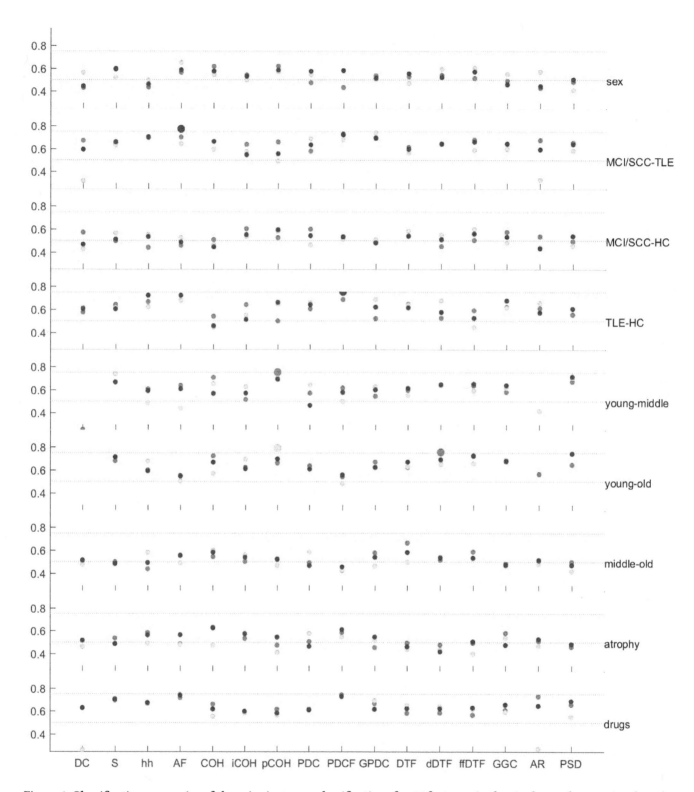

Figure 4: Classification accuracies of the pairwise group classifications for 16 features, in the single epoch scenario when the frequency range was restricted to θ, α, and β, for epochs from first EEG only (red), second EEG only (green), both EEGs pooled (blue). Horizontal lines indicate the range between 0.5 and 0.75. Larger markers indicate values ≥ 0.75.

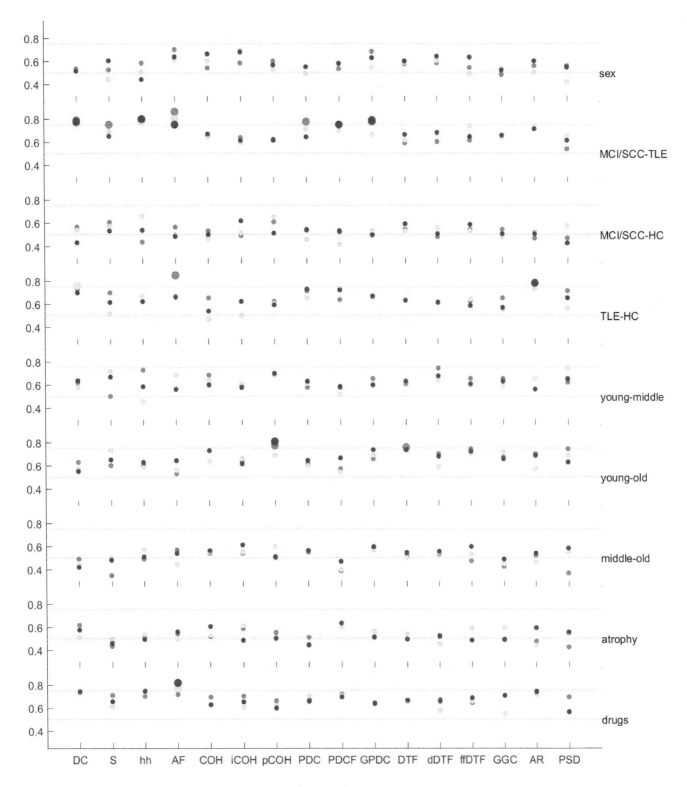

Figure 5: Classification accuracies of the pairwise group classifications for 16 features, in the template scenario for templates from first EEG only (red), second EEG only (green), both EEGs pooled (blue). Horizontal lines indicate the range between 0.5 and 0.75. Larger markers indicate values ≥ 0.75.

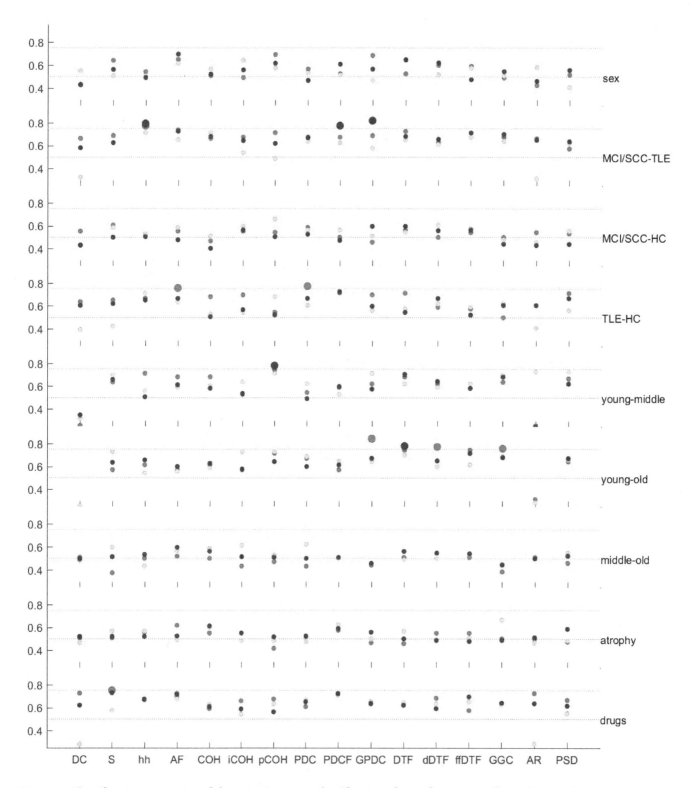

Figure 6: Classification accuracies of the pairwise group classifications for 16 features, in the in the template scenario when the frequency range was restricted to θ, α, and β, for templates from first EEG only (red), second EEG only (green), both EEGs pooled (blue). Horizontal lines indicate the range between 0.5 and 0.75. Larger markers indicate values ≥ 0.75.

exceeds the advantage of averaging multiple epochs. Because of the variation of the EEG over time, the average of multiple epochs may be more stable and contain more reliable information than the single epoch data.

The restriction of the frequency range to θ-β may be beneficial when using the system in a sample of healthy subjects. In the presented experimental sample we included neurological populations into our analysis, for which EEG activity in the low δ frequency band as well as high-frequency activity in the γ band could be identifying. As such, the restriction to this range was helpful when differentiating young from old participants. As stated in the introduction, in clinical EEG analyses, the presence of slow activity is a correlate of healthy aging, but may represent also a hint for pathological processes, as well as high-frequency activity is considered to be a marker for epileptogenicity [16].

Among the biomarkers that yielded accuracies above .75, AF and pCOH did so more consistently over the four configurations (single epochs/templates, frequency restriction) than the other markers. Both of these markers strongly emphasize the frequency content of the signal, but in contrast to a classical PSD, these markers take also the multivariate aspect of the EEG into account. In agreement with the current opinion leaders in quantitative EEG research, both, frequency content and spatial interaction of brain activity contain relevant information [10]. Despite a sample size of 60 is quite small, the presented study documents that this information might not only be interesting for clinical purposes such as diagnoses, but it should also be considered in terms of user privacy in EEG biometric systems. Future experiments with larger sample sizes might extend the present work by effective combination of promising features.

4 CONCLUSIONS

EEG features and even more so biometric templates can reveal privacy sensitive information about the subject, e.g. the diagnosis of epilepsy or the intake of drugs affecting the central nervous system. Since the sample suffering from TLE overlapped completely with the sample taking the mentioned drugs we cannot disentangle the informative aspect for the classifier. But it is also possible that both aspects contribute to the differentiability of these subjects, since the effect of epilepsy on the EEG is the main reason why EEG is a diagnostic modality in the clinics, and numerous studies document the effect of anti-epileptic drugs on the EEG [26, 30, 47, 66]. Epilepsy is a considerable burden for the affected people, specifically because of the stigma. Moreover, also age is considerably affecting the EEG; a drop in the background dominant frequency from the α frequency band into lower ranges of θ can be observed both in healthy elderly individuals, and even more so in pathological aging [46]. Thus, the information contained in the biometric templates warrants the use of protective safeguards in EEG biometric systems.

ACKNOWLEDGMENTS

The authors would like to thank Kevin Butz and Aljoscha Thomschewski for performing the data recording, and Eugen Trinka, Julia Höfler, Judith Dobesberger, Giorgi Kuchukhidze, Markus Leitinger, Margaritha Kirschner, Elisabeth Schmid, Daniela Sinadinoska, Susanne Grinzinger, Martin Scherr, and Wolfgang Staffen for recruitment of patients, and all participants for their time. The presented research was funded by the Austrian Science Fund (FWF): KLI12-B00 and by the Paracelsus Medical University Research Support Funds (PMU FFF): A-11/02/004-TRI.

REFERENCES

[1] G Al-Hudhud, MA Alzamel, E Alattas, and A Alwabil. 2014. Using brain signals patterns for biometric identity verification systems. *Computers in Human Behavior* 31 (2014), 224–229.

[2] LA Baccalá and K Sameshima. 2001. Partial directed coherence: a new concept in neural structure determination. *Biol Cybern* 84 (2001), 463–474.

[3] LA Baccalá, DY Takahashi, and K Sameshima. 2007. Generalized Partial Directed Coherence. In *Proceedings of the 15th International Conference on Digital Signal Processing (DSP); July 1-4, Wales, UK*, S Sanei, JA Chambers, J McWhirter, Y Hicks, and AG Constantinides (Eds.). IEEE, New York, 162–6.

[4] Garima Bajwa and Ram Dantu. 2016. Neurokey: Towards a new paradigm of cancelable biometrics-based key generation using electroencephalograms. *Computers & Security* 62 (2016), 95 – 113. https://doi.org/10.1016/j.cose.2016.06.001

[5] X. Bao, J. Wang, and J. Hu. 2009. Method of Individual Identification Based on Electroencephalogram Analysis. In *2009 International Conference on New Trends in Information and Service Science*. Institute of Electrical and Electronics Engineers (IEEE), Beijing, China, 390–393. https://doi.org/10.1109/NISS.2009.44

[6] SL Bressler, CG Richter, Y Chen, and M Ding. 2007. Cortical functional network organization from autoregressive modeling of local field potential oscillations. *Stat Med* 26 (2007), 3875–85.

[7] K. Brigham and B. V. K. V. Kumar. 2010. Subject identification from electroencephalogram (EEG) signals during imagined speech. In *2010 Fourth IEEE International Conference on Biometrics: Theory, Applications and Systems (BTAS)*. Washington, DC, USA, 1–8. https://doi.org/10.1109/BTAS.2010.5634515

[8] J Britton, L Frey, J Hopp, P Korb, M Koubeissi, W Lievens, E Pestana-Knight, and E Louis. 2016. *Electroencephalography (EEG): An Introductory Text and Atlas of Normal and Abnormal Findings in Adults, Children, and Infants*. American Epilepsy Society, Chicago. https://doi.org/10.1002/14651858.CD007272.pub2

[9] CP Brötzner, W Klimesch, M Doppelmayr, A Zauner, and HH Kerschbaum. 2014. Resting state alpha frequency is associated with menstrual cycle phase, estradiol and use of oral contraceptives. *Brain Research* 19 (2014), 36–44.

[10] E Bullmore and O Sporns. 2009. Complex brain networks: graph theoretical analysis of structural and functional systems. *Nat Rev Neurosci* 10 (2009), 186–98. https://doi.org/10.1038/nrn2575

[11] John Chuang, Hamilton Nguyen, Charles Wang, and Benjamin Johnson. 2013. I Think, Therefore I Am: Usability and Security of Authentication Using Brainwaves. In *Financial Cryptography and Data Security: FC Workshops, USEC and WAHC 2013, Okinawa, Japan, Revised Selected Papers*, Andrew A. Adams, Michael Brenner, and Matthew Smith (Eds.). Springer Berlin Heidelberg, Berlin, Heidelberg, 1–16. https://doi.org/10.1007/978-3-642-41320-9_1

[12] P. Cserti, B. Végsö, G. Kozmann, Z. Nagy, F. De Vico Fallani, and F. Babiloni. 2012. Methods to highlight consistency in repeated EEG recordings. *IFAC Proceedings Volumes, 8th IFAC Symposium on Biological and Medical Systems* 45, 18 (2012), 23 – 27. https://doi.org/10.3182/20120829-3-HU-2029.00078

[13] M DelPozo-Banos, J Alonso, J Ticay-Rivas, and C Travieso. 2014. Electroencephalogram subject identification: a review. *Expert Systems with Applications* 41, 15 (2014), 6537–6554.

[14] M DelPozo-Banos, C Travieso, C Weidemann, and J Alonso. 2015. EEG biometric identification: a thorough exploration of the time-frequency domain. *J Neural Eng* 12 (2015), 056019.

[15] M Eichler. 2006. On the evaluation of information flow in multivariate systems by the directed transfer function. *Biol Cybern* 94 (2006), 469–82.

[16] B Frauscher, F Bartolomei, K Kobayashi, J Cimbalnik, M A van't Klooster, S Rampp, H Otsubo, Y Höller, J Y Wu, E Asano, J Jr Engel, P Kahane, J Jacobs, and J Gotman. 2017. High-frequency oscillations: The state of clinical research. *Epilepsia* 58 (2017), 1316–1329. https://doi.org/10.1111/epi.13829

[17] W Gersch and GV Goddard. 1970. Epileptic focus location: spectral analysis method. *Science* 169 (1970), 701–2.

[18] J Geweke. 1982. Measures of Conditional Linear Dependence and Feedback Between Time Series. *J Am Stat Assoc* 77 (1982), 304–313.

[19] RE Greenblatt, ME Pflieger, and AE Ossadtchi. 2012. Connectivity measures applied to human brain electrophysiological data. *Journal for Neuroscience Methods* 207 (2012), 1–16.

[20] MJ Kaminski and KJ Blinowska. 1991. A new method of the description of the information flow in the brain structures. *Biol Cybern* 65 (1991), 203–210.

[21] M Kaminski, M Ding, WA Truccolo, and SL Bressler. 2001. Evaluating causal relations in neural systems: Granger causality, directed transfer function and statistical assessment of significance. *Biol Cybern* 85 (2001), 145–57.

[22] J Kennedy and S U Schuele. 2013. Long-term monitoring of brain tumors: when is it necessary? *Epilepsia* 9 (2013), 50–5. https://doi.org/10.1111/epi.12444

[23] J. Klonovs, C. K. Petersen, H. Olesen, and A. Hammershoj. 2013. ID Proof on the Go: Development of a Mobile EEG-Based Biometric Authentication System. *IEEE Vehicular Technology Magazine* 8, 1 (March 2013), 81–89. https://doi.org/10.1109/MVT.2012.2234056

[24] G Korbakis and P M Vespa. 2017. Multimodal neurologic monitoring. *Handb Clin Neurol* 140 (2017), 91–105. https://doi.org/10.1016/B978-0-444-63600-3.00006-4

[25] A Korzeniewska, M Maczak, M Kaminski, KJ Blinowska, and S Kasicki. 2003. Determination of information flow direction among brain structures by a modified directed transfer function (dDTF) method. *J Neurosci Methods* 125 (2003), 195–207.

[26] K Lehnertz and CE Elger. 1997. Neuronal complexity loss in temporal lobe epilepsy: Effects of carbamazepine on the dynamics of the epileptogenic focus. *Electroenceph Clin Neurophysiol* 103 (1997), 376–80.

[27] E Maiorana, D La Rocca, and P Campisi. 2016. On the Permanence of EEG Signals for Biometric Recognition. *IEEE Transactions on Information Forensics and Security* 11, 1 (Jan 2016), 163–175. https://doi.org/10.1109/TIFS.2015.2481870

[28] Emanuele Maiorana, Daria La Rocca, and Patrizio Campisi. 2016. Eigenbrains and Eigentensorbrains: Parsimonious bases for EEG biometrics. *Neurocomputing* 171 (2016), 638 – 648. https://doi.org/10.1016/j.neucom.2015.07.005

[29] S Marple. 1987. *Digital Spectral analysis with applications.* Prentice Hall, Upper Saddle River, New Jersey.

[30] KJ Meador, A Gevins, PT Leese, C Otoul, and DW Loring. 2011. Neurocognitive effects of brivaracetam, levetiracetam, and lorazepam. *Epilepsia* 51 (2011), 264–72.

[31] A G Messina, M Wang, M J Ward, C C Wilker, B B Smith, D P Vezina, and N L Pace. 2016. Anaesthetic interventions for prevention of awareness during surgery. *Cochrane Database Syst Rev* 10, CD007272 (2016). https://doi.org/10.1002/14651858.CD007272.pub2

[32] F Miraglia, F Vecchio, and P M Rossini. 2017. Searching for signs of aging and dementia in EEG through network analysis. *Behav Brain Res* 317 (2017), 292–300. https://doi.org/10.1016/j.bbr.2016.09.057

[33] K Mohanchandra, L GM, P Kambli, and V Krishnamurthy. 2013. Using brain waves as new biometric feature for authenticating a computer user in real-time. *International Journal of Biometrics and Bioinformatics (IJBB)* 7 (2013), 49–57.

[34] VK Murthy. 1963. Estimation of the Cross-Spectrum. *Ann Math Statist* 34 (1963), 1012–21.

[35] I. Nakanishi, S. Baba, and C. Miyamoto. 2009. EEG based biometric authentication using new spectral features. In *2009 International Symposium on Intelligent Signal Processing and Communication Systems (ISPACS)*. IEEE, Kanazawa, Japan, 651–654. https://doi.org/10.1109/ISPACS.2009.5383756

[36] G Nolte, O Bai, L Wheaton, Z Mari, S Vorbach, and M Hallett. 2004. Identifying true brain interaction from EEG data using the imaginary part of coherency. *Clin Neurophysiol* 115 (2004), 2292–307.

[37] M Nuwer. 1997. Assessment of digital EEG, quantitative EEG, and EEG brain mapping: Report of the American Academy of Neurology and the American Clinical Neurophysiology Society. *Neurology* 49 (1997), 277–292. https://doi.org/10.1212/WNL.49.1.277

[38] R Palaniappan. 2006. Electroencephalogram signals from imagined activities: A novel biometric identifier for a small population. In *Intelligent Data Engineering and Automated Learning*, E Corchado (Ed.), Vol. 4224. Springer-Verlag, Berlin Heidelberg, 604–611. https://doi.org/10.1007/11875581_73

[39] Ramaswamy Palaniappan and Danilo P. Mandic. 2007. EEG Based Biometric Framework for Automatic Identity Verification. *The Journal of VLSI Signal Processing Systems for Signal, Image, and Video Technology* 49, 2 (2007), 243–250. https://doi.org/10.1007/s11265-007-0078-1

[40] Ramaswamy Palaniappan and K.V.R. Ravi. 2006. Improving visual evoked potential feature classification for person recognition using PCA and normalization. *Pattern Recognition Letters* 27, 7 (2006), 726 – 733. https://doi.org/10.1016/j.patrec.2005.10.020

[41] R. Palaniappan and K. V. R. Ravi. 2003. A new method to identify individuals using signals from the brain. In *2003 Proceedings of the joint Fourth International Conference on Information, Communications and Signal Processing, and the Fourth Pacific Rim Conference on Multimedia*, Vol. 3. IEEE, Singapore, Singapore, 1442–1445. https://doi.org/10.1109/ICICS.2003.1292704

[42] CP Panayiotopoulos. 2005. . Bladon Medical Publishing, Oxfordshire, UK.

[43] M. Poulos, M. Rangoussi, V. Chrissikopoulos, and A. Evangelou. 1999. Person identification based on parametric processing of the EEG. In *Electronics, Circuits and Systems, 1999. Proceedings of ICECS '99. The 6th IEEE International Conference on*, Vol. 1. Pafos, Cyprus, Cyprus, 283–286. https://doi.org/10.1109/ICECS.1999.812278

[44] K. V. R. Ravi and R. Palaniappan. 2005. Leave-one-out Authentication of Persons Using 40 Hz EEG Oscillations. In *EUROCON 2005 - The International Conference on "Computer as a Tool"*, Vol. 2. IEEE, Belgrade, Serbia and Montenegro, 1386–1389. https://doi.org/10.1109/EURCON.2005.1630219

[45] F Rosenow, K M Klein, and H M Hamer. 2015. Non-invasive EEG evaluation in epilepsy diagnosis. *Expert Rev Neurother* 15 (2015), 425–44. https://doi.org/10.1586/14737175.2015.1025382

[46] P.M. Rossini, S. Rossi, C. Babiloni, and J. Polich. 2007. Clinical neurophysiology of aging brain: From normal aging to neurodegeneration. *Prog Neurobiol* 83 (2007), 375–400.

[47] MC Salinsky, LM Binder, BS Oken, D Storzbach, CR Aron, and CB Dodrill. 2002. Effects of gabapentin and carbamazepine on the EEG and cognition in healthy volunteers. *Epilepsia* 43 (2002), 482–90.

[48] W G Sannita. 1990. Quantitative EEG in human neuropharmacology. Rationale, history, and recent developments. *Acta Neurol (Napoli)* 12 (1990), 389–409.

[49] A Schlögl. 2006. A comparison of multivariate autoregressive estimators. *Signal Processing* 86 (2006), 2426–2429.

[50] A Schlögl and C Brunner. 2008. BioSig: A Free and Open Source Software Library for BCI Research. *Computer* 41 (2008), 44–50. Issue 10.

[51] T Schuster and U Kalliauer. 2009. Localizing the focus of epileptic seizures using modern measures from multivariate time series analysis. Diploma-Thesis at the Vienna University of Technology. (2009).

[52] G. K. Singhal and P. RamKumar. 2007. Person Identification Using Evoked Potentials and Peak Matching. In *2007 Biometrics Symposium*. IEEE, Baltimore, MD, USA, 1–6. https://doi.org/10.1109/BCC.2007.4430555

[53] H.H Stassen. 1980. Computerized recognition of persons by EEG spectral patterns. *Electroencephalography and Clinical Neurophysiology* 49, 1-2 (1980), 190 – 194. https://doi.org/10.1016/0013-4694(80)90368-5

[54] Shiliang Sun. 2008. Multitask learning for EEG-based biometrics. In *2008 19th International Conference on Pattern Recognition*. IEEE, Tampa, FL, USA, 1–4. https://doi.org/10.1109/ICPR.2008.4761865

[55] W Szurhaj, M D Lamblin, A Kaminska, H Sediri, and Sociét4 de Neurophysiologie Clinique de Langue Francaise. 2015. EEG guidelines in the diagnosis of brain death. *Neurophysiol Clin* 45 (2015), 97–104. https://doi.org/10.1016/j.neucli.2014.11.005

[56] P. Tangkraingkij, C. Lursinsap, S. Sanguansintukul, and T. Desudchit. 2009. Selecting Relevant EEG Signal Locations for Personal Identification Problem Using ICA and Neural Network. In *2009 Eighth IEEE/ACIS International Conference on Computer and Information Science*. Shanghai, China, 616–621. https://doi.org/10.1109/ICIS.2009.156

[57] J Taxidis, B Coomber, R Mason, and M Owen. 2010. Assessing cortico-hippocampal functional connectivity under anesthesia and kainic acid using generalized partial directed coherence. *Biol Cybern* 102 (2010), 327–340.

[58] P van Mierlo, E Carrette, H Hallez, K Vonck, D Van Roost, P Boon, et al. 2011. Accurate epileptogenic focus localization through time-variant functional connectivity analysis of intracranial electroencephalographic signals. *Neuroimage* 56 (2011), 1122–1133.

[59] M J van Putten and J Hofmeijer. 2016. Multimodal neurologic monitoring. *J Clin Neurophysiol* 33 (2016), 203–10. https://doi.org/10.1097/WNP.0000000000000272

[60] O Vysata, J Kukal, A Prochazka, L Pazdera, J Simko, and M Valis. 2014. Age-related changes in EEG coherence. *Neurologia I Neurochirurgia Polska* 48 (2014), 35–38.

[61] Y Wada, Y Nanbu, R Kadoshima, ZY Jiang, Y Koshino, and T Hashimoto. 1996. Interhemispheric EEG coherence during photic stimulation: sex differences in normal young adults. *Int J Psychophysiol* 22 (1996), 45–51.

[62] Y Wada, Y Takizawa, ZY Jiang, and N Yamaguchi. 1994. Gender differences in quantitative EEG at rest and during photic stimulation in normal young adults. *Clin Electroencephalogr* 25 (1994), 81–5. Issue 2.

[63] S. Yang and F. Deravi. 2017. On the Usability of Electroencephalographic Signals for Biometric Recognition: A Survey. *IEEE Transactions on Human-Machine Systems* PP, 99 (2017), 1–12. https://doi.org/10.1109/THMS.2017.2682115

[64] A. Yazdani, A. Roodaki, S. H. Rezatofighi, K. Misaghian, and S. K. Setarehdan. 2008. Fisher linear discriminant based person identification using visual evoked potentials. In *2008 9th International Conference on Signal Processing*. IEEE, Beijing, China, 1677–1680. https://doi.org/10.1109/ICOSP.2008.4697459

[65] Seul-Ki Yeom, Heung-Il Suk, and Seong-Whan Lee. 2013. Person authentication from neural activity of face-specific visual self-representation. *Pattern Recognition* 46, 4 (2013), 1159 – 1169. https://doi.org/10.1016/j.patcog.2012.10.023

[66] HP Zaveri, SM Pincus, II Goncharova, EJ Novotny, RB Duckrow, DD Spencer, H Blumenfeld, and SS Spencer. 2010. Background intracranial EEG spectral changes with anti-epileptic drug taper. *Clin Neurophysiol* 121 (2010), 311–7. https://doi.org/10.1016/j.clinph.2009.11.081

Fake Faces Identification via Convolutional Neural Network

Huaxiao Mo
Sun Yat-sen University
Guangzhou, China
mohx5@mail2.sysu.edu.cn

Bolin Chen
Sun Yat-sen University
Guangzhou, China
chenbl8@mail2.sysu.edu.cn

Weiqi Luo*
Sun Yat-sen University
Guangzhou, China
luoweiqi@mail.sysu.edu.cn

ABSTRACT

Generative Adversarial Network (GAN) is a prominent generative model that are widely used in various applications. Recent studies have indicated that it is possible to obtain fake face images with a high visual quality based on this novel model. If those fake faces are abused in image tampering, it would cause some potential moral, ethical and legal problems. In this paper, therefore, we first propose a Convolutional Neural Network (CNN) based method to identify fake face images generated by the current best method [20], and provide experimental evidences to show that the proposed method can achieve satisfactory results with an average accuracy over 99.4%. In addition, we provide comparative results evaluated on some variants of the proposed CNN architecture, including the high pass filter, the number of the layer groups and the activation function, to further verify the rationality of our method.

KEYWORDS

Image Forensics, Deep Learning, Generative Adversarial Networks (GAN), Convolutional Neural Network (CNN)

ACM Reference Format:
Huaxiao Mo, Bolin Chen, and Weiqi Luo. 2018. Fake Faces Identification via Convolutional Neural Network. In *IH&MMSec '18: 6th ACM Workshop on Information Hiding and Multimedia Security, June 20–22, 2018, Innsbruck, Austria.* ACM, New York, NY, USA, 5 pages. https://doi.org/10.1145/3206004.3206009

1 INTRODUCTION

With the rapid development of image processing technology, modifying an image without obvious visual artifacts becomes much easier. Nowadays, seeing is no longer believing. Image forensics have attracted widely attention in the last decade, and many forensic methods based on hand-crafted features such as [4, 15, 16, 19] have been proposed until now.

Different from conventional methods based on hand-crafted features, deep learning can exploit cascaded layers to adaptively learn hierarchical representations from input data. Some novel models in deep learning such as CNN and GAN have been extensively studied and have achieved great success in many image related applications, such as image style transfer [8, 11], image super-resolution [13, 18],

---

*Corresponding author.

image inpainting [10, 22] and image steganalysis [6, 21]. Up to now, several deep learning based works have been proposed for image forensics. For instance, Chen et al. [5] proposed a median filtering forensic method based on CNN; Bayar et al. [2] proposed a new CNN architecture to detect several typical image manipulations; Rao et al. [17] proposed a CNN based method to detect image splicing and copy-move; Choi et al. [7] proposed a CNN based method to detect composite forgery detection. Recently, some studies have shown that we can obtain fake face images with high visual quality (refer to Section 2 for details) based on GAN model. Since these fake face images can successfully cheat our eyes, identifying fake images becomes an very important issue in image forensics. In this paper, we propose a CNN based method to identify the fake images generated by the work [20]. In our method, we carefully design the CNN architecture, with particular attention to the high pass filter for the input image, the number of layer groups and the activation function, and then provide extensive experimental results to show the effectiveness and rationality of the proposed method. To the best of our knowledge, this is the first work to investigate this forensic problem.

The rest of the paper is organized as follows. Section 2 describes two recent GAN based works on face generation. Section 3 gives the proposed detection method based on CNN. Section 4 shows experimental results and discussions. Finally, the concluding remarks of this paper and the future works are given in Section 5.

2 FACE GENERATION WITH GAN

Generative adversarial networks (GAN) [9] is a prominent generative model, which learns the distribution form high-dimension data and produces novel sample. Typically, a GAN contains two parts: a generator and a discriminator. The generator learns to create fake data indistinguishable from the real data, while the discriminator learns to determine whether the input data is real or fake. They contest against each other during training until the generator can produce high quality fake data.

Recently, several GAN based methods are proposed to generate high quality fake face images. For instance, in [3], Berthelot et al. proposed a novel equilibrium method for balancing the two parts of GAN to generate visually pleasing face images. However, this method can only produce fake face images in low resolutions, such as 256×256. In [20], Karras et al. proposed a progressive strategy to construct and train GAN for generating high quality images. The progressive strategy is illustrated in Fig. 1. Instead of training the whole GAN on high-resolution image, they first construct a simple GAN training on low-resolution images in the beginning, and then gradually add more layers to adapt the model to high-resolution images during the training stage. Based on the experiments, most fake face images (1024×1024) generated by this method are difficult to identify with the naked eye, as illustrated

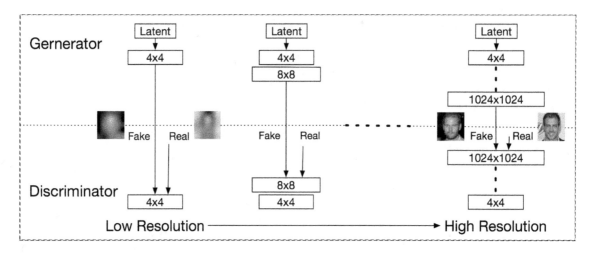

Figure 1: The progressive training strategy employed in [20]. Here $N \times N$ refers to layers operating on images of $N \times N$ resolution.

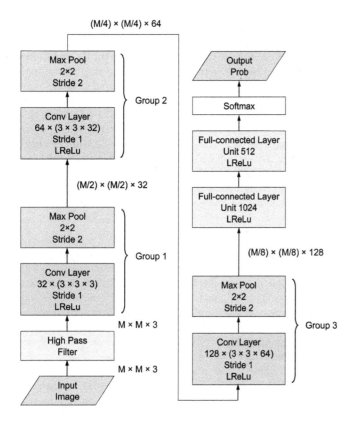

Figure 2: The proposed architecture

in the first row of Fig.8. However, some poorer results are also obtained using this method, as illustrated in the second row of Fig. 8. In this paper, we first propose a method to identify those good fake face images generated using the method [20].

3 THE PROPOSED DETECTION METHOD

Since the generator and discriminator employed in [20] are mainly based on CNN, it is natural to use a CNN based method to detect the resulting fake face images. To this end, we carefully design the architecture of the proposed CNN model, as illustrated in Fig. 2. The model input is an RGB color image with size $M \times M \times 3$. Since the contents of fake and true face images are quite similar, it is expected that the main difference between the two kinds of images would be reflected on the residual domain according to the previous research [14]. Therefore, we first transform the input images into residuals using a high pass filter. The resulting residuals are then fed into three layer groups. Each group includes a convolutional layer (3×3 size, 1×1 stride) equipped with LReLu and a max pooling layer (2×2 size, 2×2 stride). The output feature map number of the convolutional layer in the first group is 32, while that of the other convolutional layers is twice the corresponding input feature map number. The output feature maps of the last group are then aggregated and fed into two fully-connected layers. They both equipped with LReLu and consist of 1024, 512 units, respectively. Finally, the softmax layer is used to produce the output probability.

In our experiments, we implement the proposed CNN model using Tensorflow [1] and train it using Adam [12] with a learning rate of 0.0001. All the weights are initialized using a truncated Gaussian distribution with zero mean and standard deviation of 0.01. The biases is initialized as zero. L2 regularization is enabled in the fully-connected layer with the λ of 0.0005. In the training stage, we use a batch size of 64 and train the proposed CNN for 20 epochs. In addition, we shuffle the training data between epochs.

4 EXPERIMENTAL RESULTS

In this section, we first describe the image data set used in our experiments. Then we present some experiments to show the effectiveness of the proposed method in identifying fake face images. In addition, we conduct extensive experiments to show the rationality of the proposed model.

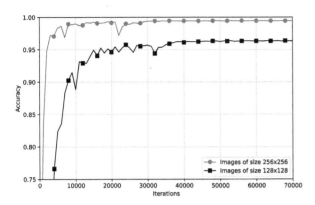

Figure 3: Comparison of different image sizes

4.1 Image Data Set

In our experiments, we use 30,000 true face images from CELEBA-HQ dataset and select 30,000 fake ones with good visual quality from the fake face image database [1] generated by [20]. All images are with 1024×1024 and stored in PNG format. In our experiments, we resize all images into 256×256 using bilinear interpolation, and compress them using lossy JPEG compression with a quality factor of 95. Finally, we divide the resulting images into training set (12,000 pairs of true-fake face images), validation set (3,000 pairs) and test set (15,000 pairs). To achieve convincing results, we randomly split the training, validation, and test set three times and report the average results in the following experiments.

4.2 Fake Face Identification

In this section, we aim to identify whether a given face image is real or generated one. As shown in the blue box in Fig. 9, we found that some background regions in some fake face images looks unnatural, which may help increase the detection performance. To reduce the influence of image backgrounds, we crop a small segment (128×128) from every image in the original image set (256×256), and ensure that each cropped segment mainly includes some facial key-points (such as eyes, nose, and mouse), as illustrated in red box in Fig. 9. Finally, we obtain two different image data set for experiments, that is original ones including face and background, and the cropped ones just including main facial region.

The experimental results evaluated on the two validation set are shown in Fig. 3. From Fig. 3, we observe that during training stage, the proposed model on both original images (green line) and cropped images (black line) can converge within 70,000 iterations, and both detection accuracies would be over 95% after 40,000 iterations. For a more convincing result, we evaluate the trained model on the test set, and obtain accuracies of over 99.4% and 96.3% on the original images and cropped images respectively, which means that we can still obtain satisfactory results after removing unnatural parts in the background.

---

[1] Available at: https://drive.google.com/drive/folders/0B4qLcYyJmiz0TXY1NG02bzZVRGs

4.3 Comparison of Variants of the Proposed Model

In this section, we present some results to validate the rationality of the proposed model in Fig.2. Three parts of our model are considered, including the high pass filter, the number of the layer groups and the activation function. The corresponding results evaluated on the validation set are shown in the following subsections.

4.3.1 High Pass Filter: In this experiment, three following high pass filters are evaluated in the model.

$$
\begin{bmatrix} -1 & 1 \end{bmatrix}
\quad
\begin{bmatrix} 0 & -1 & 0 \\ -1 & 4 & -1 \\ 0 & -1 & 0 \end{bmatrix}
\quad
\begin{bmatrix} -1 & 2 & -2 & 2 & -1 \\ 2 & -6 & 8 & -6 & 2 \\ -2 & 8 & -12 & 8 & -2 \\ 2 & -6 & 8 & -6 & 2 \\ -1 & 2 & -2 & 2 & -1 \end{bmatrix}
$$

(a) filter A   (b) filter B   (c) filter C

Figure 4: Three high pass filters

The corresponding results are shown in Fig. 5. From Fig 5, we observe the proposed model (i.e. using the filter B) can achieve highest accuracy among the three test filters. We also observe that the model using the filter A can achieve similar results with our proposed model, while the model with filter C has the lowest detection accuracy. In addition, the detection accuracy of removing the high pass filter is nearly 98%, which means that using suitable high pass filter can help improve detection performance.

4.3.2 Number of layer groups: In this experiment, we evaluate the influence of adding/removing one layer group in the proposed model. The results are shown in Fig. 6. From Fig. 6, we observe that adding one group to the proposed model does not increase the detection performance, while removing one group decreases the detection performance slightly, which means that using three layer groups in the proposed model is sufficient for the investigated problem.

4.3.3 Activation functions: Activation function is another important factor in CNN. In this experiment, six commonly used activation functions are considered in the proposed model. They are TanH, ReLu, and four variants of ReLu, including PReLu, LReLu, ELU and ReLu6. The experimental results are shown in Fig. 7. From Fig. 7, we observe that LReLu ReLu, PReLu, and ELU can achieve similar accuracy. Among six activation functions, LReLu obtains the best performance while TanH shows the worst performance.

5 CONCLUSION

In this paper, we first propose a CNN based method to identify fake face images generated with the state-of-the-art method [20], and provide extensive experimental results to show that the proposed method can effectively identify fake face images with a high visual quality from real ones. Our experimental results also indicate that even though the current GAN based methods can generate realistic looking faces (or other image objects and scenes), some obvious statistical artifacts would be inevitably introduced and can serve as evidences for fake ones.

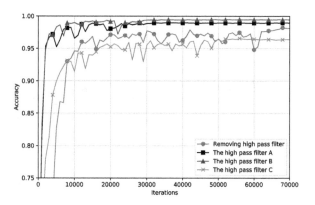

Figure 5: Comparison of using different high pass filters/without high pass filter

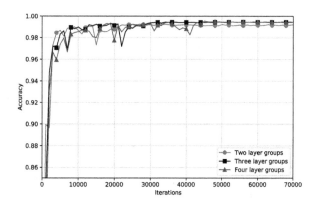

Figure 6: Comparison of different numbers of groups

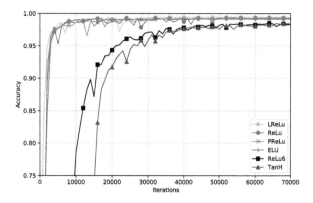

Figure 7: Comparison of different activation functions

In future, we will further investigate some inherent artifacts left by the GAN in [20] for image forensics. On the other side, we will try to propose a wise face generation method that can avoid detection.

ACKNOWLEDGMENTS

This work is supported in part by the NSFC (61672551), the Special Research Plan of Guangdong Province under Grant 2015TQ01X365, and the Guangzhou Science and Technology Plan Project under Grant 201707010167.

REFERENCES

[1] Martín Abadi, Ashish Agarwal, Paul Barham, Eugene Brevdo, Zhifeng Chen, Craig Citro, Greg S Corrado, Andy Davis, Jeffrey Dean, Matthieu Devin, et al. 2016. Tensorflow: Large-scale machine learning on heterogeneous distributed systems. *arXiv preprint arXiv:1603.04467* (2016).

[2] Belhassen Bayar and Matthew C Stamm. 2016. A deep learning approach to universal image manipulation detection using a new convolutional layer. In *Proceedings of the 4th ACM Workshop on Information Hiding and Multimedia Security*. 5–10.

[3] David Berthelot, Tom Schumm, and Luke Metz. 2017. Began: Boundary equilibrium generative adversarial networks. *arXiv preprint arXiv:1703.10717* (2017).

[4] Gang Cao, Yao Zhao, Rongrong Ni, and Xuelong Li. 2014. Contrast enhancement-based forensics in digital images. *IEEE transactions on information forensics and security* 9, 3 (2014), 515–525.

[5] Jiansheng Chen, Xiangui Kang, Ye Liu, and Z Jane Wang. 2015. Median filtering forensics based on convolutional neural networks. *IEEE Signal Processing Letters* 22, 11 (2015), 1849–1853.

[6] Mo Chen, Vahid Sedighi, Mehdi Boroumand, and Jessica Fridrich. 2017. JPEG-Phase-Aware Convolutional Neural Network for Steganalysis of JPEG Images. In *ACM Workshop on Information Hiding and Multimedia Security*. 75–84.

[7] Hak-Yeol Choi, Han-Ul Jang, Dongkyu Kim, Jeongho Son, Seung-Min Mun, Sunghee Choi, and Heung-Kyu Lee. [n. d.]. Detecting composite image manipulation based on deep neural networks. In *IEEE International Conference on Systems, Signals and Image Processing*. 1–5.

[8] Vincent Dumoulin, Jonathon Shlens, and Manjunath Kudlur. 2017. A learned representation for artistic style. In *Proceedings of International Conference on Learning Representations*.

[9] Ian Goodfellow, Jean Pouget-Abadie, Mehdi Mirza, Bing Xu, David Warde-Farley, Sherjil Ozair, Aaron Courville, and Yoshua Bengio. 2014. Generative adversarial nets. In *Advances in neural information processing systems*. 2672–2680.

[10] Satoshi Iizuka, Edgar Simo-Serra, and Hiroshi Ishikawa. 2017. Globally and locally consistent image completion. *ACM Transactions on Graphics* 36, 4 (2017), 107:1–107:14.

[11] Justin Johnson, Alexandre Alahi, and Li Fei-Fei. 2016. Perceptual losses for real-time style transfer and super-resolution. In *European Conference on Computer Vision*. Springer, 694–711.

[12] Diederik P. Kingma and Jimmy Ba. 2014. Adam: A Method for Stochastic Optimization. *CoRR* abs/1412.6980 (2014). arXiv:1412.6980 http://arxiv.org/abs/1412.6980

[13] Christian Ledig, Lucas Theis, Ferenc Huszar, Jose Caballero, Andrew Cunningham, Alejandro Acosta, Andrew Aitken, Alykhan Tejani, Johannes Totz, Zehan Wang, et al. 2017. Photo-Realistic Single Image Super-Resolution Using a Generative Adversarial Network. In *Proceedings of the IEEE Conference on Computer Vision and Pattern Recognition*. 4681–4690.

[14] Haodong Li, Weiqi Luo, Xiaoqing Qiu, and Jiwu Huang. 2018. Identification of various image operations using residual-based features. *IEEE Transactions on Circuits and Systems for Video Technology* 28, 1 (2018), 31–45.

[15] Lu Li, Jianru Xue, Zhiqiang Tian, and Nanning Zheng. 2013. Moment feature based forensic detection of resampled digital images. In *Proceedings of the 21st ACM international conference on Multimedia*. ACM, 569–572.

[16] Xiaoqing Qiu, Haodong Li, Weiqi Luo, and Jiwu Huang. 2014. A universal image forensic strategy based on steganalytic model. In *Proceedings of the 2nd ACM workshop on Information hiding and multimedia security*. ACM, 165–170.

[17] Yuan Rao and Jiangqun Ni. 2016. A deep learning approach to detection of splicing and copy-move forgeries in images. In *IEEE International Workshop on Information Forensics and Security*. 1–6.

[18] Casper Kaae Sønderby, Jose Caballero, Lucas Theis, Wenzhe Shi, and Ferenc Huszár. 2017. Amortised map inference for image super-resolution. In *Proceedings of International Conference on Learning Representations*.

[19] Matthew Stamm and KJ Ray Liu. 2008. Blind forensics of contrast enhancement in digital images. In *IEEE International Conference on Image Processing*. IEEE, 3112–3115.

[20] Samuli Laine Jaakko Lehtinen Tero Karras, Timo Aila. 2018. Progressive Growing of GANs for Improved Quality, Stability, and Variation. *International Conference on Learning Representations* (2018). https://openreview.net/forum?id=Hk99zCeAb accepted as oral presentation.

Figure 8: Fake face examples from the work [20]. The first row shows examples with a good visual quality, while the second shows ones with a poor visual quality that would be removed in our experiments.

Figure 9: Fake face vs. Background. The region in the red box includes some facial key-points; while the blue ones are located at the background with poor visual artifacts.

[21] Guanshuo Xu, Han Zhou Wu, and Yun Qing Shi. 2016. Structural Design of Convolutional Neural Networks for Steganalysis. *IEEE Signal Processing Letters* 23, 5 (2016), 708–712.

[22] Chao Yang, Xin Lu, Zhe Lin, Eli Shechtman, Oliver Wang, and Hao Li. 2017. High-resolution image inpainting using multi-scale neural patch synthesis. In *The IEEE Conference on Computer Vision and Pattern Recognition*, Vol. 1. 3.

Generalized Benford's Law for Blind Detection of Morphed Face Images

Andrey Makrushin, Christian Kraetzer, Tom Neubert and Jana Dittmann

Otto-von-Guericke University of Magdeburg, Germany

andrey.makrushin@ovgu.de,{christian.kraetzer,tom.neubert,jana.dittmann}@iti.cs.uni-magdeburg.de

ABSTRACT

A morphed face image in a photo ID is a serious threat to image-based user verification enabling that multiple persons could be matched with the same document. The application of machine-readable travel documents (MRTD) at automated border control (ABC) gates is an example of a verification scenario that is very sensitive to this kind of fraud. Detection of morphed face images prior to face matching is, therefore, indispensable for effective border security. We introduce the face morphing detection approach based on fitting a logarithmic curve to nine Benford features extracted from quantized DCT coefficients of JPEG compressed original and morphed face images. We separately study the parameters of the logarithmic curve in face and background regions to establish the traces imposed by the morphing process. The evaluation results show that a single parameter of the logarithmic curve may be sufficient to clearly separate morphed and original images.

CCS CONCEPTS

• **Security and privacy** → **Biometrics**; • **Applied computing** → *Investigation techniques*;

KEYWORDS

Face Morphing; Digital Image Forensics; Morphing Detection

ACM Reference Format:
Andrey Makrushin, Christian Kraetzer, Tom Neubert and Jana Dittmann. 2018. Generalized Benford's Law for Blind Detection of Morphed Face Images. In *IH&MMSec '18: 6th ACM Workshop on Information Hiding and Multimedia Security, June 20–22, 2018, Innsbruck, Austria.* ACM, Innsbruck, Austria, 6 pages. https://doi.org/10.1145/3206004.3206018

1 INTRODUCTION

A face image in a document is a widely established and accepted means of identity verification. Recent machine readable travel documents (MRTD) are equipped with digital portraits to automate the identity verification process. The automation saves expensive manpower and improves security due to switching from subjective (officers) to objective (automated face recognition systems) matching of faces. The benefit of automation is especially tangible in high-throughput applications like an airport border control. However, the automation entails the risk of face presentation [9] and face morphing [4] attacks.

It has been shown that blending of face images of two or more persons can lead to a face image resembling the faces of all persons involved [4, 11]. Using a blended face image as a reference in a document is referred to as face morphing attack because it enables illicit document sharing among several users. Morphing attacks have been shown to be effective in an automated border control (ABC) scenario giving a wanted criminal a chance to to cross a border [5, 17]. As long as persons are allowed to submit images to the document issuing office, the face morphing attack will remain a severe threat to photo-ID-based verification. Indeed, if an officer accepted a morphed face image, the issued document would pass all integrity checks, and if an automated face recognition (AFR) system matches a live face with a morphed document image, access will be granted to an impostor.

The risk of the morphing attack can be reduced by supporting both officers and AFR systems with a dedicated morph detector. Establishing requirements for a morph detector and the evaluation of its performance is a hot discussion topic within the biometrics and media forensics research communities. We define four such requirements for a media forensic detector integrated into ABC gates to validate the authenticity and integrity of a digital face image in MRTD: (i) high detection rate, (ii) low false alarm rate, (iii) high generalization power of the classification model, and (iv) quick classification.

Relying on the hypothesis that morphing invokes blurring and ghosting artifacts in particular regions, many blind morph detectors are based on features extracted from intensity values of images e.g. micro-textures [15], keypoints [10] or deep convolutional neural networks (DCNN) [18]. Therefore, high-contrast morphed face images without artifacts as well as low-quality unfocused original face images are likely to be misclassified.

In contrast, we propose a detection approach based on generalized Benford's law applied to locally extracted frequencies in JPEG-compressed images. We model the distribution of Benford features by a logarithmic curve and consider the characteristics of the curve as discriminative features. Benford features have been already used for morphing detection in [11]. Focusing on the requirement (iii), our contribution is a simplification of the classification model to improve its generalization power. With the Utrecht ECVP face dataset [2], the detection rate increased from approx. 87% to approx. 98% while the false alarm rate decreased to 0%.

Hereafter, the paper is organized as follows: An overview of related work is given in Section 2 including recent advances in generation and detection of face morphs. In Section 3, our modelling concept is reported. Section 4 comprises practical aspects of the realization of our morph detector. Experimental validation is presented in Section 5. Section 6 concludes the paper with the results and future work.

2 RELATED WORKS

Attacking and preventing attacks in media forensics is a cat-and-mouse game. The research on a morphing attack can be split into two reciprocal topics: morph generation and morph detection. On the one hand, it is studied how to create "good" morphs taking inspiration in the field of computer graphics. On the other hand, it is studied how morphs should be detected based on the knowledge from the fields of digital image forensics and biometrics.

Currently, there exist many free and commercial software tools to morph faces. However, a manual assistance is always required to create natural-looking morphs. In fact, manual morph generation lacks reproducibility and makes it hardly possible to get to a large number of morphs. The very first effort to manually create morphed face images aiming at attacking an ABC scenario is done in [4] using GIMP/GAP (www.gimp.org). The same authors in [5] generate 80 morphs and evaluate these in experiments with human observers and three commercial off-the-shelf (COTS) AFR systems. A similar morphing technique is applied in [15] to create 450 morphs. The proposed morph detection is based on an analysis of skin microtexture. Skin characteristics are represented by binary statistical image features (BSIF) that are classified with a linear support vector machine (SVM).

The first approach to automated generation of visually faultless morphs is reported in [11]. More than 4400 morphs are generated and evaluated in experiments with human observers and a COTS AFR system. The authors also propose a morph detector based on Benford features. The detectors for these morphs are also designed in [3, 10, 12]. In [3], topological data analysis is applied to count the number of connected components based on two-ones local binary pattern. A low number of connected components should be an indicator of morphed images. Based on the hypothesis that a face region becomes more blurry in morphed images, the authors of [10] suggest counting the number of keypoints in the face region in relation to the size of the face region. A low number of keypoints should indicate morphed images. In the degradation approach [12], an image is progressively compressed and the loss of details is measured by the changing number of detected keypoints. Due to blending, morphed images are expected to be less affected by compression. Based on similarly generated morphs, the authors of [19] make an effort to quantify the risk of the morphing attack based on extensive experiments with a state-of-the-art face recognition algorithm based on DCNN. A sophisticated face morphing approach with an optimal face cutting path is introduced in [18]. The authors compare three DCNN architectures applied to morphing detection. Both learning strategies are evaluated: learning from scratch and transfer learning.

The detection performance of morph detectors could drastically drop in case of applying post-processing filters to morphed images. In [8], the StirTrace benchmark is adopted to evaluate the robustness of a morph detector from [11].

An important issue within the framework of the ABC scenario is the re-digitalization of face images that are submitted in a printed form and when scanned at the document issuing office. This procedure destroys many forensic traces. In [17], it is demonstrated that the print-scan procedure makes the classification with BSIF features flawed increasing equal error rate (EER) form approx. 5% to approx. 20%. To support classification of print-scanned images, in [16], a DCNN is trained by transfer learning.

Referring to the ABC scenario, there are two ways of detecting morphed face images: detection in the presence of only a document image (blind detection) and detection in the presence of a document image and a live face image. The aforementioned studies address blind detection. Morphing detection in the presence of live image is addressed in [6]. The live image is subtracted from the document image and the difference image is matched against the live image. Low similarity scores should indicate morphed document images.

Despite numerous publications on face morphing detection, a fair comparison of detection approaches has not been done yet. The reason is that morph detectors are designed for particular types of morphs and may completely fail for other types of morphs. In a proper benchmark, the quality of morphed face images should be defined first and the performance of morph detectors should be reported in relationship to the morph quality. In [13], three face morphing approaches are compared addressing biometric and forensic qualities of morphed images. A first effort to generalize the morph generation process is made in [10]. The authors propose a life-cycle model for photo-ID documents and extend it by an image editing history model allowing for a formal description and comparison of morphing approaches.

3 THEORETICAL CONCEPT

Morphing is formally defined as a process of consecutive transformation of one object (source) to another (target). A morphed face image is, therefore, an image that would be generated by a morphing process while transforming one face image to another if the process stopped somewhere in between. Another requirement is that a morphed face should resemble both original faces. However, since we focus on blind detection, the similarity requirement is neglected and only forensic traces left by the morphing process are questioned. There are many ways to morph face images so that the set of possible traces cannot be formally defined. Nevertheless, the common operations in almost all morphing approaches are image warping and blending. Warping produces resampling artifacts and blending leads to a blurring effect. Note that resampling and blurring can be caused by other image editing operations. In cases like this, when the characteristics of an object to detect cannot be semantically well described, the classifier is learned from examples applying dedicated machine learning techniques.

3.1 Morphing

Here, we apply morphing approaches introduced in [11] and [13] to generate morphed face images from our face dataset (AMSL-DB) as well as from Face Research Lab London Set [1]. Moreover, we test our morph detector with morphs from the aforementioned studies.

The morphed face images proposed in [11] are called "complete" and "splicing" morphs and those proposed in [13] are called "combined" morphs. A complete morph is a result of partitioning the complete image into a triangular mesh with nodes at certain spots,

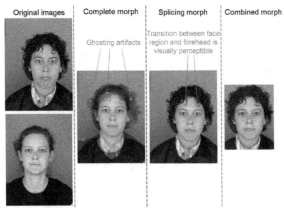

Figure 1: Examples of original and morphed (complete, splicing, combined) face images generated based on the Utrecht ECVP face dataset [2]. Adapted from [13].

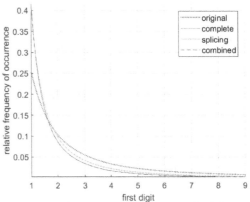

Figure 2: Average log-curves fitted to Benford features extracted from original and morphed (complete, splicing, combined) images in the AMSL database

warping triangles in both images to fit an average geometry, and blending the warped face images. A splicing morph is a composition of the background from one face image and a spliced face region that is morphed using the same procedure as for complete morphs. To get to a combined morph, the face images are roughly aligned first and then warped to the average geometry, as done for complete morphs. Afterwards, the face regions are morphed and the resulting face is spliced into a warped image, as for splicing morphs. The transition between face and background is concealed using Poisson image editing [14]. Examples of morphed faces are shown in Fig. 1.

Complete morphs are usually successfully matched against both persons involved, but suffer from apparent ghosting artifacts usually presented in the hair region. Splicing morphs are created in a way to avoid ghosting artifacts. However, in a splicing morph the face geometry is inherited from one person and thus the morph is expected to match only one person well. Combined morphs unite the advantages of complete and splicing morphs. There are no major ghosting artifacts and morphs match faces of both persons well.

3.2 Morphing Detection

We propose an approach to blind morphing detection based on fitting a logarithmic curve to Benford features. Benford features are first digits of the quantized DCT coefficients in JPEG-compressed images. Fu et al. [7] show that Benford features of single-compressed JPEG images follow the logarithmic distribution while those of double-compressed JPEG images can deviate from that.

In [11], Benford features are utilized for detection of splicing morphs. A morphed image contains blocks from the original image that have already undergone a JPEG compression as well as non-compressed blocks that are generated by the morphing process. If a morphed image was JPEG-compressed, the original blocks would become double-compressed and the morphed blocks would be single-compressed. In original images, all blocks have the same compression level. Hence, the distributions of Benford features in morphed and original images are expected to be different.

Here, we go one step further and apply generalized Benford's law [7] by fitting a logarithmic curve to Benford features. Our assumptions are that the curves should be different for morphed

and original images and the "fitting error" of original images should be higher than that of morphed images. In the case of splicing morphs, the second assumption is valid only for the face region.

Formally, a random variable satisfies the generalized Benford's law if its first digit x occurs with a probability $p(x)$:

$$p(x) = n \log_{10} \left(1 + \frac{1}{\alpha + x^\beta}\right), \ x = 1, 2, ..., 9 \tag{1}$$

where α, β are the parameters specifying the logarithmic curve and n - the normalization factor. In our further considerations, we ignore the normalization factor for practical reasons.

Let Y_i denote the i-th quantized DCT coefficient and N the number of DCT coefficients, the first digits d are computed as follows:

$$d_i = \left\lfloor \frac{Y_i}{10^{\lfloor \log_{10} Y_i \rfloor}} \right\rfloor, \ i = 1, 2, ..., N \tag{2}$$

and the Benford features b as follows:

$$b_j = \frac{1}{N} \sum_{i=1}^{N} \delta_i, \ \delta_i = \begin{cases} 1 & d_i = j \\ 0 & d_i \neq j \end{cases} \tag{3}$$

We fit the logarithmic curve $f(x, \alpha, \beta) = \log_{10}\left(1 + \frac{1}{\alpha + x^\beta}\right)$ to the nine data points $b_j, j = 1, 2, ..., 9$ by minimizing the least squares:

$$\sum_{j=1}^{9} (b_j - f(x_j, \alpha, \beta))^2 \xrightarrow{\alpha, \beta} min \tag{4}$$

Finally, we obtain α and β parameters as well as the fitting error MSE (mean squared error) separately for face and background regions. Considering the classification task, the dimensionality of the feature space reduces three times from nine (first digits) to three (α, β, MSE).

Our research hypothesis is that α, β and MSE parameters are class-specific allowing for distinguishing between original and morphed images. Average log-curves for original and morphed images in the AMSL database are shown in Fig. 2.

4 IMPLEMENTATION

The first processing step in our morph detection pipeline is image re-compression. This is done to ensure that all input images are in

JPEG format with the same level of compression. The level is set to 100% aiming at preserving the original image quality. A JPEG-compressed image is comprised of non-overlapping 8x8 pixel blocks of DCT coefficients for three color channels: Y, Cb and Cr. Next, the face region is segmented. If segmentation fails, the workflow will stop with an error. Next, nine Benford features are extracted from all three channels in the face and background regions separately using equations (2) and (3). For each nine Benford features we extract two parameters of the logarithmic curve α, β and the fitting error MSE using eq. (4) resulting in six new features α_f, β_f, MSE_f, α_b, β_b, MSE_b for face and background regions correspondingly. This is done by means of the Matlab function for nonlinear regression *nlinfit* with the standard parameterization.

Feature selection is done manually by visualizing the parameters α, β as well as MSE in two-dimensional scatter plots. Fig. 3 shows the distributions of original and morphed images in AMSL database regarding the α and β parameters. On this plot, we see that α in the face region allows for distinguishing between original and morphed images. We suggest setting the decision boundary for α_f to -0.15 and making use of the following decision rule:

$$class = \begin{cases} morphed & \alpha_f < -0.15 \\ original & \alpha_f \geq -0.15 \end{cases} \quad (5)$$

Note that for the face region, the distributions of all morph types are very similar. In contrast, for the background, the distributions of complete and combined morphs are similar while the distributions of original images and splicing morphs have an overlap confirming that α and β parameters reflect the characteristics of the morphing processes.

Fig. 4 shows that Benford features of original images tend to have strong deviation from the log-curve. However, a clear separation of original and morphed images is not possible in both face and background regions. Complete and combined morphing processes seem to destroy initial artifacts of JPEG-compression which is reflected in low MSE values in both face and background regions. The high MSE values for splicing morphs in the face region are suspect as well as the evident difference in MSE values of original images and splicing morphs in the background region.

5 EVALUATION

We apply the standard metrics for evaluating detection performance: true positive rate (TPR) also referred to as detection rate and false positive rate (FPR) also referred to as false alarm rate. TPR gives a relative number of correctly detected morphs while FPR gives a relative number of original images falsely detected as morphs. Note that morphed images are considered as positive samples and original images as negative.

5.1 Datasets

A first important step for designing a morph detector is a creation of the evaluation database. Our dataset (AMSL-DB) contains 3186 face images of 85 persons captured with one of six cameras: two instances of Canon EOS 1200D with the Canon lens EF28-105 f/4-5.6, two instances of Nikon D3300 with the Nikkor lens AF-S 50mm f/1.8G, and two instances of Nikon Coolpix A100. The resolutions of images spread from 1200x1600 to 3000x4496 pixels. The ISO-value

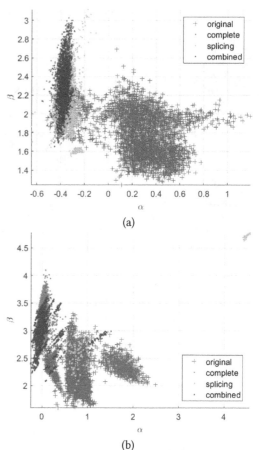

(a)

(b)

Figure 3: Scatter plots of the α (x-axis) vs. β (y-axis) log-curve parameters for the original and morphed (complete, splicing, combined) images in the AMSL database: (a) face region, (b) background

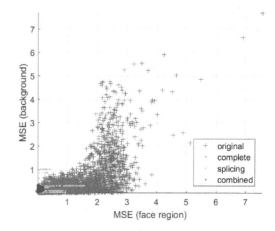

Figure 4: Scatter plot of the MSE values in the face vs. background regions for the original and morphed (complete, splicing, combined) images in the AMSL database

is 100, 200 or 400. All images follow the requirements of the ICAO standard [20] for biometric portraits. A high diversity of the image data is reached by picking face images from a large collection with a random camera instance, resolution, ISO-value and person. Based on a carefully selected subset of faces, we created 2998 complete, 2637 splicing, and 2634 combined morphs. Only plausible image pairs participate in morphing meaning that both persons are of the same sex and ethnicity. The generalization performance of our detector is evaluated with two publicly available databases: Face Research Lab London Set [1] further referred to as London-DB and Utrecht ECVP face dataset [2] further referred to as Utrecht-DB. For both databases we generated morphs from all possible pairs of frontal faces with neutral expressions. In Table 1, we summarize the numbers of original and morphed images collected for our experiments.

Table 1: Numbers of original and morphed images collected for our experiments

	#original images	#complete morphs	#splicing morphs	#combined morphs
AMSL-DB	3186	2998	2637	2634
London-DB	102	5050	9352	10100
Utrecht-DB	73	1326	2614	2652

5.2 Experiments

5.2.1 Generalization power. In order to demonstrate the generalization power of the simple decision rule based on α_f (see eq. (5)), we trained a linear SVM based on all six features (α_f, β_f, MSE_f, α_b, β_b, MSE_b) and images from AMSL-DB (3186 original and 8269 morphed images) as a reference classifier. The receiver operating characteristic (ROC) curves of both the simple decision rule and the linear SVM with the training dataset (AMSL-DB) are shown in Fig. 5. At the operational point, when the threshold for α_f is set to -0.15, the detection rate (TPR) of the simple decision rule is 99.976% and the false alarm rate (FPR) is 9.573%. At the operational point, when the threshold for α_f is set to -0.2934, the equal error rate (EER) is reached yielding 1-TPR = FNR = FPR = 5.07%. Although the detection performance of the linear SVM is significantly better with the detection rate (TPR) of 99.843% and the false alarm rate (FPR) of 6.434% at the standard operational point and the EER of 2.75%, the generalization power, evaluated in experiments with other datasets, namely London-DB and Utrecht-DB, is very low. As shown in Table 2, the linear SVM fails with drastic error rates. The false alarm rate (FPR) with the London-DB approaches 100% and detection rate (TPR) with the Utrecht-DB is less than 48%. In contrast, the simple decision rule still allows for very precise classification with detection rates higher than 98% and 0% false alarm rates. In Fig. 6, we visualize the distributions of original and morphed images in the Utrecht-DB and London-DB in two-dimensional feature space regarding the α_f and β_f log-curve parameters.

5.2.2 Comparison with state of the art. The comparison of detectors will be only reasonable if it is done with the same dataset. Since the only accessible morphs are generated based on Utrecht-DB and considered for detection challenge in several studies [10–13], we

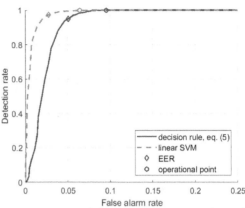

Figure 5: ROC curves of the simple decision rule eq. (5) and the linear SVM with images from AMSL-DB

Table 2: Morph detection performance of our approach with three different face databases

	Detection rate (TPR)	False alarm rate (FPR)
	simple decision rule, eq. (5)	
AMSL-DB	99.976% (8267/8269)	9.573% (305/3186)
London-DB	99.984% (24498/24502)	0% (0/102)
Utrecht-DB	98.604% (6500/6592)	0% (0/73)
	linear SVM	
AMSL-DB	99.843% (8256/8269)	6.434% (205/3186)
London-DB	100% (24502/24502)	98.039% (100/102)
Utrecht-DB	47.907% (3158/6592)	0% (0/73)

report the detection performance of our detector with the Utrecht-DB in Table 3. In comparison to its competitors, our detector has, on average, a significantly higher detection rate of 98.60% and 0% false alarm rate. Note that the detector in [13] can better detect splicing morphs, but in more than 12% of the cases fails to detect the other two morph types.

Table 3: Comparison of morph detectors using Utrecht-DB [2] images (73 original images, 1326 complete, 2614 splicing, and 2652 combined morphs)

-	Detection rate (TPR)	False alarm rate (FPR)	Approach
Our detector	98.60% complete + splicing + combined morphs (6500/6592)	0%	α parameter of the log curve fitted to Benford features
Makrushin et al. [11]	87.03% complete m. 87.89% splicing m. (1837/2090)	3.82% (20/524)	Benford features
Kraetzer et al. [10]	90.0% complete m. 98.0% splicing m.	18.7%	Keypoints
Neubert [12]	89.1% complete m. 83.1% splicing m.	80.8%	Keypoints + JPEG degradation
Neubert et al. [13]	86.07% complete m. 99.76% splicing m. 87.59% combined m.	-	Feature-level fusion of Benford features and keypoints

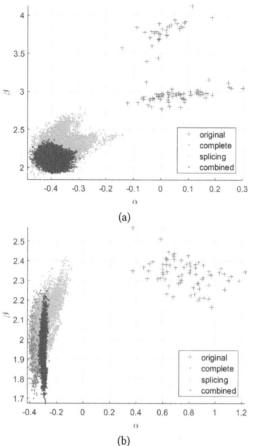

(a)

(b)

Figure 6: Scatter plot of the α (x-axis) vs. β (y-axis) log-curve parameters for the original and morphed (complete, splicing, combined) images in (a) London-DB [1] and (b) Utrecht-DB [2]

6 CONCLUSION

The Benford features derived from the quantized DCT coefficients of JPEG-compressed images have repeatedly been demonstrated to be a powerful tool for detecting image manipulations. The proposed fitting of a logarithmic curve to the nine Benford features leads to dimensionality reduction of the feature space and more plausible decision making. We figured out that the single parameter of the log-curve, that is responsible for the steepness, can be used as an indicator of face image morphing even applying a simple threshold-based decision rule. The detection performance with the training dataset is 99.976% TPR and 9.573% FPR which is significantly better than that reached with the Benford features in the former studies. The high generalization power of the proposed classification approach is shown in the experiments with two face datasets collected by other researchers with different cameras and under different environmental conditions. The TPR values are higher than 98.6% while FPR values yield 0%. This can be seen as a clear separation between original images and morphs for all three addressed morph types. Another important benefit of the dimensionality reduction in combination with the simplistic classification is a speed-up of the detection process. This is an indispensable characteristic for the life-forensics applications such as checking for morphing traces in a passport face image at ABC gates. In future research, we plan to study the influence of anti-forensic image editing on Benford features and on the parameters of the fitted logarithmic curve. The detection performance will be checked with other face morphing approaches engaging additional face databases.

ACKNOWLEDGMENTS

The work in this paper has been funded in part by the German Federal Ministry of Education and Research (BMBF) through the research programme ANANAS under the contract no. FKZ: 16KIS0509K.

REFERENCES

[1] [n. d.]. Face Research Lab London Set, Version 3, https://figshare.com/articles/Face_Research_Lab_London_Set/5047666/3, accessed 2018-02-08. ([n. d.]).
[2] [n. d.]. Utrecht ECVP, http://pics.stir.ac.uk/2D_face_sets.htm, accessed 2018-02-08. ([n. d.]).
[3] A. Asaad and S. Jassim. 2017. Topological Data Analysis for Image Tampering Detection. In *Proc. 16th Int. Workshop on Digital Forensics and Watermarking (IWDW)*. 136–146.
[4] M. Ferrara, A. Franco, and D. Maltoni. 2014. The Magic Passport. In *Proc. Int. Joint Conf. on Biometrics (IJCB)*. 1–7.
[5] M. Ferrara, A. Franco, and D. Maltoni. 2016. On the Effects of Image Alterations on Face Recognition Accuracy. In *Face Recognition Across the Imaging Spectrum*, T. Bourlai (Ed.). Springer, 195–222.
[6] M. Ferrara, A. Franco, and D. Maltoni. 2018. Face Demorphing. *Transactions on Information Forensics and Security (TIFS)* 13, 4 (2018), 1008–1017.
[7] D. Fu, Y.Q. Shi, and W. Su. 2007. A generalized Benford's law for JPEG coefficients and its applications in image forensics. In *Proc. SPIE EI 6505*.
[8] M. Hildebrandt, T. Neubert, A. Makrushin, and J. Dittmann. 2017. Benchmarking face morphing forgery detection: Application of stirtrace for impact simulation of different processing steps. In *Proc. 5th Int. Workshop on Biometrics and Forensics (IWBF)*. 1–6.
[9] ISO/IEC. 2016. *ISO/IEC 30107-1:2016, Information technology – Biometric presentation attack detection – Part 1: Framework*. Standard. International Organization for Standardization.
[10] C. Kraetzer, A. Makrushin, T. Neubert, M. Hildebrandt, and J. Dittmann. 2017. Modeling Attacks on Photo-ID Documents and Applying Media Forensics for the Detection of Facial Morphing. In *Proc. 5th ACM Workshop on Information Hiding and Multimedia Security (IHMMSec)*. 21–32.
[11] A. Makrushin, T. Neubert, and J. Dittmann. 2017. Automatic Generation and Detection of Visually Faultless Facial Morphs. In *Proc. 12th Int. Joint Conf. on Computer Vision, Imaging and Computer Graphics Theory and Applications - Volume 6: VISAPP, (VISIGRAPP)*. 39–50.
[12] T. Neubert. 2017. Face Morphing Detection: An Approach Based on Image Degradation Analysis. In *Proc. 16th Int. Workshop on Digital Forensics and Watermarking (IWDW)*. 93–106.
[13] T. Neubert, A. Makrushin, M. Hildebrandt, C. Kreatzer, and J. Dittmann. 2018. Extended StirTrace Benchmarking of Biometric and Forensic Qualities of Morphed Face Images. *IET Biometrics* (2018).
[14] P. Perez, M. Gangnet, and A. Blake. 2003. Poisson image editing. *ACM Trans. Graph.* 22, 3 (2003), 313–318.
[15] R. Raghavendra, K. B. Raja, and C. Busch. 2016. Detecting morphed face images. In *Proc. 8th Int. Conf. on Biometrics Theory, Applications and Systems (BTAS)*. 1–7.
[16] R. Raghavendra, K. B. Raja, S. Venkatesh, and C. Busch. 2017. Transferable Deep-CNN features for detecting digital and print-scanned morphed face images. In *Proc. 30th Int. Conf. on Computer Vision and Pattern Recognition Workshop (CVPRW)*. 10–18.
[17] U. Scherhag, R. Raghavendra, K. B. Raja, M. Gomez-Barrero, C. Rathgeb, and C. Busch. 2017. On the vulnerability of face recognition systems towards morphed face attacks. In *Proc. 5th Int. Workshop on Biometrics and Forensics (IWBF)*. 1–6.
[18] C. Seibold, W. Samek, A. Hilsmann, and P. Eisert. 2017. Detection of Face Morphing Attacks by Deep Learning. In *Proc. 16th Int. Workshop on Digital Forensics and Watermarking (IWDW)*. 107–120.
[19] L. Wandzik, R. Vicente Garcia, G. Kaeding, and X. Chen. 2017. CNNs Under Attack: On the Vulnerability of Deep Neural Networks Based Face Recognition to Image Morphing. In *Proc. 16th Int. Workshop on Digital Forensics and Watermarking (IWDW)*. 121–135.
[20] A. Wolf. 2018. *ICAO: Portrait Quality (Reference Facial Images for MRTD), Version 1.0*. Standard. International Civil Aviation Organization.

CNN-based Steganalysis of MP3 Steganography in the Entropy Code Domain

Yuntao Wang
State Key Laboratory of Information Security, Institute of Information Engineering, Chinese Academy of Sciences, Beijing, China 100093 School of Cyber Security, University of Chinese Academy of Sciences, Beijing, China 100093
wangyuntao2@iie.ac.cn

Kun Yang
State Key Laboratory of Information Security, Institute of Information Engineering, Chinese Academy of Sciences, Beijing, China 100093 School of Cyber Security, University of Chinese Academy of Sciences, Beijing, China 100093
yangkun9076@iie.ac.cn

Xiaowei Yi*
State Key Laboratory of Information Security, Institute of Information Engineering, Chinese Academy of Sciences, Beijing, China 100093 School of Cyber Security, University of Chinese Academy of Sciences, Beijing, China 100093
yixiaowei@iie.ac.cn

Xianfeng Zhao
State Key Laboratory of Information Security, Institute of Information Engineering, Chinese Academy of Sciences, Beijing, China 100093 School of Cyber Security, University of Chinese Academy of Sciences, Beijing, China 100093
zhaoxianfeng@iie.ac.cn

Zhoujun Xu
Beijing Information Technology Institute, Beijing, China 100094
pl_xzj@uestc.edu.cn

ABSTRACT

This paper presents an effective steganalytic scheme based on CNN for detecting MP3 steganography in the entropy code domain. These steganographic methods hide secret messages into the compressed audio stream through Huffman code substitution, which usually achieve high capacity, good security and low computational complexity. First, unlike most previous CNN based steganalytic methods, the quantified modified DCT (QMDCT) coefficients matrix is selected as the input data of the proposed network. Second, a high pass filter is used to extract the residual signal, and suppress the content itself, so that the network is more sensitive to the subtle alteration introduced by the data hiding methods. Third, the 1×1 convolutional kernel and the batch normalization layer are applied to decrease the danger of overfitting and accelerate the convergence of the back-propagation. In addition, the performance of the network is optimized via fine-tuning the architecture. The experiments demonstrate that the proposed CNN performs far better than the traditional handcrafted features. In particular, the network has a good performance for the detection of an adaptive MP3 steganography algorithm, equal length entropy codes substitution (EECS) algorithm which is hard to detect through conventional handcrafted features. The network can be applied to various bitrates and relative payloads seamlessly. Last but not the least, a sliding window method is proposed to steganalyze audios of arbitrary size.

CCS CONCEPTS

• **Security and privacy** → *Authentication*; • **Computing methodologies** → *Learning latent representations*;

KEYWORDS

CNN, entropy code, steganalysis, MP3, QMDCT coefficients, adaptive

ACM Reference Format:
Yuntao Wang, Kun Yang, Xiaowei Yi, Xianfeng Zhao, and Zhoujun Xu. 2018. CNN-based Steganalysis of MP3 Steganography in the Entropy Code Domain. In *IH&MMSec '18: 6th ACM Workshop on Information Hiding and Multimedia Security, June 20–22, 2018, Innsbruck, Austria,* Jennifer B. Sartor, Theo D'Hondt, and Wolfgang De Meuter (Eds.). ACM, New York, NY, USA, 11 pages. https://doi.org/10.1145/3206004.3206011

*Corresponding author

1 INTRODUCTION

Steganography is the art of embedding secret messages into digital files, which is widely used as a secure method of communication between two parties. On the contrary, steganalysis aims to detect hidden messages in suspicious files. With the development of multimedia technology, recording equipment and editor software popularized in people's daily life, which brings convenience to steganography. Due to the high compression rate and the high quality of MP3, these compressed digital products become one of the most influential media recently. Furthermore, facilitated by the more complex coding principle and the better concealment, MP3 is regarded as one of the most suitable carriers for data hiding.

In the past decade, many MP3 steganographic schemes have emerged gradually. Majority of them are combined with the encoder. MP3Stego [14] is a well known steganographic method. The embedding operation is completed in the inner loop of the encoding. Messages are hidden based on the parity of part_2_3_length. Moreover, Liu et al. [13] proposed a data hiding method based on the energy of MDCT coefficients in adjacent frames. Gao et al. [4] and Yan et al. [21] presented steganographic algorithms based on Huffman codes substitution respectively, which establishes a mapping relationship between secret messages and Huffman codes. And Yang et al. [22] proposed an adaptive MP3 steganographic algorithm using equal length entropy codes substitution (EECS). A content-aware distortion function is designed to achieve optimal masking effect via the psychoacoustic model in this algorithm, which makes the algorithm more secure than previous methods.

Until now, many statistical features are proposed for MP3 steganalysis, but most of them are against MP3Stego. Westfeld [19] detected MP3Stego based on the change of the part_2_3 length variance. In [15], a method for MP3Stego steganalysis was proposed, which is based on the second order differential quantized modified discrete cosine transform (QMDCT) coefficients, accumulative Markov transition features, and accumulative neighboring joint density features. Wan et al. [18] proposed a steganalytic approach based on Huffman table distribution and recoding scheme. Yan [20] found that the length of bit reservoir would change after steganography, so they presented a method based on the statistic characters of bit reservoir. For general schemes, Hamzeh et al. [5] extracted a set of features based on the reversed mel-frequency cepstral coefficients (R-MFCC) of audio and its second order differential signal. Jin et al. [10] proposed to extract Markov features from row and column of the QMDCT coefficients matrix. Besides, Ren et al. [16] extracted the Markov and joint density features of multi-order Intra and Inter frame to detect AAC steganography. All these general schemes have good versatility.

Recently, various deep learning architectures are proposed successively, which have achieved state-of-the-art results in many areas, such as computer vision, speech recognition, natural language processing, and reinforcement learning. However, very few deep learning based methods have been applied for audio steganalysis. Therein, Chen et al. [1] first proposed a novel CNN to detect ±1 LSB steganography in the time domain.

This paper presents a deep learning based method to detect MP3 steganographic algorithms in the entropy code domain. In our proposed network, we first obtain the QMDCT coefficients matrix of MP3 audio and extract the residual signal via the second order row differences to improve the sensitivity to the subtle alteration introduced by the algorithms. Then, several block convolutional layers are followed to capture the potential properties of the input data. Each block is a combination of the convolutional layer, the activation function layer, and the max pooling layer. Some blocks contain a batch normalization layer at the top of 1×1 convolutional layer. Finally, the fully connected layer and the batch normalization layer are connected in cascade at the end of the network. The performance of the architecture is optimized via fine-tuning, such as substitution of activation function and subsampling methods. Experiments demonstrate that our proposed network outperforms the traditional handcrafted features, and the performance is also good at low relative payloads especially. Besides, we introduce sliding window mechanism to steganalyze audios of arbitrary size.

Explicitly, our two contributions to MP3 steganalysis are as follows.

1. A CNN-based method is proposed which is against MP3 steganographic algorithms in the entropy domain. Our network is effective to detect MP3 data hiding methods in the entropy domain at several bitrates and relative payloads. In particular, this network can be applied to steganalyze the EECS algorithm, a novel adaptive MP3 steganography, which is hard to detect by traditional handcrafted features.

2. The 1×1 convolutional kernel and the batch normalization layer are introduced to accelerate the convergence of the back-propagation and to decrease the danger of overfitting. Besides, we analyze the effect of batch normalization layer on the final accuracy and convergence speed further. Redundant batch normalization layers will decrease the final accuracy. Thus, we finetune the batch normalization layer to make the network perform better.

The rest of this paper is organized as follows. The preliminaries are introduced in Section 2. The architecture of our network is presented in Section 3. And Section 4 shows the experimental settings and results. Finally, the conclusions are drawn in Section 5.

2 PRELIMINARIES

2.1 Overview of MP3 Encoder

The architecture of MP3 encoder is shown in Figure 1, which can be divided into six parts: framing and sub-band filter, psychoacoustic model (PAM), MDCT, quantization, Huffman encoding and bitstream formatting. The original audio is encoded using pulse code modulation (PCM), which is WAV format. The WAV audio is first segmented into frames of 1152 sample dots. The sub-band filter process divides the audio signal into 32 uniform frequency sub-bands. The PAM process analyzes the audio signal via Fast Fourier Transform (FFT) and computes the perceptual entropy (PE). The MDCT process performs the time-frequency mapping with four type of windows. Then the non-uniform quantized MDCT coefficients are encoded through Huffman encoding process. Therein, the value of SMR determines the number of bits in quantized coding. Finally, the codestream and side information are formatted into the MP3 file.

As described in Figure 2, a channel consists of 576 QMDCT coefficients, which are orderly divided into three regions: big-value region, count1 region, and zero region. For the big-value region, every two QMDCT coefficients are encoded into one Huffman code. The big-value region can be further segmented into region0, region1, and region2. Three subregions are encoded independently through the utilization of Huffman tables from Table 0 to Table 31. If the value of QMDCT coefficients is less than 15, it is coded directly. Otherwise, the exceeding value is represented by linbits. Besides, if the coefficient is nonzero, the sign bit is used. The value 0 indicates the positive number and 1 indicates the negative number. The value of QMDCT coefficients in count1 region belongs to $\{-1, 0, 1\}$, and every four coefficients are encoded into one Huffman code via Table 32 and 33. All coefficients in zero region are zero and those coefficients would not be encoded. The structure of Huffman code

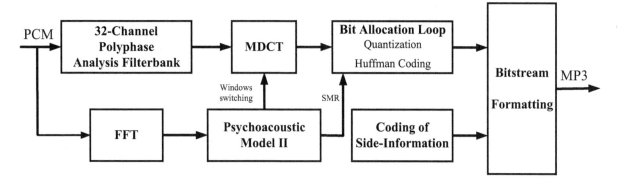

Figure 1: The procedure of MP3 encoding.

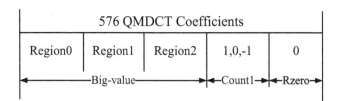

Figure 2: The structure of QMDCT coefficients in a channel.

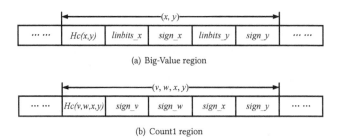

Figure 3: The structure of Huffman codestream.

is shown in Figure 3. H_c denotes a Huffman code of the QMDCT coefficient, *linbits_x* denotes the linbits of the first coefficient, *sign_x* denotes the sign bit of the first coefficient, *linbits_y* denotes the linbits of the second coefficient, *sign_y* denotes the sign bit of the second coefficient. Likewise, *sign_v*, *sign_w*, *sign_x*, and *sign_y* orderly denotes the sign bits of four QMDCT coefficients in count1 region.

2.2 Huffman Code Substitution Data Hiding Method

As more than 90% of the content of the MP3 compressed bitstream is Huffman code, the codewords are ideal steganography carrier. For Huffman code substitution algorithms (HCM), messages are directly embedded by the Huffman code substitution within the MP3 encoding, which is different from the previous MP3 data hiding method. Compared with other MP3 steganography algorithms, HCM can

obtain higher capacity, better security, and lower computational complexity.

Random modification of the codewords causes confusion in the structure of the bitstream, which makes the decoder to fail. In order to keep the statistical distribution of Huffman codes and the codestream length, the structure of codestream in Figure 3 could not be changed arbitrarily. Otherwise, the MP3 encoder would collapse. Suppose that h_i^k is the ith Hc in the kth Huffman table, (x_i^k, y_i^k) is the corresponding QMDCT coefficients pair of h_i^k. Thus if $\forall i \neq j$, h_i^k and h_j^k is a pair of substitutable codes, it satisfies the following three conditions.

1. The length of h_i^k and h_j^k is equal,

$$L(h_i^k) = L(h_j^k) \tag{1}$$

2. The number of sign bits of (x_i^k, y_i^k) and (x_j^k, y_j^k) is equal,

$$S(x_i^k, y_i^k) = S(x_j^k, y_j^k) \tag{2}$$

3. The linbits of x_i^k and x_j^k is consistent, as well as y_i^k and y_j^k,

$$G(x_i^k) = G(x_j^k), G(y_i^k) = G(y_j^k) \tag{3}$$

Suppose the set Π^k contains all Huffman codes in the kth Huffman table. For HCM algorithms, this set can be divided into two parts: Π_u^k and Π_v^k. Therein, Huffman codes in Π_v^k are available for embedding secret information. First, Π_v^k is set as $\varnothing$. For $\{\exists h_i | h_j \in \Pi^k \cap h_j \notin \Pi_v^k, (i \neq j)\}$, if (h_i, h_j) satisfies the three conditions, (h_i, h_j) moves to Π_v^k, otherwise it moves to Π_u^k. This process is repeated until Π^k is empty. Each Huffman code h_i in Π_v^k is numbered according to certain rules which keep the distribution characteristics of codewords to the utmost. The Huffman codes in Π_v^k are further divided into Π_0^k and Π_1^k. If the order of the codeword is odd, h_i is put into Π_1^k, or it is put into Π_0^k. Codes in Π_1^k indicate the bit 1 and codes in Π_0^k indicate the bit 0.

Until now, several HCM algorithms have been presented. In [4] (HCM-Gao), specific pairs of Huffman codes are extracted for substitution according to the similarities of codewords. In [21] (HCM-Yan), to minimize the modification of the QMDCT coefficients, Huffman codes are sorted in lexicographic order according to the value of the QMDCT coefficients. And, in [22] (EECS), zigzag scanning is presented in order to keep the distribution characteristics of Huffman

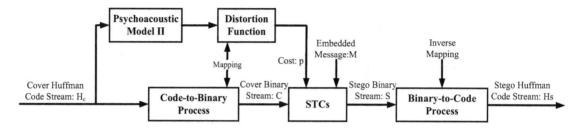

Figure 4: The procedure of EECS algorithm.

codes. Further, the EECS algorithm introduces distortion function based on PAM to hide secret messages adaptively, and the security of the algorithm is better than previous HCM algorithms. The flowchart of the EECS algorithm is shown in Figure 4. The algorithm is mainly divided into four steps: code-to-binary, distortion function, STC encode, and binary-to-code. Firstly, the cover Huffman code H_c is transformed into the cover binary stream C. Secondly, the distortion ρ is calculated according to the PAM and the distance of mapping Huffman codes. Thirdly, the secret messages M are concealed via STC [2]. Finally, the stego binary stream is mapped into stego Huffman code S.

3 THE PROPOSED CNN ARCHITECTURE

In this section, the architecture of the proposed CNN is elaborated, and every part of the network is analyzed in detail. The whole structure is shown in Figure 5.

First, the QMDCT coefficients matrix of MP3 with the size of 200×380 is extracted as the input data of the network. A high pass filter follows to get the residual signal in order to capture the minor modification introduced by the steganography algorithm better. Then, six block convolutional layers are followed in cascade. Each block is a combination of convolutional layers of 3×3 and 1×1 kernel, a Tanh activation function, and a max pooling layer. And we introduce the batch normalization layers in the last three blocks. The fully connected layers and the batch normalization layers are placed at the end. Finally, the cross-entropy loss is used to update the parameters of the network.

3.1 Input data – QMDCT Coefficients Matrix

There are three reasons why the QMDCT coefficients matrix is selected as the input data of the network. First, as described in Section 2, QMDCT coefficients are further encoded into Huffman codes, which means the substitution of Huffman codes is equivalent to the modification of QMDCT coefficients. Next, as shown in Figure 6 and Figure 7, the modification of QMDCT coefficients is larger than the modification of the sampling dots in the time domain by the data hiding methods. Finally, some paper [10, 15, 16] show that the statistical characteristics of the QMDCT coefficients matrix are effective to detect MP3 steganography algorithms. Overall, in order to steganalyze the algorithms in the entropy code domain, the QMDCT coefficients matrix is extracted as the input data. In consideration of the invariance of zero coefficients in steganography, the matrix is cropped to 200×380. To facilitate the description,

the matrix is denoted as

$$
M_Q = \begin{bmatrix} Q_{1,1} & & Q_{1,j} & & Q_{1,380} \\ & \ddots & & \ddots & \\ Q_{i,1} & & Q_{i,j} & & Q_{i,380} \\ & \ddots & & \ddots & \\ Q_{200,1} & & Q_{200,j} & & Q_{200,380} \end{bmatrix} \tag{4}
$$

where the variable $i \in \{1, 2, ..., 200\}$ is the number of selected channels and $j \in \{1, 2, ..., 380\}$ is the index of QMDCT coefficients in a channel. The range of variable i depends on the selected frames N which satisfies $i \in [0, 4N]$.

3.2 High Pass Filter

High pass filter (HPF) is used to reduce the impact of content information and capture the minor modification introduced by the data hiding methods. In many image classification tasks, CNN can effectively extract the significant features that express the properties of the content. Nevertheless, the stego signal is far weaker than the content itself in steganography, which can be seen as high-frequency noise as shown in Figure 6 and Figure 7. Thus, for steganalysis, the introduction of the HPF layer is conducive to improve the detection accuracy. The HPF layer can be seen as a "fixed convolutional layer" in the network. Because the calculation of HPF is based on CPU, we just use some simple HPFs for more quick training.

The type of HPFs has a great influence on the final detection accuracy and the convergence speed of the network. In our experiments, a group of audio files is selected from dataset randomly. For the security of algorithms and the coding principle of MP3, zero values in QMDCT coefficients will not be changed. Therefore, we just calculate the proportion of modified points in nonzero coefficients at the situation of the origin, the first order row differences (Δ_r^1), the second order row differences (Δ_r^2), the first order column differences (Δ_c^1) and the second order column differences (Δ_c^2) separately. All results are shown in the Table 1. Herein, w is the width of the parity-check matrix which satisfies $\alpha = 1/w$ and α represents the relative payload. As the results shown, the ratio can be expanded to triple of the original via the second order row differences which is selected as the HPF layer finally. Besides, a better HPF like Rich Model [3] is conducive to improve the detection accuracy significantly. It can be discussed for further study.

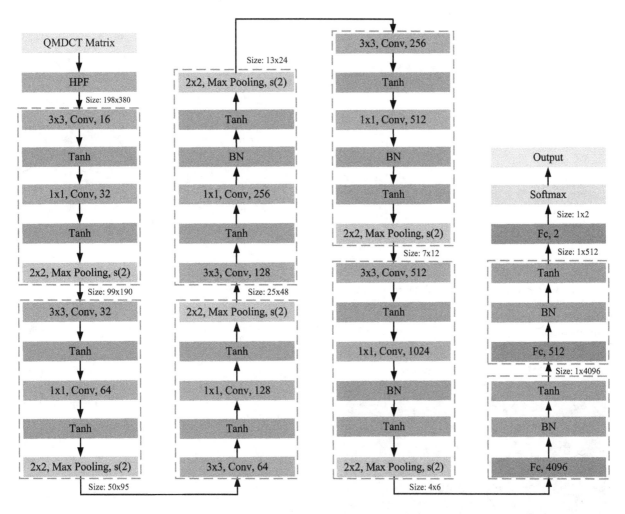

Figure 5: Structure of the proposed network. The parameters in each box are kernel size, layer type and the number of channels (the number of kernels). For example, "3x3, Conv, 32" means a convolutional layer with 3x3 kernel size and 32 output channels. s(2) means the stride of slide window is 2. "Fc, 4096" means the number of neurons in this Fc layer is 4096. "BN" and "Tanh" represents batch normalization layer and activation function respectively. The "Size 25x72" represents the output dimension of the block, which is the shape of feature maps.

The difference matrix is denoted as

$$
M_{D_2Q} = \begin{bmatrix} D_2Q_{1,1} & D_2Q_{1,j} & D_2Q_{1,380} \\ & \ddots & \ddots \\ D_2Q_{m,1} & D_2Q_{m,j} & D_2Q_{m,380} \\ & \ddots & \ddots \\ D_2Q_{198,1} & D_2Q_{198,j} & D_2Q_{198,380} \end{bmatrix} \quad (5)
$$

$$
D_2Q_{m,j} = 2 \times Q_{i+1,j} - Q_{i,j} - Q_{i+2,j} \quad (6)
$$

where the variable m and j is the row and col of the matrix separately. $m \in \{1, 2, ..., 198\}$ and $j \in \{1, 2, ..., 380\}$.

Table 1: The percentages (%) of modified points in QMDCT coefficients matrix algorithm for each pre-processing methods (EECS)

Bitrate	W	Origin	Δ_r^1	Δ_r^2	Δ_c^1	Δ_2^2
	2	8.75	16.52	**23.68**	11.70	16.89
	3	5.14	9.93	**14.46**	6.94	10.03
128	4	3.36	6.57	**9.65**	4.59	6.66
	5	2.42	4.77	**7.04**	3.32	4.81
	6	1.99	3.93	**5.81**	2.74	3.95
	2	9.53	17.81	**25.42**	12.32	18.55
	3	6.08	11.61	**16.84**	7.93	12.03
320	4	3.89	7.55	**11.06**	5.15	7.81
	5	3.24	6.29	**9.25**	4.26	6.48
	6	2.58	5.04	**7.43**	3.40	5.20

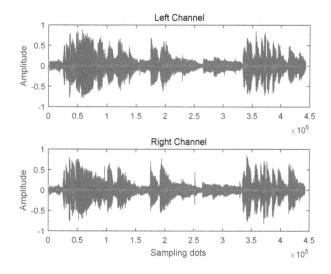

Figure 6: The waveform in the time domain (EECS, Bitrate=128kbps, W=2, and the blue line represents the cover signal, the red line represents the signal introduced by the data hiding method).

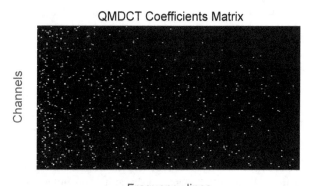

Figure 7: The diagram of the QMDCT coefficients matrix (EECS, Bitrate=128kbps, W=2, and the "white dot" represents the the signal introduced by the data hiding method).

3.3 Convolutional Layer

The convolutional layer (Conv layer) is the main component in CNN. In our proposed network, convolutional kernels of two sizes, 3×3 kernel and 1×1 kernel, are used. The convolutional layer with the 3×3 kernel is mainly used to capture the features of input data, and the convolutional layer with the 1×1 kernel is applied for the interaction and information integration across channels, as well as the reduction of network parameters. We mainly discuss the function of the 1×1 convolutional kernel in this part. The structure of our block convolutional layers and the classical convolutional layers are shown in Figure 8.

Interaction and information integration across channels. The 1×1 convolutional kernel is valued in [12]. This kernel ignores the relationship between data points and other peripheral points. It is a

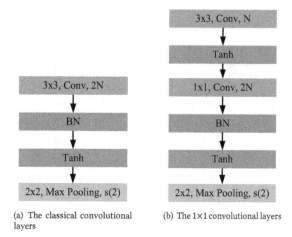

(a) The classical convolutional layers

(b) The 1×1 convolutional layers

Figure 8: The structure of different block convolutional layers.

linear combination of different feature maps so that the information can be integrated across channels.

Reduction of the network parameters. Another function of 1×1 convolutional kernel is to decrease the danger of overfitting. Suppose that the input channels of the 3×3 convolutional layer are N and the output channels are $2N$, the number of introduced parameters (including weights and biases) is

$$3 \times 3 \times N \times 2N + 2N = 18N^2 + 2N \qquad (7)$$

If the 1×1 convolutional layer is applied, the number of introduced parameters is:

$$3 \times 3 \times N \times N + N + 1 \times 1 \times N \times 2N + 2N = 11N^2 + 3N \qquad (8)$$

In this way, the number of parameters is reduced by $7N^2 - N$. When $N = 64$, the reduction of parameters is 28608.

3.4 Pooling Layer

The pooling layer is commonly used for the reduction of feature dimensions to retain main properties of input data and decrease parameters. The pooling layer can be regarded as a kind of fixed convolutional layers and it is mainly divided into two categories of max pooling and average pooling. The output of max pooling is the maximum value of the sliding window, which tends to retain the texture information. The output of average pooling is the average value of the sliding window that retains the background information. Besides, some experiments show that the convolutional layer with stride 2 or more also can be applied for subsampling. The feature extraction and subsampling are achieved at the same time. Subsampling via convolutional layer can be seen as an adaptive pooling method, but it needs more computational cost. In consideration of characteristics of steganography and complexity of models, only max pooling layer is used in our proposed network.

3.5 Activation Function

Due to the limited expression of the linear model, we introduce nonlinear factors through the activation function. For activation

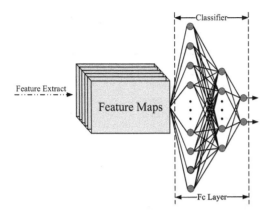

Figure 9: The structure of fully connected layer.

function, ReLu [17] is most commonly used, which can accelerate training. However, in our audio steganalysis task, Tanh is selected as the activation function given the finite range of Tanh.

3.6 Batch Normalization Layer

The Batch Normalization layer (BN layer) [9] is an effective trick widely used in CNNs, which can be placed at any position of the network, but before activation layer generally. The acceleration of convergence and increment of detection accuracy is achieved via the BN layer. The dependence on initialization method is weakened via the introduction of the BN layer. Besides, we decrease the danger of overfitting through BN layer instead of the dropout layer in our network. However, redundant BN layers will reduce the final accuracy.

3.7 Fully Connected Layer

The fully connected layer (Fc layer) acts as a role of "classifier" in the network. If the convolutional layer, the pooling layer and the activation function are used to map the input data into the hidden layer feature space, the Fc layer plays the role of mapping the features to the label space of samples as shown in Figure 9. The parameters of Fc layer accounts for 80% of the entire network. In our network, three Fc layers with the activation function Tanh are connected in cascade.

4 EXPERIMENTS

4.1 Experimental Setup

To evaluate the performance of our proposed network, a dataset which consists of 22671 stereo WAV audio clips with a sampling rate of 44.1kHz and duration of 10s is constructed. The WAV audios are encoded into MP3 files with the two common bitrates of 128kbps and 320kbps by LAME [8]. Three Huffman code substitution steganography algorithms, HCM-Gao [4], HCM-Yan [21] and EECS [22], are implemented to generate the stego MP3 audio files. For the two HCM algorithms, the secret information is embedded in the audio files during the encoding process at the relative embedding rate (RER) of 0.1, 0.3 and 0.5. The hidden messages in the EECS algorithm is encoded by Syndrome-Trellis Codes (STC), so the relative payload α is used to represent the embedding capacity.

In consideration of $\alpha = 1/W$, we use the variable W, the constraint width of the parity-check matrix, to represent the relative payload instead of α. The secret information is embedded at W of 2, 3, 4 and 5, and the constraint height of parity-check matrix is fixed at 7, so that we get 20000 cover-stego pairs respectively. In every group, 16000 pairs are set for training, and the other 4000 pairs are for validation. The rest 2671 pairs are left for test in order to compare the network with traditional handcrafted features.

We train all networks on an NVIDIA Tesla P100 GPU with 16G graphics memory. For optimization, we use Adam [11] with $\beta_1 = 0.9$, $\beta_2 = 0.999$, and $\epsilon = 10^{-8}$. The network is trained with an initial learning rate of 10^{-3} and we use exponential decay function with a decay rate of 0.9 and decay steps of 5000. The batch size of each iteration is 64 (32 cover/stego pairs) in training stage and 16 (8 cover/stego pairs) in validation stage. The weights of convolutional layers and fully connected layers are initialized via Xavier [6] method. And the initialization of biases is zero. To reduce the danger of overfitting further, we introduce the L2 regularization with the gain of 0.001. Last but not the least, all BN layers are removed at the test stage.

Two contrastive steganalysis features are used to compare with the proposed network, which are shown in experimental result tables as Ren [16] and Jin [10]. The features of these schemes are extracted from the QMDCT coefficients matrix and used to be against steganography algorithms in the compressed domain, such as MP3 and AAC. In [16], the multi-order differential coefficients of Intra and Inter-frame are calculated, then two correlation metrics including Markov transition probability and accumulative neighboring joint density are extracted for steganalysis. The threshold is fixed at 4. And in [10], the first order differential coefficients of Intra and Inter-frame is calculated and the Markov transition probability in row and column are extracted as the feature. The threshold is set to 6. All handcrafted features are trained via SVM with 10-ford validation.

4.2 The Fine-tune of Network Structure

To optimize the performance of the network, we fine-tune the structure appropriately. The type of activation function, the size of convolutional kernels, the number of batch normalization layers and the method of subsampling influence the final detection accuracy. The description, detection accuracy of each network variant and the number of iterations for convergence are shown in Table 2. Here, if the accuracy and loss of the network are almost constant in several consecutive epochs, the network can be regarded as convergence. The convergence speed of every network is not exactly the same, so we just record the final accuracy. In our experiments, it costs more time to train the network at the lower relative payload, which conforms to common sense. All experiments are implemented to detect the EECS algorithm with the bitrate of 128kbps and the relative payload W of 2. The performance of the network is measured according to the accuracy and convergence speed as shown in Table 2. And the detection curves of some networks are shown in Figure 10.

The function of BN layer. As the results shown in Table 2, the accuracy is greatly different whether there is BN layer or not.And the number of BN layers has a great impact on the final detection

Table 2: The description, detection accuracy and convergence iterations of each network variant (EECS, Bitrate=128kbps, W=2, the value of iterations is an approximate number, "-" means the network does not converge)

ID	The description of the modification	Accuracy (%)	Iterations
a	The proposed network	90.39	5000
b	Remove the batch normalization layer in the first group	84.51	4000
c	Remove the batch normalization layers in the first two groups	87.13	4500
d	Remove the batch normalization layers in the first four groups	79.46	12000
e	Remove all batch normalization layers	50.67	-
f	Remove the high pass filter layer	88.87	10000
g	Remove all 1×1 convolutional layers	86.73	7000
h	Average pooling layer is used for subsampling	56.21	-
i	Convolutional layer with stride 2 is used for subsampling	60.75	-
j	Replace the convolutional kernel with 5×5 kernel	90.36	9000
k	Introduce the ABS layer at the top of HPF layer	87.66	7000
l	Introduce the ABS layer at the bottom of HPF layer	88.35	8000
m	Replace all the activation function Tanh with ReLu and introduce the ABS layer at the top of HPF layer	58.27	-
n	Replace all the activation function Tanh with ReLu	51.09	-
o	Deepen the network to 7 blocks	88.54	7500

accuracy. The BN layer is conducive to improve the convergence speed and final accuracy of the network, but the redundant BN layers will decrease the accuracy. Thus, we remove the BN layers in the first three groups according to the results a, b, c in Table 2.

The function of HPF. From Table 2 and Figure 10(b), we can find that the high pass filter makes a great difference. Due to the similarity between cover and stego samples, it is little difficult for the network without HPF to capture some useful features efficiently. Thus, the introduction of the HPF can accelerate the convergence greatly and increase the final detection accuracy, especially at a lower relative payload. The design of HPF is independent of the network, but an effective HPF or data preprocessing method is conducive to the classification of cover and stego.

The function of 1×1 convolutional layers. As the result shown in the table 2. The detection accuracy of the network without 1×1 convolutional layers is lower than the proposed network and the iterations for convergence is more. It can be considered that the interaction and information integration across channels of 1×1 kernel as mentioned above contributes to the detection improvements. Besides, fewer parameters make the network more easily trained. Therefore, the introduction of the 1×1 convolutional layers is necessary.

The selection of the subsampling method. To analyze the influence of subsampling method on the final detection accuracy. The average pooling and the convolutional layer with stride 2 are both used for subsampling instead of the max pooling. But the detection accuracy of both networks is worse than the max pooling. It may be because the subtle secret message is hidden in the "texture region", the average pooling and convolutional pooling which tend to capture the content information are not suitable. Thus, the max pooling method is selected for subsampling.

The selection of the convolutional kernel size. In consideration of the truth that every four QMDCT coefficients in count1

region are encoded into one Huffman codeword, the 5×5 convolutional kernel is applied instead of 3×3 kernel. Besides, the LRF of 5×5 kernel is larger, which may capture some properties on a large scale. However, the detection accuracy of two kernels is similar roughly as shown in Table 2 and Figure 10(c). And the parameters of the network with 3×3 kernels are fewer, which means the network with 3×3 kernel can be trained more easily. Hence, it's enough to select 3×3 convolutional kernel in our network.

The selection of activation function and the function of ABS layer. Different activation functions will affect the final detection accuracy. We replace Tanh with ReLu, but the experimental result shows that the activation function Tanh performs far better. The network with ReLu is difficult to converge and the detection accuracy drops sharply compared with Tanh. In order to find the influence of negative value of input data on the network, we introduce the ABS layer and ReLu is still selected as the activation function. The performance of the network is promoted not well. Besides, to obtain the effect of the ABS layer further, we placed the ABS layer at the top and bottom of the HPF layer respectively, but all experimental results are worse than the proposed network. One of the results is shown in Figure 10(d). Therefore, a conclusion can be drawn that the finite of Tanh activation function contributes to the detection and the ABS layer will reduce the difference between cover and stego which is detrimental to classification.

The depth of the network. In general, more features of the input data can be captured by a deeper network. Thus, we attempt to deepen the network to 7 blocks. However, two problems influence the train of deeper networks – overfitting and vanishing gradient that can be improved by ResNet [7] later, which means it is more difficult to train a deeper network. And as the result shown in Table 2. There is no significant improvement in the performance of the network with greater depth. Therefore, it is not advisable to stack or deepen the network simply.

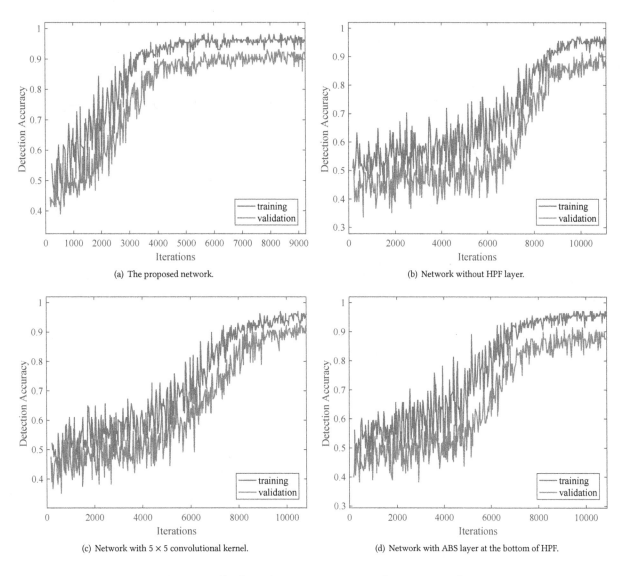

(a) The proposed network.

(b) Network without HPF layer.

(c) Network with 5 × 5 convolutional kernel.

(d) Network with ABS layer at the bottom of HPF.

Figure 10: The detection accuracy curves of some networks.

4.3 Comparison with Handcrafted Features

To assess our scheme comprehensively, two state-of-the-art handcrafted features (Ren [16] and Jin [10]) are compared with the proposed network. The results of each algorithm are shown in Table 3, 4 and 5. The experiments demonstrate that our network outperforms the traditional techniques in several bitrates and relative payloads. In the HCM-Gao algorithm, just specific codeword pairs are selected for substitution, so the embedding capacity is too little to detect. The embedding capacity of the HCM-Yan algorithm is larger and the traditional methods have a good performance for the detection of this algorithm at the RER of 0.5. But the performance is still less than the proposed network. Especially, the EECS algorithm is an adaptive steganography algorithm, which is hard to detect by the traditional method, but it can be well detected by our proposed network. For the three steganography algorithms,

the detection accuracy of the proposed network is higher than the handcrafted features. Overall, our network can effectively detect the existing MP3 steganography algorithms in the entropy domain at various bitrates and relative payloads.

Table 3: Detection accuracy (%) of the HCM-Gao algorithm

Bitrate	RER	Ours	Ren [16]	Jin [10]
	0.1	**70.72**	50.13	50.11
128	0.3	**75.18**	51.41	52.34
	0.5	**78.53**	53.75	52.79
	0.1	**73.83**	50.77	50.85
320	0.3	**77.27**	55.18	53.63
	0.5	**80.71**	62.69	59.42

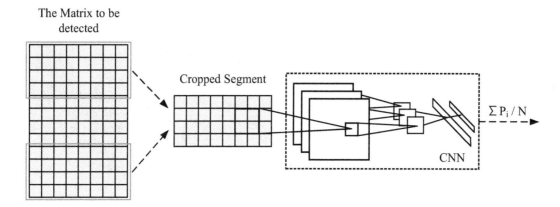

Figure 11: The procedure of steganalyzing audios of varying size.

Table 4: Detection accuracy (%) of the HCM-Yan algorithm

Bitrate	RER	Ours	Ren [16]	Jin [10]
128	0.1	**75.92**	50.94	51.25
	0.3	**81.39**	56.88	60.31
	0.5	**85.88**	76.56	72.50
320	0.1	**79.35**	64.38	54.69
	0.3	**83.09**	66.56	62.50
	0.5	**90.21**	77.81	77.19

Table 5: Detection accuracy (%) of the EECS algorithm

Bitrate	W	Ours	Ren [16]	Jin [10]
128	2	**90.39**	59.42	56.25
	3	**80.17**	53.37	53.81
	4	**67.82**	51.96	51.73
	5	**54.78**	50.56	50.35
320	2	**95.35**	71.38	69.69
	3	**83.09**	55.81	54.56
	4	**72.33**	52.24	52.13
	5	**56.46**	50.10	50.07

4.4 Steganalyzing audios of varying size

For a trained CNN, the input dimension of the Fc layer is invariant, which means the size of input data is fixed. If the size of test audios are not the same with trained audios, the network can't be used directly. In our experiments, the QMDCT coefficients matrix of 200×380 (almost duration of 1.3s) is selected as the minimum data unit. The matrix is variant on the dimension of channels as described in Section 2. Thus, a sliding window with 50% overlap is proposed to steganalyze audios of varying size as shown in Figure 11. Suppose the hidden messages are embedded into the whole audio file, otherwise this scheme is invalid. First, The matrix is cropped into several uniform fragments, and each part is 200×380. If the remaining segment does not satisfy the scale of 200×380, this segment is dropped directly. Then, the cropped segments are put

into the network successively, thus the probability of classification can be obtained. Finally, calculate the average value of all results. If the value is more than 0.5, the audio is judged as stego. Otherwise, it is cover. In our experiments, the final detection accuracy is basically equivalent to the small fragments detection.

5 CONCLUSION

In this paper, we propose an effective steganalytic scheme based on CNN to detect MP3 steganography algorithms in the entropy code domain. The performance of the network is optimized via the substitution of activation function, kernel size and other parts which may have the influence on the final accuracy. Experiments demonstrate that our network performs far better than two state-of-the-art handcrafted features. The proposed network can be applied to various steganographic algorithms, bitrates, and relative payloads. In addition, our network can be used for steganalyzing the EECS algorithm, an adaptive MP3 steganographic method, which is hard to detect by conventional handcrafted features. Last but not the least, a sliding window strategy is presented to steganalyze audios of arbitrary size. All of our source code and datasets are now available via GitHub: https://github.com/Charleswyt/tf_audio_steganalysis.

Furthermore, better networks will be designed, which can be used for steganalysis in low embedding capacities effectively, such as a more efficient HPF layer or more excellent structure.

ACKNOWLEDGMENTS

This work was supported by National Key Technology R&D Program under 2016YFB0801003, NSFC under U1636102 and U1536105, and National Key Technology R&D Program under 2016QY15Z2500

REFERENCES

[1] Bolin Chen, Weiqi Luo, and Haodong Li. 2017. Audio Steganalysis with Convolutional Neural Network. In *Proceedings of the 5th ACM Workshop on Information Hiding and Multimedia Security, IH&MMSec 2017, Philadelphia, PA, USA, June 20-22, 2017.* 85–90.
[2] Tomáš Filler, Jan Judas, and Jessica J Fridrich. 2010. Minimizing embedding impact in steganography using trellis-coded quantization. In *Media Forensics and Security II, part of the IS&T-SPIE Electronic Imaging Symposium, San Jose, CA, USA, January 18-20, 2010, Proceedings.* 754105.
[3] Jessica J Fridrich and Jan Kodovsky. 2012. Rich models for steganalysis of digital images. *IEEE Trans. Information Forensics and Security* 7, 3 (2012), 868–882.

[4] Haiying Gao. 2007. The MP3 steganography algorithm based on Huffman coding. *Acta Scientiarum Naturalium Universitatis Sunyatseni* 4 (2007), 009.

[5] Hamzeh Ghasemzadeh, Mehdi Tajik Khass, and Meisam Khalil Arjmandi. 2016. Audio steganalysis based on reversed psychoacoustic model of human hearing. *Digital signal processing* 51 (2016), 133–141.

[6] Xavier Glorot and Yoshua Bengio. 2010. Understanding the difficulty of training deep feedforward neural networks. In *Proceedings of the Thirteenth International Conference on Artificial Intelligence and Statistics, AISTATS 2010, Chia Laguna Resort, Sardinia, Italy, May 13-15, 2010.* 249–256.

[7] Kaiming He, Xiangyu Zhang, Shaoqing Ren, and Jian Sun. 2016. Deep Residual Learning for Image Recognition. In *2016 IEEE Conference on Computer Vision and Pattern Recognition, CVPR 2016, Las Vegas, NV, USA, June 27-30, 2016.* 770–778.

[8] Robert Hegemann, Alexander Leidinger, and RogÃrio Brito. 1998. LAME. https://sourceforge.net/projects/lame/files/lame/.

[9] Sergey Ioffe and Christian Szegedy. 2015. Batch normalization: Accelerating deep network training by reducing internal covariate shift. In *Proceedings of the 32nd International Conference on Machine Learning, ICML 2015, Lille, France, 6-11 July 2015.* 448–456.

[10] Chao Jin, Rangding Wang, and Diqun Yan. 2017. Steganalysis of MP3Stego with low embedding-rate using Markov feature. *Multimedia Tools and Applications* 76, 5 (2017), 6143–6158.

[11] Diederik Kingma and Jimmy Ba. 2014. Adam: A method for stochastic optimization. *CoRR* abs/1412.6980 (2014).

[12] Min Lin, Qiang Chen, and Shuicheng Yan. 2013. Network in network. *CoRR* abs/1312.4400 (2013).

[13] Wei Liu, Shuo-zhong Wang, and Xin-peng Zhang. 2004. Audio watermarking based on partial mp3 encoding. *Acta Scientiarum Naturalium Univ. Sunyatseni*

[14] Fabien Petitcolas. 2002. MP3Stego. http://www.petitcolas.net/steganography/mp3stego/.

[15] Mengyu Qiao, Andrew H Sung, and Qingzhong Liu. 2013. MP3 audio steganalysis. In *Information sciences*, Vol. 231. 123–134.

[16] Yanzhen Ren, Qiaochu Xiong, and Lina Wang. 2017. A Steganalysis Scheme for AAC Audio Based on MDCT Difference Between Intra and Inter Frame. In *Digital Forensics and Watermarking - 16th International Workshop, IWDW 2017, Magdeburg, Germany, August 23-25, 2017, Proceedings.* 217–231.

[17] Karen Simonyan and Andrew Zisserman. 2014. Very deep convolutional networks for large-scale image recognition. *CoRR* abs/1409.1556 (2014).

[18] Wei Wan, Xianfeng Zhao, Wei Huang, and Rennong Sheng. 2012. Steganalysis of MP3Stego based on Huffman table distribution and recording. *Journal of Graduate University of Chinese Academy of Science* 29, 1 (2012), 118–124.

[19] Andreas Westfeld and Andreas Pfitzmann. 1999. Attacks on steganographic systems. In *Information Hiding, Third International Workshop, IH'99, Dresden, Germany, September 29 - October 1, 1999, Proceedings.* 61–76.

[20] Diqun Yan and Rangding Wang. 2014. Detection of MP3Stego exploiting recompression calibration-based feature. *Multimedia tools and applications* 72, 1 (2014), 865–878.

[21] Diqun Yan, Rangding Wang, and Li-Guang ZHANG. 2011. A high capacity MP3 steganography based on Huffman coding. *Journal of Sichuan University (Natural Science Edition)* 6 (2011), 013.

[22] Kun Yang, Xiaowei Yi, Xianfeng Zhao, and Linna Zhou. 2017. Adaptive MP3 Steganography Using Equal Length Entropy Codes Substitution. In *Digital Forensics and Watermarking - 16th International Workshop, IWDW 2017, Magdeburg, Germany, August 23-25, 2017, Proceedings.* 202–216.

43, S2 (2004), 26–33.

Adversarial Examples Against Deep Neural Network based Steganalysis

Yiwei Zhang
CAS Key Laboratory of
Electromagnetic Space Information
University of Science and Technology
of China
Hefei, Anhui, China
zywvvd@mail.ustc.edu.cn

Weiming Zhang*
CAS Key Laboratory of
Electromagnetic Space Information
University of Science and Technology
of China
Hefei, Anhui, China
zhangwm@ustc.edu.cn

Kejiang Chen
CAS Key Laboratory of
Electromagnetic Space Information
University of Science and Technology
of China
Hefei, Anhui, China
chenkj@mail.ustc.edu.cn

Jiayang Liu
CAS Key Laboratory of
Electromagnetic Space Information
University of Science and Technology
of China
Hefei, Anhui, China
1229370169@qq.com

Yujia Liu
CAS Key Laboratory of
Electromagnetic Space Information
University of Science and Technology
of China
Hefei, Anhui, China
yjcaihon@mail.ustc.edu.cn

Nenghai Yu
CAS Key Laboratory of
Electromagnetic Space Information
University of Science and Technology
of China
Hefei, Anhui, China
ynh@ustc.edu.cn

ABSTRACT

Deep neural network based steganalysis has developed rapidly in recent years, which poses a challenge to the security of steganography. However, there is no steganography method that can effectively resist the neural networks for steganalysis at present. In this paper, we propose a new strategy that constructs enhanced covers against neural networks with the technique of adversarial examples. The enhanced covers and their corresponding stegos are most likely to be judged as covers by the networks. Besides, we use both deep neural network based steganalysis and high-dimensional feature classifiers to evaluate the performance of steganography and propose a new comprehensive security criterion. We also make a tradeoff between the two analysis systems and improve the comprehensive security. The effectiveness of the proposed scheme is verified with the evidence obtained from the experiments on the BOSSbase using the steganography algorithm of WOW and popular steganalyzers with rich models and three state-of-the-art neural networks.

KEYWORDS

Steganography; adversarial examples; deep neural network; steganalysis; security

---

*Corresponding author

ACM Reference Format:
Yiwei Zhang, Weiming Zhang, Kejiang Chen, Jiayang Liu, Yujia Liu, and Nenghai Yu. 2018. Adversarial Examples Against Deep Neural Network based Steganalysis. In *Proceedings of 6th ACM Information Hiding and Multimedia Security Workshop (IH&MMSec'18)*. ACM, New York, NY, USA, Article 4, 6 pages. https://doi.org/10.1145/3206004.3206012

1 INTRODUCTION

In recent years, information hiding researchers have proposed many advanced steganographic algorithms to hide secret information into a cover image. Most of the schemes embed secret messages in spatial domain or frequency domain, such as HUGO [16], WOW [7], S-UNIWARD [8], HILL [14], J-UNIWARAD [8] and UERD [6]. These methods can minimize a heuristically-defined embedding distortion while hiding secrets into a given image to lower the statistical detectability. And based on an oracle used to calculate the detectability map, a new steganography called ASO [13] is proposed which can preserve both cover image and sender's database distributions during the embedding process.

In order to detect whether there is hidden information in an image, the traditional method of steganalysis is divided into two steps, high-dimensional feature extraction and machine learning classifier training. An excellent steganalyzer is the Rich Model (RM), which is usually used in the first step. There are several versions of Rich Models such as Spacial Rich Model (SRM) [4] and its variants [3, 19] in spatial domain and JPEG-SRM (J-SRM) [10] in frequency domain. The most common choice of machine learning classifier is Ensemble Classifier (EC) [11]. The combination of SRM and EC has achieved excellent detection performance.

In the past two years, steganalysis based on Convolutional Neural Network (CNN) models has made a tremendous progress. Compared with the traditional methods, CNN-based steganalysis uses various network structures to learn the effective features of images to distinguish cover images and stego images. Qian [17] used a CNN architecture with Gaussian activations function to construct a model for steganalysis. Xu [23] designed another CNN structure with *tanh* activation function. Wu [20–22] proposed a CNN model made full use of the advantage of residual network for image steganalysis. Ye [24] proposed a CNN model whose first layer was initialled with the high-pass filter set used in SRM and introduced a novel activation function TLU and a selection-channel-aware scheme for CNN-based steganalysis. The performances of Ye and Wu exceed that of SRM+EC.

Therefore, deep learning steganalysis has become a severe challenge to steganography. In fact, the tasks of neural networks for steganalysis and networks for object classification are very similar. The difference between them are the structure of networks and the number of classification targets. Steganalysis is a binary classification problem while object classification has multiple category labels. Adversarial example is a technique that adds carefully crafted small adversarial noise to the input to cheat the object classification network producing incorrect outputs. Szegedy [18] and Goodfellow [5] made a seminal work and put forward a method of adversarial example construction based on neural network gradient. Then a lot of related outstanding works came up [1, 12, 15].

In a steganographic process, let C be the cover image, S be the stego and we use $\boldsymbol{m}$ to denote the secret message. An intuitive way to combine the technique of adversarial examples with steganography is to add adversarial noise $\boldsymbol{n}_{ad}$ to S in order to turn S into an adversarial example $S_{ad} = S + \boldsymbol{n}_{ad}$. We assume that the object network will judge S as cover successfully, but $\boldsymbol{n}_{ad}$ will prevent the receiver from getting the message $\boldsymbol{m}$ correctly. In a word, there is some difficulty in applying technique of adversarial examples directly to steganography.

In this paper, we propose an adversarial example construction method suitable for steganography, that is, reverse the order of adding adversarial noise and embedding messages. We first add the adversarial noise to C to construct a robust enhanced cover C', then embed the message m into C' to get S. In this way, the receiver can extract $\boldsymbol{m}$ from S successfully. Our method can make the adversarial example C' robust enough to withstand the influence of the message embedding process, so S will still be misjudged by the deep learning classifier as cover. We have also considered how to generate adversarial examples against multiple neural networks for steganalysis. However, in the process of constructing the adversarial examples, modification would be introduced to the images unavoidably. Actually, the larger modification would be likely exposed to SRM+EC. We have analyzed how to control the noise intensity to obtain a reasonable trade-off, so that the overall security of steganography is improved.

The rest of this paper is structured as follows: In Section 2 we review a method to construct adversarial examples and describe details of our adversarial training methods. Section 3 describes our experiment settings and results. Conclusions are drawn in Section 4.

2 STEGANOGRAPHY BASED ON ADVERSARIAL EXAMPLES

In this section, we introduce the technique of adversarial examples and describe our method of training robust adversarial cover images for a given network. We also illustrate ways to construct adversarial examples for multiple networks.

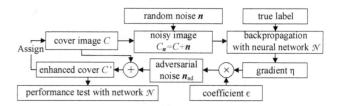

Figure 1: Diagram of the process of constructing enhanced covers using the technique of adversarial examples.

2.1 Adversarial Examples

Similar to the classic "fast gradient sign method"[5], our method to construct an adversarial example is as follows. For a given neural network $\mathcal{N}$, we use θ to denote its parameters. Let C be the input image, y be the target label associated with C (when we are constructing adversarial examples against neural network for steganalysis, the target would always be set to 0 which means cover, while 1 presents stego) and $L_{\mathcal{N}}(\theta, C, y)$ be the loss of the network. Fix θ and compute the gradient of $L_{\mathcal{N}}$ as η:

$$\eta = \nabla_C L_{\mathcal{N}}(\theta, C, y), \qquad (1)$$

A perturbation that coincides with η will make C more easily be judged as cover by $\mathcal{N}$. Note that the η could be computed efficiently by back propagation in the network. We can simply multiply the gradient η by a coefficient ϵ and add it to C to get the adversarial example C':

$$C' = C + \epsilon\eta. \qquad (2)$$

ϵ is related to the learning rate of deep learning. By choosing appropriate ϵ, C' can mislead $\mathcal{N}$ successfully. The above are the construction procedures of adversarial examples. However, just misleading the networks is far from enough. What we need are robust enhanced covers that can withstand the message embedding processing in steganography. We will discuss how to construct the enhanced covers in Section 2.2.

2.2 Adversarial Examples Against Neural Network for Steganalysis

In order to let cover images resist steganographic noise, we introduce a model which can iteratively construct enhanced covers. The model is shown in Figure 1. The process starts at cover image C. We define a noise vector, $\boldsymbol{n}$, which has a considerable strength relative to the steganographic noise that we are going to resist. We add noise $\boldsymbol{n}$ to C to get C_n. Then a gradient η is obtained by back propagation of network $\mathcal{N}$. Multiply η by the coefficient ϵ to obtain the adversarial noise $\boldsymbol{n}_{ad}$. The sum of $\boldsymbol{n}_{ad}$ and C is the enhanced cover C'. Performance test on C' with $\mathcal{N}$ is the last step in this iteration. If C' passes the test at this time, it will be used as an enhanced cover for steganography, otherwise we will assign C' to C and start the next iteration.

2.2.1 Construction Process. In order to construct C' successfully and ensure the robustness, we usually need to go through several loops to construct an enhanced cover. We set the number of required training loops to q. To ensure the stability and strength of $\boldsymbol{n}_{ad}$, there would be k iterations in each loop. Given a cover image C (C_0) and a neural network $\mathcal{N}$ with parameters θ in the i-th ($1 \leq i \leq k$) iteration of a loop, we simulate the steganography with random noise $\boldsymbol{n}_i$ on C_{i-1} (after $i-1$ rounds of iterative calculation of C) to get the noisy image C_{n_i} and then feed it to $\mathcal{N}$. After that, we can use the method described in Section 2.1 to calculate the i-th gradient η_i. Here we add the adversarial noise $\boldsymbol{n}_{ad_i} = \epsilon\eta_i$ calculated on C_{n_i} to C_{i-1} to complete the i-th update iteration, which means $C_i = C_{i-1} + \boldsymbol{n}_{ad_i}$. The modification vector Δ obtained from k iterations can be expressed as:

$$\Delta = \sum_{i=1}^{k} (\epsilon\nabla_{C+\Delta_i} L_{\mathcal{N}}(\theta, C + \Delta_i + \boldsymbol{n}_i, y)), \qquad (3)$$

where Δ_i is the cumulative modification vector after i iterations of training, that is $\Delta_i = \sum_{j=1}^{i} \boldsymbol{n}_{ad_j}$. As i increases, $C + \Delta_i$ will gradually adapt to the noise interference and η_i will convergence to a vector close to zero.

After k iterations, the pixel values would be rounded to integers and bounded to 0 to 255 so that the pixels are saved as integers and the overflows/underflows caused by changes are avoided. Then we will test the performance of C' (C_k). The testing process is as follows. Using the specific steganographic method and relative payload, we embed v group random messages on C' to obtain v stego images $\{S_1, S_2, ..., S_v\}$. When the probability that S_i ($1 \leq i \leq v$) is judged as a cover by $\mathcal{N}$ is greater than that of as a stego, S_i misleads the network $\mathcal{N}$. C' pass the test of $\mathcal{N}$ only if the corresponding stegos can mislead $\mathcal{N}$ with a probability greater than a threshold denote as Th. Otherwise C_k will be assigned to C and begin the next loop of k iterations. In this way, C' will converge to a stable, robust enhanced cover. Finally, the message m is embedded into the enhanced cover C' to generate the stego object S, which will be send to the receiver.

2.2.2 Intensity Control.
Using this method, we can implement the white-box attack [9] on current neural networks for steganalysis. Unfortunately, the noise introduced during the adversarial example construction process will be exposed to SRM+EC.

Because the L_2-norm would control the number and magnitude of image pixel modifications and it could be easily utilized by the network to calculate the gradient, we choose the L_2-norm of the modified vector as a regularizer by adding the L_2-loss to the loss function. Let T denote the number of pixels that need to be modified. We want to control the modification of the image when L_2-loss exceeds T, so we use a threshold bounded loss as the regularizer which is denoted as L_2^T. The process of calculating Δ will be changed as follows:

$$\Delta = \sum_{i=1}^{k} (\epsilon\nabla_{C+\Delta_i} (L_{\mathcal{N}}(\theta, C + \Delta_i + \boldsymbol{n}_i, y) + \epsilon L_2^T)), \qquad (4)$$

$$L_2^T = max(\|\Delta_i\|_2 - T, 0), \qquad (5)$$

where ϵ is the coefficient of L_2^T, which is used to control the strength of the regularization. With loss function (4), we can now construct robust adversarial examples for a specific neural network and control the intensity of the modification vectors.

As we already know, adversarial examples can mislead the network to recognize an input image as an object of another target

category. Because of the fact that adversarial perturbations are highly aligned with the weight vectors of a model and different models learn the similar functions in the stage of training to perform the same task, adversarial examples in object classification networks have got a generalization across different models [5]. However, steganalysis is a binary classification based on image residual feature extraction. It abandons the semantic information of images, so the generalization of adversarial examples between different models is not strong. This conclusion has been confirmed in our follow-up experiments. Then, how to get a cover image against multiple neural networks is what we are going to solve in the next subsection.

2.2.3 Against Multiple Neural Networks.
In this subsection, we focus on the problem of construction of adversarial examples against multiple neural networks. The main framework still follows the model shown in Figure 1. The differences lie in the method of gradient calculation which is shown in Figure 2 and the part of performance test.

For given h neural networks $\{\mathcal{N}_1, \mathcal{N}_2, ..., \mathcal{N}_h\}$, a stego image need to mislead all h networks to pass the performance test. We connect these h networks to form a joint network with one input and multiple outputs. For the process of gradient calculation, we take the weighted sum of the cross-entropy loss $\{loss_1, loss_2, ..., loss_h\}$ of each network as the total loss of all networks. Because we do not know the adaptability of the current image to each network, the initial values of weights $\{\alpha_1, \alpha_2, ..., \alpha_h\}$ are set to 1 and they will be updated in the construction process. If the performance test of i-th ($1 \leq i \leq q$) loop fails, the weights of failed networks will be updated. For the failed network $\mathcal{N}_t$ ($1 \leq t \leq h$), the average probability that stegos are judged as cover by network $\mathcal{N}_t$ after i training loops is represented as $p_{t,i}$. Then we use $\gamma_{t,i} = 1 - p_{t,i}$ as the update step for α_t which means that the loss weight of $\mathcal{N}_t$ would be updated to $\alpha_t + \gamma_{t,i}$.

Similarly, we can control the intensity of adversarial perturbations against multiple networks by adding L_2^T to the total loss of networks. Now the loss function of multiple networks is shown as Equation (6):

$$TotalLoss = \alpha_1 loss_1 + \alpha_2 loss_2 + \cdots + \alpha_h loss_h + \epsilon L_2^T. \qquad (6)$$

With $TotalLoss$ we can calculate C's modification vector Δ to construct an adversarial example against multiple networks.

$$\Delta = \sum_{i=1}^{k} (\epsilon\nabla_{C+\Delta_i} TotalLoss), \qquad (7)$$

3 EXPERIMENTS

In this section, we will validate the validity of the proposed model. The image dataset used for all experiments is the BOSSbase ver.1.01 [2]. The BOSSbase contains 10,000 images with the size of 512×512 and is a standard database for evaluating steganography and steganalysis. Taking the speed of operation and the amount of data into account, we cut each image of the dataset into four non-overlapping 256×256 images in our experiment. Therefore, we used a cropped BOSS containing 40,000 images to organize our experiments.

We will get different parameters of a neural network if different steganographic algorithms and relative payloads are utilized. Here

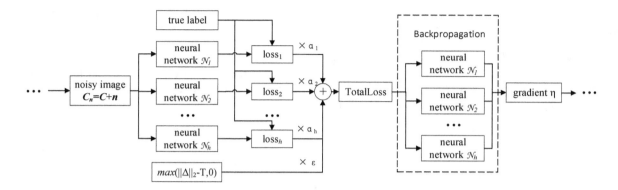

Figure 2: Diagram of gradient calculation for multiple neural network.

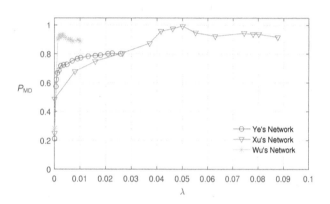

Figure 3: Testing error of adversarial examples by single network under steganography of WOW with a relative payload of 0.4 bpp.

we choose the WOW algorithm under relative payload 0.4 bpp as an example to generate 40,000 stego images. 35,000 randomly selected pairs of cover and stego images are used to train neural networks for steganalysis and SRM+EC, while the other 3000 pairs as validation dataset and the remaining 2000 pairs as testing set. Our experiments use the state-of-the-art neural networks for steganalysis of spacial images, such as Xu's [23], Ye's [24] and Wu's [22] networks. Each network uses an input image size of 256×256, while all other settings are based on the author's source code or description in their essays.

In all experiments, the learning rate is set to 1.0. The number of quantification loops per image, q, is set to 50 and the number of iterations in a loop, k, is 30. The number of testing stego images, v, is set to 300 and the value of Th is 90%. The output loss is calculated with cross-entropy. ε is set to 5×10^{-6}. In order to explore the effect of different modified intensities, we use $\lambda = \frac{T}{256 \times 256}$ as the intensity parameter of the modification and to represent the percentage of image pixel modifications. Because we are trying to generate enhanced secure covers that can accommodate unknown steganographic noise, n is set to a random matrix of -1,0 and 1.

3.1 Against Single Network

For each network, we use 2000 testing images to construct adversarial images for each λ. Then the corresponding network tests the stegos generated by these adversarial images. In most of our experiments, the training images used by networks and SRM+EC are original cover images in BOSSbase and stegos generated by WOW directly. In other words, in most experiments, we didn't use the classifiers retrained with adversarial stegos, and thus our approach does not have an impact on the false alarm rate. Therefore we evaluate the performance only with the probability of missed detection P_{MD}.

Figure 3 shows the testing error of adversarial examples. As λ increases, the performance gets better, but different networks have different effects. For Wu's network, due to the use of the residual network, we only need to change less than 1% (in fact only 0.2%) of the pixels to make an image a satisfactory adversarial example. However, for the Xu's network, we have to introduce a large number of changes to the image to achieve similar results. Modifying 2% of the pixels of an image can make the missing detection probability of Ye's network reach 80%. So when λ is large enough, the constructed images with secret messages embedded are difficult to be detected by specific neural network. This result means that we have successfully constructed adversarial cover images for a single neural network. The average number of iterations of each image is 1.31 and it takes 27.8 seconds on the GPU of NVIDIA Tesla K80.

In order to explore whether there exists generalization in our constructed images, we input images made for a specific network to other networks for steganalysis. The testing result is shown in Figure 4. G in the figure means the networks which construct the image and T means the testing networks. It can be seen is that the generalization of adversarial examples is very limited. So although the images have been modified, they still cannot effectively resist other networks.

3.2 Against Multiple Networks

Defending as many defensive systems as possible is a goal of stenographers. Similarly, constructing an adversarial example that simultaneously resists multiple neural networks for steganalysis is an important part of this paper. In order to verify the correctness of

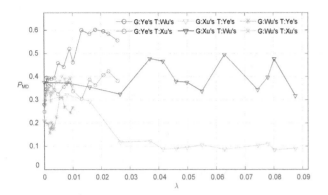

Figure 4: Testing error of adversarial examples by other networks under steganography of WOW with a relative payload of 0.4 bpp.

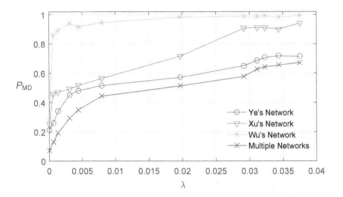

Figure 5: Testing error of multiple networks' adversarial examples under steganography of WOW with a relative payload of 0.4 bpp.

the method described in Section 2.2.3, we use multiple λ values to construct adversarial examples for multiple networks. The validation dataset is used to construct adversarial images for each λ. Each network then detects the images. It is important to emphasize that we use a strict definition of multiple networks testing error rate P_E^{Mul}, which represents the probability that all networks are misled.

The testing error of each network and multiple networks is shown in Figure 5. Multi-network adversarial examples have a very good performance for all networks and as λ increases, P_E^{Mul} can raise from 7.0% to 67.3%. And during the construction of the adversarial examples, the average number of iterations required for each image is 9.93, which will take 583s on a GPU of NVIDIA Tesla K80.

3.3 Tradeoff With SRM+EC

Since SRM+EC is an important and powerful steganalysis system, we have to consider the impact of the construction process of the adversarial images on it. We put adversarial images for multiple networks of different λ into trained SRM+EC. Unfortunately, while

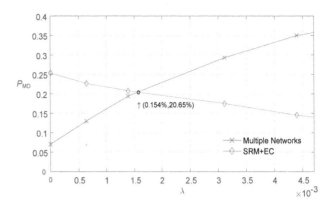

Figure 6: Testing error of multiple networks' adversarial examples by multiple networks and SRM+EC under steganography of WOW with a relative payload of 0.4 bpp.

facing SRM, the safety of the modified cover images gradually decreases as λ increases as is shown in Figure 6. It shows that the images we construct will reduce the performance against steganalysis of high-dimensional features, but we should apply the "Cask Effect Theory" to evaluate the security of steganography algorithms. In other words, if there are several steganalyazers, the security of steganographic algorithm should be defined by the minimum testing error rate. Herein, we define the security of the images as P_E^B, which is the minimum testing error rate of both systems. Our objective is to find a suitable λ that can maximize P_E^B and is stated in Equation (8):

$$\begin{aligned} & \underset{\lambda}{maximize} \; P_E^B, \\ & subject \; to \; 0 \le \lambda \le 1, \end{aligned} \qquad (8)$$

where $P_E^B = min(P_E^{SRM}, P_E^{Mul})$. From Figure 6 we can see that, increasing λ from 0% to 0.154% can increase P_E^B from 7.0% to 20.6% which is the highest value that P_E^B can reach and the correctness of the result has been verified on the testing dataset.

In addition to the construction of enhanced secure covers, we can also design a scheme against both neural network and SRM+EC steganalysis by combining the framework of minimizing distortion steganography with the proposed adversarial example technique. For instance, denote the adversarial noise on the ith pixel as $\boldsymbol{n}_i$, and the ± 1 distortion on the ith pixel as ρ_i^{+1} and ρ_i^{-1} respectively which is defined with a steganographic algorithm such as WOW or HILL. If $\boldsymbol{n}_i$ is positive, we will reduce the value of ρ_i^{+1} according to the magnitude of $\boldsymbol{n}_i$ and vice versa. Stegos generated from the modified distortion, which is called the "adversarial distortion", will have the ability to resist SRM+EC while misleading neural networks for steganalysis. Some experimental results on the adversarial distortion steganography (ADS) are shown in Table 1, in which the ADS-WOW is constructed with the adversarial distortion on the multi-CNN based steganalyzer. It can be seen that, with adversarial distortion, we can not only increase the ability of WOW to resist CNN based steganalyzers but also increase its ability to resist SRM. We also retrained SRM with stegos generated by ADS, and labeled it as SRM (retrained). As shown in the last line of Table 1, retraining

SRM significantly reduces the P_E on detecting ADS, but suffers from greatly increase of P_E on detecting the original WOW.

Table 1: Testing error of WOW and ADS-WOW under different steganalyzers with a relative payload of 0.4 bpp

Error Rate(%)	WOW			ADS-WOW		
Steganalyzer	P_{MD}	P_{FA}	P_E	P_{MD}	P_{FA}	P_E
Xu's CNN	25.54	26.60	26.07	86.71	26.60	56.66
Ye's CNN	21.34	18.55	19.95	74.26	18.55	46.41
Wu's CNN	28.04	35.17	31.61	75.34	35.17	55.26
Multi-CNN	7.01	58.43	32.72	56.28	58.43	57.36
SRM	25.23	25.77	25.50	47.81	25.77	36.79
SRM (retrained)	23.90	44.72	34.31	13.33	44.72	29.03

4   CONCLUSIONS

In this paper, we propose a method of iteratively constructing robust enhanced cover images that can resist the neural networks for steganalysis and the intensity of adversarial noise is controllable. The stegos, obtained by using the constructed images as cover, can effectively avoid the detection of network-based steganalyzers. Besides, we also consider how to simultaneously fight against network-based steganalyzers and SRM+EC and define the comprehensive security criterion P_E^B under the two systems. We have made a tradeoff between the two systems and evaluated the performance of our model using the BOSSbase dataset, the WOW steganography method and three state-of-the-art networks. Results show the effectiveness of our method and comprehensive security level has been improved.

ACKNOWLEDGMENTS

This work was supported in part by the Natural Science Foundation of China under Grant U1636201 and 61572452. The authors would like to thank DDE Laboratory of SUNY Binghamton for sharing the source code of steganography, steganalysis and ensemble classifier on the webpage (http://dde.binghamton.edu/download/).

REFERENCES

[1] Shumeet Baluja and Ian Fischer. 2017. Adversarial Transformation Networks: Learning to Generate Adversarial Examples. *arXiv preprint arXiv:1703.09387* (2017).

[2] Patrick Bas, Tomáš Filler, and Tomáš Pevný. 2011. âĂİ Break Our Steganographic SystemâĂİ: The Ins and Outs of Organizing BOSS. In *Information Hiding*. Springer, 59–70.

[3] Tomas Denemark, Vahid Sedighi, Vojtech Holub, Rémi Cogranne, and Jessica Fridrich. 2014. Selection-channel-aware rich model for steganalysis of digital images. In *Information Forensics and Security (WIFS), 2014 IEEE International Workshop on*. IEEE, 48–53.

[4] Jessica Fridrich and Jan Kodovsky. 2012. Rich models for steganalysis of digital images. *IEEE Transactions on Information Forensics and Security* 7, 3 (2012), 868–882.

[5] Ian J Goodfellow, Jonathon Shlens, and Christian Szegedy. 2014. Explaining and harnessing adversarial examples. *arXiv preprint arXiv:1412.6572* (2014).

[6] Linjie Guo, Jiangqun Ni, Wenkang Su, Chengpei Tang, and Yun-Qing Shi. 2015. Using statistical image model for JPEG steganography: uniform embedding revisited. *IEEE Transactions on Information Forensics and Security* 10, 12 (2015), 2669–2680.

[7] Vojtech Holub and Jessica Fridrich. 2012. Designing steganographic distortion using directional filters. In *Information Forensics and Security (WIFS), 2012 IEEE International Workshop on*. IEEE, 234–239.

[8] Vojtěch Holub, Jessica Fridrich, and Tomáš Denemark. 2014. Universal distortion function for steganography in an arbitrary domain. *EURASIP Journal on Information Security* 2014, 1 (2014), 1.

[9] Sandy Huang, Nicolas Papernot, Ian Goodfellow, Yan Duan, and Pieter Abbeel. 2017. Adversarial attacks on neural network policies. *arXiv preprint arXiv:1702.02284* (2017).

[10] Jan Kodovský and Jessica Fridrich. 2012. Steganalysis of JPEG images using rich models. In *Media Watermarking, Security, and Forensics 2012*, Vol. 8303. International Society for Optics and Photonics, 83030A.

[11] Jan Kodovsky, Jessica Fridrich, and Vojtěch Holub. 2012. Ensemble classifiers for steganalysis of digital media. *IEEE Transactions on Information Forensics and Security* 7, 2 (2012), 432–444.

[12] Jernej Kos, Ian Fischer, and Dawn Song. 2017. Adversarial examples for generative models. *arXiv preprint arXiv:1702.06832* (2017).

[13] Sarra Kouider, Marc Chaumont, and William Puech. 2013. Adaptive steganography by oracle (ASO). In *Multimedia and Expo (ICME), 2013 IEEE International Conference on*. IEEE, 1–6.

[14] Bin Li, Ming Wang, Jiwu Huang, and Xiaolong Li. 2014. A new cost function for spatial image steganography. In *Image Processing (ICIP), 2014 IEEE International Conference on*. IEEE, 4206–4210.

[15] Jiajun Lu, Theerasit Issaranon, and David Forsyth. 2017. Safetynet: Detecting and rejecting adversarial examples robustly. *arXiv preprint arXiv:1704.00103* (2017).

[16] Tomáš Pevný, Tomáš Filler, and Patrick Bas. 2010. Using high-dimensional image models to perform highly undetectable steganography. In *International Workshop on Information Hiding*. Springer, 161–177.

[17] Yinlong Qian, Jing Dong, Wei Wang, and Tieniu Tan. 2015. Deep learning for steganalysis via convolutional neural networks. *Media Watermarking, Security, and Forensics* 9409 (2015), 94090J–94090J.

[18] Christian Szegedy, Wojciech Zaremba, Ilya Sutskever, Joan Bruna, Dumitru Erhan, Ian Goodfellow, and Rob Fergus. 2013. Intriguing properties of neural networks. *arXiv preprint arXiv:1312.6199* (2013).

[19] Weixuan Tang, Haodong Li, Weiqi Luo, and Jiwu Huang. 2014. Adaptive steganalysis against WOW embedding algorithm. In *Proceedings of the 2nd ACM workshop on Information hiding and multimedia security*. ACM, 91–96.

[20] Songtao Wu, Shenghua Zhong, and Yan Liu. 2017. Deep residual learning for image steganalysis. *Multimedia Tools and Applications* (2017), 1–17.

[21] Songtao Wu, Sheng-Hua Zhong, and Yan Liu. 2016. Steganalysis via Deep Residual Network. In *Parallel and Distributed Systems (ICPADS), 2016 IEEE 22nd International Conference on*. IEEE, 1233–1236.

[22] Songtao Wu, Sheng-hua Zhong, and Yan Liu. 2017. Residual convolution network based steganalysis with adaptive content suppression. In *Multimedia and Expo (ICME), 2017 IEEE International Conference on*. IEEE, 241–246.

[23] Guanshuo Xu, Han-Zhou Wu, and Yun-Qing Shi. 2016. Structural design of convolutional neural networks for steganalysis. *IEEE Signal Processing Letters* 23, 5 (2016), 708–712.

[24] Jian Ye, Jiangqun Ni, and Yang Yi. 2017. Deep learning hierarchical representations for image steganalysis. *IEEE Transactions on Information Forensics and Security* 12, 11 (2017), 2545–2557.

Identification of Audio Processing Operations Based on Convolutional Neural Network

Bolin Chen
Sun Yat-sen University
Guangzhou, China
chenbl8@mail2.sysu.edu.cn

Weiqi Luo*
Sun Yat-sen University
Guangzhou, China
luoweiqi@mail.sysu.edu.cn

Da Luo
Dongguan University of Technology
Dongguan, China
luoda@dgut.edu.cn

ABSTRACT

To reduce the tampering artifacts and/or enhance audio quality, some audio processing operations are often applied in the resulting tampered audio. Like image forensics, the detection of various post processing operations has become very important for audio authentication. In this paper, we propose a convolutional neural network (CNN) to detect audio processing operations. In the proposed method, we carefully design the network architecture, with particular attention to the frequency representation for the audio input, the activation function and the depth of the network. In our experiments, we evaluate the proposed method on audio clips with 12 commonly used audio processing operations and of three different small sizes. The experimental results show that our method can significantly outperform related methods based on hand-crafted features and other CNN architectures, and can achieve state-of-the-art results for both binary and multiple classification.

KEYWORDS

Audio Forensics, Audio Processing Operations, Convolutional Neural Network

ACM Reference Format:
Bolin Chen, Weiqi Luo, and Da Luo. 2018. Identification of Audio Processing Operations Based on Convolutional Neural Network. In *IH&MMSec '18: 6th ACM Workshop on Information Hiding and Multimedia Security, June 20–22, 2018, Innsbruck, Austria.* ACM, New York, NY, USA, 5 pages. https://doi.org/10.1145/3206004.3206005

1 INTRODUCTION

With the rapid development of multimedia processing technology, it is now easier than ever to modify multimedia data without leaving any obvious perceptible artifacts. The abuse of tampered multimedia data can lead to many potential serious moral, ethical and legal problems, and multimedia forensics have therefore attracted increasing attention over the past decade.

To the best of our knowledge, most existing forensic works focus on digital images. However, there has been some work on audio forensics. In [11], for instance, Farid et al. authenticate audio signals

---

*Corresponding author.

IH&MMSec'18, June 20–22, 2018, Innsbruck, Austria
© 2018 Association for Computing Machinery.
ACM ISBN 978-1-4503-5625-1/18/06...$15.00
https://doi.org/10.1145/3206004.3206005

using higher-order statistical correlations. In [12], Grigoras argues that the Electric Network Frequency (ENF) Criterion is useful in analyzing and verifying digital audio recordings. In [21], Malik et al. describe a technique for modeling reverberation in an audio recording and show its efficacy in audio forensics. In [14], Ikram et al. present a new audio forensics method based on background noise. In [9, 10], Cuccovillo et al. present audio tampering detection methods using device analysis. In [5, 26], the authors analyze quantized MDCT coefficients to detect audio recompression. In [17], Luo et al. employ the sample repetition rate as a feature to identify AMR decompressed audio. Since audio post-processing operations are often applied to the resulting tampered audio clips, the identification of audio processing operations is very important for subsequent forensic analysis. Several works have been proposed for this forensic issue. For instance, the authors of [16] exploit coocurrence patterns in audio signals to distinguish original audio clips from those that have undergone audio processing operations. The authors of [19] employ a steganalytic feature set derived from both the time and the Mel-frequency domain to identify various audio processing operations.

Unlike the conventional methods mentioned above, deep learning can exploit cascaded layers to adaptively learn hierarchical representations from input data. It has achieved great success in various research fields such as computer vision and speech recognition. In image forensics, there are several works such as [2–4, 7] that exploit CNNs to detect common image processing operations. Recently, deep learning has also made significant progress in audio steganalysis and forensics. For instance, in [22], Paulin et al. exploit a deep belief network (DBN) to detect three audio steganographic methods. In [6], Chen et al. propose a CNN model to detect ±1 LSB matching audio steganography in the time domain. In [23], Seichter et al. train a CNN on quantized MDCT coefficients for AAC encoding detection and bitrate estimation. In [15], Lin et al. combine electric network frequency (ENF) analysis and a CNN to verify whether or not an audio recording is a recaptured one. In [18], Luo et al. propose a framework for detecting double compressed AMR audio based on the stacked autoencoder network and the universal background model–Gaussian mixture model. In this paper, we introduce a CNN to detect various audio processing operations. We carefully design the network architecture, and provide extensive results to show that the proposed method significantly outperforms the other related works in both binary and multiple classification. In addition, we provide some supplementary experiments to demonstrate the rationality about network.

The rest of the paper is organized as follows. Section 2 describes the proposed network architecture and some important hyper parameters. Section 3 presents comparative results for the detection

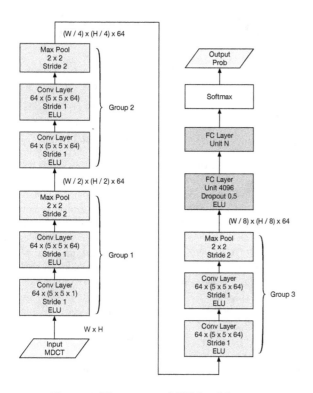

Figure 1: The proposed CNN architecture

of various audio processing operations. Finally, the concluding remarks of this paper are given in Section 4.

2 THE PROPOSED METHOD

The proposed network architecture is shown in Fig. 1. We first transform the audio clip into the MDCT domain, and feed the MDCT coefficients [1] into the network. Compared with other frequency coefficients(e.g. STFT and MFCC) or samples in the time domain [6], we can achieve better detection results using MDCT coefficients based on our extensive experiments (refer to Section III). The MDCT coefficients are then undergone three groups, each of which includes two convolutional layers and a max pooling layer. The convolutional layers use filters of square shape (5×5 size, 1×1 stride) and are equipped with the ELU [8] activation function. The first convolutional layer in the model has one input channel and 64 output channels. The other convolutional layers have both an input and output channel number of 64. The max pooling layers use small kernels (2×2 size, 2×2 stride). The output feature maps of these three groups are then aggregated and fed into two fully-connected layers. The first one consists of 4096 units equipped with ELU. Dropout [24] is applied to the first fully-connected (FC) layer to prevent overfitting with a dropout ratio of 0.5. The second one consists of N units, corresponding to the number of output classes. Finally, the softmax layer is used to produce the output probability.

In our experiments, this CNN model was implemented using Tensorflow [1]. We used Nesterov Momentum [25] with momentum of 0.9 to train the model. L2 regularization was used and the weight

---

[1]Code available at: http://mdct.readthedocs.io/en/latest/. In our method, the frame size is 256 and has a half overlap.

Table 1: Audio processing operations and their abbreviations in CoolEdit and GoldWave.

Cool Edit Pro		GoldWave	
Operation	Abbr.	Operation	Abbr.
PitchBlender(JustWindup)	PAD	Echo	ECH
Stretch(LowerPitch)	TRM	Filter high	FLH
SweepPhaser(VocalPhase)	PHS	Filter noise	FLN
DynamicProc(GateCompress)	DYN	Filter bandpass	FLB
Echo(ShowerEffect)	SHW	Mechanization	MEC
HissReduction(Standard)	HIS	Reverb	RVB

decay was 0.0005. We initialized all the weights using a Gaussian distribution with zero mean and a standard deviation of 0.01, and initialized all the biases as zero. In the training stage, the batch size was 64, and the training set was shuffled between epochs. The learning rate was initially 0.001 and this was divided by 10 when the validation accuracy stopped improving. We terminated the training stage after reducing the learning rate three times.

3 EXPERIMENTAL RESULTS AND ANALYSIS

In this section, we first present the experimental data and then compare the proposed method with other existing methods. In addition, we also present experimental results for some variants of the proposed model.

3.1 Experimental Data

We first crop 40,000 mono audio clips (16 kHz 16-bit) from audio databases TIMIT. Each audio has a duration of 1.00 s. Three different sizes of audio clips are then obtained via center cropping from the originals. Finally, we obtain 40,000 audio clips of 1.00 s, 0.50 s, and 0.05 s respectively. As in [16] and [19], we consider 12 typical operations with the default setting in two popular audio editing software packages (Cool Edit Pro and GoldWave), as illustrated in Table 1. In each class, half of the audio clips are used for training, and the rest are used for testing. At the training stage, 4,000 audio clips from each class are used for validation, and the remaining 16,000 are used to train the model. To achieve convincing results, we randomly split the training, validation and testing data three times and report the average results in the following experiments.

3.2 Comparison with Related Works

In this subsection, we compare our method with four related studies of audio forensics and/or steganalysis, including two methods based on CNN ([6, 23]) and two methods based on hand-crafted features ([16, 19]). In the following, binary and multiple classification will be evaluated separately.

3.2.1 Binary classification. In this experiment, we aim to identify whether the test sample is original or has been processed by a special operation. It should be noted that we train different binary classifiers for different processing operations. The results are shown in Tables 2 and 3. From these two tables, we can observe that the proposed method outperforms other methods in most cases and always achieves the best average detection accuracy. For example,

Table 2: Detection accuracy(%) for identifying audio processing operations in Cool Edit Pro. The best accuracy for each operation is highlighted and labeled with an asterisk (*).

Sample Size	Method Type	Detection Method	PAD	TRM	PHS	DYN	SHW	HIS	Average
1.00 s	Deep Learning-Based	Proposed Method	99.88	100.00*	99.79*	99.71*	99.53*	100.00*	99.82*
		Method [23]	99.24	99.98	98.92	97.20	53.40	99.97	91.45
		Method [6]	99.96*	100.00*	93.61	94.28	86.26	100.00*	95.69
	Hand-Crafted Features	Method [19]	99.17	99.99	92.67	97.51	81.57	99.95	95.14
		Method [16]	91.14	95.34	72.26	87.76	66.44	95.34	84.71
0.50 s	Deep Learning-Based	Proposed Method	99.75	100.00*	99.34*	99.03*	100.00*	99.99	99.69*
		Method [23]	99.23	99.98	99.24	94.81	52.93	99.93	91.02
		Method [6]	99.91*	99.99	89.13	92.10	83.41	100.00*	94.09
	Hand-Crafted Features	Method [19]	98.97	99.96	88.65	95.53	77.54	99.91	93.43
		Method [16]	87.74	91.80	68.35	84.70	63.66	92.37	81.44
0.05 s	Deep Learning-Based	Proposed Method	98.67*	99.90*	79.85*	88.70*	94.91*	99.92*	93.66*
		Method [23]	98.70	99.89	54.64	83.52	51.88	99.86	81.42
		Method [6]	98.49	99.78	68.38	82.02	66.58	99.89	85.86
	Hand-Crafted Features	Method [19]	95.39	99.06	68.45	84.06	61.67	98.66	84.55
		Method [16]	74.47	73.76	58.93	66.77	57.18	77.55	68.11

Table 3: Detection accuracy(%) for identifying audio processing operations in GoldWave. The best accuracy for each operation is highlighted and labeled with an asterisk (*).

Sample Size	Method Type	Detection Method	ECH	FLH	FLN	FLB	MEC	RVB	Average
1.00 s	Deep Learning-Based	Proposed Method	96.09*	100.00*	99.98*	100.00*	99.98	99.87*	99.32*
		Method [23]	82.29	100.00*	99.83	99.99	99.89	94.74	96.12
		Method [6]	75.63	100.00*	99.67	100.00*	100.00*	95.48	95.13
	Hand-Crafted Features	Method [19]	82.77	100.00*	99.79	100.00*	99.88	96.46	96.48
		Method [16]	78.51	99.80	89.60	99.99	96.95	82.87	91.29
0.50 s	Deep Learning-Based	Proposed Method	92.96*	100.00*	99.96*	100.00*	99.93	99.78*	98.77*
		Method [23]	58.70	100.00*	99.78	100.00*	99.76	94.67	92.15
		Method [6]	73.77	100.00*	99.44	100.00*	99.99*	90.88	94.01
	Hand-Crafted Features	Method [19]	77.70	100.00*	99.41	100.00*	99.60	93.72	95.07
		Method [16]	72.75	99.58	85.43	99.97	95.25	79.58	88.76
0.05 s	Deep Learning-Based	Proposed Method	73.21*	100.00*	99.08*	100.00*	99.64*	89.18*	93.52*
		Method [23]	54.73	100.00*	99.00	99.97	99.06	55.85	84.77
		Method [6]	60.38	100.00*	96.27	100.00*	99.59	73.30	88.26
	Hand-Crafted Features	Method [19]	64.08	100.00*	96.98	100.00*	90.53	75.86	87.91
		Method [16]	57.75	93.26	73.73	97.10	85.37	64.25	78.58

in the experiments on an audio length of 0.50 s in Table 3, the proposed method obtains very promising accuracies (over 99.5%) for all operations except ECH (92.96%). The average accuracy of the proposed method for all six operations is 98.77%, while the detection accuracies of the other four methods are all less than 95.5%. It can also be observed that even when the length of the audio sample is as small as 0.05 s, the proposed method still achieves an average detection accuracy of over 93.5%, which is significantly better than the current best work [19] based on hand-crafted features and two related works based on CNNs ([6, 23]). Similar results can be observed in Table 2.

3.2.2 Multiple classification. Compared with binary classification, multiple classification for various audio processing operations is more practical for real forensic applications. In this experiment, we aim to identify the 12 operations listed in Table 1. Due to page

limitations, we give only the confusion matrix for our method evaluated on audio clips of 0.50 s in Table 4. From Table 4, we can observe that most operations have been identified correctly with a high detection rate of over 98%. The detection rate is slightly poorer for the ECH operation, which is consistent with the results in Table 3. In this case, we obtain an average detection accuracy of 98.14% (i.e. the average result along the diagonal values in the confusion matrix). Table 5 shows the average detection accuracies for the other related methods and for different audio lengths. It can be observed that the proposed method significantly outperforms other methods. Even when the length of audio clips is as small as 0.05 s, we obtain a detection accuracy of over 84% .

Table 4: Confusion matrix for identifying the 12 audio processing operations in Cool Edit Pro and GoldWave. The asterisk (*) here means that the corresponding value is less than 1%. The average result along the diagonal line of this matrix is 98.14%.

Actual/Predicted	Ori	PAD	TRM	PHS	DYN	SHW	HIS	ECH	FLH	FLN	FLB	MEC	RVB
Ori	**91.05**	*	*	*	1.04	*	*	6.59	*	*	*	*	*
PAD	*	**99.02**	*	*	*	*	*	*	*	*	*	*	*
TRM	*	*	**99.22**	*	*	*	*	*	*	*	*	*	*
PHS	*	*	*	**98.74**	*	*	*	*	*	*	*	*	*
DYN	1.00	*	*	*	**98.38**	*	*	*	*	*	*	*	*
SHW	*	*	*	*	*	**99.99**	*	*	*	*	*	*	*
HIS	*	*	*	*	*	*	**99.09**	*	*	*	*	*	*
ECH	7.80	*	*	*	*	*	*	**91.08**	*	*	*	*	*
FLH	*	*	*	*	*	*	*	*	**100.00**	*	*	*	*
FLN	*	*	*	*	*	*	*	*	*	**99.87**	*	*	*
FLB	*	*	*	*	*	*	*	*	*	*	**100.00**	*	*
MEC	*	*	*	*	*	*	*	*	*	*	*	**99.91**	*
RVB	*	*	*	*	*	*	*	*	*	*	*	*	**99.53**

Table 5: Average results (%) along the diagonal line of the corresponding confusion matrix. The best accuracy of the five methods is highlighted and labeled with an asterisk (*).

Sample Size	Proposed Method	Method [23]	Method [6]	Method [19]	Method [16]
1.00s	**99.06***	92.92	78.69	89.53	66.44
0.50s	**98.14***	91.01	75.39	85.55	59.14
0.05s	**84.30***	75.46	61.90	64.27	35.05

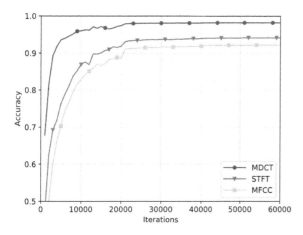

Figure 2: Comparison with different frequency inputs

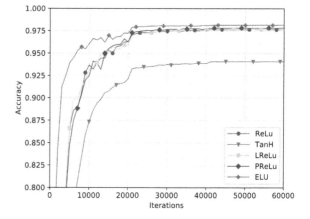

Figure 3: Comparison with different activation functions

3.3 Comparison of Variants of Our Model

To verify the rationality of the proposed CNN model, we present some supplementary results evaluated using variants of this model, including the use of different frequency inputs, activation functions and numbers of groups. The average detection accuracies evaluated on the validation data for multiple classification are given in the following subsections.

3.3.1 Input data. In this experiment, we use different frequency features of the audio as network input, including STFT [2] and MFCC

[3], which are widely used in various applications such as audio compression and classification. The results are shown in Fig. 2. From the figure, we can observe that the models using these three inputs converge within 60,000 iterations. With the MDCT input (i.e. the proposed model), the detection accuracy is as high as 98.17%. Compared with using STFT (94.11%) and MFCC (92.15%), we achieve improvements of over 4% and 6% respectively, which is a significant improvement for multiple classification.

3.3.2 Activation functions. In this experiment, we evaluate the use of different activation functions in the proposed model. Five

---

[2] Code available at:
https://docs.scipy.org/doc/scipy-0.19.1/reference/signal.html

[3] Code available at:http://python-speech-features.readthedocs.io/en/latest/

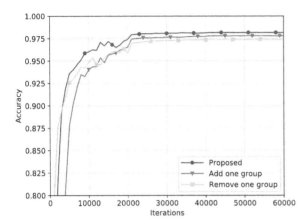

Figure 4: Comparison with different number of groups

commonly used functions are used here: TanH, ReLu, and three variants of ReLU, including LReLu [20], ELU [8] and PReLu [13]. The experimental results are shown in Fig 3. From the figure, we can observe that the proposed ELU is generally the most effective and TanH the least effective of the five activation functions, while the remaining three functions give very similar results.

3.3.3 Number of groups. In this experiment, we evaluate the influence of adding/removing one group of the convolutional layer and max pooling layer in the proposed model. The experimental results are shown in the Fig. 4. From this figure, we can observe that adding one group to the proposed model does not increase the detection performance, while removing one group decreases the detection performance slightly; this means that three groups in the proposed model is suitable for the investigated problem.

4 CONCLUSION

Different artifacts would be introduced into audio clips by different audio processing operations; it therefore seems unwise to design specific hand-crafted features for different operations, as in most conventional forensic methods. In this paper, we carefully design a CNN model for the detection of various audio processing operations, and provide extensive results to show that the proposed method can significantly outperform existing related methods based on hand-crafted features and deep learning. We obtain a significant improvement since the proposed CNN model is able to automatically learn high-level feature representations that are essential for the investigated task. In the future, we will extend the proposed model to identify the audio compression history and to detect audio splicing.

ACKNOWLEDGMENTS

This work is supported in part by the NSFC (61672551,61602318), the Special Research Plan of Guangdong Province under Grant 2015TQ01X365, and the Guangzhou Science and Technology Plan Project under Grant 201707010167.

REFERENCES

[1] Martín Abadi, Ashish Agarwal, Paul Barham, Eugene Brevdo, Zhifeng Chen, Craig Citro, Greg S Corrado, Andy Davis, Jeffrey Dean, Matthieu Devin, et al. 2016. Tensorflow: Large-scale machine learning on heterogeneous distributed systems. *arXiv preprint arXiv:1603.04467* (2016).
[2] Mauro Barni, Luca Bondi, Nicolò Bonettini, Paolo Bestagini, Andrea Costanzo, Marco Maggini, Benedetta Tondi, and Stefano Tubaro. 2017. Aligned and non-aligned double JPEG detection using convolutional neural networks. *Journal of Visual Communication and Image Representation* 49 (2017), 153–163.
[3] Belhassen Bayar and Matthew C Stamm. 2016. A deep learning approach to universal image manipulation detection using a new convolutional layer. In *Proceedings of the 4th ACM Workshop on Information Hiding and Multimedia Security.* ACM, 5–10.
[4] Belhassen Bayar and Matthew C Stamm. 2017. Design principles of convolutional neural networks for multimedia forensics. *Electronic Imaging* 2017, 7 (2017), 77–86.
[5] Tiziano Bianchi, Alessia De Rosa, Marco Fontani, Giovanni Rocciolo, and Alessandro Piva. 2013. Detection and classification of double compressed MP3 audio tracks. In *Proceedings of the first ACM workshop on Information hiding and multimedia security.* 159–164.
[6] Bolin Chen, Weiqi Luo, and Haodong Li. 2017. Audio Steganalysis with Convolutional Neural Network. In *Proceedings of the ACM Workshop on Information Hiding and Multimedia Security.* 85–90.
[7] Jiansheng Chen, Xiangui Kang, Ye Liu, and Z Jane Wang. 2015. Median filtering forensics based on convolutional neural networks. *IEEE Signal Processing Letters* 22, 11 (2015), 1849–1853.
[8] Djork-Arné Clevert, Thomas Unterthiner, and Sepp Hochreiter. 2016. Fast and accurate deep network learning by exponential linear units (ELUs). In *Proceedings of International Conference on Learning Representations.*
[9] Luca Cuccovillo, Sebastian Mann, Patrick Aichroth, Marco Tagliasacchi, and Christian Dittmar. 2013. Blind microphone analysis and stable tone phase analysis for audio tampering detection. In *Audio Engineering Society Convention 135.*
[10] Luca Cuccovillo, Sebastian Mann, Marco Tagliasacchi, and Patrick Aichroth. 2013. Audio tampering detection via microphone classification. In *IEEE International Workshop on Multimedia Signal Processing.* 177–182.
[11] Hany Farid. 1999. Detecting Digital Forgeries Using Bispectral Analysis. *Tech. Rep. AIM-1657, MIT AI Memo, Mass. Inst. Technol., Cambridge, MA, USA* (1999).
[12] Catalin Grigoras. 2005. Digital audio recording analysis–the electric network frequency criterion. *International Journal of Speech Language and the Law* 12, 1 (2005), 63–76.
[13] Kaiming He, Xiangyu Zhang, Shaoqing Ren, and Jian Sun. 2015. Delving deep into rectifiers: Surpassing human-level performance on imagenet classification. In *Proceedings of the IEEE international conference on computer vision.* 1026–1034.
[14] Sohaib Ikram and Hafiz Malik. 2010. Digital audio forensics using background noise. In *IEEE International Conference on Multimedia and Expo.* 106–110.
[15] Xiaodan Lin, Jingxian Liu, and Xiangui Kang. 2016. Audio recapture detection with convolutional neural networks. *IEEE Transactions on Multimedia* 18, 8 (2016), 1480–1487.
[16] Da Luo, Mengmeng Sun, and Jiwu Huang. 2016. Audio postprocessing detection based on amplitude cooccurrence vector feature. *IEEE Signal Processing Letters* 23, 5 (2016), 688–692.
[17] Da Luo, Rui Yang, and Jiwu Huang. 2015. Identification of AMR decompressed audio. *Digital Signal Processing* 37 (2015), 85–91.
[18] Da Luo, Rui Yang, Bin Li, and Jiwu Huang. 2017. Detection of Double Compressed AMR Audio Using Stacked Autoencoder. *IEEE Transactions on Information Forensics and Security* 12, 2 (2017), 432–444.
[19] Weiqi Luo, Haodong Li, Qi Yan, Yang Rui, and Jiwu Huang. [n. d.]. Improved Audio Steganalytic Feature and Its Applications in Audio Forensics. *ACM Transactions on Multimedia Computing, Communications, and Applications,* accepted ([n. d.]).
[20] Andrew L Maas, Awni Y Hannun, and Andrew Y Ng. 2013. Rectifier nonlinearities improve neural network acoustic models. In *Proceedings of the International conference on Machine Learning.*
[21] Hafiz Malik and Hany Farid. 2010. Audio forensics from acoustic reverberation. In *IEEE International Conference on Acoustics Speech and Signal Processing.* 1710–1713.
[22] Catherine Paulin, Sid-Ahmed Selouani, and Eric Hervet. 2016. Audio steganalysis using deep belief networks. *International Journal of Speech Technology* 19, 3 (2016), 585–591.
[23] Daniel Seichter, Luca Cuccovillo, and Patrick Aichroth. 2016. AAC encoding detection and bitrate estimation using a convolutional neural network. In *IEEE International Conference on Acoustics, Speech and Signal Processing.* 2069–2073.
[24] Nitish Srivastava, Geoffrey E Hinton, Alex Krizhevsky, Ilya Sutskever, and Ruslan Salakhutdinov. 2014. Dropout: a simple way to prevent neural networks from overfitting. *Journal of machine learning research* 15, 1 (2014), 1929–1958.
[25] Ilya Sutskever, James Martens, George Dahl, and Geoffrey Hinton. 2013. On the importance of initialization and momentum in deep learning. In *Proceedings of the International conference on Machine Learning.* 1139–1147.
[26] Rui Yang, Yun Q Shi, and Jiwu Huang. 2010. Detecting double compression of audio signal. In *Proceedings of the SPIE Media Forensics and Security II.* 75410K.

Learning Unified Deep-Features for Multiple Forensic Tasks

Owen Mayer
Drexel University
Philadelphia, PA, USA
om82@drexel.edu

Belhassen Bayar
Drexel University
Philadelphia, PA, USA
bb632@drexel.edu

Matthew C. Stamm
Drexel University
Philadelphia, PA, USA
MStamm@coe.drexel.edu

ABSTRACT

Recently, deep learning researchers have developed a technique known as *deep features* in which feature extractors for a task are learned by a CNN. These features are then provided to another classifier, or even used to perform a different classification task. Research in deep learning suggests that in some cases, deep features generalize to seemingly unrelated tasks. In this paper, we develop techniques for learning deep features that can be used across multiple forensic tasks, namely image manipulation detection and camera model identification. To do this, we develop two approaches for building deep forensic features: a transfer learning approach and a multitask learning approach. We experimentally evaluate the performance of both approaches in several scenarios and find that: 1) features learned for camera model identification generalize well to manipulation detection tasks but manipulation detection features do not generalize well to camera model identification, suggesting a task asymmetry, 2) deeper features are more task specific while shallower features generalize well across tasks, suggesting a feature hierarchy, and 3) a single, unified feature extractor can be learned that is highly discriminative for multiple forensic tasks. Furthermore, we find that when there is limited training data, a unified feature extractor can significantly outperform a targeted CNN.

KEYWORDS

Multimedia forensics, transfer learning, multitask learning

ACM Reference Format:
Owen Mayer, Belhassen Bayar, and Matthew C. Stamm. 2018. Learning Unified Deep-Features for Multiple Forensic Tasks. In *Proceedings of 6th ACM Workshop on Information Hiding and Multimedia Security (IH&MMSec '18)*. ACM, New York, NY, USA, 7 pages. https://doi.org/10.1145/3206004.3206022

1 INTRODUCTION

In recent years, there has been an explosion in deep learning research targeted at multimedia forensic tasks. For example, work in [11] shows that a convolutional neural network (CNN) can be built to detect whether an image patch has undergone median filtering. Other works have shown that resampling operations can be detected using deep learning methods [4, 10], as well as several approaches to classify multiple post-processing manipulations [1, 5, 12]. Research has also shown that CNNs can be used

to identify the source camera model of an image patch with high accuracy [2, 3, 7, 8, 20]. To date, many multimedia forensic deep learning methods have targeted several types of manipulation detection tasks and camera model identification tasks.

More recently, research has found that techniques utilizing *deep features* are also very effective for multimedia forensics tasks [4, 6, 7, 9, 15]. Deep features are the neuron responses, at a particular layer of a CNN, induced by the feeding forward an image through the network [13, 19]. In these approaches a CNN is trained for one task, and then deep features extracted from that network are utilized for a different task. For example, work by Bondi et al. in [7] showed that deep features extracted from a closed set camera model identification CNN can be used to train an SVM that classifies a different set of camera models. Mayer and Stamm [15] showed that pairs camera model deep features can be mapped to a similarity score to identify whether two images were captured by the same camera model, even if those camera models are unknown. Additionally, Bayar and Stamm [6] proposed a technique for open set camera model identification using deep features. The findings of these works suggest that deep feature representations learned for camera model identification may generalize to many different camera models, not just those in the original training set.

In research outside of multimedia forensics, deep features have been shown to generalize to seemingly unrelated tasks. For example, deep features extracted from a CNN pre-trained for scene detection can be used to train a object detection classifier and vice versa [21]. Additionally, work in the remote sensing community has shown that object recognition deep features can be trained for land-usage classification tasks [17]. These findings suggest that perhaps features learned in one specific multimedia forensics task may be applicable to other forensic tasks.

While research has shown that features learned for camera model identification generalize to other camera models [6, 7, 15], there has been no research showing that camera model identification features generalize to manipulation detection tasks, or vice versa. Additionally, very little is understood about which image features are being captured by deep learning methods. Because of this, we are led to ask several questions:

- Are features learned for one forensic task useful for another forensic task? Is it possible that forensic tasks, which are often thought of as very different, are actually very similar?

- Does an abstract hierarchical structure exist for feature generalization? That is, is it possible that low-level features generalize well across tasks but a more task-specific representation does not?

- Does there exist a single set of universal features that work for all multimedia forensic tasks?

In this paper we address these questions and show that 1) features learned for camera model identification generalize well to manipulation detection tasks, but that features learned for manipulation detection tasks do not generalize well to camera model identification tasks, suggesting a *task asymmetry*, 2) that deeper features are more task-specific, while shallower features generalize well across tasks, suggesting a *feature hierarchy*, and 3) that a single, unified feature extractor can be learned that is highly discriminative for multiple forensic tasks. Furthermore, we find that when there is limited training data, a unified feature extractor can significantly outperform a targeted CNN.

To do this, we adopt two strategies for learning deep feature extractors, and then experimentally evaluate the performance of each to demonstrate the properties that are enumerated above. In the first approach, we propse a transfer learning method where a CNN is initially learned for one forensic task. Then, the lower layers of the CNN are frozen, acting as a fixed feature extractor, while learning new upper layers that target a different task. We use this approach to experimentally demonstrate the transference of features between tasks. Furthermore, to evaluate the feature hierarchy, we experimentally vary the depth at which the CNN layers are frozen during retraining on the second task.

In the second approach, we propose a multitask learning approach where we train two CNNs simultaneously while constraining the lower layers of both networks to learn the same weights and biases. This approach effectively creates a single, unified feature extractor that is highly discriminative for multiple forensic tasks. Additionally, we find this approach to significantly outperform a targeted CNN when there is limited training data.

2 DEEP FEATURES OVERVIEW

In deep feature based approaches, classification of an image patch is broken down into two steps. In the first step, an image patch $X \in \mathbb{X}$, where $\mathbb{X}$ is the space of image patches, is mapped to an N-dimensional, real-valued feature space by a deep feature extractor function $\mathbf{f}(\cdot)$:

$$\mathbf{f} : \mathbb{X} \to \mathbb{R}^N. \tag{1}$$

The feature vector $\mathbf{f}(X)$ encodes high level forensic information about the image patch X. Next, a task classifier $g(\cdot)$ maps the deep feature vector into a classification decision

$$g : \mathbb{R}^N \to \mathbb{T}, \tag{2}$$

where $\mathbb{T}$ is the set of target classes (e.g. a set of camera models or a set of manipulations). Thus, the total system

$$y = g(\mathbf{f}(X)) \tag{3}$$

maps an input image $X \in \mathbb{X}$ to a classification decision $y \in \mathbb{T}$.

A diagram of the deep feature approach is shown in Fig. 1. An image patch X is input to a deep feature extractor $\mathbf{f}(\cdot)$, and the output deep features are input to task classifiers, $g_A(\cdot)$, $g_B(\cdot)$, $g_C(\cdot)$, which classify the image for the respective tasks A, B, and C.

In this work, we use a pre-trained CNN as the deep feature extractor $\mathbf{f}(\cdot)$. The features $\mathbf{f}(X)$ are evaluated by recording the neuron responses, at a specified layer, induced by the feed-forward of an input image patch X. Often, the last fully connected layer of the CNN is used for deep feature extraction [13, 19]. The power of using a deep feature approach is that

$$dimensionality\,(\mathbf{f}(X)) << dimensionality\,(X)\,,$$

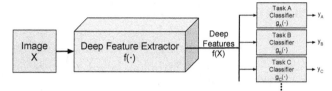

Figure 1: Diagram showing deep feature extraction and classification. A feature extractor maps an input image patch X into a deep feature space. Task classifiers then map these features into a task-specific classification decision.

which enables a task classifier $g(\cdot)$ to be trained with relatively few training samples.

However, a deep feature approach also requires that the features output by the feature extractor $\mathbf{f}(\cdot)$ are general enough to discriminate between the classes targeted by $g(\cdot)$. Ideally, the features extracted from feature extractor encode general, low-dimensional forensic information about the image patch, which allows for training task specific classifiers on many different forensic tasks.

3 CNN ARCHITECTURE

In this work, we use pre-trained CNNs to perform deep feature extraction. For each CNN, we use a network architecture proposed by Bayar and Stamm that has proven effective at both manipulation detection and source camera model identification [3, 5]. Briefly, the network consists of 5 convolutional layers and 3 fully connected layers. The first convolutional layer, labeled 'constr' is a set of 3 5x5 constrained filters where the central weight is constrained to be -1 and the rest of the weights sum to one, such that

$$\begin{cases} \mathbf{w}(0, 0) = -1 \\ \sum_{(l, m) \neq (0, 0)} \mathbf{w}(l, m) = 1 \end{cases} \tag{4}$$

where l, m are the spatial indices of each constrained filter. These constraints are designed to suppress image content while learning salient forensic features. The remaining 4 convolutional layers, labeled 'conv1'–'conv4,' each have hyperbolic tangent activation, mini-batch normalization and pooling. The network has 3 fully connected layers. The first two are labeled 'fc1' and 'fc2', each with 200 neurons and hyperbolic tangent activation. Finally, the network has an output fully connected layer with softmax function. Further details of the baseline architecture, including filter dimensions and parameter choice motivation, can be found in [5].

4 LEARNING DEEP FEATURE EXTRACTORS

The three goals of this work are to 1) propose and evaluate techniques to develop a unified set of deep features that are discriminative for multiple forensics tasks, as well as to 2) evaluate the transference of deep features between tasks and finally to 3) identify a potential abstract hierarchy of deep features. In this section, we propose two approaches for learning deep feature extractors, i.e. the mapping $\mathbf{f}(\cdot)$ described in Eq. (1).

4.1 Transfer Learning

In the first approach, we use transfer learning to learn the deep feature extractor. In transfer learning, portions of a convolutional neural network (CNN) pre-trained for one task are used to extract

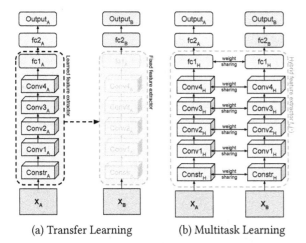

(a) Transfer Learning   (b) Multitask Learning

Figure 2: Diagrams of proposed approaches (a) transfer learning and (b) multitask learning, both using an example share depth of *fc1*. In the transfer learning approach, layers 'constr' through 'fc1' are learned for an initial task A, then 'fc2' and 'output' are retrained for a new task B. In the multitask approach, two networks are trained simultaneously on different datasets, but with layers 'constr' through 'fc1' constrained to learn the same parameters.

features for another task [16]. That is, the knowledge (feature representations) learned for one task are "transferred" to another task. In the experimental evaluation in Sec. 5.2, we use this approach to evaluate how well the features learned from one task generalize to another task. Additionally, by varying the depth of the feature extractor, we use this approach to also evaluate the hierarchical nature of feature transference.

The transfer learning process is accomplished in two training phases. In the first training phase, a *source* CNN is trained for a source task A, using a baseline architecture described in Sec. 3. Training is performed with a set of training image patches X_A that are representative of classes in $\mathbb{T}_A$. The result of this training phase is a trained network that has layers $constr_A$ through $output_A$, which is depicted by the left hand side of the diagram in Fig. 2a.

In the second training phase, we first fix the source CNN learned for task A, preventing its parameters from being updated. Then, we discard the upper layers of the source CNN, above a layer called the *share depth*. Finally, we replace the discarded layers with new layers that are then learned for target task B. A diagram of this approach with a share depth of $fc1$ is shown on the right of Fig. 2a. The fixed lower layers of the source CNN through 'fc1$_A$' are input to new layers 'fc2$_B$' and 'output$_B$' learned for the target task B.

The term *share depth* is used to signify the layers that are shared between the two tasks. The layers below and including the share depth act as the deep feature extractor $\mathbf{f}_A(\cdot)$. The layers above the share depth act as the task specific classifier.

4.2 Multitask Learning

In our second approach, we propose a method to learn a single feature extractor that outputs deep features highly discriminative for multiple forensic tasks. To do this, we train two (or more) CNNs simultaneously on two (or more) different tasks, but constrain the

lower layers of each network to learn the same parameters. This is a form of multitask learning [18]. The shared layers of these networks form a single, unified feature extractor that outputs deep features discriminative of two (or more) forensic tasks, which we call a *hybrid* feature extractor. In the experimental evaluation in Sec. 5.3, we use this approach to evaluate how well hybrid features are able to classify multiple tasks, and compare with feature extractors learned in the transfer learning approach.

A diagram of the multitask learning process is shown in Fig. 2b, which uses a share depth of *fc1*. Unlike the transfer learning process, the multitask process is accomplished in a single learning phase. One network leg has input database for task A, and the network leg has input database for task B. The bottom layers through the share depth are called *hybrid layers*. In the example shown in Fig. 2b, the hybrid layers are labeled 'constr$_H$' through 'fc1$_H$' creating a feature extractor $f_H(\cdot)$. The task A specific layers are labeled 'fc2$_A$' and 'output$_A$', and the task B specific layers are labeled 'fc2$_B$' and 'output$_B$', creating task specific classifiers $g_A(\cdot)$ and $g_B(\cdot)$.

During training, at each iteration the weights and biases of the hybrid layers are updated according to

$$w'_k = w_k + \Delta w_k, \tag{5}$$

where w_k is the original weight indexed by k, Δw_k is the weight update step, and w'_k is the updated weight. The update step is calculated by

$$\Delta w_k = \sum_{t \in T} \lambda_t \Delta w_{k,t}, \tag{6}$$

where T is the set of tasks that are being targeted, t is a specific task in that set, λ_t is a specified weight (i.e. preference) given to task t, and $\Delta w_{k,t}$ is the portion of the update step attributed to task t. In our approach, we use $\lambda_t = 1 \ \forall t$, that is each task has equal weight. The task portion of the update step is calculated according to

$$\Delta w_{k,t} = -\eta \frac{\partial L_t}{\partial w_k}, \tag{7}$$

where η is the learning rate and L_t is the loss for task t. In summary, we ensure the two network's learn the same parameters by summing together the gradient for each task-specific loss and applying the same update rule to each network.

In addition, the architecture that we use employs mini-batch normalization. After each iteration, we average the normalization parameters across network legs to ensure that each network uses the same normalization.

5 EXPERIMENTAL EVALUATION

In this section, we experimentally evaluate the following: 1) how well features learned for one task transfer to another task, specifically the tasks of camera model identification and manipulation detection, 2) whether shallower features are more generic and deeper features are more task specific, and 3) whether a set of unified features can be learned that are discriminative for multiple tasks. The first two evaluations were performed using the transfer learning approach, and the third evaluation was performed using the multitask learning approach.

To do this, we created two different databases, one for each task under investigation. The first database we created was for the manipulation detection task, following the steps used in [3]. We collected 400,000 training patches and 50,000 testing patches

Manipulation Detection, $\mathbb{T}_A$ =		
Unaltered	Median Filter (5x5)	Gauss. Blur ($\sigma = 1.1$)
AWGN ($\sigma = 2$)	Bilinear Interp. (x1.5)	JPEG (Q=70)
Camera Model Identification, $\mathbb{T}_B$ =		
Apple iPhone 4s*	Nikon Coolpix S710†	Rollei RCP-S7325XS†
Apple iPhone 6*	Nikon D200†	Samsung Gal. Note4*
Canon Ixus70†	Olympus mju-1050SW†	Samsung Gal. S4*
Casio EX-Z150†	Panasonic DMC-FZ50†	Samsung LZ74 wide†
FujiFilm FinePixJ50†	Pentax OptioA40†	Samsung NV15†
Kodak M1063†	Praktica DCZ5.9†	Sony DSC-T77†
LG Nexus 5x*	Ricoh GX100†	
Limited Training Data Camera Model Identification, $\mathbb{T}_C$ =		
HTC One M7*	Nikon D70†	Sony DSC-W170†
Mot. Droid Maxx*	Samsung Galaxy S2*	

Table 1: Classes for the three investigated tasks.
Camera models from our database*, and from the Dresden Image Database†

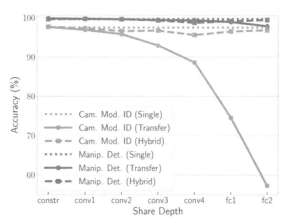

Figure 3: Accuracy, by share depth, for the single task, transfer learning, and multitask learning approaches.

of size 256×256 using 8334 images chosen at random from the publicly available Dresden Image Database [14]. The training and testing patches were created from two separate sets of images using the nine central 256×256 blocks of each image. Only the green color channel was used. Next, each block was edited using the six processing operations in the set $\mathbb{T}_A$ in Table 1.

We then created a second database for the source camera model identification task. This database is composed of image patches of size 256×256 from the set $\mathbb{T}_B$ of 20 different camera models in Table 1. The camera models were chosen such that they had at least 2 devices. For each camera model, 20,000 non-overlapping training patches were randomly selected from among all but one device. For testing, 1500 non-overlapping patches were randomly chosen from the remaining device. The camera models were also selected to create a diversity of manufacturers and camera types (e.g. point-and-shoot, DSLR, cell phone). These images were taken from the publicly available Dresden Image Database [14], and from our own database of cameras. Camera models from our database had at least 300 images per device, with images taken in diverse scene environments. In total, 400,000 training patches and 30,000 testing patches were used.

5.1 Single task baseline

To provide a measure for comparison, we trained the baseline network for each task individually, i.e. 'Single Task' training. To do this, we trained the baseline CNN network described in Sec. 3 for each task. We performed training using stochastic gradient decent with a base learning rate of 0.001, momentum of 0.9, and batch size of 40 patches. The learning rate was halved every 3 epochs, and the network was trained for 30 epochs total.[1] Single task accuracy of 97.5% was achieved for camera model identification, and 99.6% for manipulation detection.

5.2 Feature transfer and hierarchy

In this experiment, we used the transfer learning approach outlined in Sec. 4.1 to evaluate how well features learned from one forensic task transfer to another task forensic task, as well as to evaluate a feature hierarchy.

To do this, we used a pre-trained single-task network, learned above in Sec. 5.1, as a deep feature extractor. Then we retrained the upper layers, above a share depth, to target the other task. We varied the share depth between the shallowest possible of 'constr' through the deepest possible of 'fc2.' This was done for both tasks. Training was performed using stochastic gradient descent with a base learning rate of 0.005, momentum of 0.9, and a batch size of 100 patches. The learning rate was halved every 3 epochs, and the network was trained for 30 epochs total, with no early stopping.

The accuracy achieved for each transfer learning scenario, by share depth, is shown in Fig. 3. Transfer of camera model features to target the manipulation detection task is shown in solid green. Transfer of manipulation features to target the camera model identification task is shown in solid blue.

When we transfered manipulation features to the camera model identification task, an accuracy of 97.5% was achieved when using the shallowest share depth of 'constr'. Accuracy monotonically decreased as share depth was increased, and achieved an accuracy of 57.8% at the deepest share depth of 'fc2.' When we transfered camera model features to the manipulation detection task, an accuracy of 99.8% was achieved when using the shallowest share depth of 'constr'. Accuracy monotonically decreased as share depth increased, and achieved an accuracy of 97.6% for at 'fc2' share depth.

An important observation from this experiment is that when we targeted the camera model identification task using manipulation features, there was a significant drop in accuracy of 39.7 percentage points relative to the single-task baseline, at a share depth of 'fc2'. However, there was only a 2.0 percentage point drop in accuracy when we targeted the manipulation detection task using camera model features up to the same share depth.

This result suggests that a *task asymmetry* exists in the generality of forensic deep features. That is, the camera model features transfer much better to the manipulation task than manipulation features transfer to camera model identification. One possible explanation for this phenomenon is that camera model features may be much more complex than manipulation features, and thus need to discriminate a greater expanse of the forensic feature space, which may include manipulation features. Another possible explanation is that manipulation features are a subset of camera model features, but that the reverse is not true.

---

[1]Source code for this work can be found at misl.ece.drexel.edu/downloads or gitlab.com/MISLgit/unified-features-ihmmsec2018. All experiments were conducted using caffe with an Nvidia GTX 1080 or 1080ti GPU.

Target Task:	Manipulation		Camera Model	
Feature Extractor	CNN	ERT	CNN	ERT
Manipulation (*A*)	99.6%	**99.8%**	57.8%	72.5%
Camera Model (*B*)	97.6%	98.9%	97.5%	**97.7%**
Hybrid (*A* + *B*, **fc2**)	99.4%	**99.8%**	96.8%	97.6%

Table 2: Accuracy comparison of extremely randomized trees (ERT) classifier on fc2 deep features versus the single task, transfer, and hybrid networks

Another important observation from this experiment is that, for both tasks, the classification accuracy monotonically decreased as the share depth was increased. This result suggests a *feature hierarchy* of forensic features. That is, low-level features learned by the shallower layers of a network are general across tasks, i.e. higher level features for different forensic tasks can be learned from these low-level representations. By contrast, high-level features learned in the deeper layers appear to be more task specific. This result has significant implications for forensic investigators who use transfer learning methods, and shows that the choice of share depth is a critical one. We note that also as the share depth decreases, the parameters that must be retrained for the target task increases. Thus if the training dataset is small, it may not be practical to use a shallow share depth.

Another interesting observation is that classification accuracy actually improves to 99.8% for the manipulation detection task when using the 'constr' features transferred from camera model network, versus the classification accuracy of 99.6% achieved by the single-task CNN. Literature in multitask learning suggests that training on different tasks may prevent overfitting by enforcing generality of features [18], which perhaps happened in this case.

5.3 Unified deep features

In this experiment, we used the multitask learning approach outlined in Sec. 4.2 to evaluate how well unified features are able to discriminate multiple tasks. To do this, we trained hybrid networks using the multitask learning approach described in Sec. 4.2. Additionally, we varied the share depth from 'constr' through 'fc2'. For each hybrid network, we simultaneously trained on the manipulation detection and camera model identification datasets. Training was performed using stochastic gradient descent with a base learning rate of 0.001, momentum of 0.9, and batch size of 40 patches per task. The learning rate was halved every 3 epochs, and the network was trained for 30 epochs total with no early stopping.

The accuracy achieved for each task using this multitask learning approach, by share depth, is shown by the dashed lines with squares in Fig. 3. At a share depth of 'fc2,' the most difficult scenario for the transfer learning approach, an accuracy of 96.8% was achieved for the camera model identification task. This improved accuracy by 39.5 percentage points over the transfer learning method. For the manipulation detection, and accuracy of 99.4% was achieved using the multitask approach, a 1.6 percentage point improvement over the transfer learning method.

Notably, at all share depths, the multitask approach improved accuracy for the camera model identification task over the transfer learning method. Additionally, for the manipulation detection task,

Feature Extractor	CNN	ERT
Manipulation Detection (*A*)		75.0%
20 Camera Model (*B*)		88.9%
5 Camera Model (*C*)	86.6%	85.6%
Hybrid (*A* + *B*, **fc2**)		91.5%
Hybrid (*A* + *B* + *C*, **fc2**)	92.1%	**92.8%**

Table 3: Classification accuracy for the 5 camera model identification task using different feature extractors.

the multitask approach improved classification accuracy over the transfer learning approach at deep share depths of 'fc1' and 'fc2.'

While the multitask approach did not improve classification accuracy over the single-task baseline, it did improve classification accuracy over the transfer learning approach especially at deeper share depths. The results of this experiment demonstrate that unified features are much more effective for discriminating multiple forensic tasks than using a transfer learning approach.

5.3.1 Hybrid features with extremely randomized trees. In this experiment, we used extremely randomized trees (ERT) classifiers to improve classification accuracy of the unified features. Work in [4] found that the use of extremely randomized trees on deep features extracted from the last fully connected layer improved classification accuracy of resizing detection. We also compare to the transfer learning and single task approaches.

For each task we extracted 'fc2' deep features from 1) the baseline manipulation detection CNN (*A*), 2) the baseline camera model identification CNN (*B*), and 3) the hybrid network with share depth of 'fc2' (*A* + *B*). We then trained an ERT classifier on each set of features, using 800 estimators and a minimum of 3 samples required to split an internal node.

Results from this experiment are shown in Table 2, and are compared to the results from the previous, CNN-based experiments. In each case, the ERT classifier slightly improves the CNN classifier. Notably, in the manipulation detection case the hybrid features performed equally as well as the single task feature extractor case, both achieving 99.8% accuracy. For camera model identification, the hybrid features achieve an accuracy of 97.6%, which is very nearly the single task accuracy of 97.7%.

The results of this experiment shows that the hybrid feature extractor is able to learn a single, unified set of features that are highly discriminative of multiple forensic tasks.

5.4 Classification with limited training data

In this experiment we tested the efficacy of using unified features on a new task with limited training data. This experiment was conducted to simulate a scenario where a forensic investigator may employ a deep feature approach, i.e. a scenario where there is not enough training data to robustly train a full CNN from scratch.

To do this, we first created a third database for camera model identification of 5 camera models. This set of camera models is labeled by $\mathbb{T}_C$ in Table 1, and are disjoint from the 20 camera models used in the above experiments. For training and testing, we collected image patches using the procedure outlined for the 20 camera model identification task. However, for each camera model, only 10,000 patches were collected per class for training and testing, resulting in 50,000 total training patches (1/8 of the 20 camera model training data), and 50,000 testing patches. To establish a baseline classification accuracy, we trained a single task CNN to target the 5 camera models using the same setup described in Sec. 5.1. The single task classifier achieved relatively poor accuracy of 86.6%.

Additionally, we trained a new hybrid network on the three training databases simultaneously, using an 'fc2' share depth. Training was performed using stochastic gradient descent with a base learning rate of 0.001, momentum of 0.9, and batch size of 40 patches per for the manipulation detection and 20 camera model tasks, and a batch size of 5 for the 5 camera model task. This was done to ensure that number of iterations per epoch was the same across all tasks. The learning rate was halved every 3 epochs, and the network was trained for 30 epochs total.

We used the pre-trained CNNs for manipulation detection (A), 20 camera model identification (B), 5 camera model identification (C), 2-task hybrid network with fc2 share depth ($A + B$), and 3-task hybrid network with fc2 share depth ($A + B + C$) to extract the 'fc2' features from the 5 camera model training data. Then, we trained an ERT classifier on each set of deep features extracted from these networks. To train each ERT, we used 800 estimators and required a minimum of 3 samples to split an internal node.

The classification accuracy achieved by each ERT is shown in Table 3. The ERT classifier achieved 85.6% when using 'fc2' features extracted from the 5 camera model CNN, which was trained with limited training data. Classification accuracy improved to 88.9% when using an ERT trained on features from the 20 camera model identification CNN. Accuracy was further improved to 91.2% when using deep features from the 2-task hybrid network. These results show that using deep features from well trained networks generalize well to new tasks, and that enforcing task generalization also improves the ability of the deep features

Furthermore, the highest classification accuracy of 92.8% was achieved when using deep features from the 3-task hybrid network. This result shows that using hybrid, unified features that also incorporate training samples from the target class improves classification accuracy over using a targeted CNN trained with limited training samples. These results show that it is important for a forensic investigator to enforce class and task generality when targeting new tasks that have limited training data.

6　CONCLUSION

In this paper, we adopted two strategies for learning deep feature extractors; a transfer learning approach, where features from one task are transferred to another task, and a multitask learning approach, where a single feature extractor is jointly optimized on multiple tasks. We experimentally evaluated their performance in several scenarios, in which we found that: 1) features learned for camera model identification generalize well to manipulation detection tasks, but features learned for manipulation detection tasks do not generalize well to camera model identification tasks, suggesting a task asymmetry, 2) deeper features are more task-specific, whereas shallower features generalize well across tasks, suggesting a feature hierarchy and 3) a single, unified feature extractor can be learned that is highly discriminative of multiple forensic tasks. Furthermore, we found that unified feature extractors outperform a targeted CNN when there is limited training data. These results highlight several critical considerations that a forensic investigator must make when using deep feature based approaches.

7　ACKNOWLEDGMENTS

This material is based upon work supported by the National Science Foundation under Grant No. 1553610. Any opinions, findings, and conclusions or recommendations expressed in this material are those of the authors and do not necessarily reflect the views of the National Science Foundation.

REFERENCES

[1] Belhassen Bayar and Matthew C Stamm. 2016. A deep learning approach to universal image manipulation detection using a new convolutional layer. In *Proc. of the 4th ACM Workshop on Info. Hiding and Multimedia Security*. ACM, 5–10.

[2] Belhassen Bayar and Matthew C Stamm. 2017. Augmented convolutional feature maps for robust cnn-based camera model identification. In *Image Processing (ICIP), 2017 IEEE International Conference on*. IEEE, 1–4.

[3] Belhassen Bayar and Matthew C Stamm. 2017. Design principles of convolutional neural networks for multimedia forensics. *Electronic Imaging* 7 (2017), 77–86.

[4] Belhassen Bayar and Matthew C Stamm. 2017. On the robustness of constrained convolutional neural networks to jpeg post-compression for image resampling detection. In *ICASSP, 2017 IEEE*. IEEE, 2152–2156.

[5] Belhassen Bayar and Matthew C Stamm. 2018. Constrained Convolutional Neural Networks: A New approach Towards General Purpose Image Manipulation Detection. *IEEE Transactions on Information Forensics and Security* (2018).

[6] Belhassen Bayar and Matthew C Stamm. 2018. Towards open set camera model identification using a deep learning framework. In *Acoustics, Speech and Signal Processing (ICASSP), 2018 IEEE International Conference on*. IEEE, 1–4.

[7] Luca Bondi, Luca Baroffio, David Güera, Paolo Bestagini, Edward J Delp, and Stefano Tubaro. 2017. First Steps Toward Camera Model Identification With Convolutional Neural Networks. *IEEE Signal Processing Letters* (2017), 259–263.

[8] Luca Bondi, David Güera, Luca Baroffio, Paolo Bestagini, Edward J Delp, and Stefano Tubaro. 2017. A preliminary study on convolutional neural networks for camera model identification. *Electronic Imaging* 2017, 7 (2017), 67–76.

[9] Luca Bondi, Silvia Lameri, David Güera, Paolo Bestagini, Edward J Delp, and Stefano Tubaro. 2017. Tampering Detection and Localization through Clustering of Camera-Based CNN Features. In *Proceedings of the IEEE Conference on Computer Vision and Pattern Recognition Workshops*. 1855–1864.

[10] Jason Bunk, Jawadul H Bappy, Tajuddin Manhar Mohammed, Lakshmanan Nataraj, Arjuna Flenner, BS Manjunath, Shivkumar Chandrasekaran, Amit K Roy-Chowdhury, and Lawrence Peterson. 2017. Detection and Localization of Image Forgeries using Resampling Features and Deep Learning. In *Computer Vision and Pattern Recognition Workshops (CVPRW)*. IEEE, 1881–1889.

[11] Jiansheng Chen, Xiangui Kang, Ye Liu, and Z Jane Wang. 2015. Median filtering forensics based on convolutional neural networks. *IEEE Signal Processing Letters* 22, 11 (2015), 1849–1853.

[12] Davide Cozzolino, Giovanni Poggi, and Luisa Verdoliva. 2017. Recasting residual-based local descriptors as convolutional neural networks: an application to image forgery detection. In *Proceedings of the 5th ACM Workshop on Information Hiding and Multimedia Security*. ACM, 159–164.

[13] Jeff Donahue, Yangqing Jia, Oriol Vinyals, Judy Hoffman, Ning Zhang, Eric Tzeng, and Trevor Darrell. 2014. Decaf: A deep convolutional activation feature for generic visual recognition. In *Int. Conference on Machine Learning*. 647–655.

[14] Thomas Gloe and Rainer Böhme. 2010. The Dresden image database for benchmarking digital image forensics. *Jour. of Digital Forensic Practice* (2010), 150–159.

[15] Owen Mayer and Matthew C Stamm. 2018. Learned forensic source similarity for unknown camera models. In *ICASSP, 2018 IEEE*. IEEE, 1–4.

[16] Maxime Oquab, Leon Bottou, Ivan Laptev, and Josef Sivic. 2014. Learning and transferring mid-level image representations using convolutional neural networks. In *Computer Vision and Pattern Recognition (CVPR)*. IEEE, 1717–1724.

[17] Otávio AB Penatti, Keiller Nogueira, and Jeferson A dos Santos. 2015. Do deep features generalize from everyday objects to remote sensing and aerial scenes domains?. In *Proceedings of the IEEE CVPR Workshops*. 44–51.

[18] Sebastian Ruder. 2017. An overview of multi-task learning in deep neural networks. *arXiv preprint arXiv:1706.05098* (2017).

[19] Ali Sharif Razavian, Hossein Azizpour, Josephine Sullivan, and Stefan Carlsson. 2014. CNN features off-the-shelf: an astounding baseline for recognition. In *IEEE Conference on Computer Vision and Pattern Recognition Workshops*. 806–813.

[20] Amel Tuama, Frédéric Comby, and Marc Chaumont. 2016. Camera model identification with the use of deep convolutional neural networks. In *Information Forensics and Security (WIFS), 2016 IEEE International Workshop on*. IEEE, 1–6.

[21] Bolei Zhou, Agata Lapedriza, Jianxiong Xiao, Antonio Torralba, and Aude Oliva. 2014. Learning deep features for scene recognition using places database. In *Advances in neural information processing systems*. 487–495.

Image Forgery Localization based on Multi-Scale Convolutional Neural Networks

Yaqi Liu
State Key Laboratory of Information Security, Institute of Information Engineering, Chinese Academy of Sciences, Beijing 100093, China
School of Cyber Security, University of Chinese Academy of Sciences, Beijing 100093, China
liuyaqi@iie.ac.cn

Qingxiao Guan
State Key Laboratory of Information Security, Institute of Information Engineering, Chinese Academy of Sciences, Beijing 100093, China
School of Cyber Security, University of Chinese Academy of Sciences, Beijing 100093, China
guanqingxiao@iie.ac.cn

Xianfeng Zhao*
State Key Laboratory of Information Security, Institute of Information Engineering, Chinese Academy of Sciences, Beijing 100093, China
School of Cyber Security, University of Chinese Academy of Sciences, Beijing 100093, China
zhaoxianfeng@iie.ac.cn

Yun Cao
State Key Laboratory of Information Security, Institute of Information Engineering, Chinese Academy of Sciences, Beijing 100093, China
School of Cyber Security, University of Chinese Academy of Sciences, Beijing 100093, China
caoyun@iie.ac.cn

ABSTRACT

In this paper, we propose to utilize Convolutional Neural Networks (CNNs) and the segmentation-based multi-scale analysis to locate tampered areas in digital images. First, to deal with color input sliding windows of different scales, we adopt a unified CNN architecture. Then, we elaborately design the training procedures of CNNs on sampled training patches. With a set of tampering detectors based on CNNs for different scales, a series of complementary tampering possibility maps can be generated. Last but not least, a segmentation-based method is proposed to fuse these maps and generate the final decision map. By exploiting the benefits of both the small-scale and large-scale analyses, the segmentation-based multi-scale analysis can lead to a performance leap in forgery localization of CNNs. Numerous experiments are conducted to demonstrate the effectiveness and efficiency of our method.

CCS CONCEPTS

• **Computing methodologies → Neural networks; Image processing;**

KEYWORDS

Image forensics, forgery localization, multi-scale analysis, Convolutional Neural Networks.

*Corresponding author.

IH&MMSec '18, June 20–22, 2018, Innsbruck, Austria
© 2018 Association for Computing Machinery.
ACM ISBN 978-1-4503-5625-1/18/06...$15.00
https://doi.org/10.1145/3206004.3206010

Figure 1: The framework of MSCNNs. Note that the sliding windows (blue, green, red squares) and superpixels do not indicate their real sizes.

ACM Reference Format:
Yaqi Liu, Qingxiao Guan, Xianfeng Zhao, and Yun Cao. 2018. Image Forgery Localization based on Multi-Scale Convolutional Neural Networks. In *IH& MMSec '18: 6th ACM Workshop on Information Hiding and Multimedia Security, June 20–22, 2018, Innsbruck, Austria.* ACM, New York, NY, USA, 6 pages. https://doi.org/10.1145/3206004.3206010

1 INTRODUCTION

Image forgery localization is one of the most challenging tasks in digital image forensics [18]. Different from forgery detection which simply discriminates whether a given image is pristine or fake, image forgery localization attempts to detect the accurate tampered areas [16]. Different clues are investigated to locate the tampered areas, e.g., the photo-response nonuniformity noise (PRNU) [5], the artifacts of color filter array [9], the near-duplicate image analysis [11], and copy-move forgery detection [7], etc. The tampering

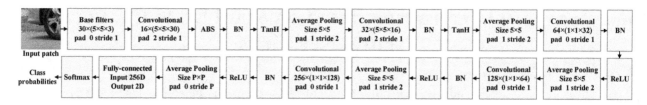

Figure 2: The architecture and parameters of the unified CNNs.

operations inevitably distort some inherent relationships among the adjacent pixels, features motivated by steganalysis [10] are frequently adopted to localize tampered areas [18]. In 2013, IEEE Information Forensics and Security Technical Committee (IFS-TC) established the First IFS-TC Image Forensics Challenge [13]. In the second phase, a complicated and practical situation for evaluating the performance of forgery localization was set up. The winner [6] and successors [11, 18] combined different clues to achieve high scores. As far as we know, the former best F1-score using a single clue from statistical features was achieved in [18] which was based on color rich models [12] and the ensemble classifier [14] (SCRM+LDA).

We focus on forgery localization utilizing statistical features extracted by Convolutional Neural Networks (CNNs) [17]. Booming in computer vision tasks, CNNs are also applied in image forensics. In [4], CNNs are applied in median filtering image forensics. In [2], a novel constrained convolutional layer is utilized to suppress the content of the image, and CNNs are adopted to detect multiple manipulations. In [20], a CNN with SRM kernels [10] for the first layer initialization is adopted for forgery detection. In [8], they show that residual-based descriptors can be regarded as a simple constrained CNN which can conduct forgery detection and localization. Numerous meaningful works have been done to improve the performance of image forensics by adopting CNNs, they try to construct different CNN architectures. While in computer vision tasks, typical CNNs are directly adopted for different purposes [19], and they mainly focus on the preprocessing and postprocessing. This kind of adoptions accelerate the development of many computer vision tasks. Thus, instead of designing a totally novel CNN, we adopt and modulate the state-of-the-art CNNs [21] to construct our framework for the task of image forgery localization. More powerful CNNs can also be adopted in the proposed framework in the future.

In this paper, an image forgery localization method based on Multi-Scale Convolutional Neural Networks (MSCNNs) is proposed, as shown in Figure 1. In our method, sliding windows of different scales are put into a set of CNNs to generate real-valued tampering possibility maps. Then, based on the graph constructed on superpixels [1], we can generate the final decision map by fusing those possibility maps. The contributions are two-fold: First, we propose to utilize multi-scale CNNs to detect forged regions. A unified CNN architecture is formulated for color patches, and multi-scale CNNs are treated as a set of "weak" classifiers to fully exploit the benefits of both the small-scale and large-scale analyses. Second, based on the fusion method in [16], the segmentation-based fusion method is proposed to efficiently process images of different sizes. Maps fusion based on conditional random fields is conducted on

the superpixel-level graph, and two strategies for superpixel-level tampering possibility maps generation are proposed and compared.

On the IFS-TC dataset, MSCNNs can achieve the best performance among the forgery localization methods which merely utilize one kind of clue for splicing detection. To the best of our knowledge, only three methods, i.e., the winner [6] and successors [11, 18], can achieve higher scores than MSCNNs, but they all combine multiple different clues. Especially, they all adopt copy-move forgery detection methods which are only effective for copy-move forgeries. MSCNNs only utilizes statistical features extracted by CNNs and can be further improved by adopting other clues, e.g. adopting copy-move forgery detection as [18]. Here, we focus on the statistical features extracted by CNNs which are effective on all kinds of splicing forgeries. Furthermore, to demonstrate the robustness of the proposed framework, we also conduct experiments on Realistic Tampering Dataset (RTD) [15, 16].

2 METHOD

2.1 CNNs Architecture

Our motivation is that we want to replace the SCRM+LDA [18] with the end-to-end CNNs to estimate the tampering probability of a given patch. Adopting the sliding window manner, we can give the tampering possibility map of the investigated image. The CNNs proposed in [21] achieve the state-of-the-art performance for steganalysis on gray-scale images. Considering the close relationship between image forensics and steganalysis, we adopt this kind of CNNs as the basic architecture in our work. In the first layer of their CNNs, a single high pass filter (we call it the base filter) is utilized to suppress the image content. In our work, to deal with color patches, two kinds of base filters are tested:

(1) Fixed SRM kernels: the base filters are fixed, and set as the SRM kernels [10]. In [20], 30 SRM kernels are adopted for the initialization of the first layer of their CNNs. We adopt all the SRM kernels as fixed base filters, and leave the task of validating their effectiveness to the backend network. Referring to [20], the 30 SRM kernels are formulated as 5×5 matrixes $\{F_1, \cdots F_{30}\}$ with zero-valued unused elements. The inputs are three-channel color patches, so we need 30×3 filters to generate 30 feature maps. For the jth feature map ($j \in \{1, 2, \cdots 30\}$), the corresponding filters are set as $\{F_1^j, F_2^j, F_3^j\} = \{F_{3k-2}, F_{3k-1}, F_{3k}\}$, where $k = ((j-1) \bmod 10) + 1$.

(2) Constrained filters: in [2], a kind of constrained filter was proposed for manipulation detection. Here, we adopt it for forgery localization. The constraint means that the filter weight at the center $f(0,0) = -1$, and $\sum_{r,c \neq 0} f(r,c) = 1$, $f(r,c)$ denotes the element in the base filter F. For fair comparisons, 90 5×5 constrained filters are adopted.

As we adopt 90 base filters, we modulate the parameters of CNNs in [21], and the unified CNN architecture can be depicted as Figure 2. For different scales of input patches, we only need to change P in the last average pooling layer, ensuring that the input of the fully-connected layer is a 256-dimensional vector. Based on the CNN depicted in Figure 2, we can train a set of CNN detectors with input patches of different scales. The detailed training procedures are introduced in Section 3.

2.2 Maps Generation

For each input image, it is analysed by the sliding window of the scale as $s \times s$ with a stride of st based on the CNN detectors described in Section 2.1. Then, we can get the tampering possibility map $\hat{\mathbf{M}}_s$ of size $h_s \times w_s$, where $h_s = \lfloor (h-s)/st \rfloor + 1$ and $w_s = \lfloor (w-s)/st \rfloor + 1$, h and w denote the height and width of the input image, and $\lfloor \cdot \rfloor$ denotes the floor function. The elements in $\hat{\mathbf{M}}_s$ denote the probabilities of the corresponding patches being fake. In order to get the possibility map $\mathbf{M}_s$ with the same size as the input image, the element $m_{i,j}^s$ in $\mathbf{M}_s$ is computed as:

$$m_{i,j}^s = \frac{1}{K} \sum_{k=1}^K \hat{m}_k^s \qquad (1)$$

where K is the number of patches containing pixel $I_{i,j}$, and $\hat{m}_k^s$ denotes the corresponding value in $\hat{\mathbf{M}}_s$. Inevitably, for some pixels, K is equal to 0, and the pixels always appear around the edges of the image. We simply set the same probabilities as the nearest pixels whose $K \neq 0$. Since we have a large stride st, there are mosaic artifacts in the possibility map generated by formula (1). Naturally, it is expected that the map for an image tends to be smoother [18]. To smooth the possibility map, the mean filtering is applied as:

$$\bar{m}_{i,j}^s = \frac{1}{s \times s} \sum_{i'=-\frac{s}{2}}^{\frac{s}{2}-1} \sum_{j'=-\frac{s}{2}}^{\frac{s}{2}-1} m_{i+i',j+j'}^s \qquad (2)$$

where s is the size of corresponding patches. Thus, we can get the smoothed possibility map $\bar{\mathbf{M}}_s$ with elements as $\bar{m}_{i,j}^s$.

2.3 Maps Fusion

With the analyses of multi-scale CNNs detectors, we can get a set of tampering possibility maps $\{\bar{\mathbf{M}}_s\}$ for each image, and s denotes the scales of input patches. The final task is to fuse possibility maps to exploit the benefits of multi-scale analyses. In [16], the multi-scale analysis in PRNU-based tampering localization was proposed. By minimizing an energy function, possibility maps fusion is formulated as a random-field problem where decision fusion resolves to finding an optimal labeling of authentication units. The optimization problem is solved by the graph cut algorithm whose worst case running time complexity is $O(ev^2)$ [3], where v is the number of nodes in the graph and e is the edge number. They consider a 2nd-order neighborhood, which means that $e \approx 4v$, so the complexity of the method is $O(v^3)$. They adopt pixels as the nodes in the graph, thus the computing time of the large image is almost unacceptable. So we propose to construct graphs on superpixels, and find the optimal labels on the superpixel level.

Simple linear iterative clustering (SLIC) [1] is a commonly used efficient superpixel segmentation method, and we adopt SLIC to conduct oversegmentation on the investigated color images. The

complexity of SLIC is linear, i.e. $O(v)$, and it is easy to generate superpixels by SLIC for large images. In the computer vision tasks, images are usually segmented into hundreds of superpixels. In the task of tampering possibility maps fusion, large superpixels can lead to information loss. Thus, thousands of superpixels must be generated in our task. Then, a graph on the superpixels is constructed, each superpixel is treated as a node in the graph and the adjacent superpixels are connected by an edge. The number of graph nodes is around several thousand, which is much easier to compute by the graph cut algorithm. Besides the efficiency of the superpixel-level computation, the segmentation-based method can also well adhere to the real boundaries, and avoid mislabeling of homogeneous pixels, resulting in the performance improvement.

As for the superpixel-level tampering possibility maps $\mathbf{M}_s^{sup}$ generation, two strategies are proposed and compared. The one is "mean", and the tampering possibility $m_{sup_l}^s$ of superpixel l under scale s is computed as:

$$m_{sup_l}^s = \frac{1}{P_l} \sum_{p=1}^{P_l} \bar{m}_p^s \qquad (3)$$

where P_l denotes the number of pixels in superpixel l, and $m_{sup_l}^s \in \mathbf{M}_s^{sup}$. $\bar{m}_p^s$ is the element in $\bar{\mathbf{M}}_s$. The other strategy called "maxa" is:

$$m_{sup_l}^s = \bar{m}_{p_0}^s, p_0 = \arg \max_{p=1,\cdots,P_l} (\mathrm{abs}(\bar{m}_p^s - \theta)) \qquad (4)$$

where $\bar{m}_p^s \in [0,1]$, so we set $\theta = 0.5$. With the superpixel-level graph and superpixel-level maps at hands, it is easy to fuse the maps by minimizing the energy function in [16]:

$$\frac{1}{S} \sum_{i=1}^N \sum_{\{s\}} E_\tau(c_i^{(s)}, t_i) + \alpha \sum_{i=1}^N t_i + \sum_{i=1}^N \sum_{j \in \Xi_i} \beta_{ij}|t_i - t_j| \qquad (5)$$

where S is the number of candidate possibility maps. In our method, N is the number of elements in $\mathbf{M}_s^{sup}$, $t_i = 1$ denotes tampered units, and $c_i^{(s)}$ denotes the element of the input candidate map with analysis windows of size s, i.e. $c_i^{(s)} = m_{sup_l}^s$. The three terms can penalize differences of different possibility maps, bias the decision towards the hypotheses and encode a preference towards piecewise-constant solutions. For space limitations, the detailed definitions and discussions of the terms are not provided here, readers can kindly refer to the seminal work [16] for details. In terms of the parameters in the energy function, we adopt the default settings of the codes provided by [16].

3 EXPERIMENTAL EVALUATION

Experiments are conducted on two publicly available datasets. In Section 3.1, we introduce the experimental results on the image corpus provided in the IFS-TC Image Forensics Challenge (IFS-TC) [13]. In Section 3.2, experiments are conducted on Realistic Tampering Dataset (RTD) [15, 16].

3.1 Experiments on IFS-TC

In the IFS-TC image dataset, there are two sets of images, i.e. 450 images in the training set with corresponding human-labeled ground truths, and 700 testing images without ground truths. The scores on the testing set have to be computed by the system provided by the IFS-TC challenge. Thus, in order to test the methods locally, we

Table 1: The numbers of patches on IFS-TC.

Patch size	32	48	64	96	128
sub-training set	275046	309690	325942	339396	341930
testing set-1	53938	61770	65704	68776	69044

randomly select 368 images for training and 75 images for testing (7 images are deserted for imperfect ground truths) from the training set of IFS-TC. For the sake of clarity, the image set of 368 images is called *sub-training set*, the image set of 75 images is called *testing set-1*, and the testing set of the IFS-TC dataset with 700 images is called *testing set-2*.

During the patches generation, we also adopt the sliding window manner. The sliding window with a fixed scale slides across the full image. We set the stride st as 8 to get plenty of sampled patches. In the training set, the tampered areas are marked as the ground truths, we can sample patches based on whether they contain tampered pixels. In [18], the patches tampered with 10% to 90% are regarded as fake patches for that discriminative features mostly appear around the contours of manipulated regions, we also adopt this strategy. The rates of the tampered areas in the full images differ greatly. In some images, more than ten thousand patches can be generated, while in some images, no patch can be generated. The imbalance of patches distribution can lead to overfitting, so we set an upper threshold T. While more than T patches are generated, we randomly select T patches, and we set $T = 500$ to make sure that we sample a similar number of patches on most images. With the sliding window sampling manner, no patch can be generated for some images. For those images, we resample patches which are centered at the tampered areas. If the tampered rates of patches are satisfied, the patches are selected. After the fake patches are generated, we sample the same number of pristine patches in the same images, and the pristine patches do not have any tampered pixels. The numbers of sampled patches are shown in Table 1. With 5 groups of sampled patches of scales as {32, 48, 64, 96, 128}, 5 independent CNNs can be trained, and all the CNNs models are trained on the *sub-training set*.

Our method is implemented via Caffe and Matlab. Minibatch gradient descent is adopted for training, the momentum is 0.99 and weight decay is 0.0005. The learning rate is initialized to 0.001 and scheduled to decrease 10% for every 8000 iterations. The convolution kernels are initialized by random numbers generated from zero-mean Gaussian distribution with standard deviation of 0.01, and bias learning is disabled. The parameters in the fully-connected layer are initialized using "Xavier". Note that the input patches for the CNNs should all subtract the mean values of each channel.

We summarize localization performance as an average F1-score [18]. As shown in Table 2, the comparisons between SCRM+LDA (codes provided by [12, 14]) and different variants of CNNs are conducted. "MF" denotes mean filtering, and it can certainly improve the F1-scores based on the experimental observation. The results in Figure 3 also corroborate that, and the main reason of the improvement achieved by MF smoothing is that the map for an image tends to be smoother without mosaic artifacts caused by sliding-window operations. The training procedure of SCRM+LDA takes too much time. Although we have a powerful CPU, it takes almost

Table 2: The comparisons on the IFS-TC *testing set-1*. Time-1 denotes the training time, and Time-2 denotes the average computing time.

Method	Size	Stride	Time-1 (s)	Time-2 (s)	F1-score
SCRM+LDA	64	16	3.20×10^5	2854.75	0.2847
SCRM+LDA+MF	64	16		2855.05	0.3123
CNN-SRM	64	8	3376.07	17.11	0.3263
CNN-SRM+MF	64	8		17.32	**0.3423**
CNN-SRM+MF	64	16	3376.07	8.38	0.3354
CNN-C-SRM+MF	64	8	3843.03	31.66	0.2816
CNN-C-GAU+MF	64	8	3849.09	31.71	0.2718

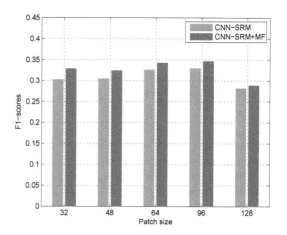

Figure 3: The F1-scores of CNNs with input patches of different sizes on IFS-TC *testing set-1*.

4 days. Furthermore, its average computing time on the images is also unacceptable. With the same patch size (64) and stride (16), the computing time of CNN is 1/340 of SCRM+LDA. CNN-SRM denotes the CNN with fixed SRM base filters, CNN-C-SRM denotes constrained filters (refer to Section 2.1) with SRM initialization and the base filters of CNN-C-GAU are constrained filters with Gaussian initialization. It can be seen that CNN-SRM can achieve higher F1-scores. We also compare the CNN-SRM models with different strides, as shown in Table 2, and the model with a small stride (8) can achieve better performance.

For the good performance of CNN-SRM, we adopt this form of CNN for multi-scale analyses, and the stride is set as 8. As shown in Figure 3, CNNs with scales as 64 and 96 can achieve higher scores. While in Figure 4, the multi-scale analysis can improve the performance significantly. As an alternative, we also conduct maps fusion on the resized pixel-level maps directly. Let w and h denote the width and height of the maps, if $w > 2000$ and $h > 2000$, the map is reduced to 1/10 of the original map; if $w < 1000$ and $h < 1000$, the map is reduced to 1/2; otherwise, it is reduced to 1/4. We call this method as "MSCNN-resize". "mean" and "maxa" represent the two strategies for superpixel-level tampering possibility maps generation. It can be seen that MSCNNs can achieve higher scores with more scales, and MSCNNs-maxa can achieve higher scores than MSCNNs-resize and MSCNNs-mean. In MSCNNs-maxa and

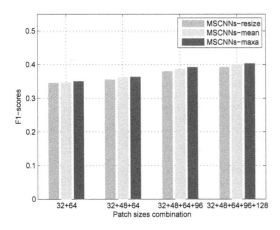

Figure 4: The F1-scores of MSCNNs with different combinations on IFS-TC *testing set-1*.

Table 3: Results on the IFS-TC *testing set-2*.

Method	F1-score	Variant	F1-score
S3+SVM [6]	0.1115	CNN-SRM32MF	0.3436
S3+LDA [18]	0.1737	CNN-SRM48MF	0.3526
PRNU [11]	0.2535	CNN-SRM64MF	0.3570
SCRM+LDA [18]	0.3458	CNN-SRM96MF	0.3423
		CNN-SRM128MF	0.3135
		MSCNNs-resize	0.4014
		MSCNNs-mean	0.4025
		MSCNNs-maxa	**0.4063**

MSCNNs-mean, all the images are empirically segmented into 4000 superpixels, and adaptive segmentation strategies for maps fusion need further research in the future.

Subsequently, we adopt five single-scale CNNs and the 5-scale MSCNNs to test on the *testing set-2*. As shown in Table 3, the right side presents the results of different variants of our method, and the left side presents results of the state-of-the-art methods for splicing detection. In another word, the compared methods are not designed for some particular cases, e.g. copy-move forgery detection, and can be utilized to detect any splicing forgeries (refer to [18]). Their results are borrowed from their papers [6, 11, 18]. SCRM+LDA adopts the sliding window manner with the scale of 64, and our CNN with $s = 64$ can achieve better performance than SCRM+LDA. Multi-scale analyses can greatly improve the performance of CNNs, and MSCNNs-maxa can achieve a similar F1-score as the winner of IFS-TC challenge [6] (0.4063 vs. 0.4072). The winner utilizes three different clues, while MSCNNs-maxa only utilizes statistical features extracted by CNNs and can be further improved by combining other clues, e.g., we can adopt copy-move clues as [18] in which SCRM+LDA and copy-move forgery detection are combined.

We evaluate the computing time on the *testing set-2* in which the sizes of images vary from 922×691 to 4752×3168 (most images are around 1024×768). Experiments are conducted on a machine with Intel(R) Core(TM) i7-5930K CPU @ 3.50GHz, 64GB RAM and

Table 4: Computing time on IFS-TC *testing set-2*.

		32	48	64	96	128
CNNs	Average time (s)	15.47	15.10	17.74	19.21	19.56
	Median time (s)	7.96	7.67	8.89	9.33	9.20
MF	Average time (s)	0.08	0.13	0.19	0.37	0.63
	Median time (s)	0.04	0.07	0.11	0.20	0.35
	multi-scales fusion: SLIC + CRF					
Fusion	Average time (s)	20.88 (5-scales: 32+48+64+96+128)				
	Median time (s)	11.75 (5-scales: 32+48+64+96+128)				

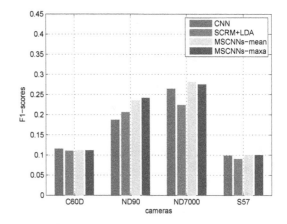

Figure 5: The F1-scores on RTD *testing set*. All the models are trained on the *sub-training set* of IFS-TC.

a single GPU (TITAN X). As shown in Table 4, the computing time of 5-scales MSCNNs is around 60 s for most images. The MF and Fusion (including SLIC) procedures are implemented on CPU which can be further accelerated by implementing on GPU.

3.2 Experiments on RTD

The RTD dataset contains 220 realistic forgeries created by hand and covers various challenging tampering scenarios involving both object insertion and removal. The images were captured by four different cameras: Canon 60D (C60D), Nikon D90 (ND90), Nikon D7000 (ND7000), Sony α57 (S57). All images are 1920×1080 px RGB uint8 bitmaps stored in the TIFF format [15, 16]. Each kind of camera contains 55 images, and we randomly select 27 as the *training set*, and the left 28 images compose the *testing set*. In another words, there are 108 images in the *training set* and 112 images in the *testing set*. We adopt the same manner to sample patches on RTD, readers can refer to Section 3.1 for details.

Firstly, we adopt the models trained on the *sub-training set* of IFS-TC to test on the RTD *testing set*. The CNN is the model based on CNN-SRM and mean filtering, and the results of SCRM+LDA are also processed by mean filtering. The size of the sliding window is 64×64, and the stride is set as 16 for fair comparison. The models based on MSCNNs are the 5-scale models as above mentioned. As shown in Figure 5, the performance of all the models decline than the performance on IFS-TC. It proves that both CNN and SCRM+LDA tend to be sensitive to the training sets for that the

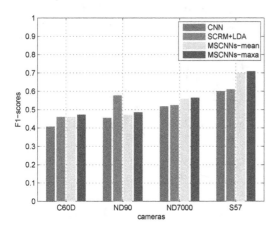

Figure 6: The F1-scores on RTD *testing set*. All the models are trained on the *training set* of RTD.

images may be captured from different cameras and the quality of manipulations may be different. In a different dataset, MSCNNs can still achieve better performance.

Then, models trained on the RTD *training set* are compared. As shown in Figure 6, it can be seen that the performance of CNN is worse than SCRM+LDA. However, with the help of multi-scale analyses, MSCNNs can achieve better performance than SCRM+LDA except for results on ND90. Furthermore, the CNN and MSCNNs are very efficient, the average computing time of CNN is 6.58 s, and the computing time of MSCNNs is 34.62 s (5 CNNs on GPU) +30.36 s (the fusion procedure on CPU), while SCRM+LDA takes 2220.45 s per image. Thus, MSCNNs is a better alternative of SCRM+LDA in the image forgery localization tasks.

4 CONCLUSIONS

In this paper, a novel forgery localization method based on Multi-Scale Convolutional Neural Networks is proposed. CNNs for color patches of different scales are well designed and trained as a set of forgery detectors. Then, segmentation-based multi-scale analysis is utilized to dig out the information given by the different-scale analyses. Full experiments on the publicly available datasets demonstrate the effectiveness and efficiency of the proposed method named MSCNNs. Although the proposed method can achieve the state-of-the-art performance, it still has a long way to go for real applications. The robustness of existing works against post compression, manipulation qualities and camera models still needs to be further studied. In the future, MSCNNs can also be improved by adopting more powerful CNNs.

ACKNOWLEDGMENTS

This work was supported by National Key Technology R&D Program under 2016YFB0801003, NSFC under U1636102, U1736214 and U1536105, Fundamental Theory and Cutting Edge Technology Research Program of IIE, CAS, under Y7Z0371102, and National Key Technology R&D Program under 2016QY15Z2500.

REFERENCES

[1] Radhakrishna Achanta, Appu Shaji, Kevin Smith, Aurelien Lucchi, Pascal Fua, and Sabine Süsstrunk. 2012. SLIC superpixels compared to state-of-the-art superpixel methods. *IEEE transactions on pattern analysis and machine intelligence* 34, 11 (2012), 2274–2282.

[2] Belhassen Bayar and Matthew C Stamm. 2016. A deep learning approach to universal image manipulation detection using a new convolutional layer. In *The 4th ACM Workshop on Information Hiding and Multimedia Security*. ACM, 5–10.

[3] Yuri Boykov and Vladimir Kolmogorov. 2004. An experimental comparison of min-cut/max-flow algorithms for energy minimization in vision. *IEEE transactions on pattern analysis and machine intelligence* 26, 9 (2004), 1124–1137.

[4] Jiansheng Chen, Xiangui Kang, Ye Liu, and Z Jane Wang. 2015. Median filtering forensics based on convolutional neural networks. *IEEE Signal Processing Letters* 22, 11 (2015), 1849–1853.

[5] Mo Chen, Jessica Fridrich, Miroslav Goljan, and Jan Lukás. 2008. Determining image origin and integrity using sensor noise. *IEEE Transactions on Information Forensics and Security* 3, 1 (2008), 74–90.

[6] Davide Cozzolino, Diego Gragnaniello, and Luisa Verdoliva. 2014. Image forgery localization through the fusion of camera-based, feature-based and pixel-based techniques. In *IEEE International Conference on Image Processing (ICIP)*. IEEE, 5302–5306.

[7] Davide Cozzolino, Giovanni Poggi, and Luisa Verdoliva. 2015. Efficient dense-field copy–move forgery detection. *IEEE Transactions on Information Forensics and Security* 10, 11 (2015), 2284–2297.

[8] Davide Cozzolino, Giovanni Poggi, and Luisa Verdoliva. 2017. Recasting residual-based local descriptors as convolutional neural networks: an application to image forgery detection. In *The 5th ACM Workshop on Information Hiding and Multimedia Security*. ACM, 159–164.

[9] Pasquale Ferrara, Tiziano Bianchi, Alessia De Rosa, and Alessandro Piva. 2012. Image forgery localization via fine-grained analysis of CFA artifacts. *IEEE Transactions on Information Forensics and Security* 7, 5 (2012), 1566–1577.

[10] Jessica Fridrich and Jan Kodovsky. 2012. Rich models for steganalysis of digital images. *IEEE Transactions on Information Forensics and Security* 7, 3 (2012), 868–882.

[11] Lorenzo Gaborini, Paolo Bestagini, Simone Milani, Marco Tagliasacchi, and Stefano Tubaro. 2014. Multi-clue image tampering localization. In *IEEE International Workshop on Information Forensics and Security (WIFS)*. IEEE, 125–130.

[12] Miroslav Goljan, Jessica Fridrich, and Rémi Cogranne. 2014. Rich model for steganalysis of color images. In *IEEE International Workshop on Information Forensics and Security (WIFS)*. IEEE, 185–190.

[13] IFS-TC. 2013. The 1st IEEE IFS-TC Image Forensics Challenge. http://ifc.recod.ic.unicamp.br/fc.website/index.py. (2013).

[14] Jan Kodovsky, Jessica Fridrich, and Vojtěch Holub. 2012. Ensemble classifiers for steganalysis of digital media. *IEEE Transactions on Information Forensics and Security* 7, 2 (2012), 432–444.

[15] Paweł Korus and Jiwu Huang. 2016. Evaluation of Random Field Models in Multi-modal Unsupervised Tampering Localization. In *Proc. of IEEE Int. Workshop on Inf. Forensics and Security*.

[16] Paweł Korus and Jiwu Huang. 2017. Multi-scale analysis strategies in PRNU-based tampering localization. *IEEE Transactions on Information Forensics and Security* 12, 4 (2017), 809–824.

[17] Alex Krizhevsky, Ilya Sutskever, and Geoffrey E Hinton. 2012. Imagenet classification with deep convolutional neural networks. In *Advances in neural information processing systems*. 1097–1105.

[18] Haodong Li, Weiqi Luo, Xiaoqing Qiu, and Jiwu Huang. 2017. Image Forgery Localization via Integrating Tampering Possibility Maps. *IEEE Transactions on Information Forensics and Security* 12, 5 (2017), 1240–1252.

[19] Yaqi Liu, Xiaoyu Zhang, Xiaobin Zhu, Qingxiao Guan, and Xianfeng Zhao. 2017. Listnet-based object proposals ranking. *Neurocomputing* 267 (2017), 182–194.

[20] Yuan Rao and Jiangqun Ni. 2016. A deep learning approach to detection of splicing and copy-move forgeries in images. In *IEEE International Workshop on Information Forensics and Security (WIFS)*. IEEE, 1–6.

[21] Guanshuo Xu, Han-Zhou Wu, and Yun-Qing Shi. 2016. Structural design of convolutional neural networks for steganalysis. *IEEE Signal Processing Letters* 23, 5 (2016), 708–712.

Densely Connected Convolutional Neural Network for Multi-purpose Image Forensics under Anti-forensic Attacks

Yifang Chen
Sun Yat-sen University
School of Electronics and Information Technology
Guangzhou, China
chenyf79@mail2.sysu.edu.cn

Xiangui Kang
Guangdong Key Laboratory of Information
Security Technology, SunYat-sen University
Guangzhou, China
isskxg@mail.sysu.edu.cn

Z. Jane Wang
University of British Colombia
Department of ECE
Vancouver, Canada
zjanew@ece.ubc.ca

Qiong Zhang
Sun Yat-sen University
School of Data and Computer Science
Guangzhou, China
zhangq39@mail.sysu.edu.cn

ACM Reference Format:
Yifang Chen, Xiangui Kang, Z. Jane Wang, and Qiong Zhang. 2018. Densely Connected Convolutional Neural Network for Multi-purpose Image Forensics under Anti-forensic Attacks. In Proceedings of 6th ACM Information Hiding and Multimedia Security Workshop (IH&MMSec'18). ACM, NY, NY, USA, 6 pages. https://doi.org/10.1145/3206004.3206012

ABSTRACT

Multiple-purpose forensics has been attracting increasing attention worldwide. However, most of the existing methods based on hand-crafted features often require domain knowledge and expensive human labour and their performances can be affected by factors such as image size and JPEG compression. Furthermore, many anti-forensic techniques have been applied in practice, making image authentication more difficult. Therefore, it is of great importance to develop methods that can automatically learn general and robust features for image operation detectors with the capability of countering anti-forensics. In this paper, we propose a new convolutional neural network (CNN) approach for multi-purpose detection of image manipulations under anti-forensic attacks. The dense connectivity pattern, which has better parameter efficiency than the traditional pattern, is explored to strengthen the propagation of general features related to image manipulation detection. When compared with three state-of-the-art methods, experiments demonstrate that the proposed CNN architecture can achieve a better performance (i.e., with a 11% improvement in terms of detection accuracy under anti-forensic attacks). The proposed method can also achieve better robustness against JPEG compression with maximum improvement of 13% on accuracy under low-quality JPEG compression.

KEYWORDS

Image forensics, anti-forensic attack, convolutional neural network, dense connectivity

1 INTRODUCTION

With the widespread use of low cost and powerful multimedia processing editing software, e.g., Adobe Photoshop, ACDsee and Hornil Stylepix, people can modify a digital image without leaving any perceptible artifact. During the past decade, multimedia forensics has been an active research area and a number of blind forensic techniques have been proposed for detecting image processing operations such as contrast enhancement [1, 2], sharpening filtering [3], median filtering [4], [5], resampling [6], and compression [7, 8], etc.

Since classic forensic methods mainly aim at deploying only one specific operation, which limits their applicability in practice, several multi-purpose forensic methods have been proposed in [9–12] on the basis of hand-crafted features. However, constructing hand-crafted features for the detection of multiple operations is labor expensive and the performance is severely affected by the size of the investigated image and the operation of JPEG compression. With the development of anti-forensics, farsighted forgers attempt to identify weaknesses of image forensics and fool the forensic investigators by using anti-forensic techniques [13–20] to remove or hide traces left by certain image processing operations. Nevertheless, most existing forensic methods which work on manual extraction of features related to the traces left by image operations may be ineffective to identify the altered image post-processed by anti-forensic operations. Therefore, it is desirable to develop a forensic approach that can automatically learn effective and robust features, for the detection of image processing operations of both with and without anti-forensic attacks.

In recent years, deep neural networks, such as Convolutional Neural Networks (CNNs), have witnessed huge successes in image

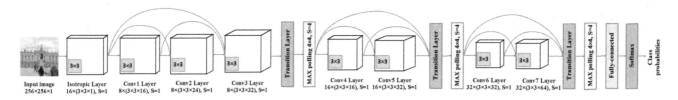

Fig. 1: Illustration of the proposed densely connected CNN architecture.

recognition due to their competence to learn features adaptively and attain classification automatically [21, 22]. There have been a growing number of approaches using CNN as the fundamental architecture for blind image forensics [23–30]. Generally, these methods aim at only one or several certain operations and take no account of anti-forensic attacks. Moreover, in response to the increasing number of CNN layers, the optimization of huge parameters needs a large amount of data. While in practice, it is always expensive to obtain such a large number of labeled samples for forensic purposes, which might lead to over-fitting inevitably. Obviously, developing CNN models for forensic tasks with a limited amount of training data is of great interest.

In this work, we propose a novel CNN-based method for the detection of image operations. The major contributions are as follows: 1). To our knowledge, it is the first attempt made to conduct multi-purpose detection of image manipulations under anti-forensic attacks, a more practical scenario. The proposed method has shown excellent performances on countering anti-forensics. 2). Different from the existing CNN architectures which have the preprocessing layer for residual extraction, the convolutional layer with the isotropic mask in [31] is introduced to adaptively learn rotation-invariant features for image manipulation detection. Thus it is more flexible to optimize the feature extraction using our method. 3). Motivated by DenseNet [32, 33], all layers with matched feature map size are directly connected with each other. This dense connectivity alleviates the vanishing gradient problem, strengthens the feature propagation especially for rotation-invariant features, and substantially reduces the number of CNN parameters.

The proposed CNN shows competence of learning strong forensic features automatically and can serve as a universal image operation detector with the capability of countering anti-forensics. The proposed method significantly outperforms the best traditional method, which is based on hand-crafted features [12], and two other related CNN-based methods [27, 28] for image forensics. We also demonstrate its robustness against JPEG compression with different quality factors.

The rest of this paper is organized as follows. Section 2 describes the structure of the proposed network. The experimental results, comparisons and analysis are included in Section 3. Finally, the concluding remarks are drawn in Section 4.

2 THE PROPOSED CNN MODEL

In this section, the overall architecture of the proposed CNN is introduced first. Then, key points in the CNN design for improved statistical modeling (e.g., dense connectivity) are described in detail.

2.1 Overall Architecture

Fig. 1 illustrates the general structure of the proposed densely connected CNN. The net contains 8 layer groups, where the first group is the isotropic convolutional layer, and the second to the eighth groups are regular convolutional layers. Besides, it has 3 transitional layers, 3 max-pooling layers and 1 fully-connected layer.

Each layer group in this network processes feature maps outputted by the previous layer in three steps: convolution, batch normalization, and rectified linear units (ReLU). We observe that using ReLU instead of TanH can yield an average improvement of 3.9%. This could be attributed to the acceleration of SGD (stochastic gradient descent) convergence of ReLU. As shown in Fig. 1, layer groups with the same size of feature maps are densely connected. As for the spatial size of convolution kernels, CNN works by modeling relationships (through convolutions) of the elements in a small local region over the whole image. We adopt 3 × 3 receptive field throughout the whole architecture. The pooling layers which facilitate down-sampling and change the size of feature maps divide the network into three dense blocks. Regarding the type of pooling layers, here we empirically choose the max pooling. Based on our experiments, the 4 × 4 max-pooling layer with a stride of 4 can reduce the error rate by around 1.1% when compared with the 4 × 4 average-pooling layer. The transition layers with 1×1 convolutions are designed to reduce the number of input feature maps and thus improve the computational efficiency.

2.2 The Proposed Isotropic Convolutional Layer

It is noteworthy that image manipulations might have the attribute of directional invariance, which can be used to learn robust and general features for detection. Filters of the convolutional layer allowing feature evolution freely into any form tend to extract some features irrelevant to the detection of image operations (e.g. the content-dependent features) [30]. Therefore, we introduce the convolutional layer with the isotropic mask in [31]. $w(i, j)$ represents the weight of a $N \times N (N > 1)$ filter at i^{th} row and j^{th} column. With the center $w(\lceil \frac{N}{2} \rceil, \lceil \frac{N}{2} \rceil)$, all the other values of $w(i, j)$ are both center symmetrical and mirror symmetrical.

The weights of a 5 × 5 isotropic filter are shown in Fig. 2, where the objects with the same shape indicate the weights with the same

Fig. 2: The weight distribution of a 5×5 isotropic filter.

value. In implementation, during each iteration, all the weights are updated based on the stochastic gradients in back-propagation, and all the average values of the weights in symmetric positions, with the same shapes as shown in Fig. 2, are calculated respectively. The isotropic constraints are enforced via assigning these average values to the corresponding weights.

No matter rotated by any multiple of 90 degrees, the filters perform the same operations on images, thereby serve as the extractors that remove anisotropic structures which usually exist in natural images but are unrelated to manipulation detection and that highlight the features that are of interest to the forensic analysis. Furthermore, the amount of CNN parameters can be significantly reduced. Take a 3 × 3 filter for instance, there are only 3 parameters in the isotropic filter which is only a third of the original one. As a result, the proposed CNN model with low complexity can be learned to extract robust and general forensic features.

2.3 Dense Connectivity

As CNN becomes increasingly deep, information extracted in preceding layers or gradients which pass by many layers may vanish by the time it reaches deeper layers. To tackle this issue, the dense connectivity pattern [32] is introduced to directly connect two adjacent layers with the same feature map size. The lth layer receives the feature maps from all preceding layers, $x_0, \cdots, x_{l-1}$, as the input:

$$x_l = H_l([x_0, x_1, \ldots, x_{l-1}]) \tag{1}$$

where $[x_0, x_1, \ldots, x_{l-1}]$ refers to the concatenation of the feature maps produced in layers $0, \cdots, l$-1. $H_l(\cdot)$ is a composite function of operations including Batch Normalization (BN), rectified linear units (ReLU) and Convolution (Conv).

Compared with L-layer traditional convolutional neural networks with L connections, the dense connectivity introduces $\frac{L(L+1)}{2}$ connections without relearning redundant feature maps. Thus, the dense pattern has better parameter efficiency than the traditional pattern in convolutional networks. Instead of drawing representational power from extremely deep or wide architectures, dense connectivity exploits the potential of the network through feature reuse. Concatenating feature maps learned by different layers increases variations in the input of subsequent layers and ensure maximum information flow between layers in the network. The advantage is more obvious in our architecture, because some general features (e.g., rotation-invariant features) which are only extracted in the preceding layers can be shared in the deeper layers. In addition, the gradients can flow directly through the identity function from the later layers to earlier layers and lead to an implicit deep supervision [32], which alleviates the vanishing-gradient problem and makes the network easy to be trained.

3 RESULTS AND DISCUSSION

In this section, experiments are carried out to demonstrate the effectiveness of the proposed CNN model. We compare it with state-of-the-art methods, including the method based on hand-crafted features [12] and two CNN related methods [27, 28] for multi-purpose forensics.

3.1 Experimental Setup

The primary database used in this study is a mixed image dataset which includes two public image databases: the BossBase V1.01 database and the BOW database, each containing 10,000 gray-scale images. All images are cropped from the center to size of 256 × 256 to construct original image set. We create five altered image sets via

Table 1: Five common image processing operations, with the parameters used in the experiments.

Altered image set	Operation type	Parameters
1 (UM_all)	Unsharp masking sharpening (UMS)	σ: 1 − 1.5, λ: 1 − 1.5
	Anti-UMS [13]	Removing overshoot artifacts in image edges and abrupt change in histogram ends with the same parameter setup in [13].
2 (GC_all)	Gamma correction (GC)	γ: 0.5, 0.6, 0.7
	Anti-GC [14]	Gaussian noise with σ=1 is introduced.
	Anti-GC [15]	Adding with noise of uniform distribution in (-0.5, 0.5).
3 (MF_all)	Median filtering (MF)	Window size: $3 \times 3, 5 \times 5, 7 \times 7$
	Anti- MF [16]	Adding with noise disturbance with the same parameter setup in [16].
	Anti- MF [17]	Adding with random noises with the same parameter setup in [17].
4 (RES_all)	Resampling (RES)	Random scaling factors: 0.6 − 2
	Anti- RES [18]	Setting the strength of distortion σ = 0.4.
5 (JPEG_all)	JPEG compression (JPEG)	Quality factor: 55 − 95
	Anti- JPEG [19]	The original images are JPEG compressed as above, then dither is added in the DCT coefficients.
	Anti- JPEG [20]	The original images are JPEG compressed as above, then modified with corresponding anti-forensic method [20].

Note: *_all is referred to the altered image set which contains altered images partially from one normal modification and partially from its corresponding anti-forensic magnification(s).

Table 2: Confusion matrix (%) for classifying multi-class operations. Here the image size is 256×256.

Test / Operation	Origin	UMS_all	GC_all	MF_all	RES_all	JPEG_all
Origin	93.70	*	4.12	*	1.52	*
UMS_all	*	98.98	*	0	*	*
GC_all	2.16	*	95.82	0	1.14	*
MF_all	*	0	*	99.64	*	*
RES_all	*	*	*	*	98.62	*
JPEG_all	*	*	*	*	*	99.52
					Average:	97.71

Table 3: Average accuracy results (%) for classifying multi-class operations from different methods. Here the different image sizes are investigated.

Method / Size	32×32	64×64	128×128	256×256
Li's method [12]	78.45	87.18	92.24	95.73
Bayar's method [27]	68.93	82.13	90.54	92.03
Yu's method [28]	78.76	88.16	93.05	95.75
Proposed method	**79.89**	**90.41**	**94.91**	**97.71**

the common image processing operations with random parameters and corresponding typical anti-forensic manipulations shown in Table 1. For each processing operation with one (or two) anti-forensic methods, one half (or one third) of randomly selected original images are normally modified and the rest are anti-forensically modified. The number of each altered set is 20,000. There are 120,000 images (20,000 pairs) in total including 20,000 original images and 100,000 images for five altered sets. In each experiment, 78,000 images (13,000 pairs) are randomly selected for training, 12,000 images (2,000 pairs) are randomly selected for validation, and the remaining 30,000 images (5,000 pairs) are used for testing. Only the training pairs contribute to updating the weights, and the validation pairs are used to determine the best CNN model.

All of the experiments using the CNN reported in this study are performed using a modified version of the Caffe toolbox on Nvidia Tesla K80 GPUs. Mini-batch stochastic gradient descent is used to solve all the CNNs in experiments. The momentum is fixed to 0.9. The learning rate is initialized to 0.001, and scheduled to decrease by 10% for every 5000 training iterations. Parameters in the convolution kernels are randomly initialized by zero-mean Gaussian distribution with a standard deviation of 0.01; bias learnings are disabled in convolutional layers and fulfilled in the BN layers. Parameters of layers are initialized using Xavier initialization. There are 10,000 training iterations in total. The input for each iteration is filled by a mini-batch of 32 images. The training set is randomly shuffled for each epoch of training.

3.2 Comparison with Different Variants

In order to investigate the influence of different components in the proposed CNN architecture, we propose different variants based on the proposed CNN and evaluate their performances for the detection of different image sizes and sources. Here we use smaller images which are cropped from the center to size of 128 × 128, 64 × 64 and 32 × 32 respectively. Except the testing images from the mixed database (BossBase-and-BOW database), images from UCID Database are also used to test the performance. There are three variants considered: Variant 1: Replace the isotropic convolutional layer with the constrained convolutional layer in [27]; Variant 2: Replace the isotropic convolutional layer with regular convolutional layer; Variant 3: Remove all the dense connectivity; Variant 4: Replace the isotropic convolutional layer with the convolutional layer and remove all dense connectivity.

The testing accuracy of different variants is shown in Fig. 3. It can be seen that the isotropic convolutional layer and the dense connectivity both help improve the detection accuracy, especially for images with smaller size. Comparing Variant 1 and Variant 2 with our proposed approach, all of them show good performance when testing on the mixed database which is from the same image source as the training database. However, our proposed approach achieves the highest accuracies than Variant 1 and Variant 2 when testing on UCID database. Therefore, using the isotropic layer in densely connected network brings more improvement of overall performance for different databases than regular convolutional layer and the constrained convolutional layer in [27].

3.3 Performance of the Proposed Scheme

In this experiment, we try to identify all types of altered operations used for a questionable image no matter whether it is normally modified or anti-forensically modified. The classification results for multiple image-altered operations are shown as confusion matrix in Table 2. The satisfactory results (more than 93%) are obtained for all altered operations and the average detection accuracy achieves 97.71%. It is also observed that the proposed method performs almost perfectly for the detection of median filtering (MF) and JPEG.

Table 4: Average classification accuracies (%) of different methods for images from different sources. Here the different image sizes are investigated.

Method / Size	32×32	64×64	128×128	256×256
Li's method [12]	70.68	81.76	86.67	89.81
Bayar's method [27]	62.75	75.79	83.08	84.83
Yu's method [28]	75.09	83.93	89.86	91.98
Proposed method	**76.33**	**86.73**	**92.05**	**93.70**

Table 5: Average classification accuracies (%) for different JPEG compression quality factors (QFs). Here the image size is 256×256.

Method / QF	N/A	JPEG(90)	JPEG(75)
Li's method [12]	95.73	81.26	70.02
Bayar 's method [27]	92.03	85.77	75.34
Yu's method [28]	95.75	87.60	77.60
Proposed method	**97.71**	**91.13**	**83.23**

We also compare the proposed method with state-of-the-art methods, including the method based on hand-crafted features [12] (which is referred to Li's method) and two other related CNN based methods [27, 28] (which are referred to Bayar's method and Yu's method respectively). For a fair comparison, the experimental conditions are the same, e.g., the same training iterations. Image operations may be practically applied on a small image patch, where we also conduct the detection tasks. The average accuracies of multiple image-altered operations on different sizes of images are shown in Table 3. It can be observed that the proposed method achieves the best performance for all detection cases. Compared with Li's method [12], the proposed CNN approach improves the accuracies by around 1%~3%, meaning that the automatically learned CNN features can work better than hand-crafted feature sets. There are significant improvements of 4%~11% when compared with Bayar's method [27], meaning the densely connected rotation-invariant features are more effective for detections under anti-forensic attacks than the constrained convolutional features in [27]. Furthermore, the number of parameters in our network is about 1200, which is only a seventh of the Bayar's method. The improvements of average accuracies are 1%~2% when compared with Yu's method [28] which is also a CNN without the preprocessing layer, and the accuracy boost may attribute to the architecture with isotropic convolutional layer and dense connectivity.

3.4 Generalization Performance and Robustness

To illustrate the better overall performance of our proposed CNN, after all CNN models have been trained on the mixed database as mentioned in Section 3.1, we test all trained models on the benchmark UCID database, which consists of a total of 1,338 gray-scale images. Table 4 shows the accuracy results of different methods in detecting images from different sources with different sizes. It is obvious that our proposed CNN model still achieves the highest accuracies than the other methods despite the discrepancy of databases for all detection cases.

The robustness against JPEG compression is evaluated on images from the mixed database with size of 256×256. We first conduct image compression with two quality factors (QF), 90 and 75, respectively, and then perform training and testing as mentioned in Section 3.1. The test results of our proposed CNN and other three

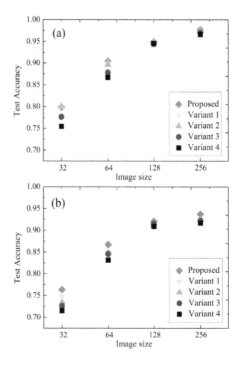

Fig. 3: Performance comparison of the proposed method and the variants for testing (a) the mixed database; and (b) UCID.

methods are reported in Table 5. It is observed that the detection performance of any of the four methods degrades after JPEG compression, and the method based on hand-crafted features (Li's method [12]) suffers the most severe decline. The accuracies of Li's method [12] decrease by 14.47% and 25.17% for QF=90 and QF=75 respectively, because the hand-crafted features are significantly affected by compression. Compared with three state-of-the-art methods, the accuracies of our proposed method are improved by around 4%~10% and 6%~13% respectively after the compression with QF=90 and QF=75. This demonstrates the robustness of the densely connected convolutional features against post-processing even under low-quality JPEG compression.

4 CONCLUSION

In this paper, we propose a novel CNN-based method for image operation detections under anti-forensic attacks. The convolutional layers with isotropic mask are designed as the first layer to automatically learn rotation-invariant features related to image manipulations detection. The dense connectivity pattern is introduced to strengthen propagation of some general features (e.g., rotation-invariant features) without relearning redundant feature maps, which helps boost the detection accuracy even under anti-forensic attacks. The state-of-the-art methods for forensic applications are used for comparisons. The proposed CNN architecture can achieve higher accuracy on mixed databases (BossBase-and-BOW database) for detecting five operations under anti-forensic attacks, and the improvement of detection accuracy can be up to about 11%. It also shows better performances on the UCID database and improved robustness against JPEG compression. In the future, we plan to extend the proposed approach for the detection of more image manipulations under anti-forensic attacks.

REFERENCES

[1] M. C. Stamm and K. J. R. Liu. 2010. Forensic estimation and reconstruction of a contrast enhancement mapping. In *Proceedings of IEEE International Conference on Acoustics, Speech and Signal Processing (ICASSP)*. Texas, USA, (2010), 1698–1701.

[2] G. Cao, Y. Zhao, and R. Ni. 2010. Forensic estimation of gamma correction in digital images. In *Proceeding of 17th IEEE Int. Conf. Image Process*. Hong Kong, (2010), 2097–2100.

[3] G. Cao, Y. Zhao, R. Ni, and A. C. Kot. 2011. Unsharp masking sharpening detection via overshoot artifacts analysis. *IEEE Signal Process. Lett* 18, 10 (2011), 603–606.

[4] H.-D. Yuan. 2011. Blind forensics of median filtering in digital images. *IEEE Trans. Information Forensics and Security* 6, 4 (2011), 1335–1345.

[5] X. Kang, M. C. Stamm, A. Peng, and K. Liu. 2012. Robust median filtering forensics based on the autoregressive model of median filtered residual. In *Proceeding of Asia-Pacific Signal and Information Processing Association Annual Summit and Conference (APSIPA)*. CA, USA, (2012), 1–9.

[6] B. Mahdian and S. Saic. 2008. Blind authentication using periodic properties of interpolation. *IEEE Trans. Information Forensics and Security* 3, 3 (2008), 529–538.

[7] W. Luo, J. Huang, and G. Qiu. 2010. JPEG error analysis and its applications to digital image forensics. *IEEE Trans. Information Forensics and Security* 5, 3 (2010), 480–491.

[8] T. Bianchi and A. Piva. 2012. Detection of nonaligned double JPEG compression based on integer periodicity maps. *IEEE Trans. Information Forensics and Security* 7, 2 (2012), 842–848.

[9] H. Zeng, X. Kang, A. Peng. 2016. A multi-purpose countermeasure against image anti-forensics using autoregressive model. *Neurocomputing* 189, (2016), 117–122.

[10] X. Qiu, H. Li, W. Luo, J. Huang. 2014. A universal image forensic strategy based on steganalytic model. In *Proceedings of ACM Workshop on Information Hiding and Multimedia Security (IH&MMSec)*. Salzburg, Austria, (2014), 165–170.

[11] W. Fan, K. Wang, and F. Cayre. 2015. General-Purpose Image Forensics Using Patch Likelihood under Image Statistical Models. In *Proceedings of IEEE International Workshop on Information Forensics and Security (WIFS)*. Rome, Italy, (2015), 1–6.

[12] H. Li, W. Luo, X. Qiu, and J. Huang. 2016. Identification of various image operations using residual-based features. *IEEE Transactions on Circuits and Systems for Video Technology* 28, 1 (2016), 31–45.

[13] Lu Laijie, Yang Gaobo, and Xia Ming. 2013. Anti-forensics for unsharp masking sharpening in digital image. *International Journal of Digital Crime and Forensics* 5, 3 (2013), 53–65.

[14] G. Cao, Y. Zhao, R. Ni, and H. Tian. 2010. Anti-forensics of contrast enhancement in digital images. In *Proceedings of 12th ACM workshop on Multimedia and security*. Rome, Italy, (2010), 25–34.

[15] C.-W. Kwok, O. Au, and S.-H. Chui. 2012. Alternative anti-forensics method for contrast enhancement. *Digital Forensics and Watermarking, ser. Lecture Notes in Computer Science. Springer Berlin Heidelberg* 7128, (2012), 398–410.

[16] Z. H. Wu, M. C. Stamm, K. J. R. Liu. 2013. Anti-Forensics of Median Filtering. In *Proceedings of IEEE Int. Conf. Acoustic, Speech, and Signal Processing*. Vancouver, Canada, (2013), 3043–3047.

[17] D. T. Dang-Nguyen, I. D. Gebru, V. Conotter, et al. 2013. Counter-forensics of median filtering. In *Proceedings of Multimedia Signal Processing (MMSP)*. Pula (Sardinia), Italy, (2013), 260–265.

[18] M. Kirchner and R. Böhme. 2008. Hiding traces of resampling in digital images. *IEEE Trans. Inf. Forensics Security* 3, 4 (2008), 582–592.

[19] M. C. Stamm, S. K. Tjoa, W. S. Lin, et al. 2010. Anti-forensics of JPEG compression. In *Proceedings of IEEE International Conference on Acoustics, Speech and Signal Processing (ICASSP)*. Texas, USA, (2010), 1694–1697.

[20] M. C. Stamm, Liu, K. J. R. 2011. Anti-forensics of digital image compression. *IEEE Trans. on Information Forensics and Security* 6, 3 (2011), 1050–1065.

[21] A. Krizhevsky, I. Sutskever, and G. E. Hinton. 2012. Imagenet classification with deep convolutional neural networks. In *Advances in Neural Information Processing Systems (NIPS)*. Lake Tahoe, (2012), 1097–1105.

[22] P. Swietojanski, A. Ghoshal, and S. Renals. 2016. Region-Based Convolutional Networks for Accurate Object Detection and Segmentation. *IEEE transactions on pattern analysis and machine intelligence* 38, 1 (2016), 142–158.

[23] J. Chen, X. Kang, Y. Liu and Z. J. Wang. 2015. Median Filtering Forensics Based on Convolutional Neural Networks. *IEEE Signal Processing Letters* 22, 11 (2015), 1849–1853.

[24] Rao Y, Ni J. 2016. A deep learning approach to detection of splicing and copy-move forgeries in images. In *Proceedings of IEEE International Workshop on Information Forensics and Security (WIFS)*. Abu Dhabi, UAE, (2016), 1–6.

[25] Bondi, Luca, et al. 2017. First Steps Toward Camera Model Identification With Convolutional Neural Networks. *IEEE Signal Processing Letters* 24, 3 (2017), 259–263.

[26] B. Bayar, M. C. Stamm. 2017. On the robustness of constrained convolutional neural networks to jpeg post-compression for image resampling detection. In *Proceedings of IEEE International Conference on Acoustics, Speech and Signal Processing (ICASSP)*. Toronto, Canada, (2017), 2152–2156.

[27] B. Bayar, M. C. Stamm. 2017. Design principles of convolutional neural networks for multimedia forensics. In *Proceedings of 2017 IS&T International Symposium on Electronic Imaging*. USA, (2017), 77–86.

[28] J. Yu, Y. Zhan, J. Yang, and X. Kang. 2017. A Multi-purpose Image Counter-anti-forensic Method Using Convolutional Neural Networks. In *Proceedings of 16th International Workshop on Digital Forensics and Watermarking (IWDW)*. Beijing, China, (2016), 3–15.

[29] M. Boroumand and J. Fridrich. 2018. Deep Learning for Detecting Processing History of Images. In *Proceedings of 2018 IS&T International Symposium on Electronic Imaging*. San Francisco, USA, (2018).

[30] B. Bayar, M. C. Stamm. 2016. A deep learning approach to universal image manipulation detection using a new convolutional layer. In *Proceedings of the 4th ACM Workshop on Information Hiding and Multimedia Security (IH&MMSec)*. Vigo, Galicia, Spain, (2016), 5-10.

[31] Y. Chen, Z. Lyu, X. Kang, and Z. J. Wang. 2017. A rotation-invariant convolutional neural network for image enhancement forensics. In *Proceedings of IEEE International Conference on Acoustics, Speech and Signal Processing (ICASSP)*. Calgary, Canada, (2018), 2111-2115.

[32] K. Q. Weinberger, Z. Liu and G. Huang. 2017. Densely Connected Convolutional Networks. In *Proceedings of 2017 IEEE Conference on Computer Vision and Pattern Recognition (CVPR)*. Hawaii, USA, (2017), 77–86.

[33] J. Yang, Y. Shi, E. K. Wong and X. Kang. 2017. JPEG Steganalysis Based on DenseNet. *arXiv preprint arXiv: 1711.09335*, (2017).

Maintaining Rate-Distortion Optimization for IPM-Based Video Steganography by Constructing Isolated Channels in HEVC

Yu Wang
State Key Laboratory of Information Security, Institute of Information Engineering, Chinese Academy of Sciences, Beijing, China 100093
School of Cyber Security, University of Chinese Academy of Sciences, Beijing, China 100093
wangyu9078@iie.ac.cn

Yun Cao*
State Key Laboratory of Information Security, Institute of Information Engineering, Chinese Academy of Sciences, Beijing, China 100093
School of Cyber Security, University of Chinese Academy of Sciences, Beijing, China 100093
caoyun@iie.ac.cn

Xianfeng Zhao
State Key Laboratory of Information Security, Institute of Information Engineering, Chinese Academy of Sciences, Beijing, China 100093
School of Cyber Security, University of Chinese Academy of Sciences, Beijing, China 100093
zhaoxianfeng@iie.ac.cn

Zhoujun Xu
Beijing Information Technology Institute, Beijing, China 100094
pl_xzj@uestc.edu.cn

Meineng Zhu
Beijing Institute of Electronics Technology and Application, Beijing, China 100091
zmneng@163.com

ABSTRACT

This paper proposes an effective intra-frame prediction mode (IPM)-based video steganography in HEVC to maintain rate-distortion optimization as well as improve empirical security. The unique aspect of this work and one that distinguishes it from prior art is that we capture the embedding impacts on neighboring prediction units, called inter prediction unit (inter-PU) embedding impacts caused by the predictive coding widespread employed in video coding standards, using a distortion measure. To avoid the emergence of neighboring IPMs mutually affecting each other within the same channel, three-layered isolated channels are established in terms of the property of IPM coding. According to theoretical analysis for embedding impacts on the current prediction unit, called intra prediction unit (intra-PU) embedding impacts on coding efficiency (both visual quality and compression efficiency), a novel distortion function purposely designed to discourage the embedding changes with impacts on adjacent channels is proposed to express the multi-level embedding impacts. Based on the defined distortion function, two-layered syndrome-trellis codes (STCs) are utilized in practical embedding implementation alternatively. Experimental results demonstrate that the proposed scheme outperforms other existing IPM-based video steganography in terms of rate-distortion optimization and empirical security.

*Corresponding author

KEYWORDS

HEVC; video steganography; prediction modes; rate-distortion

ACM Reference Format:
Yu Wang, Yun Cao, Xianfeng Zhao, Zhoujun Xu, and Meineng Zhu. 2018. Maintaining Rate-Distortion Optimization for IPM-Based Video Steganography by Constructing Isolated Channels in HEVC. In *Proceedings of 6th ACM Information Hiding and Multimedia Security Workshop (IH&MMSec'18)*. ACM, New York, NY, USA, 11 pages. https://doi.org/10.1145/3206004.3206020

1 INTRODUCTION

Steganography is the art and science of hiding communication; a steganographic system thus embeds hidden content in unremarkable cover media so as not to arouse an eavesdropper'ś suspicion [13]. In recent years, video steganography, using digital video as the empirical cover media, is emerged as an important research field that is facilitated by the booming of effective advanced video compression, especially the video coding standard H.264/Advanced Video Coding (AVC) that provides several embedding components, referred as the venues, e.g., intra prediction data [6, 17], motion data [1, 18], quantized transform coefficients [10, 11]. With the growing popularity of high definition (HD) video and the emergence of beyond-HD formats, the latest video coding standard High Efficiency Video Coding (HEVC) has been designed to address essentially all existing applications of H.264/AVC [15] and will become the mainstream of video coding standard soon, which is also creating an even stronger need for exploring the data hiding algorithms in HEVC video streams.

This paper focuses on IPM-based video steganography in HEVC mainly due to the following three reasons. First, intra-frame prediction modes generated in the stage of intra-frame prediction are lossless coded and not prone to the quantization distortion. Second, IPM-based embedding methods are proved to scarcely lead to visual artifacts in Section 4. Thirdly and the most important, IPM-based video steganography in H.264/AVC has already reached a plateau in terms of empirical security but it is a quite different case in HEVC.

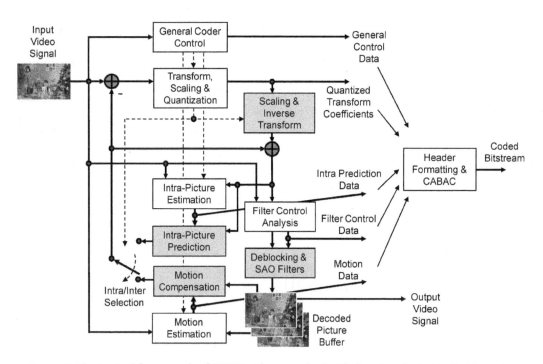

Figure 1: The typical framework of HEVC video encoder (with decoder shaded in light gray).

The IPM-based video steganography substantially affect the rate-distortion optimization, which conversely can be exploited by the detector built using IPM calibration (IPMC) [20], the state-of-the-art steganalysis of IPM-based steganography. The embedding impacts on 9 modes for intra-frame prediction of H.264/AVC shown in Figure 2(a) is easily sensed by the IPMC features. However, there exists 35 intra-frame prediction modes of HEVC shown in Figure 2(b) and the increased number of IPMs greatly improves steganographic security and decreases the detection accuracy of IPMC features.

Since the state-of-the-art literature on IPM-based steganography in HEVC video streams is still in its rudimentary phase, a review of related work is described including the related work of H.264/AVC. The cover channel intra-frame prediction mode is early employed to hide data in [7] where a blind robust algorithm of hiding data into H.264/AVC video was completed based on IPMs for copyright protection. Another early example is that Hu et al. [6] pointed out the novel channel of H.264/AVC and proposed an algorithm by modifying intra-frame prediction modes in size of 4 × 4 pixels according to the mapping between IPMs and binary message bits. Inspired by the novel channel, more analogous and optimized data hiding schemes are presented to increase embedding capacity [9], enhance the security [16] and improve embedding efficiency [17], even for real-time applications [2]. However, with the emergence of syndrome-trellis codes [3], the aforementioned literature shows relatively poor performance when compared to adaptive steganographic schemes.

The most prevalent and pragmatic steganographic schemes minimize a heuristically defined embedding distortion for preserving security. The principle of these approaches has proved extremely successful for empirical cover images including HUGO [12], WOW [4] and UNIWARD [5]. These methods cannot be directly applied to video steams without taking into account compression efficiency. As the rate-distortion is used to evaluate the coding efficiency, Zhang et al. [19] proposed an adaptive IPM-based video steganography of H.264/AVC based on cost assignment. But the design of distortion function in [19] ignores the effects of both the predictive coding and the compression efficiency, which leads to the suboptimization of rate-distortion. IPM-based embedding methods practically implemented in HEVC are pretty miserable and the existing ones like [8, 14] are non-adaptive schemes with the degraded empirical security performance.

The main contribution of this paper is the proposal of the first adaptive IPM-based steganography in HEVC by considering the effects of the predictive coding that has gained widespread popularity for video coding standards. The paper starts with the analysis of the inter-PU embedding impacts on compression efficiency and builds three-layered isolated channels in terms of the property of IPM coding. Taking into account the multi-level embedding impacts, a novel distortion function purposely designed to discourage the embedding changes with impacts on adjacent channels is proposed for practical embedding using two-layered STCs [3] within each isolated channel.

The rest of this paper is organized as follows. After introducing the preliminaries in Section 2, we model the inter-PU embedding impacts, elaborate isolated channels in Section 3 and analyse the disturbance on visual quality in Section 4. Section 5 offers a description of the distortion function and the practical implement. Section 6 shows the experimental results and the paper is closed in Section 7 where conclusions are given.

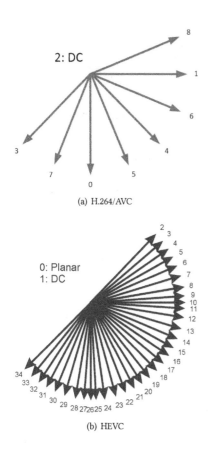

(a) H.264/AVC

(b) HEVC

Figure 2: Modes and direction orientations for intra-frame prediction.

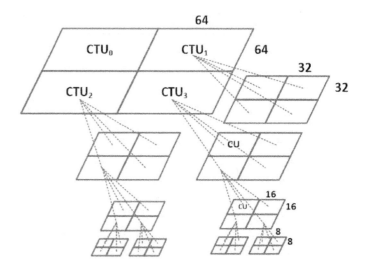

Figure 3: Subdivision of a CTU into CUs.

2 PRELIMINARIES

In this section, we detailedly describe the relevant basic knowledge of intra-frame prediction involved in the hybrid approach employed by the video coding layer of HEVC, depicted in the Figure 1. The following subsections introduce the associated syntax and the process of intra-frame prediction used to minimize the redundancy in spatial domain. Since there still exists strong correlation between adjacent IPMs and therefore we explain how to encode IPMs. For generality, we limit the scope of this paper to luminance component, the same as the vast majority of steganographic methods do.

2.1 Coding Units (CUs) and Prediction Units (PUs)

The core of the coding layer in previous standards H.264/AVC was the macroblock, in the size of 16×16 pixels, into which a picture is partitioned; whereas the analogous structure in HEVC is the new concept of coding tree unit(CTU) consisting of several CUs in the size of 64×64, 32×32, 16×16 and 8×8 pixels, depicted in the Figure 3. Each CU contains a quadtree syntax that allows for partitioning itself into multiple CUs. The quadtree split can be processed iteratively until the size reaches a minimum where the rate-distortion cost reaches a minimum and the CU is not further partitioned. Compared with the fixed array size of 16×16 pixels of

traditional macroblock in H.264/AVC, various sizes of CUs is particularly beneficial when encoding high-resolution video content.

A PU including the prediction mode contains all the information about predictive coding for the corresponding CU. The prediction mode is signaled as being intra or inter, according to whether it uses intra-frame prediction or inter-frame prediction in the picture. The block size of PU, at which the intra-frame prediction mode is established, is the same as the block size of CU for all sizes except for the smallest size. For the latter case, two types of PU partitions, referred to as PART_$2N \times 2N$ and PART_$N \times N$, are used to indicate whether the CU is partitioned into four PU quadrants. Therefore, it is seen the fact that the PUs in intra-frame prediction support square blocks of various sizes ranging from 64×64 to 4×4 pixels.

2.2 Intra-frame prediction

The goal of intra-frame prediction is essentially to reduce the spatial redundancy by taking advantage of the spatial correlation in video. The current PU, required to be encoded, used previously decoded pixels from spatially neighboring PUs to form its prediction signals. Let capital symbols stand for matrices, and as illustrated in Figure 4, the current PU, denoted as $X = \begin{bmatrix} x_{1,1} & x_{2,1} & \cdots & x_{N,1} \\ x_{1,2} & \ddots & & \vdots \\ \vdots & & \ddots & \vdots \\ x_{1,N} & \cdots & \cdots & x_{N,N} \end{bmatrix}$ in the size of $N \times N$, is a regular lattice of pixels $x_{i,j} \in I, i,j \in S, S = \{1, \ldots, N\}$. The finite set I has a dynamic range, e.g, $I = \{0, \ldots, 255\}$ for 8-bit grayscale images. Each prediction signal $\hat{x}_{i,j}$ corresponding to $x_{i,j}$ is computed by neighboring referred pixels set $\mathcal{P} = (p_{2N,0}, x_{2N-1,0}, \ldots, x_{0,0}, x_{0,1}, \ldots, x_{0,2N})$, $|\mathcal{P}| = 4N + 1$,

$$\hat{x}_{i,j} = \sum_{i=0}^{4N+1} \alpha_i Filter(p_i) \tag{1}$$

, where α_i is the prediction factor, $p_i \in \mathcal{P}$. The mapping $Filter(.)$ is the filtered value of the corresponding position. When α_i is zero,

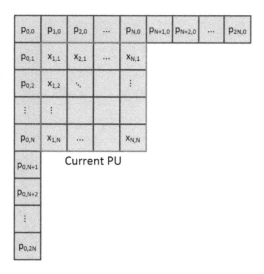

Figure 4: The signals and prediction signals of the current PU.

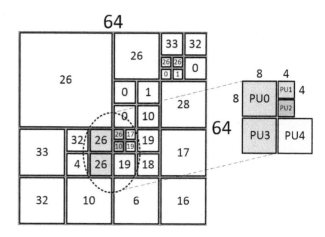

Figure 5: The IPMs and the corresponding PUs.

p_i is ignored, i.e., that the prediction signal $\hat{x}_{i,j}$ can be obtained with some neighboring referred pixels according to the adopted intra-frame prediction mode which also makes the decision of α_i.

Further, the residual, sent into the subsequent processes of transformation, quantization, entropy coding, etc., corresponding to the current pixel $x_{i,j}$, is expressed as

$$r_{i,j} = x_{i,j} - \hat{x}_{i,j} \qquad (2)$$

. To improve the intra-frame prediction accuracy and minimize the residuals, 35 intra-frame prediction modes are provided as shown in Figure 2(b). Directional prediction with 33 different directional orientations is defined for square size from 64×64 to 4×4 and the different angles are intentionally designed to reflect the different texture of video contents. Alternatively, planar prediction, applied to an amplitude surface with horizontal and vertical linear filters derived from the referred pixels, and DC prediction, applied to a flat surface with the mean value of the referred pixels, can also be used.

2.3 IPM Coding

There are 35 intra-frame prediction modes in HEVC, a total of 33 directional prediction modes denoted as Angle[k], $k \in \{2, \ldots, 34\}$ and planar prediction denoted as Planar[0] and DC prediction modes denoted as DC[1], for luma prediction for all block sizes. Besides the spatial redundancy, a significant statistical correlation between IPMs of adjacent blocks creates an urgent need to reduce the redundancy, i.e, to coding IPMs.

HEVC considers three most probable modes (MPMs) when coding the intra-frame prediction modes predictively. Among the the most probable modes, the first two are initialized by the IPMs of the above and left PUs if those PUs are available. Any unavailable prediction mode is considered to be DC prediction mode. When the first two most probable modes are the same, if the first mode is Planar[0] or DC[1], the second and the third most probable modes are assigned as Planar[0], DC[1], or Angle[26]. When the first two

most probable modes are the same, if the first mode is Angle[k], $k \in \{2, \ldots, 34\}$, the second and the third most probable modes are assigned as its neighboring modes Angle[k-1] and Angle[k+1], except that when k=2 or 34, its neighboring modes are Angle[3] and Angle[33]. When the first two most probable modes are not equal, the third mode is assigned as the one of Planar[0], DC[1] and Angle[26], in this order, which is the first one different from both the first two modes.

After most probable modes being established, if the current IPM is one of three MPMs, only the MPM index is transmitted to the decoder. Otherwise, the index of the current IPM is transmitted to the decoder at the expense of a 5-bit fixed length code.

3 CONSTRUCTION OF ISOLATED CHANNEL

In this section, we analyse the inter-PU embedding impacts of IPM-based embedding schemes on compression efficiency and then introduce a general procedure how to form three-layered isolated channels. Modeling the inter-PU embedding impacts facilitates the understanding of both the design of distortion function in Section 5 and the necessity of the isolated channel with purpose of discouraging the embedding changes with inter-PU embedding impacts.

3.1 Modeling Inter-PU Embedding Impacts

The predictive coding of IPMs in Section 2.3 is adopted to increase the compression efficiency. On the contrary, it also limits the redundancy that is used to complete the embedding schemes. To improve the empirical security, it is necessary to take the inter-PU embedding impacts caused by the predictive coding into the consideration.

For notational simplicity, we express the IPMs of an image as $\mathbf{m} = (m_1, \ldots, m_n)$, $m_l \in \mathcal{J}$, $l \in Q$, $Q = \{1, \ldots, n\}$, The finite set $\mathcal{J} = \{0, 1, \ldots, 34\}$ is virtually corresponding to all intra-frame prediction modes. To make sense of inter-PU embedding impacts, an example is given in Figure 5 where we assume that the PU_0 in the size of 8×8 is the current PU with the IPM, denoted as $m_{l_0} = 26$, $l_0 \in Q$ and the IPMs of PU_1 (4×4), PU_2 (4×4), PU_3 (8×8) and PU_4 (8×8) are successively $m_{l_1} = 26$, $m_{l_2} = 10$, $m_{l_3} = 26$ and $m_{l_4} = 19$, $l_1, l_2, l_3, l_4 \in Q$. When the current m_{l_0} is equal to one of

MPMs initialized by the above and left PUs, only one or two bits are required to encode the index of MPMs. Otherwise, 5-bit fixed length code is required to encode m_{l_0}. If m_{l_0} is modified, m_{l_1} referring to m_{l_0} is virtually polluted as well. In order to prevent the pollution, m_{l_1} is required to be re-coded at the expense of more three or four bits, i.e., reducing the compression efficiency. The overall losses of the embedding change of m_{l_0} are seen as the inter-PU embedding impacts of m_{l_0}.

We describe the inter-PU embedding impacts for the whole image as the bold symbol $\boldsymbol{\rho}_z$ and each $\rho_{z,l} \in \boldsymbol{\rho}_z$ is the distortion used to measure the inter-PU embedding corresponding to the m_l. Curiously, when dealing with m_l, we can easily get the left IPM $m_l^{\leftarrow}$ and the above $m_l^{\uparrow}$ according to the information provided by the current PU but it is quite tough to get the right and the down IPMs that all regard m_l as the referred one. Still in Figure 5, when PU_0 being processed, it is confused that which one(s) of the four PUs, i.e., PU_1, PU_2, PU_3, PU_4, regard(s) m_l as the referred one. Therefore, in Algorithm 1, $\forall \rho_{z,l} \in \boldsymbol{\rho}_z$ will be calculated. When current m_l is processed, the distortions $\rho_{z,l-\Delta_1}$ of the left $m_l^{\leftarrow} = m_{l-\Delta_1}$ and $\rho_{z,l-\Delta_2}$ of the above $m_l^{\uparrow} = m_{l-\Delta_2}$ are calculated indeed.

Algorithm 1 Cost of Inter-PU Embedding Impacts

Require: Input **m**
Ensure: Output $\boldsymbol{\rho}_z$
1: Set $\boldsymbol{\rho}_z = \{\rho_{z,1}, \rho_{z,2} \ldots \rho_{z,l}\} = 0$, counter $l = 1$
2: **while** $l \leq n$ **do**
3:     Obtain the current IPM $m_l \in \mathbf{m}$
4:     Obtain the first left IPM $m_l^{\leftarrow} = m_{l-\Delta_1}, m_{l-\Delta_1} \in \mathbf{m}$, and the
    first above IPM $m_l^{\uparrow} = m_{l-\Delta_2}, m_{l-\Delta_2} \in \mathbf{m}$
5:     **if** $m_l == m_l^{\leftarrow}$ **then**
6:         $\rho_{z,l-\Delta_1} \leftarrow \rho_{z,l-\Delta_1} + 5 - R_{mode}(m_l^{\leftarrow})$
7:     **end if**
8:     **if** $m_l == m_l^{\uparrow}$ **then**
9:         $\rho_{z,l-\Delta_2} \leftarrow \rho_{z,l-\Delta_2} + 5 - R_{mode}(m_l^{\uparrow})$
10:    **end if**
11:    $l \leftarrow l + 1$
12: **end while**

3.2 Channel Construction

In Section 3.1, we explained the embedding impacts on neighboring prediction units and modeled the impacts as $\boldsymbol{\rho}_z$. To achieve an adaptive selection strategy, three-layered isolated channels are introduced to separate the neighboring IPMs mutually affecting each other.

The overall channel is partitioned into three isolated parts within each of which the distortion w.r.t. inter-PU embedding impacts is mutually independent. The three isolated channels are denoted as $\mathbf{m}^1$, $\mathbf{m}^2$ and $\mathbf{m}^3$ successively and note that $\mathbf{m} = \mathbf{m}^1 \cup \mathbf{m}^2 \cup \mathbf{m}^3$, $|\mathbf{m}| = |\mathbf{m}^1| + |\mathbf{m}^2| + |\mathbf{m}^3|$ because $\mathbf{m}^1$, $\mathbf{m}^2$ and $\mathbf{m}^3$ are mutually disjoint channels.

Within the same channel, the blocks are supposed not to be adjacent ones avoiding affecting each other so that the left IPM $m_l^{\leftarrow}$ and the above IPM $m_l^{\uparrow}$ belong to the different channels from the current

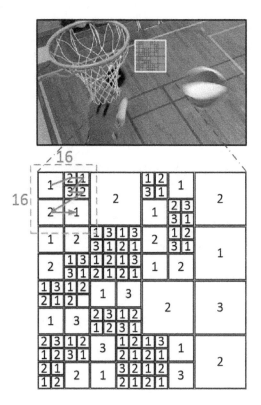

Figure 6: An example of isolated channels.

channel. Initialize the first channel $\mathbf{m}^1$, the second channel $\mathbf{m}^2$ and the third channel $\mathbf{m}^3$ to be empty and we get the serial numbers k_1 and k_2 of channels $\mathbf{m}^{k_1}$ and $\mathbf{m}^{k_2}$ that $m_i^{\leftarrow}$ and $m_i^{\uparrow}$ belongs to. Note that $m_i^{\leftarrow}$ and $m_i^{\uparrow}$ may be unavailable and we introduce the zero channel $\mathbf{M}^0$ to express the situation of unavailable IPMs. The current IPM m_l is put into the channel, denoted as $\mathbf{m}^{k_3}$, that is different from both $\mathbf{m}^{k_1}$ and $\mathbf{m}^{k_2}$ of adjacent blocks. If k_1 is equal to k_2, m_i is put into the left channel with the minor serial number. The Algorithm 2 describes the procedure of constructing the isolated channels completely.

Algorithm 2 Constructing three-layered Isolated Channels

Require: Input **m**
Ensure: Output $\mathbf{m}^1, \mathbf{m}^2, \mathbf{m}^3$
1: Set $\mathbf{m}^0 = \mathbf{m}^1 = \mathbf{m}^2 = \mathbf{m}^3 = \varnothing$, counter $l = 1$
2: **while** $l \leq n$ **do**
3:     Obtain the current IPM $m_l \in \mathbf{m}$
4:     Obtain the first left IPM $m_l^{\leftarrow} \in \mathbf{m}^{k_1}, k_1 \in \mathcal{K} = \{0, 1, 2, 3\}$,
5:     Obtain the first above IPM $m_l^{\uparrow} \in \mathbf{m}^{k_2}, k_2 \in \mathcal{K}$
6:     $k_3 \leftarrow$ the first element of the set $\mathcal{K} - \{0, k_1\} - \{k_2\}$
7:     $\mathbf{m}^{k_3} \leftarrow \mathbf{m}^{k_3} + m_l$
8:     $l \leftarrow l + 1$
9: **end while**

Figure 6 shows an example of constructing isolated channels. The top-left 16×16 PU with the red polyline is used to demonstrate the processing sequence from top to bottom, left to right. If there exists a further division in the current PU, the four sub-PUs are given a priority and processed in the same sequence. The results of the recursive process of 64×64 PU in the example is represented by the labels labelled the number of 1, 2, and 3 which are the serial numbers of isolated channels.

4　DISTURBANCE ANALYSIS OF VISUAL QUALITY

The embedding changes of IPMs will affect the coding efficiency of the corresponding PUs including two aspects of visual quality and compression efficiency. In this section, we offer a theoretical analysis for the disturbance on visual quality. A brief analysis w.r.t. bit-rate is conducted in Section 5.1.

The data is embedded into an intra-frame prediction mode m_{cur}, which intuitively leads to the perturbation of prediction signals $\hat{X}$ whose elements are obtained in (1) and further changes the values of spatial residuals R whose elements are depicted in (2). To describe the changes in spatial domain, essentially sensed by the decoder, we need to evaluate perturbation of restructured signals

$$\tilde{X} = \tilde{R} + \hat{X} \tag{3}$$

where $\tilde{R}$ is the restructured matrix of R. For simplicity, we limit to the scope of the 4×4 DCT-style transform since HEVC supports four DCT-style transform block sizes of 4×4, 8×8, 16×16 and 32×32 and for the size of 4×4, an alternative integer transform is derived from a DST. The integer DCT operation applied to spatial residuals

$$R = \begin{bmatrix} r_{1,1} & r_{2,1} & \cdots & r_{N,1} \\ r_{1,2} & \ddots & & \vdots \\ \vdots & & \ddots & \vdots \\ r_{1,N} & \cdots & \cdots & r_{N,N} \end{bmatrix}, \text{ can be formulized as follows,}$$

$$\begin{aligned}
R_D &= (H_4 R H_4^T) \otimes (E_4 \otimes E_4^T) \\
&= \left(\begin{bmatrix} 64 & 64 & 64 & 64 \\ 83 & 36 & -36 & -83 \\ 64 & -64 & -64 & 64 \\ 36 & -83 & 83 & -36 \end{bmatrix} R \begin{bmatrix} 64 & 83 & 64 & 36 \\ 64 & 36 & -64 & -83 \\ 64 & -36 & -64 & 83 \\ 64 & -83 & 64 & -36 \end{bmatrix} \right) \\
&\quad \cdot \frac{1}{128} \cdot \frac{1}{128}
\end{aligned} \tag{4}$$

where H_4 is a constant matrix called the 4×4 integer DCT matrix and H_4^T is its transpose. The symbol $\otimes$ denotes the product operation of the corresponding elements and therefore the correct matrix E_4 and its transpose E_4^T can be represented as the same constant. In practice, the twice operations $\otimes$ in (4) are integrated into the process of quantization so that we only get the $R_I = (H_4 R H_4^T)$ in the transform operation. The quantization is to compute quantized R_I,

$$R_Q = floor(R_I \otimes \frac{F}{2^{qbits+T\_shift}} \oplus f) \tag{5}$$

, where $qbits = 14 + floor(QP/6)$, $f = 1/3$,

$$F = \frac{2^{qbits}}{Q_{step}} = \begin{cases} 26214, & QP\%6 = 0 \\ 23302, & QP\%6 = 1 \\ 20560, & QP\%6 = 2 \\ 18396, & QP\%6 = 3 \\ 16384, & QP\%6 = 4 \\ 14564, & QP\%6 = 5 \end{cases} \text{ and } T\_shift \text{ stands for the}$$

scaling factor of integer DCT. QP is the quantizer factor and Q_{step} is the quantizer step size determined by QP. The symbol $\oplus$ denotes the additive operation of the corresponding elements. The function floor(.) is rounding down the number. After the inverse quantization

$$R_{Iv} = R_Q \otimes \frac{scale}{2^{shift}} \oplus \frac{1}{2} \tag{6}$$

where $shift$ stands for the scaling factor of inverse integer DCT,

$$scale = 2^6 Q_{step} = 2^{floor(QP/6)} \cdot \begin{cases} 40, & QP\%6 = 0 \\ 45, & QP\%6 = 1 \\ 51, & QP\%6 = 2 \\ 57, & QP\%6 = 3 \\ 64, & QP\%6 = 4 \\ 72, & QP\%6 = 5 \end{cases}, \text{ and the inverse}$$

integer DCT

$$\tilde{R} = \tilde{H}_4^T R_{Iv} \tilde{H}_4 \tag{7}$$

where $\tilde{H}_4$ is a constant matrix called inverse integer DCT matrix and $\tilde{H}_4^T$ is its transpose, we get the matrix of restructured residuals $\tilde{R}$ that is used to express $\tilde{X}$ according to (3).

We suppose that the decoder gets a modified IPM m'_{cur} due to the embedding change which will cause a modified prediction signals $\hat{Y}$. The difference between the original $\hat{X}$ and the modified $\hat{Y}$ is thus

$$\Delta = \hat{X} - \hat{Y} \tag{8}$$

. With (3),(4),(5),(6),(7) and (8), the deviation in spatial domain at the decoder due to the embedding change of the IPM is obtained

$$\begin{aligned}
E &= \tilde{Y} - \tilde{X} \\
&= (\tilde{R}' + (\hat{X} - \Delta)) - (\tilde{R} + \hat{X}) \\
&= \tilde{H}_4^T ((floor((H_4(R+\Delta)H_4^T) \otimes \frac{F}{2^{qbits+T\_Shift}} \oplus f) \\
&\quad - floor((H_4 R H_4^T) \otimes \frac{F}{2^{qbits+T\_Shift}} \oplus f)) \otimes \frac{scale}{2^{shift}} \oplus \frac{1}{2}) \\
&\quad \tilde{H}_4 - \Delta
\end{aligned} \tag{9}$$

where $\tilde{Y}$ and $\tilde{R}'$ are the modified restructured signals and residuals respectively. If prediction signal $\hat{X}$ is close to $\hat{Y}$, $\Delta \approx 0$, the deviation $E \approx 0$ and the change from m_{cur} to m'_{cur} is deemed to cause little impacts on visual quality. Otherwise, if $\Delta \not\approx 0$, $e_{i,j} \in E$ and $e_{i,j} \leq Q_e$ where Q_e is the quantized error caused by the process of quantization, which leads to the confusion in distinguishing embedding changes from the quantized error.

5　THE PROPOSED SCHEME

Thanks to the isolated channels, we can measure the inter-PU embedding impacts mentioned in Section 3.1 this is important for the

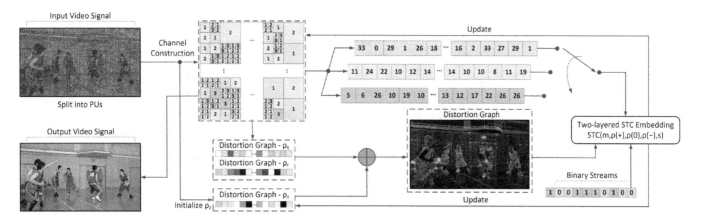

Figure 7: Alternate embedding within single intra frame.

design of the overall distortion function. In this section, we propose a distortion function reflecting multi-level embedding impacts and describe the practical implementation of our proposed scheme detailedly.

5.1 Distortion Function

The key element of the proposed scheme is the distortion, which needs to be carefully designed to indicate the applicability of each cover element m_l. The overall distortion function is calculated as followed,

$$D(\mathbf{m}, \mathbf{m}', \mathbf{x}, \tilde{\mathbf{x}}, \tilde{\mathbf{y}}) = \sum_{l=1}^{n} \rho_l(m_l, m'_l, X_l, \tilde{X}_l, \tilde{Y}_l) \quad (10)$$

where n represents the number of PUs in the current frame. Note that lowercase bold symbols stand for vectors and capital symbols stand for matrices and the variable ρ_l denotes the distortion function of m_l in the form of the addition of $\rho_{s,l}$, $\rho_{r,l}$ and $\rho_{z,l}$ in (11), the former two distortions measuring the intra-PU embedding impacts and the latter one measuring the inter-PU embedding impacts.

$$\rho_l(m_l, m'_l, X_l, \tilde{X}_l, \tilde{Y}_l) = \rho_{s,l}(X_l, \tilde{X}_l, \tilde{Y}_l) + \lambda \rho_{r,l}(m_l, m'_l) \\ + \upsilon \rho_{z,l}(m_l) \quad (11)$$

where λ and υ denote the weighting factors of $\rho_{s,l}$ and $\rho_{r,l}$ respectively. λ is essentially decided by the quantizer factor QP, $\lambda = \beta \cdot \omega \cdot 2^{(QP-12)/3.0}$ where β and ω can be seen as the constants decided by the encoder. υ is a parameter controlling the $\rho_{z,l}$ of penalizing the changes with impacts on adjacent channels. $\rho_{s,l}$, defined in (12), is to measure the impacts on visual quality.

$$\rho_{s,l}(X_l, \tilde{X}_l, \tilde{Y}_l) = \sum_{i=1}^{N} \sum_{j=1}^{N} (|x_{i,j} - \tilde{x}_{i,j}|^2 - |x_{i,j} - \tilde{y}_{i,j}|^2) \quad (12)$$

The PU with the IPM m_l has the original signals X_l, the restructured signals $\tilde{X}_l$ and the modified restructured signals $\tilde{Y}_l$ all in the size of $N \times N$ pixels. In (12), $|x_{i,j} - \tilde{x}_{i,j}|^2 - |x_{i,j} - \tilde{y}_{i,j}|^2 = (2x_{i,j} - (\tilde{x}_{i,j} + \tilde{y}_{i,j}))(\tilde{y}_{i,j} - \tilde{x}_{i,j})$ and $\tilde{y}_{i,j} - \tilde{x}_{i,j}$ is analysed in Section 4 to measure the similarity between $\tilde{X}_l$ and $\tilde{Y}_l$. Under the same similarity, $2x_{i,j} - (\tilde{x}_{i,j} + \tilde{y}_{i,j})$ is indeed to encourage $\tilde{y}_{i,j}$ to be close to $x_{i,j}$.

To evaluate the loss of bit-rate $\rho_{r,l}$, defined in (13),

$$\rho_{r,l}(m_l, m'_l) = |R_{all}(m_l) - R_{all}(m'_l)| \quad (13)$$

, all the required bits of encoding the current PU is denoted as R_{all}, containing two parts R_{coffs} and R_{mode}, the numbers of bits of encoding quantized transform coefficients and the current intra-frame prediction mode. Intuitively, a modified IPM can disturb the required bits of encoding residual coefficients and the mode so that we use the absolute difference of $R_{all}(m_l)$ and $R_{all}(m'_l)$ to express the bit-rate distortion. We give a description of $\rho_{z,l}(m_l)$ as followed

$$\rho_{z,l}(m_l) = \sum_{\psi=1}^{|\Psi|} \delta(m_l, m_{l+\psi}) \cdot (5 - R_{mode}(m_{l+\psi})) \quad (14)$$

where $\delta(,)$ is defined as $\delta(x, y) = \begin{cases} 1, & x = y \\ 0, & x \neq y \end{cases}$. Ψ is the set of neighboring PUs with each element $m_{l+\psi} \in \Psi$ and we traverse all the neighbors of m_l to obtain the value of $\rho_{z,l}(m_l)$. However, $m_{l+\psi}$ is difficult to obtain in practice and we strongly suggest calculating $\forall \rho_{z,l}(m_l) \in \boldsymbol{\rho}_z$ in Algorithm 1.

5.2 Practical Implementation

Based on the given distortion function, the practical implementation of proposed steganographic scheme using two-layered STCs is to be introduced in this subsection. Typically, the secret message bits are mapping to the binary streams and embedded in a frame-by-frame manner. The processes of embedding and extraction within one single frame are described as follows.

5.2.1 Data Embedding. The entire embedding procedure combined with intra-frame coding is illustrated as Figure 7. First, split the whole I-frame into CTUs and further obtain the PUs each of which has $m_l,, X_l$ and $\tilde{X}_l$, $l \in n$. The matrix of restructured signals $\tilde{X}_l$ is calculated according to (1), (2), (3), (4), (5), (6) and (7). Besides, secret message $\mathbf{s}$ is divided into three parts $\mathbf{s}^1$, $\mathbf{s}^2$ and $\mathbf{s}^3$.

Secondly, construct the three-layered isolated channels and initial the $\boldsymbol{\rho}_z$. Both processes described in Algorithm 2 and Algorithm 1 can be done at the same time. The purpose of that $\boldsymbol{\rho}_z$ is initialized is to reduce the computing complexity.

Table 1: Coding performance of three sequences compressed with payload $\alpha = 0$

Sequence	QP	PSNR	I-PSNR	BR	I-BR	SSIM
BQMall.yuv	22	45.483	46.784	5103.50	23230.07	0.9907
	32	39.024	39.219	1766.70	9625.44	0.9664
KristenAndSara.yuv	22	49.474	49.888	3287.67	22478.29	0.9944
	32	43.424	42.916	1191.81	9415.30	0.9841
BasketballDrive.yuv	22	46.359	48.187	22005.66	68225.16	0.9865
	32	40.830	41.196	6291.78	22623.31	0.9610

Thirdly, calculate the overall distortion of cover $\mathbf{m}^k, k \in \{1, 2, 3\}$ and repeat this step for several times to minimize the embedding impacts. For each $m_l \in \mathbf{m}^k$, $\boldsymbol{\rho}^{(+)}$ and $\boldsymbol{\rho}^{(-)}$ are respectively the overall distortions computed in (11) corresponding to two neighboring intra-frame prediction modes of m_l introduced in Section 2.3. Then execute two-layered STC($\mathbf{m}^k, \boldsymbol{\rho}^{(+)}, \boldsymbol{\rho}^{(0)}, \boldsymbol{\rho}^{(-)}, \mathbf{s}^k$) embedding with the payload α meanwhile calculate the $\boldsymbol{\rho}_z$ for the embedding next time.

Finally, the compressed frame is obtained with n IPMs carrying αn secret message bits.

5.2.2 Data Extraction. Compared to the embedding process, the data extraction is much easier. With the received frame, the recipient uses a common decoder to obtain all the IPMs $\mathbf{m}$ and divides it into three channels $\mathbf{m}^1$, $\mathbf{m}^2$ and $\mathbf{m}^3$. According to data extraction of two-layered STCs, obtain three parts of secret message bits $\mathbf{s}^1$, $\mathbf{s}^2$ and $\mathbf{s}^3$ and further the overall secret message bits $\mathbf{s} = [\mathbf{s}^1 \ \mathbf{s}^2 \ \mathbf{s}^3]$.

6 EXPERIMENTS

6.1 Experimental Setup

Our proposed embedding scheme is implemented on the well-known HEVC codec named x265. The video database is composed of 24 standard 4:2:0 YUV sequences. The raw sequences vary from 150 to 600 frames in length and are coded with 50fps frame rate.

To evaluate the visual quality, we introduce peak signal to noise ratio (PSNR) and structural similarity index (SSIM) that are regarded as perceptual metrics to quantify image quality degradation. The prefix 'I-' is used to express the meaning of only I-frame, e.g., I-PSNR actually measures the visual quality of the whole I-frames in contrast to that PSNR measures the visual quality of all the frames. The payload α is measured by the number of bits embedded per 4×4 intra-frame prediction mode (bpipm). Note that all the sizes of IPMs can be used to carry bits in our proposed scheme but in this experiment we only employ IPMs in the size of 4×4 pixels to compare performance with other embedding schemes as they do. To evaluate the compression efficiency, we define the bit-rate increase ratio (BIR) as $BIR = (BR - BR_{ori})/BR_{ori} \times 100\%$ where BR denotes the bit-rate of the embedded video and BR_{ori} denotes the bit-rate of the original compressed video without carrying messages.

For performance comparisons, Sheng's method [14] is implemented as one of typical data hiding methods of HEVC proposed in recent years. Since existing IPM-based steganographic schemes of HEVC are not quite a few and even have similar performance due

to the non-adaptive schemes, an extension of Zhang's method [19] called Ext-Zhang's, is also implemented as an adaptive steganographic scheme. For evaluating empirical security, the detector built by IPM Calibration (IPMC) features [20], which shows the best effectiveness in detecting IPM-based schemes of H.264/AVC, is leveraged against our proposed, Sheng's and Ext-Zhang's under different cases that various bit-rate including 500kbps, 1000kbps, 3000kbps and 10000kbps are considered with the achieved payloads respectively. The true negative (TN) rate and the true positive (TP) rate are computed by counting the number of detections in the test sets. By averaging TN and TP, averaged detection accuracies are obtained.

6.2 Results and Discussion

6.2.1 Coding Efficiency. Three sequences, i.e., 'BQMall.yuv', 'KristenAndSara.yuv' and 'BasketballDrive.yuv' listed in Table 1 are compressed into HEVC video streams as the original ones by $\alpha = 0$ for contrast analysis. We list the differences, denoted as ones with the prefix 'Δ', between the embedded videos with $\alpha = 0.1$ and $\alpha = 0.5$ and the ones with $\alpha = 0$ to eliminate effects caused by data compression under different QPs in Table 2. One of the conspicuous advantage of IPM-based steganographic methods is that the coding efficiency isn't affected much since values of SSIM are almost the same and the ΔPSNR and BIR are very small. Besides the theoretical analysis in Section 3.1, we attribute this satisfactory coding efficiency to that the indicators such as ΔPSNR and BIR are also affected by the P/B-frames which are not used to carry bits. Therefore, the indicators ΔI-PSNR and I-BIR are introduced to exclude the effects of P/B-frames for better embedding performance comparison in Table 2. It is observed that Sheng's method achieves the worst coding performance including both visual quality and compression efficiency among three tested methods for all QPs and all embedding rates. In most cases our proposed achieves a better performance than the extension of Zhang's method in HEVC. Curiously, when QP=22 and $\alpha = 0.1$ and QP=32 and $\alpha = 0.1$ for 'BasketballDrive.yuv', the values of PSNR are -0.002 and -0.001 respectively when compared to -0.004 and -0.002 of ours. In aforementioned two cases, we indeed outperform Ext-Zhang's method in terms of bit-rate and suppose that Ext-Zhang's method gains the visual quality at the expense of ignoring the correlation of neighboring IPMs, i.e., losses of empirical security.

Table 2: Embedding performance comparison with different QP, embedding rate α

Sequence	QP	α	Method	ΔPSNR	ΔI-PSNR	BIR(%)	I-BIR(%)	SSIM
BQMall.yuv	22	0.1	Sheng's	-0.004	-0.017	0.25	0.48	0.9906
			Ext-Zhang's	-0.003	-0.003	0.05	0.14	0.9907
			Ours	-0.001	-0.001	0.02	0.13	0.9907
		0.5	Sheng's	-0.018	-0.096	1.05	2.16	0.9906
			Ext-Zhang's	-0.006	-0.040	0.46	0.98	0.9906
			Ours	-0.004	-0.031	0.40	0.82	0.9906
	32	0.1	Sheng's	-0.002	-0.007	0.31	0.62	0.9664
			Ext-Zhang's	-0.001	-0.002	0.09	0.18	0.9664
			Ours	-0.001	-0.002	0.06	0.13	0.9664
		0.5	Sheng's	-0.015	-0.058	1.25	2.35	0.9663
			Ext-Zhang's	-0.008	-0.020	0.61	1.17	0.9664
			Ours	-0.003	-0.016	0.52	0.95	0.9664
KristenAndSara.yuv	22	0.1	Sheng's	-0.008	-0.016	0.36	0.56	0.9944
			Ext-Zhang's	-0.004	-0.005	0.10	0.17	0.9944
			Ours	-0.003	-0.002	0.09	0.16	0.9944
		0.5	Sheng's	-0.039	-0.081	1.69	2.50	0.9944
			Ext-Zhang's	-0.017	-0.032	0.71	1.07	0.9944
			Ours	-0.012	-0.028	0.59	0.88	0.9944
	32	0.1	Sheng's	-0.003	-0.009	0.49	0.67	0.9841
			Ext-Zhang's	-0.001	-0.005	0.19	0.19	0.9841
			Ours	-0.001	-0.003	0.14	0.14	0.9841
		0.5	Sheng's	-0.016	-0.049	2.09	2.67	0.9840
			Ext-Zhang's	-0.008	-0.016	1.03	1.29	0.9841
			Ours	-0.002	-0.012	0.95	1.12	0.9841
BasketballDrive.yuv	22	0.1	Sheng's	-0.005	-0.010	0.13	0.39	0.9865
			Ext-Zhang's	-0.001	-0.002	0.01	0.10	0.9865
			Ours	-0.001	-0.004	0.01	0.07	0.9865
		0.5	Sheng's	-0.006	-0.058	0.50	1.70	0.9865
			Ext-Zhang's	-0.002	-0.021	0.23	0.73	0.9865
			Ours	-0.002	-0.016	0.16	0.59	0.9865
	32	0.1	Sheng's	-0.002	-0.003	0.11	0.29	0.9610
			Ext-Zhang's	-0.001	-0.001	0.05	0.06	0.9610
			Ours	-0.001	-0.002	0.05	0.03	0.9610
		0.5	Sheng's	-0.004	-0.017	0.44	1.30	0.9610
			Ext-Zhang's	-0.001	-0.004	0.25	0.70	0.9610
			Ours	-0.001	-0.005	0.21	0.57	0.9610

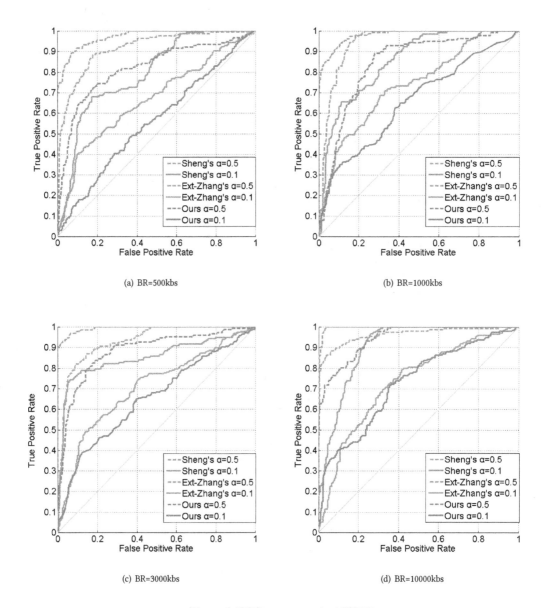

(a) BR=500kbs

(b) BR=1000kbs

(c) BR=3000kbs

(d) BR=10000kbs

Figure 8: ROC curves against IPMC

Table 3: Average detection accuracies (%) against IPMC with
$\alpha = 0.5$

Method	Video Coding Standard	TN	TP
Zhang's	H.264/AVC	91.4	90.0
Ext-Zhang's	HEVC	86.6	83.5
Ours	HEVC	80.3	76.6

6.2.2 Security. In Table 3, it is observed that with the fixed payload $\alpha = 0.5$ against the same detector built by IPMC features, Zhang's method implemented in H.264/AVC shows a worse performance than the extension of that implemented in HEVC which tells that the increased number of IPMs in HEVC indeed improves steganographic empirical security.

The receiver operation characteristic (ROC) curves are depicted in Figure 8. In comparison with ours and Ext-Zhang's, Sheng's method performs worst in all tested cases due to its non-adaptive embedding scheme that is one of typical early IPM-based embedding schemes proposed with the emergence of HEVC. Our proposed scheme outperforms Ext-Zhang's at low bit-rates of 500kps,

1000kps and 3000kps, shown in Figure 8(a), Figure 8(b) and Figure 8(c). Curiously, as bit-rate increase to 10000kps in Figure 8(d), the performance of Ext-Zhang's is quite close to ours. If the bit-rate decided by the QP increases, λ in (11) is assigned to a smaller value and $v = \lambda$ seems to be a relatively smaller weighted factor. $\rho_l(m_l, m'_l, X_l, \tilde{X}_l, \tilde{Y}_l)$ more depends on the visual quality rather than the bit-rate that leads to a fact that our proposed distortion ρ_z will be ignored. Besides, when the loss in lossy compression is less, the higher visual quality contributes to the effectiveness of the detector because high fidelity significantly promotes the accuracy of calibration features. Indeed, with the help of bit-rate high enough, the performance of all the tested methods can be inferior against the IPMC features but even so our scheme still enhances the empirical security obviously. One worth mentioning is that the empirically secure threshold value of embedding rate α is supposed to be below 0.5 and the more study on it isn't conducted in this paper.

Overall, in contrast with Sheng's and Ext-Zhang's methods, ROC curves and Table 2 indicate that our proposed method markedly improved the empirical security when testing with the detector built using IPMC features and minimized the embedding impacts on rate-distortion optimization.

7 CONCLUSION

In this paper, an adaptive IPM-based steganography of HEVC is proposed to maintain the rate-distortion optimization. To prevent the emergence of embedding impacts on the same channel, three-layered isolated channels are used complete the adaptive embedding scheme. And the practically implemented scheme using two-layered STCs is based on a novel distortion function that can describe multi-level embedding impacts including both intra-PU and inter-PU embedding impacts. In experiments against current effective steganalytic method, the proposed scheme outperforms other existing IPM-based steganographic methods in terms of empirical security and achieves the rate-distortion optimization. Besides, it is proved that HEVC indeed improves steganographic security and decreases the detection accuracy of IPMC features due to the increased number of IPMs compared to H.264/AVC.

ACKNOWLEDGMENTS

This work was supported by NSFC under U1736214 and U1636102, Fundamental Theory and Cutting Edge Technology Research Program of IIE, CAS, under Y7Z0371102čňand National Key Technology R&D Program under 2016YFB0801003 and 2016QY15Z2500.

REFERENCES

[1] Hussein A Aly. 2011. Data hiding in motion vectors of compressed video based on their associated prediction error. *IEEE Transactions on Information Forensics and Security* 6, 1 (2011), 14–18.
[2] Samira Bouchama, Latifa Hamami, and Hassina Aliane. 2012. H. 264/AVC data hiding based on intra prediction modes for real-time applications. In *Proceedings of the World Congress on Engineering and Computer Science*, Vol. 1. 655–658.
[3] Tomáš Filler, Jan Judas, and Jessica Fridrich. 2011. Minimizing additive distortion in steganography using syndrome-trellis codes. *IEEE Transactions on Information Forensics and Security* 6, 3 (2011), 920–935.
[4] Vojtech Holub and Jessica Fridrich. 2012. Designing steganographic distortion using directional filters. In *Information Forensics and Security (WIFS), 2012 IEEE International Workshop on*. IEEE, 234–239.
[5] Vojtěch Holub, Jessica Fridrich, and Tomáš Denemark. 2014. Universal distortion function for steganography in an arbitrary domain. *EURASIP Journal on Information Security* 2014, 1 (2014), 1.
[6] Yang Hu, Chuntian Zhang, and Yuting Su. 2007. Information hiding based on intra prediction modes for H. 264/AVC. In *Multimedia and Expo, 2007 IEEE International Conference on*. IEEE, 1231–1234.
[7] Cao Hua, Zhou Jingli, and Yu Shengsheng. 2005. An implement of fast hiding data into H. 264 bitstream based on intra-prediction coding. In *Proc. of SPIE Vol*, Vol. 6043. 60430I–1.
[8] Wang Jiaji, Wang Rangding, Li Wei, Xu Dawen, and Huang Meiling. 2014. An information hiding algorithm for HEVC based on intra prediction mode and block code. *Sensors & Transducers* 177, 8 (2014), 230.
[9] Chia-Hsiung Liu and Oscal T-C Chen. 2008. Data hiding in inter and intra prediction modes of H. 264/AVC. In *Circuits and Systems, 2008. ISCAS 2008. IEEE International Symposium on*. IEEE, 3025–3028.
[10] Xiaojing Ma, Zhitang Li, Hao Tu, and Bochao Zhang. 2010. A data hiding algorithm for H. 264/AVC video streams without intra-frame distortion drift. *IEEE transactions on circuits and systems for video technology* 20, 10 (2010), 1320–1330.
[11] Azadeh Mansouri, Ahmad Mahmoudi Aznaveh, Farah Torkamani-Azar, and Fatih Kurugollu. 2010. A low complexity video watermarking in H. 264 compressed domain. *IEEE Transactions on Information Forensics and Security* 5, 4 (2010), 649–657.
[12] Tomáš Pevný, Tomáš Filler, and Patrick Bas. 2010. Using high-dimensional image models to perform highly undetectable steganography. In *International Workshop on Information Hiding*. Springer, 161–177.
[13] Niels Provos and Peter Honeyman. 2003. Hide and seek: An introduction to steganography. *IEEE security & privacy* 99, 3 (2003), 32–44.
[14] Qi Sheng, Rangding Wang, Anshan Pei, and Bin Wang. 2016. An Information Hiding Algorithm for HEVC Based on Differences of Intra Prediction Modes. In *International Conference on Cloud Computing and Security*. Springer, 63–74.
[15] Gary J Sullivan, Jens Ohm, Woo-Jin Han, and Thomas Wiegand. 2012. Overview of the high efficiency video coding (HEVC) standard. *IEEE Transactions on circuits and systems for video technology* 22, 12 (2012), 1649–1668.
[16] Dawen Xu, Rangding Wang, and Jicheng Wang. 2012. Prediction mode modulated data-hiding algorithm for H. 264/AVC. *Journal of real-time image processing* 7, 4 (2012), 205–214.
[17] Gaobo Yang, Junjie Li, Yingliang He, and Zhiwei Kang. 2011. An information hiding algorithm based on intra-prediction modes and matrix coding for H. 264/AVC video stream. *AEU-International Journal of Electronics and Communications* 65, 4 (2011), 331–337.
[18] Hong Zhang, Yun Cao, and Xianfeng Zhao. 2016. Motion vector-based video steganography with preserved local optimality. *Multimedia Tools and Applications* 75, 21 (2016), 13503–13519.
[19] Lingyu Zhang and Xianfeng Zhao. 2016. An adaptive video steganography based on intra-prediction mode and cost assignment. In *International Workshop on Digital Watermarking*. Springer, 518–532.
[20] Yanbin Zhao, Hong Zhang, Yun Cao, Peipei Wang, and Xianfeng Zhao. 2015. Video steganalysis based on intra prediction mode calibration. In *International Workshop on Digital Watermarking*. Springer, 119–133.

Exploring Non-Additive Distortion in Steganography

Tomáš Pevný
Dept. of Computer Science
CTU in Prague
pevnak@gmail.com

Andrew D. Ker
Dept. of Computer Science
University of Oxford
adk@cs.ox.ac.uk

ABSTRACT

Leading steganography systems make use of the Syndrome-Trellis Code (STC) algorithm to minimize a distortion function while encoding the desired payload, but this constrains the distortion function to be additive. The Gibbs Embedding algorithm works for a certain class of non-additive distortion functions, but has its own limitations and is highly complex.

In this short paper we show that it is possible to modify the STC algorithm in a simple way, to minimize a non-additive distortion function suboptimally. We use it for two examples. First, applying it to the S-UNIWARD distortion function, we show that it does indeed reduce distortion, compared with minimizing the additive approximation currently used in image steganography, but that it makes the payload more – not less – detectable. This parallels research attempting to use Gibbs Embedding for the same task. Second, we apply it to distortion defined by the output of a specific detector, as a counter-move in the steganography game. However, unless the Warden is forced to move first (by fixing the detector) this is highly detectable.

CCS CONCEPTS

• **Security and privacy** → *Pseudonymity, anonymity and untraceability*;

KEYWORDS

Steganography, Syndrome-Trellis Codes, Distortion Minimization

ACM Reference Format:
Tomáš Pevný and Andrew D. Ker. 2018. Exploring Non-Additive Distortion in Steganography. In *IH&MMSec '18: 6th ACM Workshop on Information Hiding and Multimedia Security, June 20–22, 2018, Innsbruck, Austria*. ACM, New York, NY, USA, Article 4, 6 pages. https://doi.org/10.1145/3206004.3206015

1 MOTIVATION

The Prisoners' Problem models steganography as follows: Alice (the sender and steganographer) wishes to send secret messages to Bob (the receiver) without raising the suspicion of the warden Eve (the steganalyst), who inspects all messages for illicit content. Alice and Bob use steganography to hide their secret messages inside

innocuous-looking objects, as invisibly as possible, while Eve wants to detect hidden messages as accurately as possible. Thus Alice and Eve have antagonistic goals.

In steganography by cover modification the embedding function

$$f_{\text{emb}} : \mathcal{X} \times \mathcal{M} \times \mathcal{K} \mapsto \mathcal{X}$$

accepts the cover object $\mathbf{x} \in \mathcal{X}$, message $\mathbf{m} \in \mathcal{M}$, and secret key $k \in \mathcal{K}$, and produces a stego object $\mathbf{y} \in \mathcal{X}$ containing the hidden message. This can be extracted by a function

$$f_{\text{ext}} : \mathcal{X} \times \mathcal{K} \mapsto \mathcal{M}$$

provided with the correct key k. The sets $\mathcal{X}$, $\mathcal{M}$, and $\mathcal{K}$ correspond to the spaces of cover and stego objects (in this paper, digital images), messages, and keys respectively.

Current state of the art embedding functions (steganographic algorithms) are built on the principle of distortion minimization [6]: while embedding the message $\mathbf{m}$ into $\mathbf{x}$, Alice tries to minimize some *distortion function*

$$f_{\text{dis}} : \mathcal{X} \times \mathcal{X} \mapsto \mathbb{R}_0^+.$$

The distortion function should be related to detectability, i.e. the smaller the distortion $f_{\text{dis}}(\mathbf{x}, \mathbf{y})$, the smaller the chance that Eve detects covert communication. During embedding the algorithm therefore tries to solve the following optimization problem

$$\arg \min_{\mathbf{y} \in \mathcal{X}} f_{\text{dis}}(\mathbf{x}, \mathbf{y}) \text{ subject to } f_{\text{ext}}(\mathbf{y}, k) = \mathbf{m}.$$

This is an NP-complete problem for general extraction and distortion functions, and remains NP-complete when – as is often the case – the extraction functions are restricted to linear maps $f_{\text{ext}}(\mathbf{y}, k) = \mathbf{H}\mathbf{P}_k\mathbf{m}$, where $\mathbf{P}_k$ is some key-dependent permutation matrix, and $\mathbf{H}$ a fixed parity-check matrix of some linear code (so-called *syndrome coding*). However, for *additive* distortion functions, given by the sum of local distortions caused by changing individual pixels independently, Syndrome-Trellis Coding (STC) [6] allows finding a solution, typically within 5–7% of the optimum [20]. The computational efficiency and near-optimality of STC have narrowed the design of new steganographic algorithms to the search for better additive distortion functions, as the coding seems to be solved.

There does exist a technique for optimizing non-additive distortion functions, the Gibbs Embedding method of [5], much more complex than STCs, requires multiple sweeps through the stego object (of an uncertain number), and is restricted to the class of distortion functions which are *sums of local potentials*. It was used to boost the performance of the additive distortion in HUGO in [9], and for HILL [11] and MVG [19] to promote changes of nearby pixels in the same direction in [4, 12]. In [8] it was applied to the non-additive S-UNIWARD distortion function [9], but this failed to improve on the additive version, due in part to a technical limitation of the Gibbs sampler.

This paper explores another method for minimizing non-additive distortion functions, a variation on the STC algorithm (Sect. 2). It does *not* find optimal solutions but it avoids some of the limitations of Gibbs Embedding: it is easy to understand, relatively cheap to implement, and does not suffer the same technical limitation.

We will test this so-called *variable-cost STC* against the non-additive S-UNIWARD distortion function, that is typically minimized only in an additive approximation via the standard STC algorithm (Sect. 3). Our method does not fail in the same way that Gibbs embedding appears to in [8], but we will discover parallel results: we will find lower distortion than the additive approximation, but the stego objects will be more detectable. This casts doubt on the link between UNIWARD distortion (do not confuse with its additive approximation) and detectability.

We also show how our method can be used if the embedder knows exactly the detector that Eve uses: a kind of adversarial embedding (Sect. 4), something not necessarily possible even with Gibbs Embedding. It allows the embedder to optimize against one specific detector, although this only makes them more detectable by others.

This work is aimed at exploring some consequences of non-additive distortion. We do not claim that the variable-cost STC method is optimal, or even particularly good, and the results for S-UNIWARD distortion raise more questions than they answer. We simply hope that these questions stimulate research different from micro-optimization of additive distortion functions.

2 SYNDROME-TRELLIS CODES

Our codes will use alphabet $\Sigma = \{0, 1, 2, \ldots, q - 1\}$ and all operations will be performed in mod q arithmetic unless otherwise specified. Let cover and stego objects be represented as vectors $\mathbf{x} \in \Sigma^n$, $\mathbf{y} \in \Sigma^n$ respectively, with n being the number of pixels. For simplicity of notation, we assume that the cover and stego object have already been subject to some key-dependent permutation. This is independent of the rest of the procedure and the key will be omitted from now on.

The communicated message is also a q-ary vector $\mathbf{m} \in \Sigma^m$ with $m < n$ being the length of the message. The cover object $\mathbf{x}$ is modified to $\mathbf{y}$ such that the message $\mathbf{m}$ is communicated as a syndrome of a parity check matrix $\mathbf{H} \in \Sigma^{m,n}$, i.e.

$$\mathbf{Hy} = \mathbf{m}.$$

Since $m < n$, the solution of $\mathbf{Hy} = \mathbf{m}$ is not unique. This freedom is used to select $\mathbf{y}$ which not only communicates the message but also minimizes distortion measured by the function $f_{\text{dis}}(\mathbf{y}, \mathbf{x})$.

Ref. [6] proposed the Viterbi algorithm to solve the above problem, provided that *(i)* the distortion function is additive, i.e.

$$f_{\text{dis}}(\mathbf{x}, \mathbf{y}) = \sum_{i=1}^{n} f_{\text{dis}}(\mathbf{x}, \mathbf{y}_i),$$

where $f_{\text{dis}}(\mathbf{x}, \mathbf{y}_i)$ is a distortion between cover image $\mathbf{x}$ and stego image $\mathbf{y}$ differing from $\mathbf{x}$ only at the i-th pixel, and *(ii)* $\mathbf{H}$ is a sparse block-diagonal matrix constructed by repeatedly placing sub-matrix

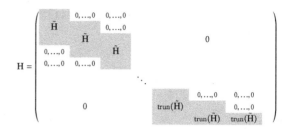

Figure 1: Block diagonal matrix used in Syndrome-Trellis Codes, as proposed in [20]. trun($\tilde{\mathbf{H}}$) denotes $\tilde{\mathbf{H}}$ with bottom rows appropriately removed.

$\tilde{\mathbf{H}} \in \Sigma^{h \times \frac{n}{m}}$ next to each other and shifted down by one (see Figure 1)[1]. The parameter h is known in convolutional codes as the *constraint height*, and its value affects the performance of the algorithm: larger h will find solutions with lower distortion, at higher computational cost.

2.1 The Viterbi Algorithm

We now use the following notation. For $\mathbf{x}$ a vector of length n, and $0 < i \leq j \leq n$ integers, $\mathbf{x}_{i:j}$ is the sub-vector of $\mathbf{x}$ consisting of elements $(\mathbf{x}_i, \mathbf{x}_{i+1}, \ldots, \mathbf{x}_j)$. If this happens to access a vector beyond its length, which will happen as our embedding reaches the end of the cover object, we can pad the answer with zeros. $\mathbf{e}_i$ will denote the i-th basis vector (with n implicit). Let $\mathbf{H} \in \Sigma^{m,n}$ be a matrix and i, j as before, then $\mathbf{H}_{i:j}$ is a sub-matrix containing only columns $(i, i + 1, \ldots, j)$ of $\mathbf{H}$. Finally, $\mathbf{H}_i$ represents the single column i of $\mathbf{H}$.

We will describe the Viterbi algorithm in a style different from [6], avoiding explicit construction of the trellis. Perverse as it may seem to remove the Trellis from Syndrome-Trellis Code, it will present a classical algorithm from an alternative view, and also allow us to show simply the modification to non-additive distortions, albeit not optimally minimized.

The algorithm maintains three variables:

$$\begin{aligned} i &\in \mathbb{N}, \\ j &\in \mathbb{N}, \\ \mathcal{S} &\subseteq \Sigma^n \times \mathbb{R} \times \Sigma^h, \end{aligned}$$

where i represents the number of cover pixels completed, j the number of payload symbols correctly and optimally encoded, and $(\mathbf{y}, d, \mathbf{s}) \in \mathcal{S}$ if stego object $\mathbf{y}$ encoded such payload, with distortion d, and $\mathbf{s} = (\mathbf{H}_{1:i}\mathbf{y}_{1:i})_{(j+1):(j+h)}$. This last quantity is called the *partial syndrome* in [6], where its evolution is traced by the trellis.

We can express these properties formally by invariants $0 \leq i \leq n$, $0 \leq j \leq m$, and $(\mathbf{y}, d, \mathbf{s}) \in \mathcal{S}$ implies $(\mathbf{Hy})_{1:j} = \mathbf{m}_{1:j}$, $d = f_{\text{dis}}(\mathbf{x}, \mathbf{y})$, $\mathbf{s} = (\mathbf{H}_{1:i}\mathbf{y}_{1:i})_{(j+1):(j+h)}$, and if $\mathbf{y}'$ satisfies the same properties then $f_{\text{dis}}(\mathbf{x}, \mathbf{y}) \leq f_{\text{dis}}(\mathbf{x}, \mathbf{y}')$. The invariant is established with *initialization*

$$i := 0, \ j := 0, \ \mathcal{S} := \{(\mathbf{x}, 0, \mathbf{0})\}.$$

---

[1] For clarity of explanation it is assumed that the payload length m is an integer divisor of the cover size n. Otherwise, the banded structure of the matrix $\mathbf{H}$ can be achieved by interleaving sub-matrices $\tilde{\mathbf{H}}$ of different widths, and some of the indexing in the algorithm must be adapted accordingly.

At each stage we explore the space of possible partial syndromes, in what we might call an *expansion step*: set $i := i + 1$, identify the column of $\tilde{\mathbf{H}}$ corresponding to i^{th} pixel[2] and call it $\mathbf{h}$, then set

$$\mathcal{S} := \left\{ \left(\mathbf{y} + k_i \mathbf{e}_i, f_{\text{dis}}(\mathbf{x}, \mathbf{y} + k_i \mathbf{e}_i), \mathbf{s} + k_i \mathbf{h} \right) \middle| (\mathbf{y}, d, \mathbf{s}) \in \mathcal{S},\ k_i \in \Sigma \right\}.$$

Then we perform a *greedy decimation step*, keeping only the optimal stego objects for each partial syndrome: for each pair $(\mathbf{y}_1, d_1, \mathbf{s}) \in \mathcal{S}$ and $(\mathbf{y}_2, d_2, \mathbf{s}) \in \mathcal{S}$, keep only the first if $d_1 < d_2$, otherwise keep the second (ties may be broken arbitrarily). This ensures that $|\mathcal{S}| \le q^h$, as there are only q^h distinct partial syndromes.

There is one further step in the case that we reached the final column of a block in $\mathbf{H}$.[3] In such cases we perform a *payload matching step*: set $j := j + 1$, then remove stego objects which do not match the first j payload symbols and restore the invariant by setting

$$\mathcal{S} := \left\{ (\mathbf{y}, d, \mathbf{s} \ll 1) \middle| (\mathbf{y}, d, \mathbf{s}) \in \mathcal{S} \wedge \mathbf{s}_1 = \mathbf{m}_j \right\},$$

where $\ll 1$ denotes a left-shift operation on a vector in Σ^h, padding with zero on the right. The condition ensures correctness of payload symbol j because of the invariant and the banded structure of $\mathbf{H}$. Note that $\mathcal{S}$ is nonempty as long as the first row of $\tilde{\mathbf{H}}$ is not all zeros.

The sequence *expansion*, *greedy decimation*, and sometimes *payload matching*, are iterated until $i = n$ and $j = m$. Then choose the l such that d_l is least in $(\mathbf{y}_l, d_l, \mathbf{s}_l) \in \mathcal{S}$; the corresponding $\mathbf{y}_l$ is the stego object that, by the invariant, correctly encodes payload $\mathbf{m}$ with lowest distortion. The optimality of the solution relies on the *Principle of Optimality* of dynamic programming: if $\mathbf{y}$ is the optimal solution to the entire problem then $\mathbf{y}_{1:n'}$ is necessarily the optimal solution to the subproblem consisting of the first $n' < n$ pixels (and the corresponding length of payload). Thus the greedy decimation step, which filters such solutions, cannot exclude an optimal solution to the entire problem.

In the case of additive distortion, a simplification may be made. We precalculate per-change costs

$$c_{i,k} = f_{\text{dis}}(\mathbf{x}, \mathbf{x} + k\mathbf{e}_i)$$

and at the expansion step we need not recalculate $f_{\text{dis}}(\mathbf{x}, \mathbf{y} + k\mathbf{e}_i)$ since, by additivity, it must equal $f_{\text{dis}}(\mathbf{x}, \mathbf{y}) + c_{i,k}$. In this case we could recover the trellis of the classical Viterbi algorithm by storing, instead of the entirety of $\mathbf{y}$ for each member of $\mathcal{S}$, the sequence of k_i: at the end of the algorithm then performing a *backward pass* through the trellis to recover $\mathbf{y}$.

2.2 Variable-Cost STCs

With our description the entire stego object is available at each i and for each partial syndrome $\mathbf{s}$. This allows recalculating the distortion function at each expansion step, applying the same procedure to the case of non-additive distortion functions. The algorithm becomes a heuristic, and optimality is not necessarily (or even probably) still true: in non-additive distortion, the Principle of Optimality does not hold. If the optimal solution to the entire problem is $\mathbf{y}$, it is not necessarily the case that $\mathbf{y}_{1:n'}$ is the optimal solution to the subproblem consisting of the first $n' < n$ pixels, since early sub-optimal decisions might unlock better solutions further along.

But the method can still be used for steganography because the correctness of the payload remains true.

This version of the algorithm will be called the *variable-cost* STC, as it corresponds to the classical STC in which outgoing costs are updated at every state of the trellis. Note that the time complexity of the original STC is $O\left(nhq^{h+1}\right)$ arithmetic operations to maintain $\mathcal{S}$ (n expansion steps, each with up to q^h partial syndromes, each with q outgoing edges; by storing only k_i these operations can all be on vectors of length at most h) and only $O\left((q-1)n\right)$ calls on the distortion function when the costs are precomputed for each location. For the variable-cost STC, there are the same number of vector operations, but because we maintain a complete stego object at each step they are vectors of length n: thus $O\left(n^2 q^{h+1}\right)$ arithmetic operations to maintain $\mathcal{S}$. More significantly, we now require $O\left(nq^{h+1}\right)$ calls on the distortion function, one for each possible change for each partial syndrome. Since in the practice of digital image steganography, distortion functions involve multiple filters on the entire image, this is a significant overhead, as will be reported in Section 3.

This method can be contrasted with Gibbs Embedding [5]. It is conceptually much simpler, and can be accomplished with minor modifications to the standard STC algorithm. It does not require multiple sweeps; indeed, at the start of the cover image it functions rather like the first Gibbs sweep, and at the end rather like the second. There is no need to divide the payload amongst sublattices, nor does *erasure entropy* penalize us when the changes are clustered: we will explore this in the next section.

3 OPTIMIZATION OF S-UNIWARD

The variable-cost STC was tested in spatial domain steganography using S-UNIWARD [9] with ternary alphabet $q = 3$, implemented as ± 1 embedding changes. The layered construction [6] was *not* used, as it causes additional coding loss.

The reasons for choosing this distortion function are *(i)* it is still a leading steganographic scheme, *(ii)* it was derived from a non-additive cost function that depends on the entire cover and stego object, unlike other leading cost-assignment rules [11, 18] which are pixel-wise and additive by design, and *(iii)* a similar experiment was attempted with Gibbs Embedding in [8].

The UNIWARD distortion function originally proposed in [9] is

$$f_{\text{dis}}(\mathbf{x}, \mathbf{y}) = \sum_{k=1}^{3} \sum_{u=1}^{n_1} \sum_{v=1}^{n_2} \frac{|W_{uv}^{(k)}(\mathbf{x}) - W_{uv}^{(k)}(\mathbf{y})|}{|W_{uv}^{(k)}(\mathbf{x}) + 1|}, \tag{1}$$

where $W_{uv}^{(k)}(\mathbf{x})$ are u, v pixels of the image $\mathbf{x}$ convolved with a kth filter; the exact filters are irrelevant to this paper so we direct the reader to [9] for details.

Because UNIWARD was designed for Syndrome-Trellis Codes, it must make an additive approximation to the non-additive distortion function (1). In the case of spatial-domain images and ± 1 embedding changes, the reference implementation of S-UNIWARD[4] uses $f_{\text{dis}}(\mathbf{x}, \mathbf{y}) = \sum_{u,v} \rho_{uv}(\mathbf{x}, \mathbf{y})$, where

$$\rho_{uv}(\mathbf{x}, \mathbf{y}) = \sum_{k=1}^{3} \frac{|x_{uv} - y_{uv}|}{|W_{uv}^{(k)}(\mathbf{x}) + 1|}, \tag{2}$$

---

[2]When m is an integer divisor of n, it is $\tilde{\mathbf{H}}_k$ with $k = (i - 1) \bmod (n/m) + 1$.

[3]When m is in an integer divisor of n, if $i = kn/m$ for integer k.

is the distortion at pixel location (u, v).

In [8], the Gibbs Embedding algorithm was applied to the original, non-additive, UNIWARD distortion function, and the results compared against the additive approximation. Gibbs Embedding can be applied because the form of (1) is a sum of local potentials. To paraphrase the results obtained, more sweeps of the Gibbs algorithm caused *increased* distortion, and the cause was traced to a limitation of the Gibbs sampler: it only achieves the *erasure entropy* of the conditionally-independent subfields [5, VI.C], which is strictly lower than the entropy of the entire Gibbs field. In the case of this distortion function, the sampler attempts to cluster changes very tightly, which in turn reduces the erasure entropy, forcing higher numbers of embedding changes.

We can use variable-cost STCs to investigate the same question: with this heuristic, the erasure entropy problem is not present. We also need not perform multiple sweeps and try to guess when to stop. On the other hand, unlike Gibbs Embedding we do not converge to a true optimum. Compared with standard STCs optimizing the additive approximation we pay a price in complexity, because there are many more distortion computations: Table 1 shows that it is approximately 15 times slower for this size of image and distortion function, even after we optimized the calculation of distortion so that only the part of the image affected by each embedding change is updated, and we must admit that our algorithm will not find the global minimum distortion. Nonetheless, the results tell a story, and parallel observations in [8].

Using both the additive S-UNIWARD distortion function (2), and the non-additive original (1), we embedded payloads corresponding to 0.1, 0.2, and 0.3 bits per pixel into the 10000 never-compressed images of BOSSBase v1.01 [1]. To isolate unnecessary variation, for each image we generated a random payload, random sub-matrix $\hat{\mathbf{H}}$, and random permutation of the pixels; then used the same choices for both STC and variable-cost STC embedding of that image.

The height of the sub-matrix $\hat{\mathbf{H}}$ was set to three, which means that the algorithm explored $3^3 = 27$ partial syndromes. This low number was used to reduce the computational complexity, but we must admit that it may take both versions of the STC far from the optimum. In order to estimate this effect (called coding loss), the same relative payload was embedded using *simulated optimal coding* for the additive distortion function (we call this *additive optimal* simulation). According to [6], the optimal probability of making change $k\mathbf{e}_i$, i.e. adding $k \in \Sigma$ to location i, is

$$\pi_i(k) = \frac{e^{-\lambda f_{\text{dis}}(\mathbf{x}, \mathbf{x}+k\mathbf{e}_i)}}{\sum_{k' \in \Sigma} e^{-\lambda f_{\text{dis}}(\mathbf{x}, \mathbf{x}+k'\mathbf{e}_i)}} \qquad (3)$$

where λ is determined by $\sum_{i=1}^{n} \sum_{k \in \Sigma} -\pi_i(k) \log_2 \pi_i(k) = m$.

The detectability of each steganographic scheme, at each payload, has been estimated by the probability of error of a Fisher Linear Classifier [2] that has used the full set of 34671 dimensional SRM steganalytic features [7]. These features are one of the standard benchmarks for contemporary steganalysis, amongst those that do not exploit knowledge of the selection channel. The classifier was trained for each embedding method separately following the standard setting, where half of the images were left for testing and the tolerance parameter was optimized by grid-search on values $\{10^{-5}, 10^{-4}, \dots, 10^{15}\}$, with the probability of error estimated by five-fold cross-validation.

method	payload (bpp)		
	0.1	0.2	0.3
embedding time (mm:ss)			
additive	1:07	1:06	1:07
non-additive	17:07	16:30	16:04
distortion achieved			
additive	18871	35973	57089
non-additive	11747	24184	40953
additive optimal	13196	27408	42231

Table 1: Average embedding time per image, and distortion as measured by Equation (1), **for different payload sizes. The images were grayscale** 512×512, **and times measured on Amazon's AWS** m4.2xlarge **instance (Intel® Xeon® CPU E5-2686 with 32Gb of RAM).**

Table 1 shows the average distortion of stego-images measured by Equation (1) for the three compared methods on the three payloads. As expected, minimizing the additive approximation results in total distortion which is higher than minimizing the true non-additive distortion via variable-cost STC. The non-additive version optimizing the true distortion is on average better by 30%. We can be sure that this is not simply a poor performance by the standard STC due to the relatively small value of h, because the distortion the variable-cost STC is still lower than the optimal distortion calculated by (1). This demonstrates that the proposed variable-cost modification of STC is able to find better solutions when minimization of the original UNIWARD distortion is the aim.

However, Figure 2 (left) shows the error of steganalyzers for these steganographic schemes. Optimizing original UNIWARD, despite giving lower distortion, is more detectable. (The only exception is on the payload 0.3 bpp, where it is better by an insignificant 0.3%.) This parallels the results in [8], though in our case it is not due to the erasure entropy limitation of Gibbs samplers. Instead, it suggests that UNIWARD distortion (1) is simply not as related to steganographic security (as measured by this detector) as was originally thought. Its additive approximation is a better measure.

Similarly to [8], we explored the number and patterns of changes caused by minimizing the non-additive distortion. Figure 2 (right) shows the average number of embedding changes for all three schemes on all three payloads. The non-additive algorithm makes more embedding changes, apparently finding ways to reduce distortion by adding changes that, to some extent, cancel out the effects of others. An additive approximation, when the costs are all positive, never makes such a choice, implicitly regularizing the number of embedding changes. In this sense, the additive approximation corrects a flaw of the S-Uniward's distortion function.

We also explored whether the non-additive distortion function tends to cluster its changes or align nearby changes in the same direction: such synchronization has been recently proposed in [4, 12, 21], as an adjunct to additive distortion functions. Figure 3 shows changes of the image under a single message. A closer look shows that changes of the non-additive version are slightly more clustered and aligned. We measured these by, for each changed pixel, counting the number of aligned versus non-aligned changes in its

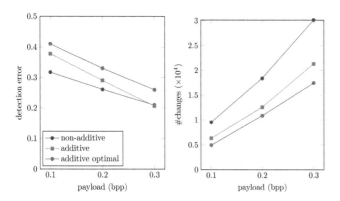

Figure 2: Error of linear detectors (left), and number of changes made during embedding (right), for additive cost via STC, non-additive costs via variable-cost STC, and simulated optimal additive costs.

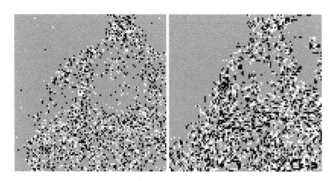

Figure 3: Embedding changes made during embedding of a message of 0.3 bpp, using additive (left) and non-additive (right) S-UNIWFeRD distortion function, in a crop from image number 1013 from BOSSBase v1.01. A white pixel indicates a positive change, grey indicates no change, and a black pixel indicates a negative change.

3×3 neighborhood. For the additive S-UNIWARD, the proportion is $0.760 : 0.758$, whereas the same ratio for the non-additive method is $1.941 : 1.098$. This is more evidence in favor of the principle of synchronizing nearby changes [4, 12, 21]. To some extent these parallel the results seen at the end of Chapter 6 of [8], but comparing with its Figure 6.4.2 we see that variable-cost STCs cluster and align changes to a much lesser degree than Gibbs Embedding. This provides probably because it does not find an optimal solution to the minimum distortion.

4 DISTORTION DEFINED BY A DETECTOR

Consider a scenario where Alice knows the steganalytic detector used by Eve. Strange as it may sound, it occurs in security domains and commonly-used antivirus software is a prime example: miscreants can (and do) use them to test detectability of their new malicious products, and there are even specialized services for this job. Another example are Oracle attacks [3] in watermarking where the attacker has unrestricted access to the detector (oracle).

Early steganographic algorithms implicitly considered this scenario, as they frequently targeted a particular type of steganalysis. For example, OutGuess's [15] statistical restoration aimed to preserve first-order statistics of DCT coefficients in JPEG images. Similarly, Model-Based Steganography [17] aimed to preserve first order statistics of individual DCT modes and statistics of pixels on the border of DCT blocks (avoiding 'blockiness' artifacts).

Subsequent work of a similar nature assumed Eve to base her detector on a particular steganalytic feature set, and attempted to stay undetectable with respect detectors utilizing them. HUGO [14] used a heuristically-defined distortion measure based on SPAM features [13]. This has been further improved by [10, 20], defining pixelwise costs from the error of L2-Support Vector Machines or Fisher Linear Discriminant classifiers. More generally, when particular detectors are used to assess the security of new algorithms that depend on parameters, such parameters are implicitly being optimized towards undetectability by those detectors.

A steganographic detector can be represented as a function $f : \mathcal{X} \mapsto \mathbb{R}$. If the output exceeds some threshold, then the object is classified as stego, otherwise as cover. Given a method for optimizing arbitrary functions while coding a message, such f can be used as a distortion function itself. But the distortion is no longer a proper name of f, because f measures *probability* or *likelihood* of image being classified as stego. By minimizing its output Alice tries to create objects that will not trip the detector, even if they are not close to covers. The same idea can be applied to any detector: those based on a combination of steganalytic features and machine-learning classifiers [7], or those based on convolutional neural networks (CNN) [16]. But STCs and Gibbs Embedding cannot be used, because the distortion is unlikely to be additive or a sum of local potentials. Variable-cost STCs could provide a method, albeit being suboptimal. It is not necessary to understand the inner workings of the detector, as it can be treated as an oracle; all that is needed is a optimization heuristic.

To demonstrate the application of variable-cost STCs to this problem, we set Eve's detector as a linear classifier utilizing the 3588 first-order part of SRM features [7] (choosing only the subset for reasons of computational complexity). Denoting by $\phi(x)$ the SRM feature extraction function, the detector is implemented as $f(x) = w^T\phi(x)$, where w is the solution of L_2-regularized Fisher's Linear Discriminant [2] detecting stego images created by additive S-UNIWARD with payload 0.3 bpp. The regularization parameter was chosen such that it minimizes error on unseen images, estimated by five-fold cross-validation. This detector has error rate 0.28 on images embedded by S-UNIWARD with payload 0.3.

Figure 4 shows the distributions of outputs of the detector on cover images, stego images embedded by S-UNIWARD with payload 0.3, and stego images created by the proposed variable-cost STC hiding the same payload. For reasons of complexity, the last class only contained 500 images. Stego images created by S-UNIWARD have higher values of $w^T\phi(x)$, which is consistent with the aims of the detector. Cover images are located closer to the center, and a practical detector will have a threshold to the cover distribution. Finally, stego images created by Alice knowing Eve's detector are far off to the left, with very low values of $w^T\phi(x)$. For this specific detector, they would be classified as covers.

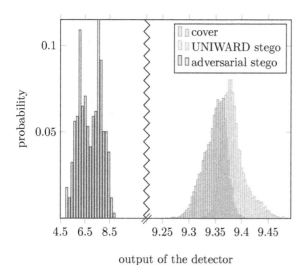

output of the detector

Figure 4: Histogram of outputs of the detector on cover images, images containing 0.3 bpp embedded by additive S-UNIWARD, and images containing the same message embedded by variable-cost STC minimizing the output of the detector ('adversarial stego'). The detector is targeted to the S-UNIWARD images, and uses first-order SRM features.

Of course, they are detectable. As is evident from the histogram, even the exact same detector, but swapping the sign of its output, would classify them as stego objects with perfect accuracy. The embedding method in this form can only be recommended if Alice is completely certain that Eve has fixed her detector. How to use it in practice is a subject for further research.

5 CONCLUSION

By re-presenting Syndrome-Trellis Codes without a trellis, we have demonstrated that the same algorithm can be used as a heuristic for minimizing non-additive distortion functions. An application was to optimize S-UNIWARD, which is normally only be minimized in its additive approximation, and where Gibbs Embedding did not succeed. The variable-cost STC does indeed reduce distortion, but we observed the same result as in [8]: detectability does not reduce. Although we do not cluster changes too tightly, as Gibbs Embedding tries to, a similar feature to [8] is that the non-additive distortion makes additional changes, presumably in the belief that they partially cancel each other out.

Although sub-optimal, the variable-cost STC is relatively simple to run, and we hope that it will spur research into non-additive distortion functions that can take advantage of it. The paucity of such functions limits the applicability of our method.

The same method can be used for distortion functions that evade a specific detector, in the case that Alice knows Eve's exact behaviour, something not necessarily possible even with Gibbs Embedding. Such a scheme cannot properly be called undetectable because it is highly detectable by anyone else! Most literature is concerned with the reverse situation, where the detector knows everything about the embedder save whether they are active or not.

Both scenarios, and the equilibrium case where each knows the other's behaviour, deserve scrutiny, and benchmarks for steganalysis should not focus purely on one case.

ACKNOWLEDGMENT

The authors thank Patrick Bas and Christy Kin-Cleaves for fruitful discussions.

The work of Tomás Pevný was supported by OP VVV Research Center for Informatics no. CZ.02.1.01/0.0/0.0/16_019/0000765.

REFERENCES

[1] Patrick Bas, Tomáš Filler, and Tomáš Pevný. 2011. "Break Our Steganographic System": The Ins and Outs of Organizing BOSS. In *International Workshop on Information Hiding*, Vol. 6958, LNCS. Springer Berlin Heidelberg, 59–70.

[2] Rémi Cogranne, Vahid Sedighi, Jessica Fridrich, and Tomáš Pevný. 2015. Is ensemble classifier needed for steganalysis in high-dimensional feature spaces?. In *IEEE International Workshop on Information Forensics and Security (WIFS)*. 1–6.

[3] Pedro Comesana, Luis Pérez-Freire, and Fernando Pérez-González. 2006. Blind newton sensitivity attack. *IEE Proceedings-Information Security* 153, 3 (2006), 115–125.

[4] Tomáš Denemark and Jessica Fridrich. 2015. Improving Steganographic Security by Synchronizing the Selection Channel. In *Proceedings of the 3rd ACM Workshop on Information Hiding and Multimedia Security (IH&MMSec '15)*. ACM, 5–14.

[5] Tomáš Filler and Jessica Fridrich. 2010. Gibbs construction in steganography. *IEEE Transactions on Information Forensics and Security* 5, 4 (2010), 705–720.

[6] Tomáš Filler, Jan Judas, and Jessica Fridrich. 2011. Minimizing additive distortion in steganography using syndrome-trellis codes. *IEEE Transactions on Information Forensics and Security* 6, 3 (2011), 920–935.

[7] Jessica Fridrich and Jan Kodovsky. 2012. Rich models for steganalysis of digital images. *IEEE Transactions on Information Forensics and Security* 7, 3 (2012), 868–882.

[8] Vojtěch Holub et al. 2014. *Content Adaptive Steganography: Design and Detection*. Ph.D. Dissertation.

[9] Vojtěch Holub, Jessica Fridrich, and Tomáš Denemark. 2014. Universal distortion function for steganography in an arbitrary domain. *EURASIP Journal on Information Security* 2014, 1 (2014), 1.

[10] Sarra Kouider, Marc Chaumont, and William Puech. 2013. Adaptive steganography by oracle (ASO). In *IEEE International Conference on Multimedia and Expo (ICME)*. 1–6.

[11] Bin Li, Ming Wang, Jiwu Huang, and Xiaolong Li. 2014. A new cost function for spatial image steganography. In *IEEE International Conference on Image Processing (ICIP)*. 4206–4210.

[12] B. Li, M. Wang, X. Li, S. Tan, and J. Huang. 2015. A Strategy of Clustering Modification Directions in Spatial Image Steganography. *IEEE Transactions on Information Forensics and Security* 10, 9 (Sept 2015), 1905–1917.

[13] Tomáš Pevný, Patrick Bas, and Jessica Fridrich. 2010. Steganalysis by subtractive pixel adjacency matrix. *IEEE Transactions on information Forensics and Security* 5, 2 (2010), 215–224.

[14] Tomáš Pevný, Tomáš Filler, and Patrick Bas. 2010. Using high-dimensional image models to perform highly undetectable steganography. In *International Workshop on Information Hiding*, Vol. 6387, LNCS. Springer Berlin Heidelberg, 161–177.

[15] Niels Provos. 2001. Defending Against Statistical Steganalysis.. In *Usenix security symposium*, Vol. 10. 323–336.

[16] Yinlong Qian, Jing Dong, Wei Wang, and Tieniu Tan. 2015. Deep learning for steganalysis via convolutional neural networks. In *Media Watermarking, Security, and Forensics 2015*, Vol. 9409. 94090J.

[17] Phil Sallee. 2005. Model-based methods for steganography and steganalysis. *International Journal of Image and graphics* 5, 01 (2005), 167–189.

[18] Vahid Sedighi, Rémi Cogranne, and Jessica Fridrich. 2016. Content-Adaptive Steganography by Minimizing Statistical Detectability. *IEEE Transactions on Information Forensics and Security* 11, 2 (2016), 221–234.

[19] Vahid Sedighi, Jessica Fridrich, and Rémi Cogranne. 2015. Content-adaptive pentary steganography using the multivariate generalized Gaussian cover model. In *Media Watermarking, Security, and Forensics 2015*, Vol. 9409. 94090H.

[20] Jessica Fridrich Tomáš Filler. 2011. Design of adaptive steganographic schemes for digital images. (2011), 7880 - 7880 - 14 pages.

[21] Wenbo Zhou, Weiming Zhang, and Nenghai Yu. 2017. A New Rule for Cost Reassignment in Adaptive Steganography. *IEEE Transactions on Information Forensics and Security* 12, 11 (2017), 2654–2667.

On the Relationship Between Embedding Costs and Steganographic Capacity

Andrew D. Ker
Department of Computer Science
University of Oxford
Oxford, UK
adk@cs.ox.ac.uk

ABSTRACT

Contemporary steganography in digital media is dominated by the framework of additive distortion minimization: every possible change is given a cost, and the embedder minimizes total cost using some variant of the Syndrome-Trellis Code algorithm. One can derive the relationship between the cost of each change c_i and the probability that it should be made π_i, but the literature has not examined the relationship between the costs and the total capacity (secure payload size) of the cover. In this paper we attempt to uncover such a relationship, asymptotically, for a simple independent pixel model of covers. We consider a 'knowing' detector who is aware of the embedding costs, in which case $\sum \pi_i^2 c_i$ should be optimized. It is shown that the total of the inverse costs, $\sum c_i^{-1}$, along with the embedder's desired security against an optimal opponent, determines the asymptotic capacity. This result also recovers a Square Root Law. Some simple simulations confirm the relationship between costs and capacity in this ideal model.

KEYWORDS

Adaptive steganography; optimal embedding; square root law

ACM Reference Format:
Andrew D. Ker. 2018. On the Relationship Between Embedding Costs and Steganographic Capacity. In *IH&MMSec '18: 6th ACM Workshop on Information Hiding and Multimedia Security, June 20–22, 2018, Innsbruck, Austria.* ACM, New York, NY, USA, 6 pages. https://doi.org/10.1145/3206004.3206017

1 INTRODUCTION

In steganography, *additive distortion minimization* is a framework for selecting steganographic changes, aiming to choose the least detectable combination. Each possible change is enumerated – in images, this might include incrementing or decrementing each pixel or transform coefficient – and each change is assigned a *cost*. Then the combination of changes is selected which both encodes the desired payload and minimizes total cost, most famously using the

Syndrome-Trellis Code (STC) algorithm [3]. With different heuristics for cost, this is the dominant method in digital media steganography at this time: the UNIWARD methods [4] and HILL [7] are the standard benchmarks for still image steganography, and STCs are now also used in audio [8] and video [10] steganography.

When the attacker (Warden, steganalyst) is aware of the costs, minimizing total cost is not optimal. Such a situation was examined in [6], which derives optimal behaviour for the the embedder against this so-called *knowing attacker*.

Against either an ignorant or a knowing attacker, there are simple calculations showing the relationship between the *cost* of a change and the *probability* of making such a change, in a single steganographic embedding. What the results do not show is the relationship between a cover's entire *set* of costs and its *capacity* (by which we mean secure payload size), yet one would expect such a relationship to exist: if most costs are large, most locations are difficult to hide in (and easy to detect changes of), so the capacity should be low; conversely if plenty of costs are low, the capacity should be high. This paper shows that the relationship is, asymptotically, rather simple.

We restrict our attention to a simple independent pixel model of covers, and the case of a knowing attacker: our result is an asymptotic analysis of the optimization problem derived in [6]. Note that this is *not* the most common optimization problem encountered in steganography, where the coding is typically solved by STCs, but it is the correct behaviour against a detector that knows the embedding costs. Indeed, this work is not strictly a result about steganography, rather about the asymptotic solutions to a certain optimization problem that has applications in steganography.

In Sect. 2 we will summarise the theoretical result of [6], describing the model at hand and the optimal behaviour of payload- and distortion-limited senders, as well as identifying some pathological cases to exclude. We state the result in Sect. 3, and prove it in Sect. 4. Some simple simulations are performed in Sect. 5 to confirm the result, and we discuss further directions in Sect. 6.

1.1 Asymptotic Notation

Throughout the paper we write asymptotic relationships

$$f(x) \sim g(x) \text{ as } x \to a$$

($a \in \mathbb{R}$ or $a = \pm\infty$; the limit may be one-sided) to mean

$$\frac{f(x)}{g(x)} \to 1$$

in the same limit. Recall that $f(x) \sim g(x)$ as $x \to a$ implies $(f \circ h)(x) \sim (g \circ h)(x)$ as $x \to h^{-1}(a)$, at least if h^{-1} exists and is continuous at a (or continuous approaching a from the relevant side, in the case of one-sided limits).

2 OPTIMAL EMBEDDING AGAINST A KNOWING ATTACKER

We adopt the model from [6], and we briefly summarise the definition and pertinent results here.

Consider a cover generated as n random elements (which we call pixels, but they need not be) taking values $x_1, \ldots, x_n$ in some finite alphabet Σ. We suppose that the pixels are independent, but not identically distributed: each x_i has a potentially-different mass function p_i.

We imagine that embedding consists of two stages: embedding locations are selected, then a fixed operation is applied at the selected locations. (This model only covers binary embedding, but see Sect. 6 for more on this.) This process is determined by the hidden payload, but if the payload is unknown it can be modelled probabilistically: location i will be selected with probability π_i. When selected, the pixel distribution is changed to some other distribution q_i. The embedder's strategy is to choose the probabilities π_i. The distributions p_i and q_i are assumed to be public knowledge.

The attacker wants to distinguish cover and stego objects. A *knowing attacker* is granted knowledge of the embedder's strategy $\pi_1, \ldots, \pi_n$, and will adjust their detector accordingly. In [6] the zero-sum payoff is modelled by the *deflection* of a linear detector, between the cases of cover and stego object, which determines (amongst other things) the large-sample false positive rate when the true detection rate is 50%. It is shown that a) linear detectors are an optimal subclass under Neyman-Pearson criteria, and b) at this game's equilibrium between embedder and attacker, the squared deflection is

$$\sum \pi_i^2 c_i$$

for some constants c_i called *costs* determined from p_i and q_i, and hence known to both players.

The paper contrasts this with the result when the attacker is not granted knowledge of the embedder's strategy $\pi_1, \ldots, \pi_n$, the so-called *ignorant* attacker: there the deflection is proportional to $\sum \pi_i c_i$ for the same costs c_i, which justifies the minimization of total average distortion in such a case. But in this work we only consider the knowing attacker.

Our starting point, then, is the following optimal embedding paradigm. Given n pixels in which to hide, and corresponding costs $c_1, \ldots, c_n$, a *distortion limited sender*, who wants to hide the maximum payload subject to a deflection constraint[1], solves the constrained optimization problem

$$\arg\max_{\pi_1, \ldots, \pi_n} m = \sum_{i=1}^n H(\pi_i) \text{ subject to } \sum_{i=1}^n \pi_i^2 c_i \leq D. \quad \textbf{(DLS)}$$

Here D is the maximum permissible squared deflection, and then m is the resulting length of payload: the relative entropy of the stego object given the cover which, thanks to the Gel'fand-Pinsker theorem, is the capacity of the cover to convey hidden payload under perfect coding. Although it is optimistic to assume that perfect coding exists, linear codes approach such capacity asymptotically [3], justifying this assumption.

Alternatively, a *payload limited sender* has a fixed payload length to communicate, and solves the constrained optimization problem

$$\arg\min_{\pi_1, \ldots, \pi_n} \delta^2 = \sum_{i=1}^n \pi_i^2 c_i \text{ subject to } \sum_{i=1}^n H(\pi_i) \geq M, \quad \textbf{(PLS)}$$

where M is the desired payload size, and then δ^2 is the resulting squared deflection.

We highlight a few properties of these two convex optimization problems, adapting arguments used for the ignorant detector [3]. We may exclude any $\pi_i > \frac{1}{2}$, since such a choice can never be optimal: $1 - \pi_i$ would reduce distortion for the same entropy. Within this range, both $\sum \pi_i^2 c_i$ and $\sum H(\pi_i)$ are increasing in each π_i, so at the optimum the constraints of (**DLS**) and (**PLS**) hold with equality. Furthermore, both (**DLS**) and (**PLS**) have (up to reparameterizing of the multiplier) the same Lagrangian

$$\mathcal{L}(\pi_1, \ldots, \pi_n, \lambda) = \sum H(\pi_i) + \lambda \sum \pi_i^2 c_i.$$

Therefore, setting its gradient to zero, they both have the same solution, occurring when, for each i,

$$\frac{\pi_i}{H'(\pi_i)} = \frac{1}{\lambda c_i}. \quad (1)$$

2.1 Exclusion of Pathological Cases

In the theory of steganographic capacity, two types of pathological case are typically excluded; they were identified in [5] as conditions termed *no free bits* and *no determinism*. We have similar conditions for the result here.

We cannot have too many cases of $c_i = 0$: each represents a 'free bit' for the embedder, who can set $\pi_i = 0.5$ to carry a payload bit while contributing nothing to the total cost. A regular supply of free payload bits will break the square root law, and contradicts the result of this paper. We also need to ban weird asymptotic behaviour where some non-negligible subset of c_i are not zero, but tend to it (which might happen if, for example, the pixels' dynamic range depends on n). Our *no free bits* condition can be simply

$$\exists \underline{c} > 0. \ \forall i. \ c_i > \underline{c}, \quad \textbf{(A)}$$

but in fact we need not always ban free bits completely. It suffices for their number to be asymptotically negligible, compared with the steganographic capacity. Such a weaker *no free bits* condition is

$$\exists \underline{c} > 0. \ \frac{\#\{c_i < \underline{c}\}}{\sqrt{n} \log n} \to 0 \text{ as } n \to \infty. \quad \textbf{(A')}$$

Clearly (**A**) implies (**A'**), and the reverse is also true if c_i are generated from some stationary ergodic[2] process, but otherwise the second condition is weaker.

We also cannot have too many $c_i = \infty$: these are unusable locations for the embedder, either because the corresponding cover location is deterministic, or because altering it would violate some constraint of the cover. We also need to ban weird asymptotic behaviour where most of the c_i are not infinite, but tend to infinity. We need not ban unusable locations completely, nor even have

---

[1]This is referred to as the *detectability limited sender* in [2].

[2]Ergodic in the sense that the ensemble mean equals the time-average mean: a cost with strictly positive probability happens linearly often, with probability 1.

them happen negligibly-often: we only need at least linearly many usable locations. So for this paper the *no determinism* condition is

$$\exists \bar{c}. \quad \frac{\#\{c_i > \bar{c}\}}{n} \to \kappa < 1 \text{ as } n \to \infty. \tag{B}$$

3 RESULT

Our result concerns the asymptotic behaviour of solutions to (**DLS**) and (**PLS**), as $n \to \infty$. In the first case, we have a fixed acceptable deflection and determine how the costs influence the rate at which m grows; in the second we have a fixed payload size and determine how the costs influence the rate at which δ^2 diminishes.

THEOREM 1. *Suppose that $c_1, c_2, \ldots$ is a fixed infinite sequence of costs (perhaps drawn from some stationary distribution, but this need not be the case) satisfying conditions (**A**) and (**B**). Write $C = \sum_{i=1}^{n} 1/c_i$ for the total inverse cost in a cover of size n, which we call the **capacity coefficient**.*

(a) *Fix D. As $n \to \infty$, the solution to (**DLS**) satisfies*

$$m \sim \frac{\sqrt{DC}}{2} \log_2(C/D). \tag{2}$$

(b) *Fix M. As $n \to \infty$, the solution to (**PLS**) satisfies*

$$\delta^2 \sim \frac{M^2}{C\left(\log_2(C/M)\right)^2}. \tag{3}$$

(c) *We may weaken the assumption that D is fixed, to $D/n \to 0$, and in (b) to $M/n \to 0$. Furthermore, (a) also holds with (**A**) weakened to (**A'**), but (b) does not.*

So in both cases the behaviour of payload/distortion is determined by the capacity coefficient C, which is the total of the inverse costs in the cover. This uncovers the asymptotic relationship between capacity, security, and the set of costs.

The result makes intuitive sense. Parts of the cover with higher costs contribute relatively little to the overall capacity, because they must be seldom used; as the cost tends to infinity, its contribution to capacity tends to zero; infinite cost locations contribute nothing.

The generalization of (a) to the case of negligibly-many zero costs is helpful since, in the real world, we might encounter a few such locations. Allowing D or M to diminish with n is practically useful since the embedder may wish to increase M with n (but sublinearly!). Indeed, probing this relationship further, we recover the famous Square Root Law by simple manipulation of (3):

COROLLARY. *If*

(i) *$m \sim r\sqrt{n} \log \sqrt{n}$, and*

(ii) *the costs are ergodic, so that $C \sim an$ where a is the **average inverse cost** $\lim \frac{1}{n} \sum 1/c_i$, then*

$$\delta^2 \to \frac{r^2}{a}. \tag{4}$$

This result shows that, even in the adversarial model where the detector knows the embedder's costs, the critical rate for embedding is $r\sqrt{n} \log \sqrt{n} = \frac{r}{2}\sqrt{n} \log n$, and the asymptotic deflection can be determined from the 'root rate' (here 'root-times-log rate') r and the average inverse cost. If m grows asymptotically strictly faster than $\sqrt{n} \log n$ then (3) ensures that the deflection tends to infinity, and if m grows strictly slower than the critical rate then the deflection tends to zero.

4 PROOF

Define the following four functions:

$$H(x) = -x \log_2 x - (1-x) \log_2(1-x), \quad J(x) = \frac{x}{\log_2 x},$$

$$G(x) = \frac{x}{H'(x)} = \frac{x}{\log_2(1-x) - \log_2 x}, \quad K(x) = \frac{x}{(\log_2 x)^2},$$

extended to $H(0) = G(0) = J(0) = K(0) = 0$. These functions are continuous approaching zero from above.

LEMMA.

(i)	$G^{-1}(x)$	$\sim$	$-x \log_2 x$	as $x \to 0^+$,
(ii)	$(H \circ G^{-1})(x)$	$\sim$	$x(\log_2 x)^2$	as $x \to 0^+$,
(iii)	$J^{-1}(x)$	$\sim$	$x \log_2 x$	as $x \to \infty$,
(iv)	$K^{-1}(x)$	$\sim$	$x(\log_2 x)^2$	as $x \to \infty$.

PROOF. For (i), compute

$$\frac{-G(x) \log_2 G(x)}{x} = \frac{-1}{H'(x)} \log\left(\frac{x}{H'(x)}\right)$$

$$= \frac{\log_2 x}{\log_2 x - \log_2(1-x)} + \frac{\log H'(x)}{H'(x)}.$$

Since $H'(x) \to \infty$ as $x \to 0^+$, the first term tends to one and the second to zero, establishing $-G(x) \log_2 G(x) \sim x$. Composing both sides with the continuous (at zero from above) function G^{-1} gives the first result. Then (ii) follows by composing $H(x) \sim -x \log_2 x$ with the previous result.

(iii) follows from

$$\frac{J(x) \log_2 J(x)}{x} = \frac{\log_2 x - \log_2 \log_2 x}{\log_2 x} \to 1, \tag{5}$$

as $x \to \infty$, so $J(x) \log_2 J(x) \sim x$. Compose with J^{-1} for the result. (iv) is similar. □

PROOF OF THEOREM 1(a). Write (1) as $\pi_i = G^{-1}(\frac{1}{\lambda c_i})$, but also rewrite it as $\pi_i c_i = \frac{H'(\pi_i)}{\lambda}$. Note that m, C, λ and the optimal solution $\pi_1, \ldots, \pi_n$ all depend on n, but we leave this dependence implicit for tidiness of notation. Now observe: G is increasing, $G(1/3) = 1/3$, H' is decreasing, and $H'(1/3) = 1$; therefore

$$H'(\pi_i) \geq 1 \iff \pi_i \leq \frac{1}{3} \iff \frac{1}{\lambda c_i} \leq \frac{1}{3} \iff c_i \geq \frac{3}{\lambda}.$$

Now consider the total distortion, bounding below:

$$\sum \pi_i^2 c_i \geq \sum_{i: c_i \leq \frac{3}{\lambda}} \pi_i^2 c_i + \sum_{i: \frac{3}{\lambda} \leq c_i \leq \bar{c}} \frac{H'(\pi_i)^2}{\lambda^2 c_i}$$

$$\geq \frac{n_1 \underline{c}}{9} + \frac{n_2}{\bar{c}\lambda^2},$$

where n_1 is the number of $c_i \leq \frac{3}{\lambda}$ and n_2 the number of $\frac{3}{\lambda} \leq c_i \leq \bar{c}$. By (**B**), $n_1 + n_2$ is linear in n. It follows that, if

$$\sum \pi_i^2 c_i \leq D, \text{ for all } n, \tag{6}$$

with D fixed, then $\lambda \to \infty$ as $n \to \infty$.

Now we know that $1/\lambda c_i \to 0$ for each i, $\pi_i \to 0$ so that any particular embedding change has diminishing probability, we can use the asymptotics of G^{-1} to obtain

$$\pi_i = G^{-1}\left(\frac{1}{\lambda c_i}\right) \sim \frac{1}{\lambda c_i} \log_2 \lambda c_i.$$

We wish to draw conclusions about $\sum \pi_i^2 c_i$ and $\sum H(\pi_i)$, but it is not in general true that $a_i \sim b_i$ for all i implies $\sum a_i \sim \sum b_i$[3]. In this case, however, because c_i is bounded below by $\underline{c}$, the arguments x_i to each G^{-1} are bounded above by $1/\underline{c}\lambda$, which tends to zero. Therefore the convergence of π_i to $-x_i \log_2 x_i$ is uniform in i, so it follows that

$$D = \sum \pi_i^2 c_i \sim \sum \frac{(\log_2 \lambda c_i)^2}{\lambda^2 c_i}. \tag{7}$$

On the other hand, use the asymptotics of $H \circ G^{-1}$ and consider the payload:

$$m = \sum H(\pi_i) = \sum (H \circ G^{-1})\left(\frac{1}{\lambda c_i}\right) \sim \sum \frac{(\log_2 \lambda c_i)^2}{\lambda c_i}. \tag{8}$$

Comparing (7) and (8), we see that the payload is asymptotically equal to λD. It remains to determine the asymptotics of λ. We get this by expanding (7),

$$D \sim \frac{1}{\lambda^2}\left[(\log_2 \lambda)^2 \sum \frac{1}{c_i} + (\log_2 \lambda) \sum \frac{\log_2 c_i}{c_i} + \sum \frac{(\log_2 c_i)^2}{c_i}\right].$$

Note that $\sum \frac{1}{c_i}$ is at least linear in n, thanks to (**B**), whereas both $\sum \frac{\log_2 c_i}{c_i}$ and $\sum \frac{(\log_2 c_i)^2}{c_i}$ are at most linear in n, because $|\log x|/x$ and $(\log x)^2/x$ are bounded for x bounded away from zero, and (**A**) ensures that c_i is bounded away from zero. Therefore the first term dominates and

$$D \sim \frac{(\log_2 \lambda)^2}{\lambda^2} \sum \frac{1}{c_i} = \frac{C}{J(\lambda)^2},$$

giving $\lambda \sim J^{-1}\left(\sqrt{C/D}\right)$ and hence

$$m \sim \lambda D \sim D J^{-1}\left(\sqrt{C/D}\right). \tag{9}$$

Plugging in the asymptotics of J^{-1} gives the result. □

PROOF OF THEOREM 1(b). Follows a similar argument. To get started we must show $\lambda \to \infty$, this time using the fact that the optimum of (**PLS**) occurs when the constraint is equality. Bounding the payload size below:

$$\sum_{c_i < \overline{c}} H(\pi_i) \geq \sum (H \circ G^{-1})\left(\frac{1}{\lambda c_i}\right) \geq n_1 (H \circ G^{-1})\left(\frac{1}{\lambda \overline{c}}\right).$$

By (**B**), n_1 is linear in n, and by monotonicity of $H \circ G^{-1}$ it follows that $\lambda \to \infty$.

By exactly the same calculations as before, $\delta^2 \sim M/\lambda$, and the asymptotics of $H \circ G^{-1}$ also give

$$M = \sum H(\pi_i) \sim \sum \frac{(\log_2 \lambda c_i)^2}{\lambda c_i} \sim \sum \frac{(\log_2 \lambda)^2}{\lambda} \frac{1}{c_i}.$$

Therefore $\lambda \sim K^{-1}(C/M)$ and hence

$$\delta^2 \sim M/\lambda \sim M/K^{-1}(C/M). \tag{10}$$

Plugging in the asymptotics of K^{-1} gives the result. □

PROOF OF THEOREM 1(c). First note that C is linear in n, since $\frac{n(1-\kappa)}{\overline{c}} \leq C \leq \frac{n}{\underline{c}}$. This follows from (**A**) and (**B**).

To see that the assumption in (a) may be weakened to $D/n \to 0$, observe that we only needed to control D at two places: after (6) to ensure $\lambda \to \infty$, which is still true as long as D is sublinear in n,

and after (9) to ensure $C/D \to \infty$, true since C is linear in n. The same applies for PLS.

To weaken (**A**) to (**A'**) in the DLS case, note that for fixed D, $m = \Theta(\sqrt{n} \log n)$. If we have a sequences of costs where (**A'**) holds, but not (**A**): set all costs below $\underline{c}$ to zero, embed one bit for free in each such location, and then remove those locations from consideration. (**A**) is now true for the rest of the locations, and we can apply the previous result. By (**A'**), giving the embedder this many free bits increased the payload m by asymptotically strictly less than $\sqrt{n} \log n$, so m was unchanged asymptotically compared with (2). The same does not hold for the PLS case when M is fixed, because the free (or asymptotically free) bits could be enough to cover the entire payload. It would be true for cases where M grows strictly between $\Omega(\sqrt{n} \log n)$ and $O(n)$. □

5 SIMULATIONS

We now perform simulations to confirm the theoretical results. Ideally we would wish to demonstrate their significance in steganalysis, for example in the case of PLS comparing the performance of detectors against the predictions for δ^2 as a function of M and C. However, the theory applies to knowing detectors against embedders using statistically accurate costs (see discussion in [6, §6]); there are some empirically-determined knowing detectors, but there is no reason to believe that they are optimal, and there are no embedders based on true statistical costs: the closest would be MiPOD [9], which is optimal only for an independent nonstationary Gaussian model of cover pixels. We will have to wait for the development of truly optimal cost-based steganography and steganalysis.

But recall that our result is not only about steganography: it gives asymptotic behaviour of solutions to a class of optimization problems. We do not need to perform steganalysis to confirm the asymptotic behaviour of the solutions to (**DLS**) and (**PLS**), for values of the parameters informed by realistic steganographic examples.

Most of our tests relate to (**DLS**), where we anticipate that the relationship with inverse cost would be most applicable (informing a steganographer how much they can safely embed). We will generate a sequence of costs, fix a maximum tolerable square deflection D, and compare the payload achieved at the optimum of (**DLS**) with (2). We will also compare with the more precise result (9). The latter still connects m with C and D, but it will turn out to be more accurate because the asymptotics of J^{-1}, used to derive (2), only converge very slowly[4]. The experiments will be performed for cover sizes $n \in \{100, 200, 400, 1000, 2000, \ldots, 10^8\}$.

Our first experiment simulates discrete costs. We drew a sequence c_i independently from a Poisson distribution with parameter 5, adding 1 to avoid zero costs. We set $D = 2$. We plot the true and estimated maximum payloads in Fig. 1. The more precise equation (9) converges rapidly to the true solution and is more accurate than (2), but for large n even the latter is no more than a small constant multiple from the true value.

For a second experiment we simulated continuous, *statistically accurate* costs. Following [6, §4] we generated covers of independent binary pixels, where p_i the probability for pixel i is itself drawn from a Beta(5, 50) distribution; the true costs are then $c_i = (1 - 2p_i)^2/p_i(1 - p_i)$ (see Eq. (7) of [6], but note that it contains a typo).

---

[3]Take for example $a_i = (1 + i/n)$ and $b_i = 1$ for all i.

[4]Looking at (5), only as fast as $(\log_2 \log_2 x)/\log_2 x \to 0$.

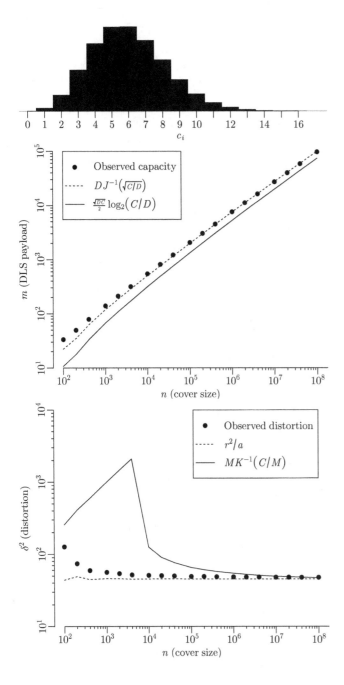

Figure 1: Top: costs drawn from $\mathrm{Poi}(5) + 1$. Middle: true maximum payloads under DLS, and those estimated using (2) and (9), for different cover sizes and $D = 2$. Bottom: squared deflection for the PLS case, when $m \sim 3\sqrt{n}\log\sqrt{n}$, compared to the theoretical predictions (10) and (4). Log-log axes.

This cost distribution has a very long tail, the extent of which cannot be seen in the histogram in Fig. 2: 0.35% of the costs are over 50 and the largest is approximately 600. (A tail of high costs is often observed in image and video steganography.) This time we chose $D = 1$. Since the costs are statistically accurate for the generated

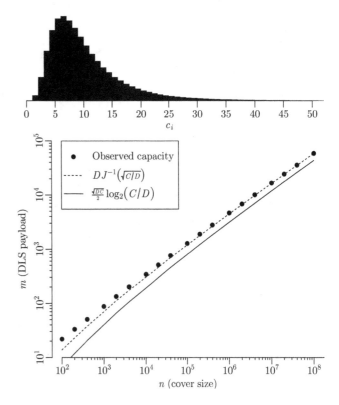

Figure 2: Above: statistically accurate costs for artificial binary images. Below: true maximum payloads, and those estimated using (2) and (9), for different cover sizes and $D = 1$. Log-log axes.

covers, we can interpret D as the square deflection of an optimal detector, who therefore in this case must make approximately 15.9% false positives if they make 50% true positive detections. Subject to this constraint, payloads are plotted in Fig. 2; as in the previous experiment, adherence to the theory is observed.

We also tested against a set of costs used in typical image steganography, the S-UNIWARD costs (with parameter $\sigma = 1$ [4]) from a single BOSSBase image [1]. About 5.7% of these costs are infinite. Drawing with replacement, we sampled them to get the sequence c_i. We know that these are not true statistical costs, so we set a deflection that makes sense in practice: $D = 1000$ gives a secure payload of around 0.1 bits per pixel for covers sized like the BOSS-Base images, which is the order of magnitude typically tested in steganalysis literature (e.g. [4, 7]), so this seems appropriate. True and estimated payloads are plotted in Fig. 3. The formulae predict nonsense answers for small n, but converge rapidly to the true answer for reasonable n.

Finally, we also tested the PLS version of our result, in this case focussing on the root rate calculation (4). For the same set of cover sizes, and using the Poisson cost sequence, we set each payload size at $M = r\sqrt{n}\log_2\sqrt{n}$ for $r = 3$, plotting the observed square deflection obtained in Fig. 1 (bottom). These distortion values, found

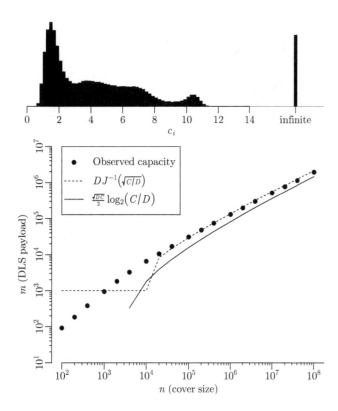

Figure 3: Above: genuine S-UNIWARD costs from one of the BOSSBase images. Below: true maximum payloads, and those estimated using (2) and (9), for different cover sizes and $D = 1000$. Log-log axes.

at the optimum of (**PLS**), converge rapidly to the theoretically-predicted[5] limit $r^2/a = 45/(1 - e^{-5})$. It is curious that they do so even faster than the prediction of (10), perhaps the result of fortuitous cancellation of log log factors.

Similar behaviour occurs for the other cost distributions, as long as r is not too large, but we omit the graphs for lack of space.

6 FURTHER DIRECTIONS

This short paper uncovers the relationship between a cover's costs and its capacity, highlighting the significance of the *capacity coefficient* $C = \sum 1/c_i$. We presented an asymptotic result (skimming some of the mathematical details) and some simple simulations. There are several further directions.

We can conceive one more asymptotic result, for what we call the *distortion- and payload-limited sender*, who varies the size of the cover to meet both distortion and payload bounds. We postpone it to further work.

In this paper we only considered binary embedding. In fact, similar asymptotic results hold for arbitrary k-ary embedding, and

the asymptotic capacity is unchanged. The k-ary equivalent of 'inverse cost' is complex, however, and it depends on cost interactions within each pixel; this requires more space for a proper exposition. Furthermore, the choices of *which* k-ary changes are made turn out to be insignificant to payload size: consider a distribution of possible changes in one pixel $((1 - \pi), \pi a_1, \ldots, \pi a_k)$, where π represents the probability that a change is made, and $a_1, \ldots, a_k$ the relative weights on each possible change. The entropy of this distribution is, asymptotically as $\pi \to 0$, only $-\pi \log_2 \pi$: most of the information is encoded in whether a change happens, not which change it is. Such a limit applies for any sublinear payload. This is not to say that the choices of k-ary changes do not matter to detectability.

Given that embedding minimizing total cost dominates the literature, a natural question is whether the same results hold when distortion $\sum \pi_i^2 c_i$ is replaced by $\sum \pi_i c_i$ (modelling the ignorant detector). There is an upper bound in terms of C, but in the limit as $D/n \to 0$ the capacity is governed by $\min c_i$ and all changes cluster in the cheapest locations. This is a slightly absurd conclusion that only emphasises how exploitable is steganography that optimizes $\sum \pi_i c_i$.

Finally, we intend to examine whether these results are observed in practice, even with non-optimal steganography and steganalysis: if they were as practically-robust as the Square Root Law seems to be, the knowledge that total inverse cost determines capacity would be key information for steganographers.

ACKNOWLEDGMENTS

The author thanks Patrick Bas and Jessica Fridrich, who independently asked him about the relationship between embedding capacity and costs, prompting this work.

REFERENCES

[1] P. Bas, T. Pevný, and T. Filler. 2011. BOSSBase: Break Our Steganographic Scheme. http://webdav.agents.fel.cvut.cz/data/projects/stegodata/BossBase-1.01-cover.tar.bz2. (May 2011).

[2] R. Cogranne, V. Sedighi, and J. Fridrich. 2017. Practical Strategies for Content-Adaptive Batch Steganography and Pooled Steganalysis. In *In Proc. IEEE International Conference on Acoustics, Speech and Signal Processing (ICASSP '17)*. IEEE, 2122–2126.

[3] T. Filler, J. Judas, and J. Fridrich. 2011. Minimizing Additive Distortion in Steganography using Syndrome-Trellis Codes. *IEEE Transactions on Information Forensics and Security* 6, 3 (2011), 920–935.

[4] V. Holub, J. Fridrich, and T. Denemark. 2014. Universal Distortion Function for Steganography in an Arbitrary Domain. *EURASIP Journal on Information Security* 2014, 1 (2014), 1–13.

[5] A. D. Ker. 2017. The Square Root Law of Steganography: Bringing Theory Closer to Practice. In *Proc. 5th Workshop on Information Hiding and Multimedia Security (IH&MMSec '17)*. ACM, New York, NY, 33–44.

[6] A. D. Ker, T. Pevný, and P. Bas. 2016. Rethinking Optimal Embedding. In *Proc. 4th Workshop on Information Hiding and Multimedia Security (IH&MMSec '16)*. ACM, New York, NY, 93–102.

[7] B. Li, M. Wang, J. Huang, and X. Li. 2014. A New Cost Function for Spatial Image Steganography. In *Proc. IEEE International Conference on Image Processing (ICIP)*. IEEE, 4206–4210.

[8] W. Luo, Y. Zhang, and H. Li. 2017. Adaptive Audio Steganography Based on Advanced Audio Coding and Syndrome-Trellis Coding. In *Proc. International Workshop on Digital Forensics and Watermarking (Lecture Notes on Computer Science)*, Vol. 10431. Springer, 177–186.

[9] V. Sedighi, R. Cogranne, and J. Fridrich. 2016. Content-Adaptive Steganography by Minimizing Statistical Detectability. *IEEE Transactions on Information Forensics and Security* 11, 2 (2016), 221–234.

[10] P. Wang, H. Zhang, Y. Cao, and X. Zhao. 2016. A Novel Embedding Distortion for Motion Vector-Based Steganography Considering Motion Characteristic, Local Optimality and Statistical Distribution. In *Proc. 4th ACM Workshop on Information Hiding and Multimedia Security (IH&MMSec '16)*. ACM, New York, NY, 127–137.

---

[5]For this cost distribution, a can be determined analytically: the expectation of $1/X$, where $X \sim 1 + \text{Poi}(\lambda)$, is

$$\sum_{i=0}^{\infty} e^{-\lambda} \frac{\lambda^i}{i!(i+1)} = \frac{1}{\lambda} \sum_{i=1}^{\infty} e^{-\lambda} \frac{\lambda^i}{i!} = \frac{1}{\lambda}\left(1 - e^{-\lambda}\right).$$

Real or Fake: Mobile Device Drug Packaging Authentication

Rudolf Schraml, Luca Debiasi, Andreas Uhl
University of Salzburg
Department of Computer Sciences
rschraml@cs.sbg.ac.at,ldebiasi@cs.sbg.ac.at,uhl@cs.sbg.ac.at

ABSTRACT

Shortly, within the member states of the European Union a serialization-based anti-counterfeiting system for pharmaceutical products will be introduced. This system requires a third party enabling to track serialized and enrolled instances of each product from the manufacturer to the consumer.

An alternative to serialization is authentication of a product by classifying it as being real or fake using intrinsic or extrinsic features of the product. Thereby, one approach is packaging material classification using images of the packaging textures. While the basic feasibility has been proven recently, it is not clear if such an authentication system works with images captured with mobile devices. Thus, in this work mobile device drug packaging authentication is investigated. The experimental evaluation provides results on single- and cross-sensor scenarios. Results indicate the principal feasibility and acknowledge open issues for a mobile device drug packaging authentication system.

ACM Reference Format:
Rudolf Schraml, Luca Debiasi, Andreas Uhl. 2018. Real or Fake: Mobile Device Drug Packaging Authentication. In *IH&MMSec '18: 6th ACM Workshop on Information Hiding and Multimedia Security, June 20–22, 2018, Innsbruck, Austria.* ACM, New York, NY, USA, 6 pages. https://doi.org/10.1145/3206004.3206016

1 INTRODUCTION

As the global markets get flooded with counterfeited products regulations and technical solutions for product authentication get implemented in various sectors of the economy. According to a report by the European Intellectual Property Office 4.4% of the sales and € 10 billion in the pharmaceutical sector correspond to counterfeited medicines [2]. Moreover, counterfeit drugs pose a significant risk to consumer or patient welfare. As a countermeasure against this problem the Falsified Medicines Directive (FMD) 2011/62/EU should be operational until 2019 within all member states of the European Union. The main purpose is to protect patients by reducing the risk of counterfeits entering the supply chain. Therefore, an anti-counterfeiting system based on product serialization will be implemented. Each drug package will be assigned a unique identifier (2D barcode) and secured by a tamper-proof seal. This enables to track and verify each drug package along the supply chain from the manufacturer to the consumer. As a drawback, a central database managed by the European Medicines Verification Organisation (EMVO) is required. Manufacturers need to register new packages at the EMVO and pharmacies have to check-out each sold package. Actually, it is planned that additional costs are covered by the manufacturers but it is likely that those are passed to the consumers. Finally, a centralized system is exposed to getting compromised by forgers, e.g. by entering 2D barcodes from forged packages.

An alternative to serialization is packaging authentication based on classification which is inspired by physical object identification approaches relying on the concept of physically unclonable functions (PUFs). A PUF is a mapping between a challenge and response function which depends on the physical nature of a object. By definition a PUF is unique and cannot be reproduced. Related to packaging authentication various works dealt with Paper PUFs. Paper PUFs either rely on extrinsic or intrinsic PUFs, i.e. which are attached to the product or can be derived from a part of the product itself. However, PUFs are intended to identify an object. In case of classification-based authentication, it is assumed that the packaging of a product shows constant but discriminative intrinsic features. Instead of identifying each single package instance, it can be classified if the product is packaged with a specific packaging material or not. The focus in our research is on drug pills which are packaged in a blister and housed in a cardboard. Recently, in [3, 8] we investigated the basic feasibility of drug packaging authentication. In [3] we showed that cardboard textures of 9 different drugs from 3 manufacturers can be classified with 100% accuracy in a closed multi-class scenario. The utilized dataset was fairly small and packaging material authentication is in fact a simplistic binary classification problem, i.e. a single class has to be distinguished from all other classes. For the training stage only a limited subspace of known other classes is available which is referred to as open-set recognition. Thus, in [8] we focused on the open-set recognition problem and we investigated two basic pre-requirements for classification-based drug packaging authentication: positional invariance and instance generalisation of the packaging material texture. Based on a substantial database, with images of 45 different drugs from multiple instances (packages), both pre-requirements were proved successfully. However, all images were taken with a DSLR camera in an optimal setting and such imagery will not be available in case of a mobile device based authentication system. Thus, for this work in addition to a DSLR camera two smartphones were used to acquire a substantial dataset.

Based on this dataset in this work mobile-sensor as well as cross-sensor drug packaging authentication is investigated. Furthermore, in [8] only the particular classification accuracies for different parts of the packaging material were presented. For an authentication system it is assumed that the fusion of the particular classification results will increase the overall accuracy. Based on a simple majority voting approach, in this work the impact of fusion as well as feature selection will be elaborated. Finally, a closer look on possible authentication error sources will be presented. For example, it is assumed that parts of the packaging material from different drugs which are from the same manufacturer can be the same.

First, in Section 2 a possible scheme for a mobile device based drug packaging authentication system is introduced. Section 3 introduces the acquired database. The classification pipeline is outlined in Section 4. Experiments and results are presented in Section 5 and Section 6 concludes this paper.

2 MOBILE DEVICE DRUG PACKAGING AUTHENTICATION SYSTEM

A schematic illustration for a mobile-device based drug package authentication system is illustrated in Fig. 1. In order to proof the authenticity of a given drug the consumer will be guided by a mobile application. First, the user needs to disassemble the drug and to capture the textures of the cardboard (CB) and the blister top (BT) and blister bottom (BB) side. These three textures of the packaging material are denoted as modalities. The captured images are denoted as I_{CB}, I_{BT} and I_{BB}. Additionally, the user is advised to take a picture of the product code (I_{PC}), e.g. the European article number or the barcode printed on the cardboard. However, the product number can be entered manually or the respective drug can be selected from a list too. These four images compose the authentication vector $\hat{AV} = (I_{CB}, I_{BT}, I_{BB}, I_{PC})$ which is processed by the authentication system. First, the textural images I_{CB}, I_{BT} and I_{BB} are preprocessed. Preprocessing includes segmentation of the textural area and enhancement of the textural pattern. Subsequently, from each preprocessed image one patch is extracted for which a feature descriptor is computed. The product code image I_{PC} is used to determine the product code. Based on the product code, the system selects the corresponding precomputed classification models M_{CB}, M_{BT}, M_{BB} from a model repository. If the required models are not available on the mobile device they could be requested from a remote repository. Based on the corresponding models M_{CB}, M_{BT}, M_{BB} for each feature vector $FV_{CB}, FV_{BT}, FV_{BB}$ a probability score P_{CB}, P_{BT}, P_{BB} between [0, 1] is computed. The closer to 1 the more likely the given feature vector is from a real sample, the closer to 0 the higher is the probability that the feature vector was computed from fake material. Finally, a decision function $f(P_{CB}, P_{BT}, P_{BB}) = (v, p)$ needs to be defined, where $v \in \{1, -1\}$ gives the final authenticity vote of the authentication system and $p \in [0, 1]$ specifies a probability score for the final vote which is then presented to the user.

3 DRUG PACKAGINGS TEXTURE DATABASE

For this study the same database as used in [8] and additional data captured with two different smartphones was utilized. Therefore, a Samsung S5 Mini & an IPhone 5 were utilized to capture images for a set of selected drugs. Therefore, mainly drugs with more than four instances from various manufacturers were selected. The acquisition setup is illustrated in Fig. 2f. Same as for the DSLR camera, the smartphones were mounted on a tripod and in addition a macro lens was utilized. For illumination a light source was placed laterally. An exemplary disassembled drug package is shown in

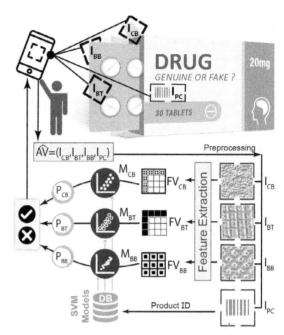

Figure 1: Mobile device drug packaging authentication

Fig. 2a. The initial dataset consists of images from 45 drugs from 28 different manufacturers which were captured with a Canon 70D. For each drug between 1 and 15 package instances are available. The Canon 70D was mounted on a tripod and a 100mm lens and a flashlight were utilized (see Fig. 2e). From each drug instance images from the corresponding CB,BT&BB modalities were captured. For CB the inner side, showing the fibre structure was captured. For BT,BB the corresponding blister textures were captured. Thereby, it was ensured that the images were taken from different and non-overlapping regions. Examples depicting the variety of the different samples for each modality are shown in Fig. 2b-2d. All captured images were manually cropped ensuring that just texture remains. The images in the 1st row in Fig.3 illustrate exemplary images from each modality captured with the different sensors.

4 CLASSIFICATION PIPELINE

Data selection is essential for the subsequent cross-validation procedure. Due to the varying number of instances and the corresponding CB,BT&BB images per drug, a keypoint selection strategy has been employed. Therefore, a fixed number of data (k) to be sampled is predefined. Data relates to image texture patches of CB,BT&BB. For patch sampling, each CB,BT&BB image is subdivided into a grid which is specified by the size of the feature descriptor. According to the results presented in [8] 256×256 pixel patches are utilized. The 2nd row in Fig. 3 depicts sample images for CB,BT&BB for which the image patch grids are shown. Basically, k patches are selected from each instance of each drug and modality. However, k is only an upper bound of patches which are selected. For example, in this work k=1000 and especially for BT and BB there are drugs where less patches are available.

Image Enhancement. Prior to feature extraction the images are converted to grey-scale and Contrast Limited Adaptive Histogram Equalization (CLAHE) [10] is applied to each patch (parameters: block radius=50, bins=256, slope=40). Exemplary CLAHE enhanced

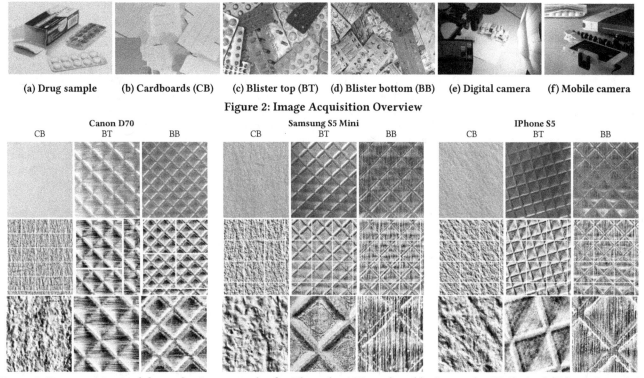

(a) Drug sample (b) Cardboards (CB) (c) Blister top (BT) (d) Blister bottom (BB) (e) Digital camera (f) Mobile camera

Figure 2: Image Acquisition Overview

Figure 3: Preprocessing and data selection examples for Thrombo ASS produced by Lannacher Heilmittel (F1): 1st Row: Original images, 2nd Row: Preprocessed images showing the keypoint grid, 3rd Row: Exemplary 256×256 pixel patches from the top left keypoint in each image of the 2nd row.

images and selected patches for each modality and camera are shown in the 2nd and 3rd row of Fig. 3, respectively.

4.1 Feature Extraction and Feature Encoding

For each selected patch a feature vector using each of the following feature extraction approaches is computed: Local Binary Pattern (LBP) [5], Local Ternary Pattern (LTP) [9], Li Local Binary Pattern (LiLBP) [4], Speeded Up Robust Features (SURF) [1]. As noted in [8] IO and memory constraints are crucial when it comes to high dimensional features like SIFT and SURF. Furthermore, high dimensional feature vectors are computationally problematic in case of kernel-based SVM classifiers. As a first consequence the x,y step size for dense SURF method was increased to 16 pixel and we decided to compute both in a pyramid at three scales (1, 2, 4). Consequently, for each patch #768 × SURF feature descriptors are computed. In case of SURF this results in a feature vector dimension of 98304. In preliminary tests it turned out that this feature vector size is suited for the classification experiments if a linear SVM classifier is utilized but not applicable in case of kernel SVMs.

Furthermore, image classification research showed that feature vector encoding schemes are beneficial for the classification accuracy. In case of SURF it was shown that the fisher vector (FV) encoding scheme [6] combined with linear classifiers improves the classification performance. The FV scheme encodes a set of vectors into a single vector which is composed by the first and second order residuals of the vectors from a Gaussian mixture model (GMM). Basically, the dimensionality of the fisher vector output is $2 \times K \times D$. K is the number of GMM components and D gives the feature vector dimensionality. Commonly, the FV encoding scheme

is combined with a dimensionality reduction approach like Principial Component Analysis (PCA). Thereby, PCA is used to reduce the size of a feature vector to a predefined number of principal components. For this work, the input feature vector is reduced to 80 components. For a reduced input feature vector dimensionality of $D = 80$ and $K = 256$ Gaussian components a single FV with the size of $2 \times 80 \times 256 = 40960$ is produced. In case of SURF the FV encoding reduces the dimension of the SVM input vector by more than the half.

4.2 Data partitioning

In order to provide reliable results cross-validation (CV) based classification is performed. For each drug a number of instances (=packages) from each modality is available. Thus, a nested leave-one-package-out (LOPO) CV procedure is well suited to avoid overfitting and to force the computation of unbiased evaluation results.

The acquired database is composed by a set of drugs $D = \{d_1, ..., d_{45}\}$ produced by different $DM = \{dm_1, ..., dm_{28}\}$ drug manufacturers. $fdm(d_i) : D \rightarrow DM$ specifies the drug manufacturer for each drug. $M = \{CB, BT, BB\}$ specifies the packaging modalities. Furthermore the drugs and modalities were captured with different sensors $S = \{CANON = S1, SAMSUNG = S2, IPHONE = S3\}$ and different feature extraction methods $FE = \{fe_1, ..., fe_n\}$ are utilized in the experiments. The feature vector sets for a certain drug $d \in D$ and modality $m \in M$, for the k-patches from sensor $s \in S$ computed with feature extraction method $fe \in F$, are given by $FV_{(d, m, s, fe)} = \{fv_1, ..., fv_k\}$.

For binary classification it is required to specify a target class, i.e. the drug and the corresponding modality which we want to authenticate. In the scope of this work various classification configurations (CCs) are computed for each target drug d which are given by the following tuple: $CC = (d \in D, m \in M, s \in S, fe \in FE)$. The respective set of feature vector sets for a CC is given by $FV_{CC} = \{FV_{(d_1, m, s, fe)}, ..., FV_{(d_{45}, m, s, fe)}\}$ which is composed by the CC specific feature vector sets from each drug. The positive training data $P_{CC} = FV_{(d, m, s, fe)}$ is specified by the target drug d in CC. The negative training data $N_{CC} = \{FV_{CC}\} \setminus \{FV_{(d, m, s, fe)}\}$ is composed by all feature vector sets of all other drugs. The positive and negative training data P_{CC}, N_{CC} are then used for nested cross-validation using a SVM classifier.

4.3 Cross-validation strategy

The overall goal of the CV strategy is to avoid two different types of over-fitting. The first ensures that no training data is used for evaluation as this leads to overestimation of the classification accuracy. CV excludes this type of over-fitting. The second type of over-fitting is crucial and concerns the training of the model. Thereby, hyperparameter selection plays a significant role in case of SVMs. The overall goal is to find parameters for a model which generalizes to the evaluation data, i.e. the ability of the model to classify unseen data. However, in binary open-set classification and especially in case of the considered drug authentication problem optimization is a trade-off between over- and under-fitting. Unseen data is composed by known data from the target drug and all other known drugs as well as a large set of data from unknown drugs. If the model is over-fitted to the training data it is likely that unseen evaluation data from other packages of the target drug are not recognized. On the other-hand under-fitting increases the risk that unseen as well as unknown packages from other drugs are misclassified as being the target drug.

Basically, for CV the positive and negative training data P_{CC} and N_{CC} for a certain CC are provided as input. For the LOPO CV strategy P_{CC} is split into n-folds $\{P_1, ..., P_n\}$ where each fold contains the feature vectors from a certain instance (=drug package sample). Thus, the number of folds n is given by the number of instances for the target drug d in CC which are available in the database. Same as in [8] the negative training N_{CC} data is split into known negatives KN_{CC} and unknown negatives $UN_{CC} = N_{CC}/KN_{CC}$. Therefore, for KN_{CC} the feature vector sets from a fixed number of drugs are selected, where the manufacturers are different to the target drug manufacturer of d in CC. The aim of this procedure is to simulate the real world, where only a limited set of other known drugs (faked and original ones) are available to train a classifier.

For the nested CV strategy in the outer loop we iterate over the n positive training folds. The current loop index is given by the variable i. In each iteration for KN_{CC} the features are split into two folds KN_1, KN_2 packagewise for each of the contained classes. Hence, half of the packages and the corresponding feature vectors of each class are contained in each fold. Subsequently, the ith positive and 2nd negative fold is selected for evaluation. The evaluation set is given by $E_{i,2} = P_i \cup KN_2 \cup UN_{CC}$. The unknown drugs UN_{CC} are only used for evaluation. The training set is composed by $T_{i,1} = \{P_1, ..., P_k\} \setminus \{P_i\} \cup \{KN_1\}$. Preliminary, $\{KN_1\}$ is reduced to a fixed number of feature vectors which are sampled equally distributed from all contained drug classes (=6) and the respective instances.

In the inner CV loop for each $T_{i,1}$ the best hyperparameters are determined using a grid search approach. Same as in the outer loop, k-fold validation is performed repeatedly in order to test a set of SVM parameters. For this purpose, the known negative training data in $T_{i,1}$ is split classwise into two folds TKN_1 and TKN_2 (training known negatives). One fold simulates known negatives (=3 classes) and the other one unknown negatives (=3 classes) in the inner loop. While the known negatives are further used for training as well as for validation, the unknown negatives are just used for validation. It is assumed that this strategy is beneficial for the generalisation of the classifier. Hence, in the grid search procedure hyperparameters delivering a good classification accuracy in terms of the target class as well as known and unknwon classes accuracy are prioritized. As a measure for the performance the F-Measure is utilized which is well suited to balance between specialisation and generalisation in binary classification tasks. The utilized SVM classifiers assign each prediction a probability. In the inner loop, the probabilities are used to determine a threshold which maximizes the F-Measure. The SVM parameters and threshold delivering the highest F-Measure are selected for the outer loop. Those are then used to train and evaluate a classifier with the training and evaluation data from the outer loop, respectively.

5 EXPERIMENTS

For data selection at maximum $k=1000$, 256×256 pixel patches were selected from each modality and sensor. For each patch feature vectors are computed with all features listed in Section 4.1. In the experiments the LIBSVM linear SVM and kernel SVM with a radial basis function are utilized as classification approaches. Both are applied in combination with FISHER feature vector encoding (FVE=FISHER) and without (FVE=NULL) to cross-validate all CC combinations. Basically, the employed CV strategy requires that only drugs with at least 5 instances can be selected as target drugs, ie. the drug which should be authenticated by the classifier. An overview on suited drugs is presented in Table 2. The table shows that for each selected target drug various numbers of instances are available and each was captured with a set of sensors (S1,S2,S3). For each target drug and sensor all CCs are computed using the outlined LOPO CV strategy. For each LOPO CV the positive data is split into 2-folds, in the inner and outer CV loop. 6 drugs are selected for the known negative training data KN_{CC}. In order to assess the cross-sensor scenario, for evaluation in the outer CV loop data from all different sensors are utilized. For training data from only one sensor are utilized. For example, in case of Mexalen (A3) in the outer loop in each LOPO iteration the evaluation is performed with #1.75k-2k features of the target drug and >#100m features from all other drugs and cameras. For a fair evaluation of the different classification approaches and features the data splits are stored and reused.

5.1 Single-sensor evaluation

An overview on the particular results for the different sensors, all modalities and classification approaches is presented in Table 1. For each CC and modality the averaged results over all target drugs (Table 2) are shown. Considering the results for different CCs, it can be concluded that the F-Measure differences between the elaborated classifiers are not significant. For L-SVM and FISHER encoding it

CC		Canon - S1			Samsung - S2			IPhone - S3		
FVE	CA	CB	BT	BB	CB	BT	BB	CB	BT	BB
NULL	RBF-SVM	*LTP* 0.87 ±6.9	*LTP* 0.94 ±3.5	*LiLBP* 0.84 ±17.6	*LTP* 0.92 ±6.8	*LTP* 0.96 ±4.0	*LiLBP* 0.91 ±5.8	*LBP* 0.83 ±6.1	*LTP* 0.95 ±6.5	*LTP* 0.88 ±8.1
	L-SVM	*LTP* 0.87 ±7.4	*LBP* 0.92 ±4.7	*LiLBP* 0.83 ±13.5	*LTP* 0.92 ±6.3	*LTP* 0.94 ±4.1	*LiLBP* 0.9 ±5.6	*LBP* 0.83 ±6.9	*LTP* 0.95 ±6.2	*LTP* 0.8 ±12.6
FISHER	L-SVM	*LiLBP* 0.84 ±7.4	*SURF* 0.93 ±3.8	*SURF* 0.89 ±10.6	*LBP* 0.88 ±9.3	*SURF* 0.97 ±4.8	*SURF* 0.91 ±4.9	*SURF* 0.82 ±6.3	*SURF* 0.95 ±7.9	*SURF* 0.84 ±12.0

Table 1: Single-sensor performances: For each sensor and all CCs the mean F-Measure and the StDev[%] for the best features of each modality are presented.

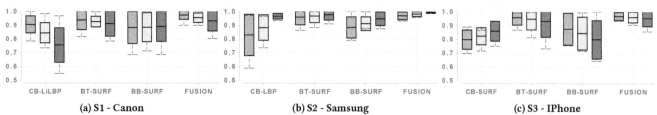

(a) S1 - Canon   (b) S2 - Samsung   (c) S3 - IPhone

Figure 4: Single-sensor results for FISHER L-SVM: For each sensor and modality the performances for the best features as well as for modality fusion are depicted. TPR = $\frac{TP}{TP+FN}$, TNR = $\frac{TN}{TN+FP}$ [Y-Axis: Mean, min, max, standard deviation].

seems that SURF as high level feature does not improve the performance as expected. Furthermore, the F-Measures are comparable to the results presented in [8]. However, in [8] less data was selected for training which shows that doubling the parameter k to 1000 does not improve the classification performance.

When comparing the F-Measures between the different sensors the values are in the same range, surprisingly. Basically, for the mobile sensors fewer drugs were available for evaluation, i.e. no unknown drugs remain for evaluation. Thus, it would be assumed that less variety (=closed-set) in the evaluation data improves the classification performance. This new finding is interesting because this increases the chance that the classification performances are robust in a real world application.

Modality fusion. In the experiments in [8] only the modality performances were considered. As shown in the exemplary drug packaging authentication scheme in Fig. 1 the three probability scores from each modality (P_{CB}, P_{BT}, P_{BB}) should be combined to a final decision. For this purpose, a simple majority voting approach

Manufacturer/Drug	#Samples		Camera		
	CB	BT&BB	Canon (S1)	IPhone (S2)	Samsung (S3)
(A) ratiopharm					
(A1) Danselle	10	10	✓	-	-
(A2) Danseo	9	9	✓	-	-
(A3) Mexalen	8	8	-	✓	✓
(F) Lannacher					
(F1) Thrombo ASS	5	5	✓	✓	✓
(I) Kwizda Pharma					
(I1) Liberel mite	15	15	✓	-	-
(I2) Delia	11	11	✓	✓	✓
(J) Rotexmedia					
(J1) Dexamethason	5	0	✓	-	-
(N) Gynial					
(N1) Bilinda	6	6	✓	✓	✓
(X) Pelpharma					
(X1) Peliette	17	17	✓	✓	✓

Table 2: List of drugs with at least 5 instances which were selected as target drugs. Only drugs which were captured with the corresponding sensors show a check-mark.

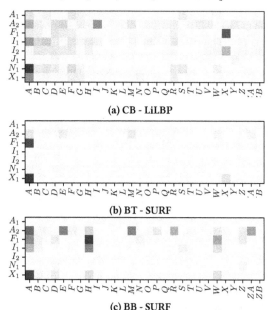

(a) CB - LiLBP

(b) BT - SURF

(c) BB - SURF

Figure 5: Single-sensor results for Canon (S1) FISHER L-SVM: (FN+FP) Error matrix for each modality. [X-Axis: Producers from the evaluation data, Y-Axis: Target Drugs]. The darker the cell, the higher is the classification error.

is applied which still offers possibilities for optimization. Initially, the modality specific classifier thresholds are used to determine a decision vector $\hat{D} = (D_{CB}, D_{BT}, D_{BB})$ from the probability scores. The decision values are either 1 or -1. In case that at least two decision values are 1 the final decision is that the package material is from a real package, i.e. it is not a fake sample. For the selection of the features which achieve the highest F-Measure SFFS (Sequential Floating Forward Selection) [7] is applied. For this purpose, the particular modality decisions are randomly shuffled to to get a set of decision vectors. The shuffling is repeated several times in order to compute the averaged classification performances of the modality fusion. For each sensor the particular modality performances as well

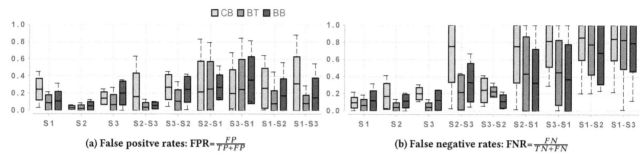

(a) False positve rates: FPR=$\frac{FP}{TP+FP}$

(b) False negative rates: FNR=$\frac{FN}{TN+FN}$

Figure 6: Cross-sensor performances for FISHER L-SVM: For all training and evaluation sensor combinations the FPR and FNR for each modality are shown. For each combination and modality the results for the best feature were selected. [Y-Axis: FPR/FNR mean, min, max and standard deviation].

as the fusion performance is illustrated in Fig. 4. It can be concluded that modality fusion significantly improves the classification and authentication accuracy.

Error sources. Basically, it is assumed that other drugs from the same or different manufacturer might have the same packaging material, e.g. if two different manufacturers have the same cardboard or blister supplier. The error matrix plots in Fig. 5 visualize the number of false positive (FP) + false negative (FN) votes for each target drug and the evaluated drugs which are grouped into manufactures. The darker the higher the amount of misclassification's. FP votes are from samples which are incorrectly authenticated and FN votes are from samples which were incorrectly not authenticated. When considering the columns it can be observed how likely the drugs of a certain manufacturer cause FP or FN votes. FN votes are only possible when the target drug (e.g. A1) and the manufacturer (A) in the columns are the same. For example, for all three modalities the drugs of ratiopharm (A) cause FP votes for drugs from other manufacturers as well as FN votes for A1 and A2. Furthermore, each target drug and the corresponding row can be considered. The darker the more FP and FN votes were observed in the CV strategy. In case of CB, the drug A2 shows a high amount of errors. Furthermore, in each error matrix there are some dark spots which show up high error rates. For example, for BB a high amount of samples from manufacturer H are incorrectly classified as drug F1 = FP votes. Comparing the error matrices for all three modalities it is obvious that the most errors are visible in case of CB and BB and there are less errors for the BT textures.

5.2 Cross-sensor evaluation

In order to assess the cross-sensor performances, all CCs were evaluated with data from other sensors. Thereby, the classifier was always trained with data from only one sensor. The two charts in Fig.6 show the FP and FN rates which were achieved for different training and evaluation sensor combinations. Actually, S1,S2&S3 show the single sensor FPR and FNR for each modality. All other combinations show results where the classifier has been trained with data from one sensor and has been evaluated with data from another sensor, i.e. cross-sensor results. The single-sensor error rates are in general lower than the cross-sensor results for almost all modalities. Especially, the cross-sensor combinations where either the DSLR or a mobile camera are used for training and the other camera type is used for evaluation show inferior FNR values and also worse FPR values. This could be attributed to the different texture scales in case of images acquired with the DSLR camera and images acquired with the mobile devices (see Fig. 3). Backing

for this argument is that the error rates for the mobile-device cross-sensor combinations are better. Furthermore, the cross-sensor FNR values are inferior to the FPR values compared to the single sensor results. Thus, in the considered cross-sensor scenario it is easier for the classifier to reject samples from other drugs than to detect samples from the same drug captured with a different sensor.

6 CONCLUSION

In this work different aspects for a mobile device based drug packaging authentication system were considered. Results showed that data captured with mobile devices and low level features are principally suited for drug packaging authentication. Furthermore, modality fusion improves the performance significantly. However, if different sensors are used and the imaging conditions get more realistic the authentication performance degrades significantly.

Future work on a mobile device based application needs to deal with all issues caused by unconstrained imaging conditions (scale, rotation, tilt & illumination variations). Furthermore, more sophisticated approaches for modality fusion, state-of-the art features and a CNN-based solution should be employed.

REFERENCES

[1] Herbert Bay, Andreas Ess, Tinne Tuytelaars, and Luc Van Gool. 2008. Speeded-Up Robust Features (SURF). *Comput. Vis. Image Underst.* 110 (June 2008), 346–359. Issue 3. https://doi.org/10.1016/j.cviu.2007.09.014

[2] EUIPO. 2016. The economic cost of IPR infringement in the pharmaceutical industry. http://authenti-city.eu/wp-content/uploads/2016/10/The-Economic-Cost-of-IPR-Infringement-in-the-Pharmaceutical-Industry-EN.pdf. (2016).

[3] Christof Kauba, Luca Debiasi, Rudolf Schraml, and Andreas Uhl. 2016. Towards Drug Counterfeit Detection Using Package Paperboard Classification. In *Advances in Multimedia Information Processing – Proceedings of the 17th Pacific-Rim Conference on Multimedia (PCM'16)* (September 15 - September 16) (Springer LNCS), Vol. 9917. Xi'an, CHINA, 136–146. https://doi.org/10.1007/978-3-319-48896-7_14

[4] Z. Li, G. Liu, Y. Yang, and J. You. 2012. Scale- and Rotation-Invariant Local Binary Pattern Using Scale-Adaptive Texton and Subuniform-Based Circular Shift. *IEEE Transactions on Image Processing* 21, 4 (April 2012), 2130–2140.

[5] T. Ojala, M. Pietikäinen, and T. Mäenpää. 2002. Multiresolution Gray-Scale and Rotation Invariant Texture Classification with Local Binary Patterns. *IEEE Transactions on Pattern Analysis and Machine Intelligence* 24, 7 (July 2002), 971–987.

[6] F. Perronnin and C. Dance. 2007. Fisher Kernels on Visual Vocabularies for Image Categorization. In *Proceedings of the IEEE Conference on Computer Vision and Pattern Recognition (CVPR'07)*. 1–8.

[7] P. Pudil, J. Novovicova, and J. Kittler. 1994. Floating Search Methods In Feature-Selection. *Pattern Recognition Letters* 15, 11 (November 1994), 1119–1125.

[8] Rudolf Schraml, Luca Debiasi, Christof Kauba, and Andreas Uhl. 2017. On the feasibility of classification-based product package authentication. In *IEEE Workshop on Information Forensics and Security (WIFS'17)*. Rennes, FR.

[9] Xiaoyang Tan and Bill Triggs. 2007. Enhanced Local Texture Feature Sets for Face Recognition under Difficult Lighting Conditions. In *Analysis and Modelling of Faces and Gestures (LNCS)*, Vol. 4778. 168–182.

[10] K. Zuiderveld. 1994. Contrast Limited Adaptive Histogram Equalization. In *Graphics Gems IV*, Paul S. Heckbert (Ed.). Morgan Kaufmann, 474–485.

Forensic Analysis and Anonymisation of Printed Documents

Timo Richter*, Stephan Escher*, Dagmar Schönfeld, Thorsten Strufe

TU Dresden

Dresden, Germany

\<firstname\>.\<lastname\>@tu-dresden.de

ABSTRACT

Contrary to popular belief, the paperless office has not yet established itself. Printer forensics is therefore still an important field today to protect the reliability of printed documents or to track criminals. An important task of this is to identify the source device of a printed document. There are many forensic approaches that try to determine the source device automatically and with commercially available recording devices. However, it is difficult to find intrinsic signatures that are robust against a variety of influences of the printing process and at the same time can identify the specific source device. In most cases, the identification rate only reaches up to the printer model. For this reason we reviewed document colour tracking dots, an extrinsic signature embedded in nearly all modern colour laser printers. We developed a refined and generic extraction algorithm, found a new tracking dot pattern and decoded pattern information. Through out we propose to reuse document colour tracking dots, in combination with passive printer forensic methods. From privacy perspective we additional investigated anonymization approaches to defeat arbitrary tracking. Finally we propose our toolkit *deda* which implements the entire workflow of extracting, analysing and anonymisation of a tracking dot pattern.

KEYWORDS

Printer identification, Multimedia forensics, Digital Forensics, Laser Printer, Yellow Dots, Tracking Dots

ACM Reference Format:

Timo Richter*, Stephan Escher*, Dagmar Schönfeld, Thorsten Strufe. 2018. Forensic Analysis and Anonymisation of Printed Documents. In *Proceedings of 6th ACM Workshop on Information Hiding and Multimedia Security (IH&MMSec '18)*. ACM, New York, NY, USA, 12 pages. https://doi.org/10.1145/3206004.3206019

1 INTRODUCTION

Still today, in our digitalised world, printed documents are used everywhere. Contracts, tickets, money, letters, invoices or analogue archives are just a small selection of examples. As a result printed documents are often an issue in crimes, like Fake IDs, copyright theft or as evidence in a criminal case. Hence, identifying the

Thanks to BMWi for funding.

*equal contribution.

source printer of such documents is an important feature for evaluating their reliability or for tracking criminals. The research field of printer forensics provides solutions for this. Tools and algorithms developed in this area can basically be distinguished between active and passive methods [3].

Active forensic methods focuses on hidden information, called extrinsic signatures, that has been explicitly added to the document before or at the printing process. These information, e.g. the serial number of the printer device or a secure hash of the document, can then be used to identify the printer or to detect forgery. Examples in this field are the intentional adding of banding frequencies [20], colour-tile deterrents [13] or tracking dots [7].

In contrast, passive forensics does not require any explicitly added features. The quality of print outs is influenced by the corresponding printer mechanism and its components. This as well as several imperfections of such components produces artifacts within the printed document. Passive printer forensic methods try to find such artifacts or individual printing characterisics which are stable over several iterations, distinguishable among different printers and robust against influences. These artifacts can be used as identification features, called intrinsic signatures, of a specific printer technology, brand, model or the device itself. Traditional technologies in this area, such as physical [12], chemical [28] or microscopic [22, 23] methods, can give good results but are slow, require specialized equipment, educated employees and may destroy the document itself. Digital forensic science aims to improve the analysis in such a way that it can be carried out cost-effectively and automatically with standard commercial scanners. Depending on the type of document different signatures are important or extractable in order to be able to make relevant statements. Methods focusing on text documents mainly analyse the differences of texture and structure of printed characters (e.g. microtexture within the character, edge roughness, etc.). These features can be used to identify the source printer technology [5, 14, 25, 26] as well as the specific printer brand and model [8, 11, 29, 34, 36]. Geometrical distortion is another artifact which could be used as intrinsic signature for text [15, 35] as well as for image prints [1, 2, 16]. For images, the different implementations of the halftoning process [17, 18, 26] as well as the different colour representations [4, 30] are important features for an intrinsic analysis. Furthermore, there are methods that analyse the paper itself or extract traces left on the paper by the paper feed construction.

However, the complex printing process not only produces usable distinguishable signatures but even could change these signatures itself. Many variable parameters like different driver settings (e.g. toner save modi or resolution), age of the toner, change of components, used paper (plain vs. recycled), different font types and many others could potentially influence the intrinsic signatures (e.g. [10]). Furthermore these methods can differentiate at most up to the printer model (including technology and brand) but not between printers of the same model. After all, a database with such an intrinsic signature of all existing printers is necessary for real forensic use, as otherwise misallocations may occur.

Active methods on the other side give clear results but are only usable for documents where the printing process can be controlled. An exception are methods implemented directly in the printer, like tracking dots which are used in nearly all colour laser printers. Through the constant existence of this signature, we propose to re-use these forensic patterns, e.g. in combination with passive printer forensic algorithms.

While the characteristics and information content of these patterns is chiefly unknown, we describe our analysis of these patterns in the following for reusability. Additionally we explore anonymisation approaches against this extrinsic signature to defeat arbitrary tracking. Finally we present our toolkit which implements the entire workflow of extracting, analysing and anonymisation of such a tracking dot pattern.

2 DOCUMENT COLOUR TRACKING DOTS

Many colour laser printer models print tiny and systematic yellow dots on each page. These are being generated at the firmware level [9] and represent encoded information such as the serial number of the printer or the date of the print [7]. This information can be read and decoded automatically. On the one hand, such tracking data is a helpful way of active forensics e.g. as a counterfeit protection system for bank notes. On the other hand, the tracking data is a lack of privacy. Theoretically it can not only be used by official authorities but also by any third party.

Since the origin and content of these yellow dots is largely unknown, we looked for answers from some printer manufacturers. We only received an official statement from one manufacturer, in which they called the yellow dots "Document Colour Tracking Dots". Unfortunately, they were not able to give any answer and referred us to the Central Bank Counterfeit Deterrence Group (CB-CDG), which also could not answer our request because it is "not a CBCDG product/technology". Finally we worked on decoding the data by ourselves and found 4 distinct *tracking dot pattern* (TDP). Patterns 2, 3 and 4 had been mentioned in previous literature [33]. Pattern 4 had also been decoded by the Electronic Frontier Foundation (EFF) [7]. Here we introduce pattern 1 to the public for the first time, analyse the code and structure for each TDP and explain the information in one further code word from pattern 4.

2.1 Definitions

The *tracking dot matrix* (TDM) is one prototype of tracking dots in a matrix of $n_i \times n_j$ cells which is printed repeatedly over the whole sheet of paper with a cell distance of Δ_i inches horizontally and Δ_j inches vertically. Each cell of the matrix stores one bit where a yellow dot represents "1" and an empty space represents "0". A *tracking dot pattern* (TDP) is a format of storing tracking information. It uses a certain code, produces a TDM of a certain size and may include marking dots and a mask of empty cells. The TDP of a printer can be described as $(n_i, n_j, \Delta_i, \Delta_j)$.

A code could be algebraic or non-algebraic. In *algebraic* codes, A is the set of all code words. An information word a^* can be encoded

Figure 1: Two interleaved (4,3,2) even parity codes

000	0
011	0
111	1
100	1

in a code word $a \in A$ so that it is possible to detect or even correct a certain amount of erroneous bits. This is helpful when transferring data via a distorted channel such as yellow dots on a sheet of paper. A code described by the parameters (n, l, d_{min}) encodes information words of length l and adds $k = n - l$ redundant bits to the code words of length n. The amounts of ones in a code word a is called weight and noted as $w(a)$. The minimal weight among $2^l - 1$ nonzero code words is the minimal Hamming distance d_{min}. Binary codes can detect $f_e = d_{min} - 1$ errors in a distorted word $b = a \oplus e$ where e is the error word. A distorted word can only be reconstructed if the error word e has a weight of $f_k = \lfloor (d_{min} - 1)/2 \rfloor$ or less.

An even parity code $(n, l = n - 1, d_{min} = 2)$ is a systematic code where the parity bit k is calculated by $k = \oplus_{i=1}^{l} u_i, u_i \in \{0, 1\}$. The weight of such code words is always even. An odd parity code is a parity code where the parity bit is $k = k \oplus 1$.

A product code (n, l, d_{min}) with an interconnected block interleaver (see fig. 1) is a code chain that consists of an outer code $(n_1, l_1, d_{min,1})$, an interleaver and an inner code $(n_2, l_2, d_{min,2})$ where $n = n_1 \cdot n_2$, $l = l_1 \cdot l_2$ and $d_{min} \geq d_{min,1} \cdot d_{min,2}$. An outer code writes code words of length n_1 row by row into a matrix before an inner code reads the words column by column of length l_2 and encodes them [19].

A "one hot encoding" $(n, n, 2)$ is a type of *non-algebraic* constant-weight code. It consists of one "1" and $n - 1$ zeros so that the weight of a code word a is $w(a) = 1$. Any error word e can certainly be detected with $w(e) \in [1..n] \setminus \{2\}$.

Example. Let $a = (01000)$ be a code word of a "one hot encoding" $(5, 5, 2)$, then the error word $e_1 = (01100)$ with weight 2 produces another code word: $b = a \oplus e_1 = (00100) \in A$. But the error word $e_2 = (00110)$ produces a word $b = a \oplus e_2 = (01110)$ with $b \notin A$.

2.2 Dataset

The tracking dots of 1286 prints by 106 printer models from 18 different manufacturers have been analysed (tab. 1), a total of 141 printers. This covers the majority of the world's most successful printer manufacturers [21]. For each printer model we considered up to three different printers. The data and prints were obtained from an archive by the DFKI [6] and from printers in the department of computer science of the TU Dresden. The DFKI data set contains prints from 132 printers. It provides the printer's manufacturer, model and serial number. Our TU Dresden data set additionally contains the date of the printing, information about the used driver, resolution and toner. Each print out has been digitalised with a common scanning device (Epson Perfection V30, 800dpi). The content of the documents consists of either images or text.

Table 1: Printer manufacturer in data set

Manufacturer	Analysed printers	Dots found
Brother	1	no
Canon	10	yes
Dell	4	yes
Epson	8	some models
Hewlett-Packard	43	some models
IBM	1	yes
Konica Minolta	21	some models
Kyocera	4	yes
Lanier	1	yes
Lexmark	6	some models
NRG	1	yes
Okidata	9	some models
Ricoh	6	yes
Samsung	5	no
Savin	1	yes
Tektronix	4	no
Unknown	1	yes
Xerox	15	some models

Canon, Brother, Hewlett-Packard, Konica Minolta, Ricoh and Xerox have signed an agreement of the Angloamerican Secret Service to fulfill "document identification requests" [32] which might have caused the tracking dots

Table 2: Automatically detected TDP

Pattern	n_i	n_j	Δ_i	Δ_j
1	32	32	0.02 in	0.02 in
2	18	23	0.03 in	0.03 in
3	24	48	0.02 in	0.02 in
4	16	32	0.04 in	0.04 in

Figure 2: Steps of the extraction workflow

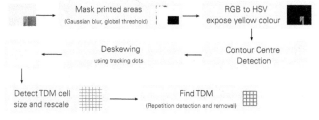

2.3 Tracking Dot Extraction

This section will describe the method on reading arbitrary TDP and transforming a sheet into a list of TDM for further analysis of previously unknown TDP. The entire workflow can be practically tested with our deda toolkit (see section 6).

In comparison to previous work by van Beusekom et al. [33], our method maps the tracking dots into a grid and therefore transforms them into a matrix. For each two prints, van Beusekom et al. aimed at deciding whether they come from the same printer or not. To achieve this, they did not extract the TDM as a matrix but as an image – using a pixel threshold to match a TDM's repetitions on the sheet. For later decoding though, numerical TDMs are needed. Furthermore our extraction algorithm is independent regarding the content of the printed document.

First, the empty areas of the document must be detected, as the yellow dots in these areas are visible. Therefore we mask the printed areas using Gaussian Blur and a global threshold. After a colour space conversion to HSV and exposure of the yellow colour range, the set D of all recognised yellow dots can be created by a contour detection algorithm [27].

Next, the page needs to be aligned so that the tracking dots can be separated by straight lines into a grid. Because of the manual scanning process, the sheet might have been skewed by $\alpha \in \mathbb{R}$ degrees and must be corrected by a rotation of $-\alpha°$. It is possible to correct a skew up to 45° by taking advantage of the fact that on the sheet a TDM is being repeated many times in a straight line. Remember that the set D of yellow dots might be distorted. To approximate α, we calculate the angles between each two dots from D, quantise them and find the most occurring value.

When mapping the dots into a matrix, the cell separating grid might be shifted due to inaccuracies caused by a limited scan resolution and therefore skip a column or row each few centimetres. To prevent this, we segment the sheet into overlapping blocks of 7.5 cm per page. Each block is then processed separately and the block with the most dots is selected.

Afterwards the tracking dots are mapped from the page block into a grid. In a matrix, all cells of the same column are exactly one below the other. Due to imperfections in the scanning and/or printing process, the x coordinates of dots from the same column vary slightly. We call this bias. Let's assume Δ_1 and Δ_2 are the two smallest local maxima of the neighbouring dots' horizontal distances' frequency with $\Delta_1 < \Delta_2$. Δ_1 typically is the biased distance between dots of the same column and Δ_2 is the distance between dots of neighbouring columns: $\Delta_i = \Delta_2$. The vertical dot distance Δ_j can be calculated analogously. The grid shall be placed in a way so that the most occurring x coordinate of D is in the center of a cell and the most occurring y coordinate is in the center of a row. The cells have the size $\Delta_i \times \Delta_j$ inches. The tracking data yields "1" where there is a yellow dot in the grid cell and "0" everywhere else.

The TDM has been printed repeatedly over the whole sheet. Its dimensions should be detected given the matrix of all yellow dots. Let's assume a function that calculates the likelihood of two columns being identical. Then for each column c we calculate the median distance to each column $\hat{c}$ where the likelihood that the content of c and $\hat{c}$ is above a given threshold. The most occurring distance is assumed to be horizontal separation distance n_i cells. The vertical separation distance n_j can be calculated analoguously. If the sheet is being cut into pieces where each contains $n_i \times n_j$ cells, a list of (possibly distorted) TDMs result. For TDPs using a redundancy code (see 2.1), all TDMs shall be removed from that list where the redundancy check fails. Otherwise a TDM prototype can be estimated by overlapping all found TDMs and setting the value "0" or "1" by a majority decision.

3 FORENSIC ANALYSIS

Four different TDP tuples were detected in our dataset using the proposed extraction algorithm (see tab. 2). The patterns may appear rotated (90° steps) and/or flipped. The companies Lanier and Savin

Table 3: Patterns by manufacturer

Manufacturer	Pattern
Lanier	1
NRG	1
Ricoh	1
Savin	1
Hewlett-Packard	2
Kyocera	2
Lexmark	2
Okidata	2
Ricoh	2
Epson	3
Konica Minolta	3
Dell	4
Epson	4
Xerox	4

Figure 3: All matrices of pattern 3 united

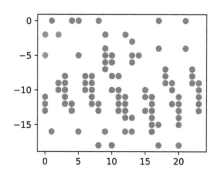

Figure 4: Pattern 1: Marking (red) and other tracking dots (blue)

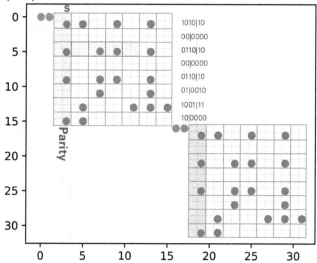

belong to the company of Ricoh [24] which use pattern 1 together with the company NRG. Pattern 2 is being used by 5 different independent manufacturers (tab. 3). The patterns 1, 2 and 3 are constant for each printer and do not vary by each print. Hence we assume that they contain fixed information like the printer's serial number but not the date. Many Canon printers showed a pattern that is not constant but seems to repeat its TDM in a rotated transformation. This pattern has not been analysed further because of its unusual irregularity.

All other detected TDPs were analysed and some matrices decoded. The patterns were evaluated according to their information density, capacity, error detection rate and conspicuousness. We also analysed the number of yellow dots generated by each pattern in the best, worst and average case, depending on the content of the TDM.

For a TDM, let *col* be the column and *row* the row index number. All patterns use a kind of repetition code because their matrices are spread over the whole sheet of paper. Therefore forward error correction can be achieved using the repetitions of a matrix. The amount of repetitions depends on the size of the printed area and the size of the matrix.

Each section relates to only one prototype of the matrix. The same statements always apply to its repetitions.

3.1 Analysis Methods on TDP

The structures of all patterns have been determined by analysing a bigger amount of TDMs.

Due to the repetitions of a pattern over the entire printout, each pattern is likely to contain marker of its beginning. To find possible markers, we overlapped all TDMs of the same pattern from different printers such that the resulting matrix shows only a dot where all matrices show a dot. Dots that appear in all TDM samples do not contain information and can be used as orientation markers therefore (red in figures).

Furthermore a TDP may contain empty cells, rows or columns that need to be skipped when reading the data. To determine them, all TDMs of one pattern were overlapped so that the resulting matrix shows a dot where at least one matrix shows a dot (fig. 3). Thereby the cells become visible that are empty on all TDMs. They

may mark spaces between data blocks. If there is only one dot in each of these blocks of size *n*, then its data may be stored in a "one hot encoding" of length n – written row by row or column by column.

The information stored in a matrix was attempted to reveal by analyzing the inference of metadata (e.g. the printer's serial number) to the matrix. For the printers, for which both the serial number and the TDP were known, a known-plaintext attack could be achieved.

3.2 Pattern 1

The first pattern is printed offset (fig. 4). Therefore its dimension is detected as 32×32 cells although the unique matrix with the spacing uses $32 \times 16 = 512$ cells. This section deals with the prototype of the matrix in rows 0-15 and columns 0-15. The pattern marks its beginning with two neighbouring dots (red in figure) and stores information in every second column in every second row. All even rows do not contain any dot except the marking ones. Each row is one code word. Let *s* be the index of the first column that contains the first code word bit in the row. s is either 2 or 3 depending on the printer. In our figure s is 3. This pattern has been discovered on 7 different devices.

Redundancy check. The pattern uses a $(7,6,2)$ even parity code. It stores 8 code words row by row which contain $8 \cdot 6 = 48$ information bits in total. A TDM is considered as valid if the amount of dots is even in all rows. Error words with an even weight produce code words. To detect them, all valid TDMs have to be compared and chosen by a majority decision.

Example. Row 31 contains the code word (1100000) and passes the parity check. The correct word might have been (0000000) as well united with the error word $e = (1100000)$. This error with $w(e) > 2$ cannot be detected.

To improve the error detection one could check the condition that on the one hand every second column from $s - 1$ to 15 is empty and on the other hand that each even row from 2 to 14 is empty as well. Using this condition the probability of decoding a word wrong due to burst errors, e.g. through printing/scanning artifacts, is much lower.

Decoding. The pattern contains the printer's serial number as 4 binary bit blocks in the said $(7,6,2)$ even parity code. Being a systematic code makes it easily readable. For the rows $1, 3, 5, ..., 15$, column $s = 3$ contains the parity bit and the information bits can be found in every second column from $s + 2$ to 15. A binary chain has to be read from left to right starting with the bottom row. Each 4 bits of this chain represent a binary number. The 11 binary numbers before the last one are the printer's serial number. The first and fifth number may represent letters, where "9" stands for "P" and "0" stands for "W" or "Q".

Example. Figure 4 contains the words (1101010), (0000000), (1011010), (0000000), (1011010), (0010010), (0100111) and (1100000). The information bits without the leading parity bit are (101010), (000000), (011010), ..., (100000). Splitting this chain into 4 bit chunks results in (1010), (1000), (0000), (0110), ..., (0000). Reading the chain as well as the chunks backwards and transforming them into decimal numbers gives us the string "079496016015".
The serial number is W**794**P**601601**.

Conspicuousness. The amount of dots per code word a is determined by its even weight $w(a) \in \{0, 2, 4, 6\}$. From 64 code words with an equal probability of occurrence, 35 have a weight of 4 (54,7%)[1]. This makes 8 code words $\cdot$ 4 dots + 2 marking dots = 34 dots per matrix at average (0.67 dots per bit).

3.3 Pattern 2

Pattern 2 uses $18 \times 23 = 414$ cells (fig. 5) and was found on 51 devices. Depending on the printer, each dot in the figure is represented by one or two printed dots. Three dots in the first two rows mark the beginning (red in figure). The TDM consists of eight blocks named A to H (from left to right) situated in rows 2-6, 7-11, 12-16, 17-21 and columns 1-8 and 10-17. Row 22 as well as columns 0 and 9 are separators. The pattern considers every second column in rows with an even index and every first column otherwise, so all cells are

---
[1]Calculated with binomial distribution

Figure 5: Pattern 2: Marking (red) and other tracking dots (blue) aligned into blocks A-H with parity. The estimated grid has been added to this figure for readability

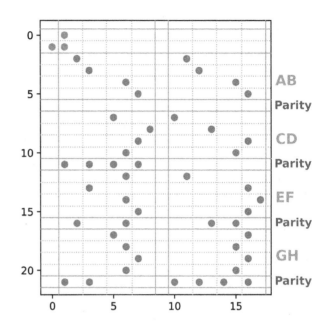

being considered where $(col \bmod 9 + row) \bmod 2 = 0$. This pattern stores 4 signs from a $(4,4,2)$ "one hot encoding" and interleaves it in a $(5,4,2)$ odd parity code. This results in a $(20,16,4)$ product code where each code word can differentiate between 4^4 different states. The pattern consists of 8 code words, so it stores $4^{4 \cdot 8}$ different states in total. This is equivalent to storing 64 bits.

Example. Block G contains
$$\begin{array}{|c|}\hline 0010 \\ 0010 \\ 0001 \\ 0010 \\ \hline 1100 \\ \hline \end{array}$$
the last row is the parity.

Redundancy Check. Each of the first four rows of each block contains information bits as a "one hot encoding". The fifth row contains the parity bits of the outer encoding which make an odd amount of dots in each column of each block. This helps to detect errors e with $w(e) = 2$ which are not detected by the "one hot encoding". Each inner code word contains exactly one "1", so 1, 3 or 4 faulty bits can be detected. The product code can detect any number of faulty bits that is 2 or odd. Moreover, error correction is possible.

Example. If $a = (1000\,0100\,0010\,0001\,0000)$ from block A is being distorted with an error word $e = (1100\,1100\,0000\,0000\,0000)$ then e is one of the few error words with weight 4 that produces a code word which matches the parity bits with $b = a \oplus e = (0100\,1000\,0010\,0001\,0000) \in A$.

Table 4: TDM's block A by manufacturer

Manufacturer	HP	Kyocera	Lexmark	Okidata	Ricoh	Ricoh
Block A	3021	0123	0213	3210	2310	0132

Decoding. Block A equals block B in all samples. They correlate to the printer's manufacturer. Printers using this pattern have serial numbers like CNBB002529, CNBC55MOPR, JPGMC52527, etc. Blocks C and D correlate to the 2nd, 3rd and 4th letter from the serial number. But these blocks are ambiguous: one can conclude them from the serial number but not vice versa. The information of blocks E-H is uncertain. It may contain encrypted digits from the serial number or some other data. To obtain the information part from the matrix, the first four rows of each block can be interpreted as a number in $\mathbb{Z}_4$ (translate "0001" into "0", "0010" into "1" etc.).

Example. Block A from our figure contains the information bits $(1000\ 0100\ 0010\ 0001)$. These represent the numbers 3, 2, 1, 0 and signify an Okidata printer.

From the information in block A, the printer manufacturer can be concluded (tab. 4). Obviously there has been a preference for chains of distinct digits to identify the manufacturer. The advantage of these numbers is that they produce less dots. Only if a block consists of all distinct numbers, the amount of added parity dots is minimal.

Conspicuousness. The amount of dots per code word ranges from 4 to 8. If one word produces 4 dots, it consists of 4 different inner code words and all parity bits are 0. In the worst case one word produces 8 dots: This occurs when all parity bits are being set to 1. The average amount of dots from all code words is 6. There are $4^4 = 256$ different code words per block. 192 of these either contain three identical numbers and one different one (example 3.1) or two identical numbers and two other numbers of which both differ (example 3.2). Both cases produce exactly 2 parity bits which are 1. All code words contain exactly 4 dots from the information bits. This sums up to 4 information dots + 2 parity dots = 6 dots. For the whole pattern this means $8 \cdot 6 + 3$ marking dots = 51 dots at average (0.80 dots per bit).

Example 3.1. The inner code words (1000), (1000), (1000), (0100) produce an outer code word where the parity bits are (0011). Two parity bits are being set.

1000
1000
1000
0100
0011

Example 3.2. The inner code words (1000), (1000), (0100), (0010) produce the parity bits (1001). Again two parity bits are being set.

3.4 Pattern 3

Pattern 3 (fig. 6) consists of 27 blocks of 6 bits where each block uses 2 columns and 3 rows. The pattern's beginning is marked by three dots (red in figure) which do not fit into one block. The pattern is being repeated over the whole sheet. Its detected shape is 24×48

Figure 6: Pattern 3: Marking (red) and other tracking dots (blue). Rectangles have been added to this figure to mark our detected code word blocks. The solid boxes indicate the pattern's offset.

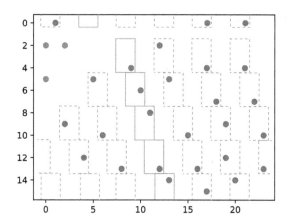

cells because each vertical repetition of the pattern is being shifted by +8 columns. The unique pattern consists of $24 \times 16 = 384$ cells.

Redundancy Check. The source alphabet contains 6 elements which are being encoded with a $(6,6,2)$ "one hot encoding". The pattern consists of 27 blocks where each block stores one code word. A code word weights "1" and therefore produces exactly one tracking dot.

Decoding. Currently we found no correlation with any of the printer's know properties.

Conspicuousness. Considering the markers, there are $27 + 3 = 30$ tracking dots in total (0.43 dots per bit). The pattern can differentiate between 6^{27} states in total. This is equivalent to storing $\ln(6^{27})/\ln(2) \approx 69.8$ bits.

3.5 Pattern 4

Pattern 4 (fig. 7) is being used by Dell, Epson and Xerox printers. According to a research fellow at Xerox, the U.S. government and his company have a „good relationship" [31] which might be the origin of this pattern. Pattern 4 uses $16 \times 16 = 256$ cells and is being repeated offset (16×32 cells in total). This section relates to the matrix in rows 0-15 and columns 0-7. There are 3 or 7 marking dots (sometimes called "separators") in row 6 although they are missing on some printers. The pattern encodes words with a $(8,7,2)$ odd parity code and interleaves 14 code words in a $(15,14,2)$ odd parity code. This results in a $(120,98,4)$ product code. The parity bits are in row 15 as well as in column 0. For some printers the outer parity does not cover the inner parity bits (e.g. see fig. 7 col 0, row 15). The pattern stores 98 information bits in total. Overall 16 devices in our dataset use this pattern.

Figure 7: Pattern 4: Marking (red) and other tracking dots (blue)

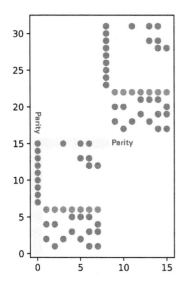

Table 6: Pattern Comparison

| Pattern | Δ_i | Size | | Capacity | Density | | Dots/in² |
		Cells	in²		Bits/cell	Bits/in²	avg / max
1	0.02 in	512	0.21	48 bits	0.09	234.38	166 / 244
2	0.03 in	414	0.37	64 bits	0.15	171.77	137 / 180
3	0.02 in	384	0.15	69 bits	0.18	454.43	195 / 195
4	0.04 in	256	0.41	98 bits	0.38	239.02	112 / 186

Table 7: Code parameters

Pattern	Dots per word avg / max	(n, l, d_{min})	f_e	f_k	f_e
1	34 / 50	(7,6,2)	1	0	14%
2	51 / 67	(20,16,4)	3	1	15%/100%[1],[2]
3	30 / 30	(6,6,2)	6[1]	0	100%[1]
4	46 / 76	(120,98,4)	3	1	14%[2]

1) An error of two bits per code word might not be detected in any case. Presence of parity bits has not been revealed.
2) For the inner code of the code chain

3.6 Evaluation of the Patterns

Table 6 gives an overview over the detected patterns. It notes the amount of cells of one unique matrix including the spacing to its closest repetition. The capacity for storing information bits is given as well as the amount of bits that one table cell and one square inch can store. The density is the quotient of the capacity and the size. The amount in bits per cell shows the efficiency of the patterns regardless of the cell distance whereas the number in bits per square inch does consider the cell distance. The more dots per square inch are printed the more visually conspicuous the matrix is on the paper. The amount of dots per matrix depends on the encoded information. Its minimum, average and maximum are given in dots/in², divided by the pattern's size. The (n, l, d_{min}) code description (tab. 7) follows with the amounts f_e and f_k of faulty bits that can be detected and/or restored correctly (forward error correction).

Comparison. Comparing the patterns leads to the following observations: Pattern 1 encodes information per in² very densely because it uses the binary system and produces few redundancy so it only detects single faulty bits and cannot correct errors at all. Pattern 4 is similar to pattern 1 but adds error correction and therefore displays information less densely. The density per cell of pattern 4 is higher than of pattern 1 because pattern 1 leaves nearly every second column and row empty, assuming a cell distance of $\Delta_i = 0.02$ in. Pattern 2 uses the "one hot encoding" and a parity code. The "one hot encoding" with length 4 still can display information quite densely and can detect distributed erroneous bits quite well. On the other hand it only detects at maximum 4 faulty bits whereas a "one hot encoding" with a higher length has a lower information density but can detect errors of a higher weight. The parity bits lead to a high redundancy.

Pattern 3 uses a "one hot encoding" with length 6. The presence of parity bits has not been found so we assume that all bits are information bits. A "one hot encoding" with length 6 stores little

Table 5: Number in TDM's row 12 by manufacturer

Manufacturer	Dell	Epson	Xerox	Xerox
Row 12	20	3	0	4

Redundancy Check. Code words in rows 1 to 14 as well as each of columns 1 to 7 must show an odd amount of dots. The product code allows error correction.

Decoding. Each row has to be transcribed into a binary number excluding the leading parity column. The resulting number can be transformed into the decimal system. The TDM contains the date and time of the print. The manufacturers Epson and Xerox add 6 digits of the serial number as well. Dell's TDMs do not include them. The minutes can be found in row 14, the hour in row 11, the day in row 10, the month in row 9 and the year in row 8. The middle of the serial number is a concatenation of the numbers from rows 3, 4, 5. Row 12 correlates with the manufacturer (tab. 5) and row 7 has been constantly empty (except parity bit). The meaning of the information in rows 1, 2 and 13 does not correlate with any of the printer's known features. Row 15 contains parity bits and row 0 is always empty.

Conspicuousness. If we assume that the pattern stores an arbitrary serial number and a date where the hour ranges from 0-23, the minutes from 0-59, the day from 1-31, the month from 1-12 and the year from 0-127 then it produces between 12 and 76 tracking dots. At average it makes 46 tracking dots (0.47 dots per bit).

Table 8: Redundancy check for known patterns from 300 dpi scans of each printer from our dataset

Pattern	Passed	Out of
1	7	7
2	47	50
3	17	23
4	15	15
-	0	46

information per sign but the absence of additional redundancy helps this pattern to create a higher density than pattern 2. The "one hot encoding" allows 6 faulty bits to be detected. Pattern 1 can be the least conspicuous one because it produces the lowest amount of dots per in^2 in the best case. Though the worst case is likely to occur if the pattern is being used to store a big variety of information. Pattern 2 produces at maximum 180 yellow dots per in^2 which is the lowest maximum for all patterns. Pattern 3 produces just 15 dots more but stores 2.6 times of the information of pattern 2 per in^2. Pattern 4 does not use an explicit marker. It can be aligned by the definition of the free space of its offset pattern but this is a lot more computationally expensive than finding the three marking dots of pattern 2. Code words of Pattern 1 can be created by the random distortion on the paper. This makes it difficult to find unambiguous information and also to determine whether a sheet does or does not contain this pattern.

Conclusion. The most efficient pattern is pattern 3. Storing more than 454 bits per in^2, it has the highest density. Because error correction can be achieved using the repetitions anyway, it is reasonable to focus on a high error detection capability rather than on forward error correction. This pattern has the highest error detection capability. A small cell distance of 0.02 in is useful to allow many cells per area. This is possible due to the few dots produced by the "one hot encoding". In the worst case 195 tracking dots are being produced which is similar to the other patterns. Pattern 3 has enough capacity to store the same information as in all other patterns without time and date information. Pattern 2 minimises its dots because it sets the parity to an odd amount of ones. Blocks where all four inner code words are different occur a lot more often than a block where all code words are the same. Therefore the outer parity code deals with odd amounts of "1" more often and sets "0" as the parity bit in this case.

4 REFINED EXTRACTION ALGORITHM

This is a very resilient method for classifying tracking information and comparing tracking information of different printers. In the code comparison in [33], each two prints from the same or different printers were analysed to classify a common or a distinct origin. To achieve this, all dots that did not appear in many of the TDM's repetitions have been removed greedily. This may allow false positives: The prints from two different printers might be detected as from the same origin if significant dots were removed. In contrast, this method uses the code's redundancy check. Comparing only valid TDMs, a classification of two different printers as identical is very unlikely.

To find a valid TDM, the tracking dots must be extracted. Different yellow colour ranges may be tried. Then any repetition of the TDM must be selected from the sheet. Initially it must be shifted so that the marking dots are on the desired place (top left corner). If an offset TDP does not provide marking dots, the matrix can be shifted according to its empty space. An offset repetition has to be removed from the extracted matrix if it contains any. Next, markers and spaces have to be removed from the matrix so that it only contains cells that belong to the code word. The result's redundant bits can be checked according to the code's description. If the check fails, the algorithm has to be repeated using another prototype from the TDM repetitions on the sheet until a valid TDM has been found.

The table 8 shows the amount of printers where the prints' tracking information passed the redundancy check successfully at least once on at least one sheet out of 10. It shows the amount of printers belonging to a pattern as well. Each of the printer's sheets has been tried a redundancy check on for all patterns. The last row tells us that pages without any known or without any TDP at all did not pass redundancy checks. From pattern 1 the extraction of a TDM often is ambiguous. A randomly distorted matrix could be valid according to the redundancy check by pattern 1. Especially the markers from pattern 2 are valid markers for pattern 1 and can therefore be interpreted as a pattern 1 matrix more easily. The spots around valid dots have to be checked carefully before deciding on pattern 1 for a sheet. The prints of which the tracking information could not be decoded showed sparse matrices or were scanned unluckily. Especially pattern 3 prints were hardly distorted on the scan.

Furthermore, we evaluated the extraction of the printers' manufacturer and serial number from a valid TDM. 100% of the extracted serial numbers are part of the printer's actual serial number. The manufacturers for all but one printer could be decoded correctly. The erroneous printer[2] has possibly been labelled wrong in the dataset.

A comparison to the evaluation in [33] might not be helpful because the used test scenario cannot reveal the advantages of our method. There, only printers were considered where the tracking dots differ heavily. Van Beusekom et al. did not find the patterns' codes and therefore could not use the redundancy check to extract a distortionless TDM. Instead they compare only the most certain dots in a TDM which are being concluded from a scan using the TDM's repetitions and a threshold to separate true dots from distortion. In our tests, this often lead to a distorted TDM that contains only few dots. The results of the evaluation by van Beusekom et al. is quite good because their method is sufficient to spot printers with a very different TDM and their dataset does not include many TDMs that differ only slightly. In a huge dataset, printers with a similar TDM might appear which could be detected as identical. Our method makes it possible to spot the difference between printers that produce very similar TDMs. A false detection of two printers as identical is very unlikely for our method because we require any true TDM to pass the redundancy check. This extraction method is also included in the deda toolkit (section 6).

---

[2]Sample 99 in the DFKI dataset

Figure 8: A scan before (*p*) and after (*p̃*) automatic tracking dot removal. Yellow colours are darkened equally on *p* and *p̃* for better visibility

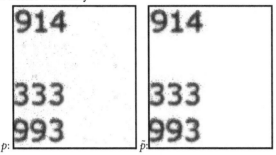

Figure 9: Pattern 1 mask example (green)

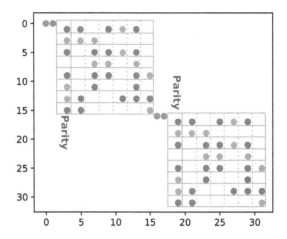

5 AN ANONYMISATION APPROACH

Tracking dots on a sheet reveal information about the printer and are therefore a lack of privacy. Tracking dots information have no controlled access and can theoretically be read and decoded by anyone. It is possible to conclude the printer of a sheet which is often owned by the author. This would be a disaster e.g. in case the sheet is a critical leaflet about the government in a dictatorship. For this reason we introduce methods for removing tracking data from scanned prints and for masking tracking data on prints. Each anonymisation method was successfully tested using our deda toolkit.

5.1 Removing Tracking Dots on Scans

When scanned documents are being sent via the internet, they might contain tracking information. Tracking dots may have a strong effect: In 2017, a document by the NSA has been published without authorisation[3]. The most probable reason for having identified the publisher is the tracking dots. Tracking dots can mostly be removed from scans (fig. 8) by clearing the original document's empty areas as detected in section 2.3.

5.2 Masking Tracking Dots on Prints

A custom TDM shall be added as a mask on top of the printer's TDM to prevent restoring a word *b* correctly. The ambiguity of correcting *b* must be high enough to allow many possibilities on restoring a masked TDM: Some code words can be detected as wrong by their content, e.g. if a decoded word contains a month greater than 12 or an invalid serial number. Wesselman et al. [9] have mentioned to print a full unit matrix on the sheet to prevent an unambiguous decoding of a pattern 4 matrix. Their mask puts a dot on all possible cells. Though, printing a yellow dot in all cells makes the TDM very conspicuous and uses a lot more toner. This might not be necessary. Because we know the codes used by the different patterns, for a given TDM we want to find a mask that has as few dots as possible but makes the decoding ambiguous when it is being united with the original TDM. The mask has the same size as the printer's TDM and must cover all of the TDM's repetitions on the sheet constantly. For each pattern there is a different algorithm to create a mask. The

Figure 10: Pattern 1 practical mask example. From left to right: original TDM, masked TDM, fully dotted TDM

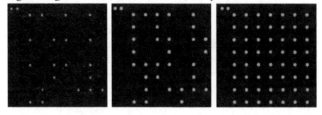

offset patterns 1 and 4 must not apply the mask on the empty areas because otherwise the mask could be concluded and therefore be removed by subtracting it from its union with the original TDM.

5.2.1 Pattern 1. The mask (fig. 9 and 10) is being created as follows. Let $s = 3$ if the information dots are placed in the odd columns and $s = 2$ otherwise. On each of the rows 1, 3, 5, 7, 9, 11, 13 and 15, one empty cell has to be chosen at random where the cell number must be one of $s, s + 2, s + 4, s + 6, s + 8, s + 10, s + 12$. These cells must carry a dot on the mask. The parity will be broken and the adversary does not know which dot has been added. From rows containing exactly one dot, it is unambiguous which dot we added. If we added two dots to each row that was empty on the original TDM, the parity would reveal that we have added an even amount of dots which must be smaller or equal than two. Therefore empty rows must be added three dots. Exactly the same mask starting at column 0, row 0 has to be repeated from column 16, row 16. This adds at least 8 dots to each TDM.

If our algorithm is known to the adversary and he wants to restore the masked TDM, there are $\prod_{r=1,3,\dots,15} d(r) \geq 3^8 \approx 2^{12.7}$ possible code words where $d(r)$ is the amount of dots in row r with $d(r) \geq 3$. If the parity bit in row r is not being set, the adversary will remove one of each of the dots. On rows where the parity bit is being set, itself might as well be considered as the flipped bit from our mask.

---

[3]https://qz.com/1002927/computer-printers-have-been-quietly-embedding-tracking-codes-in-documents-for-decades

Figure 11: Pattern 4 mask example (green)

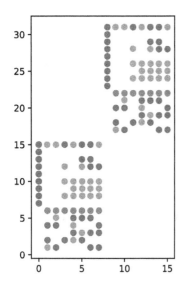

word b with weight $w(b) \in [3..\infty)$ there are $s(w)$ different possible code words a such that $a \oplus e = b$ with

$$s(b) = \sum_{w(e)=1,3,\ldots,w-1-w'} \binom{w(b)}{w(e)+w'(b)} \text{ where } w'(b) = w(b) \bmod 2.$$

PROOF. For a word b_1 with an odd weight $w(b_1)$, the parity is being satisfied and $w'(b_1)$ is 1. Because the code word a also satisfies the parity condition, an even amount of "1" has to be flipped to create another code word. $w(e)$ is one of $\{2, 4, \ldots, w(b_1) - 1\}$. There are $\binom{w(b_1)}{w(e)}$ possibilities for choosing e and restoring $a_1 = b_1 \oplus e$. For a word b_2 of an even weight $w(b_2)$ (with $w'(b_2) = 0$), the amount $w(e)$ of changed bits must be odd for the word to originate from a valid code word. So $w(e) \in \{1, 3, \ldots, w(b_2) - 1\}$. For any word $b = a \oplus e$ with an even or odd weight, $w(e)$ is one of $\{1 + w'(b), 3 + w'(b), \ldots, w(b) - 1\}$. Considering all possible $w(e)$ the result is

$$s(b) = \sum_{w(e)=1+w'(b),3+w'(b),\ldots,w(b)-1} \binom{w(b)}{w(e)} = \sum_{w(e)=1,3,\ldots,w(b)-1-w'(b)} \binom{w(b)}{w(e)+w'(b)}$$
$$\square$$

Example. A distorted word is $b = (1110)$. It has three "1" so $w(b) = 3$. The weight is odd so b is a code word. There are $s(3) = 3$ different code words that might have caused b: $a_1 = 0010$, $a_2 = 0100$ or $a_3 = (1000)$. Note that (1110) cannot have caused b because according to the proposition the error word has a weight of at least 1 but $w((1110)) = w(b)$. (1100) and (0000) would not be code words because they do not satisfy the parity condition.

The serial number is separated into the rows 3, 4 and 5. Let's assume each of these rows has been added at least one dot but enough dots to contain min_d dots in total. Let b_r be the word in row r with $w(b_r) \geq min_d$. The amount of different possible serial numbers an adversary can conclude from a masked TDM is $\hat{s}(b_3) \cdot \hat{s}(b_4) \cdot \hat{s}(b_5)$ where

$$\hat{s}(b) = \begin{cases} w(b) & \text{if } w(b) > min_d \\ & \vee w(b) \leq 2 \\ \sum_{w(e)=1,3,\ldots,w(b)-1-(w(b)\bmod 2)} \binom{w(b)}{w(e)+(w(b)\bmod 2)} & \text{otherwise} \end{cases}$$

If for a word $b = a \oplus e$, $w(b)$ is bigger than min_d and the adversary does not know e, then he can conclude that e contains one "1" which could be any of the $w(b)$ dots giving $w(b)$ possibilities to find it. If $w(b)$ is 1 or 2 then there are only 1 resp. 2 possibilities for determining a. Otherwise $w(a)$ is not shown to the adversary and the amount of possibilities for choosing a is a sum (prop. 5.1). The date is totally being hidden in the TDM, though if the date can be concluded from the printed content and the outer parity bits were not masked, in the worst case the outer parity could help to separate the original TDM from the mask.

Example. If the masked TDM is

Using this interpretation, an additional possible code word can be concluded from the unchanged information bits. The ambiguity can be low if each of the the original TDM's rows contain very few dots. To increase it, to each row a dot can be added at a randomly chosen cell. The parity in these rows will be correct.

5.2.2 Patterns 2 and 3. Because the information in the code words is not completely known to the public and might use a further error correcting code, filling all blocks completely with dots is a safe option to anonymise the TDM (see fig. 10 right TDM).

5.2.3 Pattern 4. The mask (fig. 11) for columns 0-7, rows 1-5 shall carry a dot on a randomly chosen empty cell for each row and fill the outer parity row 15 completely with dots between columns 0 and 7. To obscure the manufacturer, row 12 has to be modified. All known manufacturers use one of the numbers 3, 4 or 20 resp. binary numbers 11, 100 and 10100. From their disjunction 10111, none of the original number can be concluded. So it is sufficient to fill columns 7, 6, 5 and 3 of row 12. To hide the date of the printing process, rows 8, 9 and 10 have to be treated in a specific way: Filling columns 3-7 in row 8 hides the domain of the year, filling columns 4-7 in row 9 hides the domain of the month and filling columns 3-7 in row 10 hides the domain of the day. The hour and minute without the date are irrelevant and not being considered any further here. If rows 3, 4 and 5 are filled so that each row contains at least s dots, then at least s^3 different serial numbers can be concluded from the TDM. A copy of the mask shall be placed on columns 8-15, rows 17-30. This adds between 6 and 8+5+4+5+2+12=36 dots to each TDM.

Proposition 5.1. *Let's assume a parity code that makes the weight of a code word odd. If a distortion flips at least one "0" to a "1" but never vice versa and the error word e is unknown, then for a distorted*

	01234567
15	11111111
14	00110000
13	00110000
12	00110000
11	00110000
10	00110000
9	00110000
8	00110000
7	00110000
6	00110000
5	00100100
4	00100010
3	00100001
2	00110000
1	00110000

then the parity bits in the top row inform that there are errors in columns 5, 6 and 7. The parity bits in column 0 point at a distortion in rows 1-14. Moreover the adversary knows that one "0" per row has been changed to a "1". Therefore the ones in rows 3-5, columns 5-7 must have been changed by the mask. It is possible to restore rows 3, 4 and 5:

	01234567
5	00100000
4	00100000
3	00100000

These rows contain the printer's serial number (see section 3.5). To prevent the support by the outer parity bits, they are all being set to "1" to remove information.

6 DEDA TOOLKIT

The entire workflow of TDM extraction, retrieving the known information content and the generation of an anonymisation pattern could be obtained with our provided Dot Extraction, Decoding and Anonymisation toolkit *deda*. The code is freely available at dfd.inf.tu-dresden.de[4]. For further guidance have a look at our toolkit's README file. For the print anonymisation part a calibration sheet has to be printed and scanned. The printer's TDM is being read from this scan and an anonymisation mask is being created on top. This calibration step is described in the following. After generation of the anonymisation pattern it can be merged with the document to be printed. Note that it has to be printed borderless. If this is not possible, the margins have to be cut off, otherwise TDMs might be reconstructed.

Calibrating the TDM's location. The mask needs to be printed in a way to join the printer's native tracking dots although their position on the sheet is unknown. If a test image has been printed that contains markers in each edge on the Cartesian points A, B, C, D, then its scan can be aligned so that its coordinate system matches the test image's coordinates. An additional marker O is located in one edge of the page and used to maintain the page orientation. A contour detection algorithm [27] is used to find the markers in the scan. It is recommended to use the printer toner's colours cyan and magenta. Yellow is already used by the tracking dots and black is being displayed at the border of the scanned page. All other

colours are not recommended because they would be printed using halftones.

First, the scan needs to be rotated so that point O is in the same edge as in the test image. Then all other points A', B', C', D' need to be matched against the markers at A, B, C, D in the test image by filtering markers according to coordinate ranges and focusing on the smallest x and y coordinate for each marker. After applying a perspective transform mapping A' to A, B' to B etc., any point $Z \in \{A, ..., D\}$ on the scan would represent Z' on the test image so that $Z = Z'$. The process of scanning a document causes geometrical distortions. These distortions are minimal near the alignment markers A, B, C, D. Let's assume the printer's TDP has the parameters $n_i, n_j, \Delta_i, \Delta_j$. Now we need to find the offset coordinates x_o, y_o near the top left corner where the first TDM begins. If four valid TDMs have been found at points $\hat{A}, \hat{B}, \hat{C}, \hat{D}$ where $\hat{A} = (x_{\hat{A}}, y_{\hat{A}})$ is close to A, $\hat{B} = (x_{\hat{B}}, y_{\hat{B}})$ is close to B, etc. then the best estimation of x_o is the average of the TDM's offsets at $\hat{A}, \hat{B}, \hat{C}, \hat{D}$. We use modulo to calculate the offset given the coordinate. If the pattern's offset is close to 0, a constant $c \in \mathbb{R}$ must be chosen so that all x values can be mapped into a range $(x + c)\mathrm{mod}(n_i \cdot \Delta_i)$ that allows us to calculate a meaningful average.

$$x_o = \mathrm{average}((x_{\hat{A}} + c)\mathrm{mod}(n_i \cdot \Delta_i), (x_{\hat{B}} + c)\mathrm{mod}(n_i \cdot \Delta_i),$$
$$(x_{\hat{C}} + c)\mathrm{mod}(n_i \cdot \Delta_i), (x_{\hat{D}} + c)\mathrm{mod}(n_i \cdot \Delta_i))$$

y_o can be calculated analogously. If a page shall be printed and anonymised, the calculated mask shall be transformed into an image having cell distances of Δ_i, Δ_j. It must be printed at $(x_o|y_o)$ and at all points where a repetition of the TDM begins: $\{(x_o + x \cdot \Delta_i \cdot n_i | y_o + y \cdot \Delta_j \cdot n_j) | x, y \in \mathbb{Z}\}$. Now the tracking dots information has been made ambiguous. Note that the page margin must be identical for printing the test image and the anonymised document. If the margin has not been zero, there might remain unmasked tracking dots on it.

7 CONCLUSION

In this work we analysed document colour tracking dots, an extrinsic signature embedded in nearly all colour laser printers. From printer forensics point of view we propose to reuse these forensical patterns in combination with existing passive printer forensic algorithms. Since the properties and information content is chiefly unknown, we have researched methods of analysis for reusability. In total, we discovered 4 patterns and succeeded in automatically extracting and decoding the structure of the patterns as well as interpreting patterns 1, 4 and partially pattern 2. Further investigations are required to interpret the total information content for Patterns 2 and 3, e.g. on printers firmware level[5]. From a privacy point of view we explored anonymisation approaches to prevent arbitrary tracking. The whole workflow is provided with our freely available toolkit *deda*.

REFERENCES

[1] Gazi N Ali, Aravind K Mikkilineni, Jan P Allebach, Edward J Delp, Pei-Ju Chiang, and George T Chiu. 2003. Intrinsic and extrinsic signatures for information hiding and secure printing with electrophotographic devices. In NIP & Digital

---

[4]or https://github.com/dfd-tud/deda

[5]https://events.ccc.de/congress/2011/Fahrplan/events/4780.en.html; 08/02/2018

Fabrication Conference, Vol. 2003. Society for Imaging Science and Technology, 511–515.

[2] Orhan Bulan, Junwen Mao, and Gaurav Sharma. 2009. Geometric distortion signatures for printer identification. In Acoustics, Speech and Signal Processing, 2009. ICASSP 2009. IEEE International Conference on. IEEE, 1401–1404.

[3] Pei-Ju Chiang, N. Khanna, A. Mikkilineni, M.V.O. Segovia, Sungjoo Suh, J. Allebach, G. Chiu, and E. Delp. 2009. Printer and scanner forensics. IEEE Signal Processing Magazine 26, 2 (March 2009), 72–83. https://doi.org/10.1109/MSP.2008.931082

[4] Jung-Ho Choi, Hae-Yeoun Lee, and Heung-Kyu Lee. 2013. Color laser printer forensic based on noisy feature and support vector machine classifier. Multimedia Tools and Applications 67, 2 (Nov. 2013), 363–382. https://doi.org/10.1007/s11042-011-0835-9

[5] M. Uma Devi, C. Raghvendra Rao, and M. Jayaram. 2014. Statistical Measures for Differentiation of Photocopy from Print technology Forensic Perspective. International Journal of Computer Applications 105, 15 (2014). http://search.proquest.com/openview/5acf04697ebccb072c71b71e5ab30c47/1?pq-origsite=gscholar

[6] DFKI. 2015. Datasets for Document Analysis. (2015). http://madm.dfki.de/downloads 03/08/2017.

[7] Electronic Frontier Foundation. 2005. DocuColor Tracking Dot Decoding Guide. (2005). https://w2.eff.org/Privacy/printers/docucolor/index.php#program 21/07/2017.

[8] Sara Elkasrawi and Faisal Shafait. 2014. Printer Identification Using Supervised Learning for Document Forgery Detection. IEEE, 146–150. https://doi.org/10.1109/DAS.2014.48

[9] Maya Embar, Louis F. McHugh IV, and William R. Wesselman. 2014. Printer watermark obfuscation.. In RIIT, Becky Rutherfoord, Lei Li, Susan Van de Ven, Amber Settle, and Terry Steinbach (Eds.). ACM, 15–20. http://dblp.uni-trier.de/db/conf/riit/riit2014.html#EmbarMW14; http://doi.acm.org/10.1145/2656434.2656437

[10] Stephan Escher and Thorsten Strufe. 2017. Robustness Analysis of a passive printer identification scheme for halftone images. In IEEE International Conference on Image Processing (ICIP).

[11] Anselmo Ferreira, Luiz C. Navarro, Giuliano Pinheiro, Jefersson A. dos Santos, and Anderson Rocha. 2015. Laser printer attribution: Exploring new features and beyond. Forensic Science International 247 (Feb. 2015), 105–125. https://doi.org/10.1016/j.forsciint.2014.11.030

[12] Lukas Gal, Michaela Belovičová, Michal Ceppan, Michal Oravec, and Miroslava Palková. 2013. Analysis of Laser and Inkjet Prints Using Spectroscopic Methods for Forensic Identification of Questioned Documents. In Symposium on Graphic Arts, Vol. 10.

[13] Matthew D. Gaubatz and Steven J. Simske. 2009. Printer-scanner identification via analysis of structured security deterrents. In Information Forensics and Security, 2009. WIFS 2009. First IEEE International Workshop on. IEEE, 151–155. http://ieeexplore.ieee.org/xpls/abs_all.jsp?arnumber=5386463

[14] Johann Gebhardt, Markus Goldstein, Faisal Shafait, and Andreas Dengel. 2013. Document Authentication Using Printing Technique Features and Unsupervised Anomaly Detection. IEEE, 479–483. https://doi.org/10.1109/ICDAR.2013.102

[15] Hardik Jain, Gaurav Gupta, Sharad Joshi, and Nitin Khanna. 2017. Passive Classification of Source Printer using Text-line-level Geometric Distortion Signatures from Scanned Images of Printed Documents. arXiv preprint arXiv:1706.06651 (2017).

[16] Weina Jiang, Anthony TS Ho, Helen Treharne, and Yun Q Shi. 2010. A novel multi-size block Benford's law scheme for printer identification. In Pacific-Rim Conference on Multimedia. Springer, 643–652.

[17] Do-Guk Kim, Jong-Uk Hou, and Heung-Kyu Lee. 2017. Learning deep features for source color laser printer identification based on cascaded learning. arXiv preprint arXiv:1711.00207 (2017).

[18] Do-Guk Kim and Heung-Kyu Lee. 2014. Color laser printer identification using photographed halftone images. In Signal Processing Conference (EUSIPCO), 2014 Proceedings of the 22nd European. IEEE, 795–799. http://ieeexplore.ieee.org/xpls/abs_all.jsp?arnumber=6952258

[19] Herbert Klimant, Rudi Piotraschke, and Dagmar Schönfeld. 2006. Informations- und Kodierungstheorie (3 ed.). Teubner.

[20] Aravind K. Mikkilineni, Pei-Ju Chiang, George TC Chiu, Jan P. Allebach, and Edward J. Delp. 2007. Channel model and operational capacity analysis of printed text documents. In Electronic Imaging 2007. International Society for Optics and Photonics, 65051U–65051U. http://proceedings.spiedigitallibrary.org/proceeding.aspx?articleid=1298973

[21] CNN Money. [n. d.]. Fortune Global 500. ([n. d.]). http://fortune.com/global500/list 31/08/2017.

[22] Thong Q. Nguyen, Yves Delignon, Lionel Chagas, and François Septier. 2014. Printer identification from micro-metric scale printing. In 2014 IEEE International Conference on Acoustics, Speech and Signal Processing (ICASSP). IEEE, 6236–6239.

[23] John Oliver and Joyce Chen. 2002. Use of signature analysis to discriminate digital printing technologies. In NIP & Digital Fabrication Conference, Vol. 2002. Society for Imaging Science and Technology, 218–222.

[24] Ricoh. [n. d.]. Going global, Company History about Ricoh. ([n. d.]). http://www.ricoh.com/about/company/history/2000_2009; http://www.ricoh.com/about/company/history/1985_1999 31/08/2017.

[25] Marco Schreyer, Christian Schulze, Armin Stahl, and Wolfgang Effelsberg. 2009. Intelligent Printing Technique Recognition and Photocopy Detection for Forensic Document Examination.. In Informatiktage, Vol. 8. 39–42. https://www.researchgate.net/profile/Sebastian_Magnus/publication/221388729_Ein_Rahmenwerk_fur_Genetische_Algorithmen_zur_Losung_erweiterter_Vehicle_Routing_Problems_VRPSPDMUTW/links/0a85e52fca0dcedffb000000.pdf#page=40

[26] Shize Shang, Nasir Memon, and Xiangwei Kong. 2014. Detecting documents forged by printing and copying. EURASIP Journal on Advances in Signal Processing 2014, 1 (2014), 1–13. http://link.springer.com/article/10.1186/1687-6180-2014-140

[27] S. Suzuki and K. Abe. 1985. Topological Structural Analysis of Digitized Binary Images by Border Following. CVGIP 30, 1 (1985), 32–46.

[28] Małgorzata Szafarska, Renata Wietecha-Posłuszny, Michał Woźniakiewicz, and Paweł Kościelniak. 2011. Application of capillary electrophoresis to examination of color inkjet printing inks for forensic purposes. Forensic Science International 212, 1-3 (Oct. 2011), 78–85.

[29] Min-Jen Tsai, Chien-Lun Hsu, Jin-Sheng Yin, and Imam Yuadi. 2016. Digital forensics for printed character source identification. In Multimedia and Expo (ICME), 2016 IEEE International Conference on. IEEE, 1–6. http://ieeexplore.ieee.org/abstract/document/7552892/

[30] Min-Jen Tsai, Jung Liu, Chen-Sheng Wang, and Ching-Hua Chuang. 2011. Source color laser printer identification using discrete wavelet transform and feature selection algorithms. In Circuits and Systems (ISCAS), 2011 IEEE International Symposium on. IEEE, 2633–2636. http://ieeexplore.ieee.org/xpls/abs_all.jsp?arnumber=5938145

[31] Jason Tuohey. 2004. Government Uses Color Laser Printer Technology to Track Documents. PCWorld (nov 2004). https://www.pcworld.com/article/118664/article.html 25/09/2017.

[32] United States Secret Service. 2012. Re: Freedom of Information Act Appeal. (Feb. 2012). https://www.scribd.com/doc/81897582/microdots-pdf 25/09/2017.

[33] Joost van Beusekom, Faisal Shafait, and Thomas M. Breuel. 2013. Automatic authentication of color laser print-outs using machine identification codes. Pattern Analysis and Applications 16, 4 (Nov 2013), 663–678.

[34] Changyou Wang, Xiangwei Kong, Shize Shang, and Xin'gang You. 2013. Photocopier forensics based on arbitrary text characters, Adnan M. Alattar, Nasir D. Memon, and Chad D. Heitzenrater (Eds.). 86650G. https://doi.org/10.1117/12.2005524

[35] Yubao Wu, Xiangwei Kong, Xin'gang You, and Yiping Guo. 2009. Printer forensics based on page document's geometric distortion. In Image Processing (ICIP), 2009 16th IEEE International Conference on. IEEE, 2909–2912.

[36] Luo Xiao, Qinghu Chen, and Yuchen Yan. 2015. Printed Characters Texture Identification Based on Two-factor Analysis. Journal of Computational Information Systems 14, 11 (2015), 5199–5207. https://doi.org/10.12733/jcis14760

138

Applicability of No-Reference Visual Quality Indices for Visual Security Assessment

Heinz Hofbauer
University of Salzburg
Department of Computer Sciences
hhofbaue@cosy.sbg.ac.at

Andreas Uhl
University of Salzburg
Department of Computer Sciences
uhl@cosy.sbg.ac.at

ABSTRACT

From literature it is known that full-reference visual quality indices are a poor fit for the estimation of visual security for selective encryption. The question remains whether no-reference visual quality indices can perform where full reference indices falter. Furthermore, no-reference visual quality indices frequently use machine learning to train a model of natural scene statistics. It would be of interest to be able to gauge the impact of learning statistics from selectively encrypted images on performance as quality estimators for encryption. In the following we will answer these two questions.

ACM Reference Format:
Heinz Hofbauer and Andreas Uhl. 2018. Applicability of No-Reference Visual Quality Indices for Visual Security Assessment. In *IH&MMSec '18: 6th ACM Workshop on Information Hiding and Multimedia Security, June 20–22, 2018, Innsbruck, Austria.* ACM, New York, NY, USA, 6 pages. https://doi.org/10.1145/3206004.3206007

1 INTRODUCTION

Selective encryption (SE) is the encryption, utilizing state of the art ciphers like AES, of a *selected* part of a media file or stream. The goal is to secure the content, or parts thereof, while still maintaining the file format, that is the file is still usable as the media file or stream it actually is. An example of this is would be surveillance cameras, which are more and more common and pose some privacy concerns since a malicious actor could track a person. A solution for this is to encrypt identity revealing information like faces or license plates. On the other hand, an observer should still be able to see the rest of the video(-stream) in high quality to be able to identify suspicious behaviour. If such behaviour is identified and a law enforcement agent is notified the identity containing portion of the video can be decrypted. There are a number of papers dealing with problems like this, focusing on the technical side of performing encryption without destroying the rest of the video through drift errors and similar things, e.g., [2–4, 22].

It is well known that SE is secure, Lookabaugh and Sicker [12] showed how it relates to Shannon's work [16]. Potential insecurity come from the information left in plaintext to achieve the other objectives, e.g., the rest of the video outside a region of identity

should be error free and the media should be format-compliant. In essence some information will leak, this is unavoidable with the other goals in mind, the amount of leakage is another question though. The goal of SE can be stated as a destruction of quality in the encrypted part such that it can not be exploited in a malicious fashion. Which directly leads to the formulation of the security evaluation of the SE: "To what extent can the information left in plain text be used to reconstruct an image or video?"

It is expensive and time-consuming to use human observer experiments, to gauge recognizability and remaining quality, so image metrics or visual quality indices (VQI) are used instead as they represent a model of the human visual system. While such methods can be, and are, used to evaluate SE methods it has been shown that their performance suffers on low quality images [6]. Furthermore, there is a subset of VQIs specifically designed to evaluate SE methods, created in conjuction with a specific SE method. These SE-VQIs usually work well for the design target but are even worse than regular VQIs for all other applications [8]. Up to now the focus VQI regarding security evaluation are on full-reference VQIs (FR-VQI), i.e., metrics which have access to both the original and distorted (encrypted) image. Even evaluation of the fitness of VQI for security evaluation of SEs focus almost exclusively on FR-VQI, with one exception in [8] which is based on local entropy to evaluate the distance to a random signal.

An alternative are no-reference VQIs (NR-VQI) which only use the distorted image and statistics based on natural images. The benefit of NR-VQIs over FR-VQIs for security evaluation is threefold. NR-VQIs use a statistical approach which is better fit to deal with the artefacts resulting from encryption, which should look like a random signal, while FR-VQIs consist of models of image structure and the HVS. The second benefit of NR-VQIs is that the rely on a statistical model of images and distortions. This model is the result of a machine-learning process and can, as opposed to a fixed model (as used by most FR-VQIs), be adjusted by learning the statistics of encrypted images. Thirdly, the view of NR-VQIs is the same view an attacker has, i.e., only the encrypted image. As such it is, theoretically, a very accurate way of estimating residual content and structure in the encrypted image, which is exactly the goal of evaluating an SE method.

In this paper we will ask, and answer, two questions:

(1) *How do NR-VQIs fare in the evaluation methodology for visual security metrics, as outlined in [8]?*
(2) *Can the specific statistics of encrypted images be learned to improve the NR-VQIs for the evaluation of SE methods?*

Section 2 gives an overview over the VQIs used in this paper. Section 3 recaps the evaluation methodology from [8] and in Section 4.1 the VQIs are evaluated based on this methodology. In Section 4.2 we will use one VQI to learn, with different fitness criteria, the statistics of encrypted images and gauge the improvement for security evaluation. Finally, Section 5 will recap the results and conclude the paper.

2 OVERVIEW OF VISUAL QUALITY INDICES

In the following we will describe the visual quality indices/image metrics (VQI) which are used in this paper. The methods are primarily chosen based on available implementations, of those more recent were preferred. Further, VQIs based on different features or features from different domains, e.g., spatial versus DCT, were chosen over different VQIs using similar features.

BIQAA [5] is the blind image quality assessment based on anisotropy. The generalized Rènyi entropy is used to calculate local entropy histograms by associating a distribution for each pixel of the image. After normalization a windowed pseudo-Wigner distribution (PWD) can be approximated as a probability distribution function. This PWD is computed in a 1-D oriented window, allowing a measure of the entropy in a selected direction. Differences in the directional entropy are taken to measure image anisotropy and hence to estimate of the image quality.

BLIINDS-II [15] uses a Bayesian approach based on model parameters of generalized Gaussian distributions of various features. The features are derived from groups of AC coefficients of the local 2-D DCT transform of the image (on multiple scales). The AC coefficients are grouped into radial as well as circular clusters, orienting from the DC coefficient.

BRISQUE [13] is a quality evaluator which is based on learned regression, via scalable vector regression methods (SVR). The target values are the MOS values in the (LIVE) database and the features are based on localized luminance distribution and directional statistics. The features are calculated on two scales and are based on mean subtracted contrast normalized (MSNC) values. The MSNC values are taken directly as well as the difference values in horizontal, vertical and the two diagonal directions. An asymmetric generalized Gaussian distribution (AGGD) is fitted to each distribution and the values from the AGGD are used as features.

Global phase coherence (GPC),

Sharpness Index (sharp), and

Simplified sharpness index (SI) [10] are based on the observation that structural information in an image is encoded in the phase of its Fourier transformation. Impairment of the image affects the phase of the Fourier transform and changes phase coherence. Basically all three indices are based on the same model, they measure the (logarithmic) probability of the total variance, of the signal in phase space, diverging from the total variance of a 'random' image to denote structure (or quality). The notion of 'random' is where the three measures differ, the GPC uses a uniform random phase function as a model, sharp and SI use Gaussian white noise

with the SI only using an approximation which changes it slightly but is much faster to calculate.

NIQE [14] uses directional MSNC values similar to BRISQUE. The main difference are a) that these values are taken from local patches which show a high local variance. And b) the model is a multivariate Gaussian based on the same statistics from regular images, which means unlike the BRISQUE no human observer information is taken into account.

SSEQ [11] uses the distribution, expressed by mean and skew, of spatial and spectral entropies as features. The entropies are calculated on a block by block partition of the image and on multiple scales. The features are trained using an SVR to conform to human judgement.

In addition to the NR-VQIs we also will present the two best full-reference VQIs (FR-VQI) from literature [8], the local edge gradient image metric (**LEG**) [7] and the visual information fidelity (**VIF**) [17]. The comparison will show how the NR-VQIs compare to the full-reference VQIs in a baseline configuration. Further, since the NR-VQIs are usually based on machine learning of statistical features, we will adapt one, the BRISQUE, and retrain for better performance on low-quality images. This will show the potential of using NR-VQIs when the target application of the VQI is known prior to training.

With respect to implementations, we used only image metrics for which the code is publicly available (for reproducible research). The three features GPC, SI, and sharp are available from the webpage of Lionel Moisan at the Université Paris Descaterse[1]. An implementation for BIQAA (version 1.0 by Gabarda was used) is available at MathWorks[2]. The remaining NR-VQIs and the VIF are available from the webpage of the Laboratory of Image and Video Encryption at the University of Texas (Austin)[3]. The LEG source code is available from the visual quality index implementation (VQI) of the University of Salzburg Wavelab group webpage[4].

3 EVALUATION METHODOLOGY

We will follow the proceedings described in [8], using the same methods and databases, however, we will briefly recap them here. Note that an illustrated guide to the evaluation method is available online [9].

The main goal of these evaluations is to find how well an visual quality index (VQI) reflects the human visual system (HVS) based on the mean opinion scores (MOS). The following assumes that a low MOS indicates low quality and that the VQIs are impairment indices, a low score implies good quality.

Application Domain. is the domain to apply the VQI, either on the decoding of an encrypted image (*encrypted domain*) or on the decoding of an 'attacked', i.e., reducing/removing the impact of the encryption, encrypted image (*extracted domain*).

This is done by generating a set of image pairs, consisting of two encrypted images with clearly different quality. Then the VQI is tasked to order each image pair based on quality. This is done

---

[1] http://www.math-info.univ-paris5.fr/~moisan/sharpness/
[2] https://it.mathworks.com/matlabcentral/fileexchange/
30800-blind-image-quality-assessment-through-anisotropy
[3] http://live.ece.utexas.edu/research/Quality/index.htm
[4] http://wavelab.at/sources/VQI

in both extracted and encrypted domain, the percentage of correct orderings is used as score, 0.5 (50%) being the worst outcome, akin to a coin flip per pair. In case of referenced VQIs the groundtruth of the image is used as a reference for both cases.

Correspondence to HVS: Monotonicity. measures the correlation of the VQI to the HVS. Since the HVS, and most VQIs, are non-linear rank order correlation is used instead of linear correlation, specifically, Spearman's rank order coefficient (SROC) [20].

Since high correlation over the full quality range does not imply a high correlation over the low quality range [6], we will give the SROC over the full, high and low quality range.

Correspondence to HVS: Confidence. gives a more in depth analysis of the signal shape and divergence of VQI and the HVS which is only coarsely captured by the SROC. The confidence, for a given MOS value D, measures the VQI values $v(i)$ over all images i where zero false negatives, $V_{min}(D)$ such that $\forall i : MOS(i) > D \implies v(i) > V_{min}(D)$, and zero positives, $V_{max}(D)$ such that $\forall i : v(i) > V_{max}(D) \implies MOS(i) > D$, occur. The confidence score C for a given MOS value D is $C_D := |V_{max}(D) - V_{min}(D)|$. This function is condensed into the following values for easier representation: the average and standard deviation over C_D, $\mu_{D \in S}(C_D)$ and $\sigma_{D \in S}(C_D)$.

Similar to SROC the confidence is not constant over the full quality range. Therefore, we also give a signal shape which describes the shape of the C_D function. Outliers based on the z score of a data point D are calculated as $z_D = {}^{C_D - \mu(C_D)}/\sigma(C_D)$. If $z_D < -1$ it is a *high outlier*, and if $z_D > 1$ it is a *low outlier*. Based on the distribution of high and low outliers we can specify the shape of the signal as follows. A signal is **stable** if there are no outliers, and it is **biased** if the high and low outliers are separable by a single threshold (D_t). Specifically, the shape is denoted **biased towards high quality** if $z_D < -1 \implies D < D_t$ or **biased towards low quality** if $z_D > 1 \implies D < D_t$. A signal which is neither stable nor biased is considered **unstable**.

4 EVALUATION

In this section we will evaluate the VQIs based on the same data as was used in [8]. Specifically, the LIVE and IVC-SelectEncrypt databases.

The LIVE database, [19], does not contain encrypted images. However, the images in the low quality range exhibit strong distortions which can be equated to encrypted images in the sense that strong distortions mask a lot of the visual information. The test sets contained in the LIVE database (and their abbreviation in plots and figures) are JPEG 2000 compression (jp2k), JPEG compression (jpeg), white noise (wn), Gaussian blur (gblur), and bit errors in JPEG2000 bit stream transmission over a simulated fast fading Rayleigh Channel (fastfading), for detailed information see [18]. The threshold to separate low and high quality is set to a mean opinion score (MOS) value of 40 for our experiments. The MOS is the mean quality judgment based on a number of human observers opinions, the range of MOS depends on the database.

The IVC-SelectEncrypt database [1] contains various instances of JPEG 2000 transparent encryption, using different encryption

techniques. The test sets contained in the IVC-SelectEncrypt database (and their abbreviation) are traditional encryption (trad), truncation of the code stream (trunc), window encryption without error concealment (iwind_nec), window encryption with error concealment (iwind_ec), and wavelet packet encryption (res), for detailed information see [21]. The low/high quality threshold is set to a MOS of 3 for the following experiments.

4.1 Evaluation of No-Reference VQI

For reasons of brevity all the results are summarized in Table 3. In tables the results are marked for good (bold) and bad (italics) performance. For the application domain results in $[0.4, 0.6]$ are considered bad and those in $[0, 0.1] \cup [0.9, 1]$ are considered good. For SROC values lower than 0.5 are considered bad and those higher then 0.9 are considered good results. For $\mu(C_D)/\sigma(C_D)$ 0.3/0.1 are good results and 0.5/0.2 are bad, with a difference of signal shapes over the two databases also being considered bad.

The final score is simply a sum of individual performances, starting at 0, bad (those in italics) performances distract 1, good (in bold) performances add 1. This allows for a simple ranking of the VQIs.

Application Domain. The performance of the NR-VQIs in this test was extremely bad. It was expected that they perform badly in the encrypted domain, since errors introduced by the encryption have been shown to mislead VQIs. What is kind of interesting is the fact that the clearly different qualities in the extracted domain, see Figure 1, can not be sorted correctly. There are exceptions, BLIINDS-II does the sorting extremely well and SSEQ shows quite some improvement in the extraction domain. For the rest the improvements are slight (GPC, sharp, SI) to non-existing (NIQE, BIQAA, BRISQUE). That is not to say that the NR-VQIs can be applied in the encrypted domain, only that they (for the most part) also fail in the extraction domain. The most likely reason for this is that even the medium encryption still destroys much of the features the statistics are base on. However, the fact that BLIINDS-II does not make a single error in the extracted domain indicates that this is not true for all features.

Figure 1: Residual information in the extracted domain of a (high, medium) and (medium, low) quality pair.

Correspondence to HVS: Monotonicity. The SROC for the full and low-quality range is given in Table 1. The per test set SROC scores for the low-quality range is given in Table 3.

As pointed out in [6] the SROC over the full-quality range does not give any indication about the performance in the low-quality range. Compare the BLIINDS-II and the VIF on the IVC-SelectEncrypt database, the VIF low-quality performance is far worse than for the full-quality range, for the BLIINDS-II the performance over the low-quality range is higher than for the full-quality case. It

Table 1: The Spearman rank order for the full- and low-quality range for the LIVE and IVC-SelectEncrypt databases.

LIVE		VQI	IVC-SelectEncrypt	
full	low		full	low
0.930	0.641	LEG	0.893	*0.492*
0.963	0.788	VIF	**0.914**	*0.285*
0.270	*0.098*	BIQAA	*0.139*	*0.100*
0.912	0.711	BLIINDS-II	0.501	0.690
0.950	0.765	BRISQUE	0.642	*0.304*
0.427	*0.080*	GPC	0.703	0.504
0.445	*0.086*	sharp	0.708	0.532
0.445	*0.086*	SI	0.708	0.532
0.907	0.585	NIQE	0.632	*0.479*
0.897	0.539	SSEQ	0.511	*0.285*

should also be noted that, apart from the BLIINDS-II on the IVC-SelectEncrypt database, all VQIs perform worse on the low-quality range.

Another noteworthy tendency is the performance over regular impairments as given on the LIVE database versus the performance on encrypted images. All VQIs apart from those based on phase coherence perform worse for the encryption test sets. For most NR-VQIs this could be explained with their respective training with human judgement of regular image impairment (as given in the LIVE database). However, NIQE also does not utilize human judgement in the training phase and still performs worse on the IVC-SelectEncrypt database. The fact that phase coherence encodes structure and encryption is usually aimed at destroying structure would be a likely explanation. However, given that the phase coherence based VQIs behave very differently on the iwind test set with and without error concealment, see Table 3, invalidates this argument. The error concealment should only reduce noise in the image and is not able to reconstruct structural information. As such it is as of yet unclear what the reason for this behaviour is, however, it should be noted that the phase coherence based VQIs show some desirable traits for visual security VQIs.

Correspondence to HVS: Confidence. The confidence of the NR-VQIs overall is very bad, owing to a high average spread, the only exception is the NIQE, which is noteworthy by itself. Recall, that the confidence score gives the range of zero false negatives and zero false positives in relation to human judgement. The NIQE is the best of the NR-VQIs in this regard, even though it does not utilize information about human judgement during training.

When compared to full reference VQIs the NR-VQIs exhibit a very bad performance, except for the NIQE. Interestingly, the NR-VQIs, with the exception of those based on phase coherence, maintain their signal shape; this is something the FR-VQIs frequently fail at.

4.2 Learning SE statistics

Since a lot of the NR-VQIs are based on machine learning, to better conform to human judgement, an obvious question is how much

Table 2: Per test set comparison of SROC for the low-quality range as well as overall SROC for the full- and low-quality range on the IVC-SelectEncrypt database.

SROC on	BRISQUE	BRISQUE cross	BRISQUE low
iwind ec	0.598	0.485	0.408
iwind nec	0.143	0.709	0.676
resolution	0.107	0.321	0.393
trad	0.560	0.437	0.723
truncation	0.885	0.657	0.750
full-qualtiy	0.642	0.767	0.745
low-qualtiy	0.304	0.364	0.636

the performance improves when the learning is done on a database with encrypted distortions. For this we will use the BRISQUE, which uses the LIBSVM, and learn it on the IVC-SelectEncrypt database. In order to fairly evaluate it we will use cross validation, where we iteratively evaluate a test set which is disjoint from the training set. The folds are constructed by taking an original image and all its distorted versions for evaluation and all other images for training.

The parameters for the scalable vector regression (SVR) were searched on a grid in logarithmic space with different fitness functions. The basic version *BRISQUE cross* uses the full-quality SROC and the *BRISQUE low* uses the SROC over the low-quality range as fitness function.

The results, given in Table 2, expose an interesting behaviour. The improvement is a tradeoff in which test sets with horrible performances (iwind nec and resolution) are greatly improved at the cost of a performance reduction on relatively well performing test sets (truncation). This basically shifts all test sets towards a rather mediocre score. This is true for both target fitness functions. As such the training clearly improves the performance by a lot, compare e.g. the full- and low-quality results of BRISQUE low with the pre-trained BRISQUE, but at the cost of individual strength. As such it is recommended to train as specifically or as generally, i.e., on a large database with different distortions, as possible.

In conclusion the overall performance of LEG and VIF is still better. However, if the application scenario is known the learning approach can yield a metric which is better than LEG and VIF which are, by nature, fixed in their performance.

5 CONCLUSION

We initially asked two questions, and the answer can be summarized as follows.

How do NR-VQIs fare in the evaluation methodology for visual security metrics, as outlined in [8]? The no-reference VQIs behave overall very similar to most FR-VQIs. Some are more fit as VQIs for visual security (NIQE), some less (GPC, sharp, SI, BIQAA). But more importantly VIF and LEG also outperform the NR-VQIs, so the recommendation is to use VIF or LEG, if time is a constraint, still stands.

Can the specific statistics of encrypted images be learned to improve the NR-VQIs for the evaluation of SE methods? We used the

Table 3: Summary of Evaluation

Good performances are marked in **bold**, bad ones in *italic*. Application Domain: results in [0.4, 0.6] are bad / results in [0, 0.1] ∪ [0.9, 1] are good. SROC: values lower than 0.5 are bad / those higher then 0.9 are good. Confidence: $\mu(C_D) < 0.3$ and $\sigma(C_D) < 0.1$ are good / and $\mu(C_D) > 0.5$ $\sigma(C_D) > 0.2$ are bad. A difference of signal shapes over the two databases is also bad.

	LEG	VIF	BIQAA	BLIINDS-II	BRISQUE	GPC	sharp	SI	NIQE	SSEQ
Application Domain										
Encryption	*0.334*	*0.454*	*0.555*	*0.512*	*0.504*	*0.496*	*0.452*	*0.453*	*0.473*	*0.457*
Extraction	**0.994**	**0.988**	*0.535*	**0.000**	*0.503*	*0.435*	*0.432*	*0.428*	*0.537*	*0.754*
Confidence on the LIVE database										
$\mu(C_D)$	**0.291**	**0.285**	*0.934*	*0.504*	*0.387*	*0.724*	*0.855*	*0.857*	**0.174**	*0.564*
$\sigma(C_D)$	**0.070**	*0.110*	**0.089**	*0.122*	*0.137*	*0.202*	*0.101*	*0.100*	*0.168*	*0.125*
Signal Shape	*Bias Low*	*Bias Low*	*Stable*	*Bias High*	*Bias High*	*Bias Low*	*Bias Low*	*Bias Low*	*Bias Low*	*Bias High*
Confidence on the IVC-SelectEncrypt database										
$\mu(C_D)$	**0.268**	**0.277**	*0.322*	*0.569*	*0.597*	*0.668*	*0.699*	*0.699*	*0.415*	*0.554*
$\sigma(C_D)$	**0.077**	**0.098**	*0.239*	*0.201*	*0.190*	*0.306*	*0.333*	*0.334*	*0.166*	*0.130*
Signal Shape	*Bias High*	*Bias High*	*Stable*	*Bias High*	*Bias High*	*Stable*	*Stable*	*Stable*	*Bias Low*	*Bias High*
Low Quality SROC on the LIVE database										
fastfading	0.893	**0.937**	0.527	*0.496*	*0.465*	*0.511*	0.546	0.550	0.699	0.528
gblur	0.872	**0.920**	0.720	0.681	0.873	0.845	0.819	0.821	0.872	0.845
jp2k	0.617	0.646	*0.122*	0.599	*0.367*	0.534	*0.436*	*0.439*	*0.469*	0.616
jpeg	0.699	0.829	*0.287*	0.715	0.819	*0.380*	*0.368*	*0.368*	0.768	*0.196*
wn	0.804	**0.911**	0.554	0.826	**0.957**	0.725	0.874	0.873	**0.908**	0.817
Low Quality SROC on the IVC-SelectEncrypt database										
iwind ec	*0.141*	0.518	*0.194*	0.584	0.598	*0.098*	*0.001*	*0.001*	*0.012*	0.699
iwind nec	0.823	0.732	0.687	0.717	*0.143*	0.615	0.516	0.516	0.676	0.648
resolution	*0.490*	0.823	*0.393*	*0.286*	*0.107*	0.571	*0.429*	0.607	*0.036*	*0.107*
trad	0.652	**0.913**	0.805	0.805	0.560	0.676	0.876	**0.907**	0.764	*0.437*
truncation	*0.181*	0.832	*0.407*	0.685	0.885	0.868	0.868	0.868	0.797	0.558
Comparison Score, -1 or +1 for insufficient or good performance, -1 for conflict in signal shape										
Score	1	6	-8	-5	-6	-9	-10	-8	-3	-6

BRISQUE, which uses LIBSVM with a SVR kernel, to try and learn the specific distortions as introduced the IVC-SelectEncrypt database. It is clear that the learning improves the overall performance quite a lot. Specifically, there are test sets where the learned version of the BRISQUE outperforms LEG and VIF. So if the specific application is known and training data is available the trained NR-VQI can be a better choice. As a general purpose VQI for security metrics the VIF and LEG still are a better choice.

Future Work

Certain metrics show desirable traits: good confidence (NIQE), good overall and low quality performance on encrypted images (phase coherence based) or good performance for specific (hard) test sets like SSEQ on the iwind ec test set. It would be interesting to see if the specific traits of single metrics can be transfered and combined by using a bag of features approach.

ACKNOWLEDGMENTS

This work was partially supported by the Austrian Science Fund, project no. P27776.

REFERENCES

[1] Autrusseau, F., Stütz, T., and Pankajakshan, V. Subjective quality assessment of selective encryption techniques, 2010. http://www.irccyn.ec-nantes.fr/~autrusse/Databases/.

[2] Bergeron, C., and Lamy-Bergor, C. Compliant selective encryption for H.264/AVC video streams. In *Proceedings of the IEEE Workshop on Multimedia Signal Processing, MMSP'05* (Oct. 2005), pp. 1–4.

[3] Boult, T. E. PICO: Privacy through invertible cryptographic obscuration. In *IEEE/NFS Workshop on Computer Vision for Interactive and Intelligent Environments* (Lexington, KY, USA, Nov. 2005), pp. 27–38.

[4] Dufaux, F., and Ebrahimi, T. Scrambling for privacy protection in video surveillance systems. *IEEE Transactions on Circuits and Systems for Video Technology 18*, 8 (2008), 1168–1174.

[5] Gabarda, S., and Cristóbal, G. Blind image quality assessment through anisotropy. *Journal of the Optical Society of America A 24*, 12 (2007), B42–B51.

[6] Hofbauer, H., and Uhl, A. Visual quality indices and low quality images. In *IEEE 2nd European Workshop on Visual Information Processing* (Paris, France, July

2010), pp. 171–176.

[7] Hofbauer, H., and Uhl, A. An effective and efficient visual quality index based on local edge gradients. In *IEEE 3rd European Workshop on Visual Information Processing* (Paris, France, July 2011), p. 6pp.

[8] Hofbauer, H., and Uhl, A. Identifying deficts of visual security metrics for images. *Signal Processing: Image Communication 46* (2016), 60 – 75.

[9] Hofbauer, H., and Uhl, A. How to calculate the spearman rank order correlation, confidence and signal shape. Online at http://wavelab.at/papers_supplement/Hofbauer16c_supplement.pdf, 2017.

[10] Leclaire, A., and Moisan, L. No-reference image quality assessment and blind deblurring with sharpness metrics exploiting fourier phase information. *Journal of Mathematical Imaging and Vision 52*, 1 (2015), 145–172.

[11] Liu, L., Liu, B., Huang, H., and Bovik, A. C. No-reference image quality assessment based on spatial and spectral entropies. *Signal Processing: Image Communications 29*, 8 (2014), 856–863.

[12] Lookabaugh, T. D., and Sicker, D. C. Selective encryption for consumer applications. *IEEE Communications Magazine 42*, 5 (2004), 124–129.

[13] Mittal, A., Moorthy, A. K., and Bovik, A. C. Blind/referenceless image spatial quality evaluator. In *In Asilomar Conference on Signals, Systems and Computers* (2011), IEEE, pp. 723–727.

[14] Mittal, A., Soundararajan, R., and Bovik, A. C. Making a completely blind image quality analyzer. *Signal Processing Letters, IEEE 20*, 3 (2013), 209–212.

[15] Saad, M. A., Bovik, A. C., and Charrier, C. Blind image quality assessment: A natural scene statistics approach in the DCT domain. *Image Processing, IEEE Transactions on 21*, 8 (2012), 3339–3352.

[16] Shannon, C. E. Communication theory of secrecy systems. *Bell System Technical Journal 28* (Oct. 1949), 656–715.

[17] Sheikh, H. R., and Bovik, A. C. Image information and visual quality. *IEEE Transactions on Image Processing 15*, 2 (May 2006), 430–444.

[18] Sheikh, H. R., Sabir, M. F., and Bovik, A. C. A statistical evaluation of recent full reference image quality assessment algorithms. *IEEE Transactions on Image Processing 15*, 11 (Nov. 2006), 3440–3451.

[19] Sheikh, H. R., Wang, Z., Cormack, L., and Bovik, A. C. LIVE image quality assessment database release 2. http://live.ece.utexas.edu/research/quality.

[20] Spearman, C. The proof and measurement of association between two things. *The American Journal of Psychology 100*, 3/4 (1904), 441–471.

[21] Stütz, T., Pankajakshan, V., Autrusseau, F., Uhl, A., and Hofbauer, H. Subjective and objective quality assessment of transparently encrypted JPEG2000 images. In *Proceedings of the ACM Multimedia and Security Workshop (MMSEC '10)* (Rome, Italy, Sept. 2010), ACM, pp. 247–252.

[22] Unterweger, A., Van Ryckegem, K., Engel, D., and Uhl, A. Building a Post-Compression Region-of-Interest Encryption Framework for Existing Video Surveillance Systems – Challenges, obstacles and practical concerns. *Multimedia Systems 22*, 5 (2015), 617–639.

Author Index

NOTES